React Cookbook
Recipes for Mastering the React Framework

David Griffiths and Dawn Griffiths

Beijing · Boston · Farnham · Sebastopol · Tokyo

React Cookbook

by David Griffiths and Dawn Griffiths

Copyright © 2021 Dawn Griffiths and David Griffiths. All rights reserved.

Published by O'Reilly Media, Inc., 1005 Gravenstein Highway North, Sebastopol, CA 95472.

O'Reilly books may be purchased for educational, business, or sales promotional use. Online editions are also available for most titles (*http://oreilly.com*). For more information, contact our corporate/institutional sales department: 800-998-9938 or *corporate@oreilly.com*.

Acquisitions Editor: Amanda Quinn
Development Editor: Corbin Collins
Production Editor: Kate Galloway
Copyeditor: Kim Wimpsett
Proofreader: Kim Sandoval

Indexer: Ellen Troutman-Zaig
Interior Designer: David Futato
Cover Designer: Karen Montgomery
Illustrator: Kate Dullea

August 2021:   First Edition

Revision History for the First Edition
2021-08-11:   First Release

See *http://oreilly.com/catalog/errata.csp?isbn=9781492085843* for release details.

978-1-492-08584-3

[LSI]

Table of Contents

Preface

This book contains a collection of code that we've found helpful over several years of building React applications. Like recipes you would use in the kitchen, we've designed them to be starting points or inspirations for your own code. You should adjust them to match your situation and replace any ingredients (such as example servers) with those that seem more appropriate for your needs. The recipes range from general web development tips to larger pieces of code that you could generalize into libraries.

Most of the recipes are built with Create React App, as this is now the common starting point for most React projects. It should be straightforward to convert each recipe for use in Preact or Gatsby.

To keep the code compact, we have generally used hooks and functions rather than class components. We have also used the Prettier tool to apply standard code formatting throughout. We have used Prettier's default options, other than narrower indents and line lengths, to fit the code neatly onto the printed page. You should adjust the code format to match your preferred standard.

We have used many libraries in the creation of these recipes:

Tool/library	Description	Versions
Apollo Client	GraphQL client	3.3.19
axios	HTTP library	0.21.1
chai	Unit test support library	4.3.0
chromedriver	Browser automation tool	88.0.0
Create React App	Tool for generating React apps	4.0.3
Cypress	Automated test system	7.3.0
Cypress Axe	Automated accessibility testing	0.12.2
Gatsby	Tool for generating React apps	3.4.1
GraphQL	API query language	15.5.0
jsx-a11y	ESLint plugin for accessibility	6.4.1

Tool/library	Description	Versions
Material-UI	Component library	4.11.4
Node	JavaScript runtime	v12.20.0
npm	The Node package manager	6.14.8
nvm	Tool for running multiple Node environments	0.33.2
nwb	Tool for generating React apps	0.25.x
Next.js	Tool for generating React apps	10.2.0
Preact	Lightweight React-like framework	10.3.2
Preact Custom Elements	Library to create custom elements	4.2.1
preset-create-react-app	Storybook plugin	3.1.7
Rails	Web development framework	6.0.3.7
Razzle	Tool for generating React apps	4.0.4
React	Web framework	17.0.2
React Media	Media queries in React code	1.10.0
React Router (DOM)	Library for managing React routes	5.2.0
React Testing Library	Unit testing library for React	11.1.0
react-animations	React CSS animation library	1.0.0
React Focus Lock	Library to capture keyboard focus	2.5.0
react-md-editor	Markdown editor	3.3.6
React-Redux	React support library for Redux	7.2.2
Redux	State management library	4.0.5
Redux-Persist	Library to store Redux state	6.0.0
Ruby	Language used by Rails	2.7.0p0
selenium-webdriver	Browser testing framework	4.0.0-beta.1
Storybook	Component gallery system	6.2.9
TweenOne	React animation library	2.7.3
Typescript	Type-safe extension to JavaScript	4.1.2
Webpacker	Tool for adding React to Rails apps	4.3.0
Workbox	Library to create service workers	5.1.3
Yarn	Another Node package manager	1.22.10

Conventions Used in This Book

The following typographical conventions are used in this book:

Italic
> Indicates new terms, URLs, email addresses, filenames, and file extensions.

`Constant width`
> Used for program listings, as well as within paragraphs to refer to program elements such as variable or function names, databases, data types, environment variables, statements, and keywords.

`Constant width bold`
> Shows commands or other text that should be typed literally by the user.

`Constant width italic`
> Shows text that should be replaced with user-supplied values or by values determined by context.

 This element signifies a tip or suggestion.

 This element signifies a general note.

 This element indicates a warning or caution.

Using Code Examples

Supplemental material (code examples, exercises, etc.) is available for download at *https://github.com/dogriffiths/ReactCookbook-source*.

If you have a technical question or a problem using the code examples, please send email to *bookquestions@oreilly.com*.

This book is here to help you get your job done. In general, if example code is offered with this book, you may use it in your programs and documentation. You do not need to contact us for permission unless you're reproducing a significant portion of the code. For example, writing a program that uses several chunks of code from this book does not require permission. Selling or distributing examples from O'Reilly books does require permission. Answering a question by citing this book and quoting example code does not require permission. Incorporating a significant amount of example code from this book into your product's documentation does require permission.

We appreciate, but generally do not require, attribution. An attribution usually includes the title, author, publisher, and ISBN. For example: "*React Cookbook* by David Griffiths and Dawn Griffiths (O'Reilly). Copyright 2021 Dawn Griffiths and David Griffiths, 978-1-492-08584-3."

If you feel your use of code examples falls outside fair use or the permission given above, feel free to contact us at *permissions@oreilly.com*.

O'Reilly Online Learning

 For more than 40 years, *O'Reilly Media* has provided technology and business training, knowledge, and insight to help companies succeed.

Our unique network of experts and innovators share their knowledge and expertise through books, articles, and our online learning platform. O'Reilly's online learning platform gives you on-demand access to live training courses, in-depth learning paths, interactive coding environments, and a vast collection of text and video from O'Reilly and 200+ other publishers. For more information, visit *http://oreilly.com*.

How to Contact Us

Please address comments and questions concerning this book to the publisher:

O'Reilly Media, Inc.
1005 Gravenstein Highway North
Sebastopol, CA 95472
800-998-9938 (in the United States or Canada)
707-829-0515 (international or local)
707-829-0104 (fax)

We have a web page for this book, where we list errata, examples, and any additional information. You can access this page at *https://oreil.ly/react-cb*.

Email *bookquestions@oreilly.com* to comment or ask technical questions about this book.

For news and information about our books and courses, visit *http://oreilly.com*.

Find us on Facebook: *http://facebook.com/oreilly*

Follow us on Twitter: *http://twitter.com/oreillymedia*

Watch us on YouTube: *http://www.youtube.com/oreillymedia*

Acknowledgments

We want to thank our very patient editor Corbin Collins for his help and advice over the past year. His calm, good humor has been a steadying influence during the writing process. We would also like to thank Amanda Quinn, senior contents acquisition editor at O'Reilly Media, for commissioning the book, and Danny Elfanbaum and the production team at O'Reilly for making the physical and electronic versions a reality.

Special thanks also to Sam Warner and Mark Hobson for their very rigorous review of the material in this book.

We are also grateful to the developers working on the many open source libraries that support the React ecosystem. We are grateful to them all, particularly for the speed at which they responded to bug reports or pleas for help.

If you find these recipes useful, it is primarily because of the work of these people. If you find errors in the code or the text, that is entirely our responsibility.

CHAPTER 1

Creating Applications

React is a surprisingly adaptable development framework. Developers use it to create large JavaScript-heavy Single-Page Applications (SPAs) or to build surprisingly small plug-ins. You can use it to embed code inside a Rails application or generate a content-rich website.

In this chapter, we look at the various ways of creating a React application. We also look at some of the more valuable tools you might want to add to your development cycle. Few people now create their JavaScript projects from scratch. Doing so is a tedious process, involving an uncomfortable amount of tinkering and configuration. The good news is that you can use a tool to generate the code you need in almost every case.

Let's take a whistle-stop tour of the many ways of starting your React journey, beginning with the one most frequently used: `create-react-app`.

1.1 Generate a Simple Application

Problem

React projects are challenging to create and configure from scratch. Not only are there numerous design choices to make—which libraries to include, which tools to use, which language features to enable—but manually created applications will, by their nature, differ from one another. Project idiosyncrasies increase the time it takes a new developer to become productive.

Solution

`create-react-app` is a tool for building SPAs with a standard structure and a good set of default options. Generated projects use the React Scripts library to build, test, and run the code. Projects have a standard Webpack configuration and a standard set of language features enabled.

Any developer who has worked on one `create-react-app` application instantly feels at home with any other. They understand the project structure and know which language features they can use. It is simple to use and contains all the features that a typical application requires: from Babel configuration and file loaders to testing libraries and a development server.

If you're new to React, or need to create a generic SPA with the minimum of fuss, then you should consider creating your app with `create-react-app`.

You can choose to install the `create-react-app` command globally on your machine, but this is now discouraged. Instead, you should create a new project by calling `create-react-app` via `npx`. Using `npx` ensures you're building your application with the latest version of `create-react-app`:

```
$ npx create-react-app my-app
```

This command creates a new project directory called *my-app*. By default, the application uses JavaScript. If you want to use TypeScript as your development language, `create-react-app` provides that as an option:

```
$ npx create-react-app --template typescript my-app
```

Facebook developed `create-react-app`, so it should come as no surprise that if you have the `yarn` package manager installed, then your new project will use `yarn` by default. To use `npm`, you can either specify the `--use-npm` flag or change into the directory and remove the *yarn.lock* file and then rerun the install with `npm`:

```
$ cd my-app
$ rm yarn.lock
$ npm install
```

To start your application, run the `start` script:

```
$ npm start # or yarn start
```

This command launches a server on port 3000 and opens a browser at the home page, as shown in Figure 1-1.

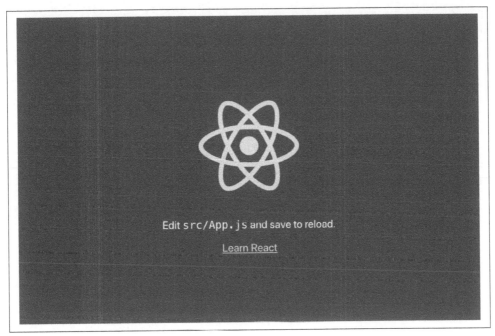

Figure 1-1. The generated front page

The server delivers your application as a single, large bundle of JavaScript. The code mounts all of its components inside this `<div/>` in *public/index.html*:

```
<div id="root"></div>
```

The code to generate the components begins in the *src/index.js* file (*src/index.tsx* if you're using TypeScript):

```
import React from 'react'
import ReactDOM from 'react-dom'
import './index.css'
import App from './App'
import reportWebVitals from './reportWebVitals'

ReactDOM.render(
  <React.StrictMode>
    <App />
  </React.StrictMode>,
  document.getElementById('root')
)

// If you want to start measuring performance in your app, pass a function
// to log results (for example: reportWebVitals(console.log))
// or send to an analytics endpoint. Learn more: https://bit.ly/CRA-vitals
reportWebVitals()
```

This file does little more than render a single component called `<App/>`, which it imports from *App.js* (or *App.tsx*) in the same directory:

```
import logo from './logo.svg'
import './App.css'

function App() {
  return (
    <div className="App">
      <header className="App-header">
        <img src={logo} className="App-logo" alt="logo" />
        <p>
          Edit <code>src/App.js</code> and save to reload.
        </p>
        <a
          className="App-link"
          href="https://reactjs.org"
          target="_blank"
          rel="noopener noreferrer"
        >
          Learn React
        </a>
      </header>
    </div>
  )
}

export default App
```

If you edit this file while the application is `start`-ed, the page in the browser automatically updates.

When you're ready to ship the code to production, you need to generate a set of static files that you can deploy on a standard web server. To do this, run the `build` script:

```
$ npm run build
```

The `build` script creates a *build* directory and then publishes a set of static files (see Figure 1-2).

```
build
├ asset-manifest.json
├ favicon.ico
├ index.html
├ logo192.png
├ logo512.png
├ manifest.json
├ robots.txt
└ static
  ├ css
  ├ js
  └ media
```

Figure 1-2. The generated contents in the build directory

The build copies many of these files from the *public/* directory. The code for the app is transpiled into browser-compatible JavaScript and stored in one or more files in the *static/js* directory. Stylesheets used by the application are stitched together and stored in *static/css*. Several of the files have hashed IDs added to them so that when you deploy your application, browsers download the latest code rather than some old cached version.

Discussion

`create-react-app` is not just a tool for generating a new application but also a platform to keep your React application up-to-date with the latest tools and libraries. You can upgrade the `react-scripts` library as you would any other: by changing the version number and rerunning `npm install`. You don't need to manage a list of Babel plugins or postcss libraries, or maintain a complex *webpack.config.js* file. The `react-scripts` library manages them all for you.

The configuration is all still there, of course, but buried deep within the *react-scripts* directory. In there, you will find the *webpack.config.js* file, containing all the Babel configuration and file loaders that your application will use. Because it's a library, you can update React Scripts just as you would any other dependency.

If, however, you later decide to manage all of this yourself, you're free to do so. If you eject the application, then everything comes back under your control:

```
$ npm run eject
```

However, this is a one-time-only change. Once you have ejected your application, there is no going back. You should think carefully before ever ejecting an application. You may find that the configuration you need is already available. For example, developers would often eject an application to switch to using TypeScript. The `--template typescript` option now removes the need for that.

Another common reason for ejecting was to proxy web services. React apps often need to connect to some separate API backend. Developers used to do this by configuring Webpack to proxy a remote server through the local development server. You can now avoid doing this by setting a proxy in the *package.json* file:

```
"proxy": "http://myapiserver",
```

If your code now contacts a URL that the server cannot find locally (*/api/thing*), the `react-scripts` automatically proxies these requests to *http://myapiserver/api/thing*.

 If you can, avoid ejecting your application. Look through the `create-react-app` documentation (*https://oreil.ly/99Ied*) to see if you can make the change some other way.

You can download the source for this recipe in JavaScript (*https://oreil.ly/UK0dZ*) or TypeScript (*https://oreil.ly/oOSo9*) from the GitHub site.

1.2 Build Content-Rich Apps with Gatsby

Problem

Content-rich sites like blogs and online stores need to serve large amounts of complex content efficiently. A tool like `create-react-app` is not suitable for this kind of website because it delivers everything as a single large bundle of JavaScript that a browser must download before anything displays.

Solution

If you are building a content-rich site, consider using Gatsby.

Gatsby focuses on loading, transforming, and delivering content in the most efficient way possible. It can generate static versions of web pages, which means that the response times of Gatsby sites are often significantly slower than, say, those built with `create-react-app`.

Gatsby has many plugins that can load and transform data efficiently from static local data, GraphQL sources, and third-party content management systems such as WordPress.

You can install `gatsby` globally, but you can also run it via the `npx` command:

```
$ npx gatsby new my-app
```

The `gatsby new` command creates a new project in a subdirectory called *my-app*. The first time you run this command, it asks which package manager to use: either `yarn` or `npm`.

To start your application, change into the new directory and run it in development mode:

```
$ cd my-app
$ npm run develop
```

You can then open your application at *http://localhost:8000*, as shown in Figure 1-3.

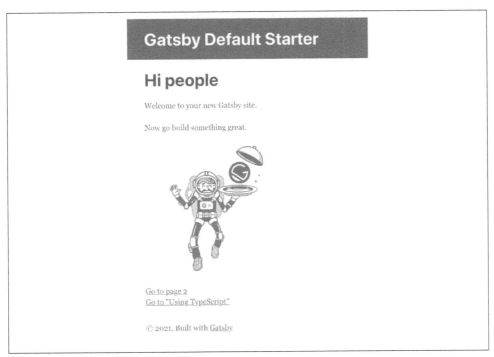

Figure 1-3. Gatsby page at http://localhost:8000

Gatsby projects have a straightforward structure, as shown in Figure 1-4.

```
Project
├ LICENSE
├ README.md
├ gatsby-browser.js
├ gatsby-config.js
├ gatsby-node.js
├ gatsby-ssr.js
├ node_modules/
├ package-lock.json
├ package.json
└ src
  ├ components
  ├ images
  └ pages
```

Figure 1-4. The Gatsby directory structure

The core of the application lives under the *src* directory. Each page within a Gatsby app has its own React component. This is the front page of the default application in *index.js*:

```
import * as React from "react"
import { Link } from "gatsby"
import { StaticImage } from "gatsby-plugin-image"
```

```
import Layout from "../components/layout"
import Seo from "../components/seo"

const IndexPage = () => (
  <Layout>
    <Seo title="Home" />
    <h1>Hi people</h1>
    <p>Welcome to your new Gatsby site.</p>
    <p>Now go build something great.</p>
    <StaticImage
      src="../images/gatsby-astronaut.png"
      width={300}
      quality={95}
      formats={["AUTO", "WEBP", "AVIF"]}
      alt="A Gatsby astronaut"
      style={{ marginBottom: `1.45rem` }}
    />
    <p>
      <Link to="/page-2/">Go to page 2</Link> <br />
      <Link to="/using-typescript/">Go to "Using TypeScript"</Link>
    </p>
  </Layout>
)
```

```
export default IndexPage
```

There is no need to create a route for the page. Each page component is automatically assigned a route. For example, the page at *src/pages/using-typescript.tsx* is automatically available at *using-typescript*.[1] This approach has multiple advantages. First, if you have many pages, you don't need to manage the routes for them manually. Second, it means that Gatsby can deliver much more rapidly. To see why, let's look at how to generate a production build for a Gatsby application.

If you stop the Gatsby development server,[2] you can generate a production build with the following:

```
$ npm run build
```

This command runs a `gatsby build` command, which creates a *public* directory. And it is the *public* directory that contains the real magic of Gatsby. For each page, you find two files. First, a generated JavaScript file:

```
1389 06:48 component---src-pages-using-typescript-tsx-93b78cfadc08d7d203c6.js
```

---

1 And yes, this means that Gatsby has TypeScript support built-in.

2 You can do this in most operating systems by pressing Ctrl-C.

Here you can see that the code for *using-typescript.tsx* is just 1,389 bytes long, which, with the core framework, is just enough JavaScript to build the page. It is not the kind of include-everything script that you find in a `create-react-app` project.

Second, there is a subdirectory for each page containing a generated HTML file. For *using-typescript.tsx*, the file is called *public/using-typescript/index.html*, containing a statically generated version of the web page. It contains the HTML that the *using-typescript.tsx* component would otherwise render dynamically. At the end of the web page, it loads the JavaScript version of the page to generate any dynamic content.

This file structure means that Gatsby pages load as quickly as static pages. Using the bundled `react-helmet` library, you can also generate `<meta/>` header tags with additional features about your site. Both features are great for search engine optimization (SEO).

Discussion

How will the content get into your Gatsby application? You might use a headless content management system, a GraphQL service, a static data source, or something else. Fortunately, Gatsby has many plugins that allow you to connect data sources to your application and then transform the content from other formats, such as Markdown, into HTML.

You can find a complete set of plugins on the Gatsby website (*https://oreil.ly/9GwLv*).

Most of the time, you choose the plugins you need when you first create the project. To give you a head start, Gatsby also supports *start templates*. The template provides the initial application structure and configuration. The app we built earlier uses the default starter template, which is quite simple. The *gatsby-config.js* file in the root of the application configures which plugins your application uses.

But there are masses of Gatsby starters available, preconfigured to build applications that connect to various data sources, with preconfigured options for SEO, styling, offline caching, progressive web applications (PWAs), and more. Whatever kind of content-rich application you are building, there is a starter close to what you need.

There is more information on the Gatsby website about Gatsby starters (*https://oreil.ly/vwUd8*), as well as a cheat sheet (*https://oreil.ly/f7xbF*) for the most useful tools and commands.

You can download the source for this recipe from the GitHub site (*https://oreil.ly/DzLSy*).

1.3 Build Universal Apps with Razzle

Problem

Sometimes when you start to build an application, it is not always clear what the significant architectural decisions will be. Should you create an SPA? If performance is critical, should you use server side r? You will need to decide what your deployment platform will be and whether you will write your code in JavaScript or TypeScript.

Many tools require that you answer these questions early on. If you later change your mind, modifying how you build and deploy your application can be complicated.

Solution

If you want to defer decisions about how you build and deploy your application, you should consider using Razzle (*https://oreil.ly/3pZic*).

Razzle is a tool for building Universal applications (*https://oreil.ly/C496O*): applications that can execute their JavaScript on the server. Or the client. Or both.

Razzle uses a plugin architecture that allows you to change your mind about how you build your application. It will even let you change your mind about building your code in React, Preact, or some other framework entirely, like Elm or Vue.

You can create a Razzle application with the `create-razzle-app` command:[3]

```
$ npx create-razzle-app my-app
```

This command creates a new Razzle project in the *my-app* subdirectory. You can start the development server with the `start` script:

```
$ cd my-app
$ npm run start
```

The `start` script will dynamically build both client code and server code and then run the server on port 3000, as shown in Figure 1-5.

---

3 The name is intentionally similar to `create-react-app`. The maintainer of Razzle, Jared Palmer, lists `create-react-app` as one of the inspirations for Razzle.

Figure 1-5. The Razzle front page at http://localhost:3000

When you want to deploy a production version of your application, you can then run the `build` script:

```
$ npm run build
```

Unlike `create-react-app`, this will build not just the client code but also a Node server. Razzle generates the code in the *build* subdirectory. The server code will continue to generate static code for your client at runtime. You can start a production server by running the *build/server.js* file using the `start:prod` script:

```
$ npm run start:prod
```

You can deploy the production server anywhere that Node is available.

The server and the client can both run the same code, which makes it *Universal*. But how does it do this?

The client and the server have different entry points. The server runs the code in *src/server.js*; the browser runs the code in *src/client.js*. Both *server.js* and *client.js* then render the same app using *src/App.js*.

If you want to run your app as an SPA, remove the *src/index.js* and *src/server.js* files. Then create an *index.html* file in the *public* folder containing a `<div/>` with an ID of `root`, and rebuild the application with this:

```
$ node_modules/.bin/razzle build --type=spa
```

 To build your application as an SPA every time, add `--type=spa` to the `start` and `build` scripts in *package.json*.

You will generate a full SPA in *build/public/* that you can deploy on any web server.

Discussion

Razzle is so adaptable because it is built from a set of highly configurable plugins. Each plugin is a higher-order function that receives a Webpack configuration and returns a modified version. One plugin might transpile TypeScript code; another might bundle the React libraries.

If you want to switch your application to Vue, you only need to replace the plugins you use.

You can find a list of available plugins on the Razzle website (*https://oreil.ly/UXwPv*).

You can download the source for this recipe from the GitHub site (*https://oreil.ly/rBR9r*).

1.4 Manage Server and Client Code with Next.js

Problem

React generates client code—even if it generates the client code on the server. Sometimes, however, you might have a relatively small amount of application programming interface (API) code that you would prefer to manage as part of the same React application.

Solution

Next.js is a tool for generating React applications and server code. The API endpoints and the client pages use default routing conventions, making them simpler to build and deploy than they would be if you manage them yourself. You can find full details about Next.js on the website (*https://nextjs.org*).

You can create a Next.js application with this command:

```
$ npx create-next-app my-app
```

This will use yarn as the package manager if you have it installed. You can force it to use the npm package manager with the --user-npm flag:

```
$ npx create-next-app --use-npm my-app
```

This will create a Next.js application in the *my-app* subdirectory. To start the app, run the dev script (see Figure 1-6):

```
$ cd my-app
$ npm run dev
```

Welcome to Next.js!

Get started by editing `pages/index.js`

Documentation →

Find in-depth information about
Next.js features and API.

Learn →

Learn about Next.js in an interactive
course with quizzes!

Examples →

Discover and deploy boilerplate
example Next.js projects.

Deploy →

Instantly deploy your Next.js site to
a public URL with Vercel.

Powered by ▲Vercel

Figure 1-6. A Next.js page running at http://localhost:3000

Next.js allows you to create pages without the need to manage any routing configuration. If you add a component script to the *pages* folder, it will instantly become available through the server. For example, the *pages/index.js* component generates the home page of the default application.

This approach is similar to the one taken by Gatsby,[4] but is taken further in Next.js to include server-side code.

Next.js applications usually include some API server code, which is unusual for React applications, which are often built separately from server code. But if you look inside *pages/api*, you will find an example server endpoint called *hello.js*:

```
// Next.js API route support: https://nextjs.org/docs/api-routes/introduction

export default (req, res) => {
  res.status(200).json({ name: 'John Doe' })
}
```

The routing that mounts this to the endpoint *api/hello* happens automatically.

---

4 See Recipe 1.2.

Next.js transpiles your code into a hidden directory called .next, which it can then deploy to a service such as Next.js's own Vercel (*https://vercel.com*) platform.

If you want, you generate a static build of your application with:

```
$ node_modules/.bin/next export
```

The export command will build your client code in a directory called *out*. The command will convert each page into a statically rendered HTML file, which will load quickly in the browser. At the end of the page, it will load the JavaScript version to generate any dynamic content.

 If you create an exported version of a Next.js application, it won't include any server-side APIs.

Next.js comes with a bunch of data-fetching options, which allow you to get data from static content, or via headless content management system (CMS) sources (*https://oreil.ly/Xmia8*).

Discussion

Next.js is in many ways similar to Gatsby. Its focus is on the speed of delivery, with a small amount of configuration. It's probably most beneficial for teams that will have very little server code.

You can download the source for this recipe from the GitHub site (*https://oreil.ly/9gbJs*).

1.5 Create a Tiny App with Preact

Problem

React applications can be large. It's pretty easy to create a simple React application that is transpiled into bundles of JavaScript code that are several hundred kilobytes in size. You might want to build an app with React-like features but with a much smaller footprint.

Solution

If you want React features but don't want to pay the price of a React-size JavaScript bundle, consider using Preact.

Preact is *not* React. It is a separate library, designed to be as close to React as possible but much smaller.

The reason that the React framework is so big is because of the way it works. React components don't generate elements in the Document Object Model (DOM) of the browser directly. Instead, they build elements within a *virtual DOM* and then update the actual DOM at frequent intervals. Doing so allows basic DOM rendering to be fast because the actual DOM needs to be updated only when there are actual changes. However, it does have a downside. React's virtual DOM requires a lot of code to keep it up-to-date. It needs to manage an entire synthetic event model, which parallels the one in the browser. For this reason, the React framework is large and can take some time to download.

One way around this is to use techniques such as SSR, but SSR can be complex to configure.[5] Sometimes, you want to download a small amount of code. And that's why Preact exists.

The Preact library, although similar to React, is tiny. At the time of writing, the main Preact library is around 4KB, which is small enough that it's possible to add React-like features to web pages in barely more code than is required to write native JavaScript.

Preact lets you choose how to use it: as a small JavaScript library included in a web page (the *no-tools* approach) or as a full-blown JavaScript application.

The no-tools approach is basic. The core Preact library does not support JSX, and you will have no Babel support, so you will not be able to use modern JavaScript. Here is an example web page using the raw Preact library:

```html
<html>
    <head>
        <title>No Tools!</title>
        <script src="https://unpkg.com/preact?umd"></script>
    </head>
    <body>
        <h1>No Tools Preact App!</h1>
        <div id="root"></div>
        <script>
         var h = window.preact.h;
         var render = window.preact.render;

         var mount = document.getElementById('root');

         render(
            h('button',
              {
```

---

5 See Recipes 1.2 and 1.3.

```
            onClick: function() {
                render(h('div', null, 'Hello'), mount);
            }
        },
        'Click!'),
    mount
);
    </script>
  </body>
</html>
```

This application will mount itself at the `<div/>` with an ID of `root`, where it will display a button. When you click the button, it will replace the contents of the root `div` with the string `"Hello"`, which is about as basic as a Preact app can be.

You would rarely write an application in this way. In reality, you would create a simple build-chain that would, at the least, support modern JavaScript.

Preact supports the entire spectrum of JavaScript applications. At the other extreme, you can create a complete Preact application with `preact-cli`.

`preact-cli` is a tool for creating Preact projects and is analogous to tools like `create-react-app`. You can create a Preact application with:

```
$ npx preact-cli create default my-app
```

 This command uses the default template. Other templates are available for creating projects using, for example, Material components or TypeScript. See the Preact GitHub page (*https://oreil.ly/IVQua*) for more information.

This command will create your new Preact application in the *my-app* subdirectory. To start it, run the `dev` script:

```
$ cd my-app
$ npm run dev
```

The server will run on port 8080, as shown in Figure 1-7.

Figure 1-7. A page from Preact

The server generates a web page, which calls back for a JavaScript bundle made from the code in *src/index.js*.

You now have a full-scale React-like application. The code inside the Home component (*src/routes/home/index.js*), for example, looks very React-like, with full JSX support:

```
import { h } from 'preact';
import style from './style.css';

const Home = () => (
    <div class={style.home}>
        <h1>Home</h1>
        <p>This is the Home component.</p>
    </div>
);

export default Home;
```

The only significant difference from a standard React component is that a function called h is imported from the preact library, instead of importing React from the react library.

 The JSX within the Preact code will be converted into a series of calls to the h function, which is why it needs to be imported. For the same reason, applications created with create-react-app prior to version 17 also required the import of the react object. From version 17 create-react-app switched to use the JSX transform (*https://oreil.ly/HOwS9*), doing away for the need to import react every time. It's always possible that future versions of Preact will make a similar change.

However, the size of the application has increased: it is now a little over 300KB. That's pretty large, but we are still in dev mode. To see the real power of Preact, stop the dev server by pressing Ctrl-C, and then run the build script:

```
$ npm run build
```

This command will generate a static version of the application in the *build* directory. First, this will have the advantage of creating a static copy of the front page, which will render quickly. Second, it will remove all unused code from the application and shrink everything down. If you serve this built version of the app on a standard web server, the browser will transfer only about 50–60KB when it's opened.

Discussion

Preact is a remarkable project. Despite working in a very different way from React, it provides virtually the same power at a fraction of the size. And the fact that you can use it for anything from the lowliest inline code to a full-blown SPA means it is well worth considering if code size is critical to your project.

You can find out more about Preact on the Preact website (*https://preactjs.com*).

You can download the source for the no-tools example (*https://oreil.ly/N9PKf*) and the larger Preact example (*https://oreil.ly/F0tW9*) from the GitHub site.

If you would like to make Preact look even more like React, see the preact-compat (*https://oreil.ly/3YXOv*) library.

Finally, for a project that takes a similar approach to Preact, look at InfernoJS (*https://infernojs.org*).

1.6 Build Libraries with nwb

Problem

Large organizations often develop several React applications at the same time. If you're a consultancy, you might create applications for multiple organizations. If you're a software house, you might create various applications that require the same look and feel, so you will probably want to build shared components to use across several applications.

When you create a component project, you need to create a directory structure, select a set of tools, choose a set of language features, and create a build chain that can bundle your component in a deployable format. This process can be just as tedious as manually creating a project for an entire React application.

Solution

You can use the nwb toolkit to create complete React applications or single React components. It can also create components for use within Preact and InfernoJS projects, but we concentrate on React components here.

To create a new React component project, you will first need to install the nwb tool globally:

```
$ npm install -g nwb
```

You can then create a new project with the nwb command:

```
$ nwb new react-component my-component
```

If instead of creating a single component, you want to create an entire nwb application, you can replace react-component in this command with react-app, preact-app, or inferno-app to create an application in the given framework. You can also use vanilla-app if you want to create a basic JavaScript project without a framework.

When you run this command, it will ask you several questions about the type of library you want to build. For example, it will ask you if you're going to build ECMA-Script modules:

```
Creating a react-component project...
? Do you want to create an ES modules build? (Y/n)
```

This option allows you to build a version including an export statement, which Webpack can use to decide if it needs to include the component in a client application. You will also be asked if you want to create a Universal Module Definition (UMD):

```
? Do you want to create a UMD build? (y/N)
```

That's useful if you want to include your component in a <script/> within a web page. For our example, we won't create a UMD build.

After the questions, the tool will create an nwb component project inside the *my-component* subdirectory. The project comes with a simple wrapper application that you can start with the start script:

```
$ cd my-component
$ npm run start
```

The demo application runs on port 3000, as shown in Figure 1-8.

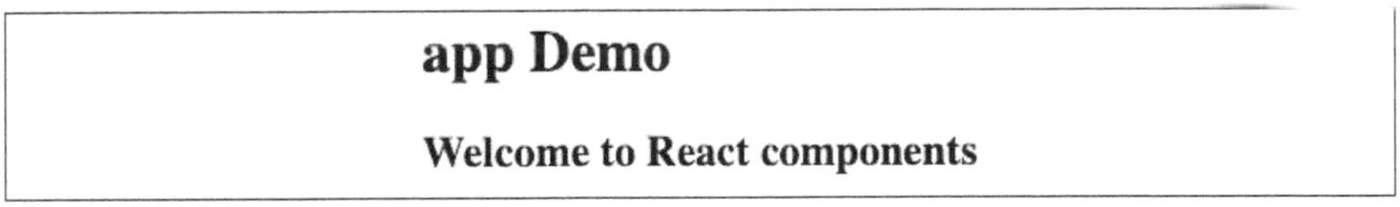

---

app Demo

Welcome to React components

Figure 1-8. An nwb component

The application will contain a single component defined in *src/index.js*:

```
import React, { Component } from 'react'

export default class extends Component {
  render() {
    return (
      <div>
        <h2>Welcome to React components</h2>
      </div>
    )
```

```
      }
   }
```

You can now build the component as you would any React project. When you are ready to create a publishable version, type:

```
$ npm run build
```

The built component will be in *lib/index.js*, which you can deploy to a repository for use within other projects.

Discussion

For further details on creating nwb components, see the nwb guide to developing components and libraries (*https://oreil.ly/XHrQa*).

You can download the source for this recipe from the GitHub site (*https://oreil.ly/P4Xzj*).

1.7 Add React to Rails with Webpacker

Problem

The Rails framework was created before interactive JavaScript applications became popular. Rails applications follow a more traditional model for web application development, in which it generates HTML pages on the server in response to browser requests. But sometimes, you may want to include more interactive elements inside a Rails application.

Solution

You can use the Webpacker library to insert React applications into Rails-generated web pages. To see how it works, let's first generate a Rails application that includes Webpacker:

```
$ rails new my-app --webpack=react
```

This command will create a Rails application in a directory called *my-app* that is pre-configured to run a Webpacker server. Before we start the application, let's go into it and generate an example page/controller:

```
$ cd my-app
$ rails generate controller Example index
```

That code will generate this template page at *app/views/example/index.html.erb*:

```
<h1>Example#index</h1>
<p>Find me in app/views/example/index.html.erb</p>
```

Next, we need to create a small React application that we can insert into this page. Rails inserts Webpacker applications as *packs*: small JavaScript bundles within Rails. We'll create a new pack in *app/javascript/packs/counter.js* containing a simple counter component:

```
import React, { useState } from 'react'
import ReactDOM from 'react-dom'

const Counter = (props) => {
  const [count, setCount] = useState(0)
  return (
    <div className="Counter">
      You have clicked the button {count} times.
      <button onClick={() => setCount((c) => c + 1)}>Click!</button>
    </div>
  )
}

document.addEventListener('DOMContentLoaded', () => {
  ReactDOM.render(
    <Counter />,
    document.body.appendChild(document.createElement('div'))
  )
})
```

This application updates a counter every time a user clicks the button.

We can now insert the pack into the web page by adding a single line of code to the template page:

```
<h1>Example#index</h1>
<p>Find me in app/views/example/index.html.erb</p>
<%= javascript_pack_tag 'counter' %>
```

Finally, we can run the Rails server on port 3000:

```
$ rails server
```

 At the time of writing, you will need the `yarn` package manager installed when starting the server. You can install `yarn` globally with `npm install -g yarn`.

You will see the *http://localhost:3000/example/index.html* page in Figure 1-9.

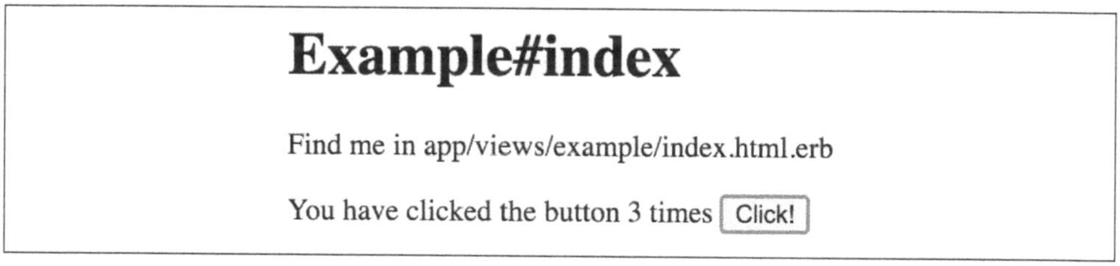

Figure 1-9. A React app embedded in http://localhost:3000/example/index.html

Discussion

Behind the scenes, as you have probably guessed, Webpacker transforms the application using a copy of Webpack, which you can configure with the *app/config/webpacker.yml* config file.

Webpacker is used alongside Rails code rather than as a replacement for it. You should consider using it if your Rails application requires a small amount of additional interactivity.

You can find out more about Webpacker on the Webpacker GitHub site (*https://oreil.ly/aYZ0h*).

You can download the source for this recipe from the GitHub site (*https://oreil.ly/H3q1F*).

1.8 Create Custom Elements with Preact

Problem

There are sometimes circumstances where it is challenging to add React code into existing content. For example, in some CMS configurations, users are not allowed to insert additional JavaScript into the body of a page. In these cases, it would be helpful to have some standardized way to insert JavaScript applications safely into a page.

Solution

Custom elements are a standard way of creating new HTML elements you can use on a web page. In effect, they extend the HTML language by making more tags available to a user.

This recipe looks at how we can use a lightweight framework like Preact to create custom elements, which we can publish on a third-party server.

Let's begin by creating a new Preact application. This application will serve the custom element that we will be able to use elsewhere:[6]

```
$ preact create default my-element
```

Now we will change into the app's directory and add the `preact-custom-element` library to the project:

```
$ cd my-element
$ npm install preact-custom-element
```

The `preact-custom-element` library will allow us to register a new custom HTML element in a browser.

Next, we need to modify the *src/index.js* file of the Preact project so that it registers a new custom element, which we will call *components/Converter/index.js*:

```
import register from 'preact-custom-element'
import Converter from './components/Converter'

register(Converter, 'x-converter', ['currency'])
```

The `register` method tells the browser that we want to create a new custom HTML element called `<x-converter/>` that has a single property called `currency`, which we will define in *src/components/Converter/index.js*:

```
import { h } from 'preact'
import { useEffect, useState } from 'preact/hooks'
import 'style/index.css'

const rates = { gbp: 0.81, eur: 0.92, jpy: 106.64 }

export default ({ currency = 'gbp' }) => {
  const [curr, setCurr] = useState(currency)
  const [amount, setAmount] = useState(0)

  useEffect(() => {
    setCurr(currency)
  }, [currency])

  return (
    <div className="Converter">
      <p>
        <label htmlFor="currency">Currency: </label>
        <select
          name="currency"
          value={curr}
          onChange={(evt) => setCurr(evt.target.value)}
        >
```

---

6 For more information on creating Preact applications, see Recipe 1.5.

```
            {Object.keys(rates).map((r) => (
              <option value={r}>{r}</option>
            ))}
          </select>
      </p>
      <p className="Converter-amount">
        <label htmlFor="amount">Amount: </label>
        <input
          name="amount"
          size={8}
          type="number"
          value={amount}
          onInput={(evt) => setAmount(parseFloat(evt.target.value))}
        />
      </p>
      <p>
        Cost:
        {((amount || 0) / rates[curr]).toLocaleString('en-US', {
          style: 'currency',
          currency: 'USD',
        })}
      </p>
    </div>
  )
}
```

 To be compliant with the custom elements specification, we must choose a name for our element that begins with a lowercase letter, does not include any uppercase letters, and contains a hyphen.[7] This convention ensures the name does not clash with any standard element name.

Our Converter component is a currency converter, which in our example uses a fixed set of exchange rates. If we now start our Preact server:

```
$ npm run dev
```

the JavaScript for the custom element will be available at *http://localhost:8080/bundle.js*.

To use this new custom element, let's create a static web page somewhere with this HTML:

```
<html>
    <head>
        <script src="https://unpkg.com/babel-polyfill/dist/polyfill.min.js">
```

---

7 See the WHATWG specification (*https://oreil.ly/KOjmP*) for further details on custom elements and naming conventions.

```
        </script>
        <script src="https://unpkg.com/@webcomponents/webcomponentsjs">
        </script>
        <!-- Replace this with the address of your custom element -->
        <script type="text/javascript" src="http://localhost:8080/bundle.js">
        </script>
    </head>
    <body>
        <h1>Custom Web Element</h1>
        <div style="float: right; clear: both">
            <!-- This tag will insert the Preact app -->
            <x-converter currency="jpy"/>
        </div>
        <p>This page contains an example custom element called
            <code>&lt;x-converter/&gt;</code>,
            which is being served from a different location</p>
    </body>
</html>
```

This web page includes the definition of the custom element in the final <script/> of the <head/> element. To ensure that the custom element is available across both new and old browsers, we also include a couple of shims from *unpkg.com*.

Now that we've included the custom element code in the web page, we can insert <x-converter/> tags into the code, as if they are part of standard HTML. In our example, we are also passing a currency property to the underlying Preact component.

 Custom element properties are passed to the underlying component with lowercase names, regardless of how we define them in the HTML.

We can run this page through a web server, separate from the Preact server. Figure 1-10 shows the new custom element.

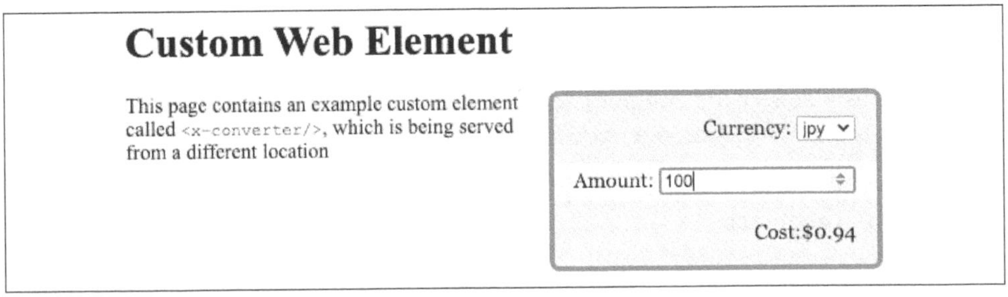

Custom Web Element

This page contains an example custom element called <x-converter/>, which is being served from a different location

Currency: [jpy ▾]

Amount: [100   ⬍]

Cost: $0.94

Figure 1-10. The custom element embedded in a static page

Discussion

The custom element does not need to be on the same server as the web page that uses it, which means that we can use custom elements to publish widgets for any web page. Because of this, you might want to check the `Referer` header on any incoming request to the component to prevent any unauthorized usage.

Our example is serving the custom element from Preact's development server. For a production release, you would probably want to create a static build of the component, which will likely be significantly smaller.[8]

You can download the source for this recipe from the GitHub site (*https://oreil.ly/aB7BP*).

1.9 Use Storybook for Component Development

Problem

React components are the stable building material of React applications. If we write them carefully, we can reuse the components in other React applications. But when you build a component, it takes work to check how it works in all circumstances. For example, in an asynchronous application, React might render the component with undefined properties. Will the component still render correctly? Will it show errors?

But if you are building components as part of a complex application, it can be tough to create all of the situations with which your component will need to cope.

Also, if you have specialized user experience (UX) developers working on your team, it can waste a lot of time if they have to navigate through an application to view the single component they have in development.

It would be helpful if there were some way of displaying a component in isolation and passing it example sets of properties.

Solution

Storybook is a tool for displaying libraries of components in various states. You could describe it as a gallery for components, but that's probably selling it short. In reality, Storybook is a tool for component development.

How do we add Storybook to a project? Let's begin by creating a React application with `create-react-app`:

---

8 For further details on shrinking Preact downloads, see Recipe 1.5.

```
$ npx create-react-app my-app
$ cd my-app
```

Now we can add Storybook to the project:

```
$ npx sb init
```

We then start the Storybook server with yarn or npm:

```
$ npm run storybook
```

Storybook runs a separate server on port 9000, as you can see in Figure 1-11. When you use Storybook, there is no need to run the actual React application.

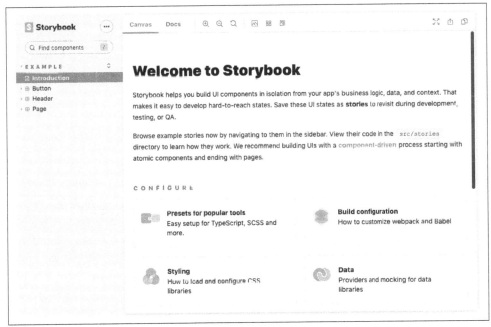

Figure 1-11. The welcome page in Storybook

Storybook calls a single component rendered with example properties a *story*. The default installation of Storybook generates sample stories in the *src/stories* directory of the application. For example, this is *src/stories/Button.stories.js*:

```
import React from 'react';

import { Button } from './Button';

export default {
  title: 'Example/Button',
  component: Button,
  argTypes: {
    backgroundColor: { control: 'color' },
  },
```

```
};

const Template = (args) => <Button {...args} />;

export const Primary = Template.bind({});
Primary.args = {
  primary: true,
  label: 'Button',
};

export const Secondary = Template.bind({});
Secondary.args = {
  label: 'Button',
};

export const Large = Template.bind({});
Large.args = {
  size: 'large',
  label: 'Button',
};

export const Small = Template.bind({});
Small.args = {
  size: 'small',
  label: 'Button',
};
```

Storybook watches for files named *.stories.js in your source folder, and it doesn't care where they are, so you are free to create them where you like. One typical pattern places the stories in a folder alongside the component they are showcasing. So if you copy the folder to a different application, you can include stories as living documentation.

Figure 1-12 shows what Button.stories.js looks like in Storybook.

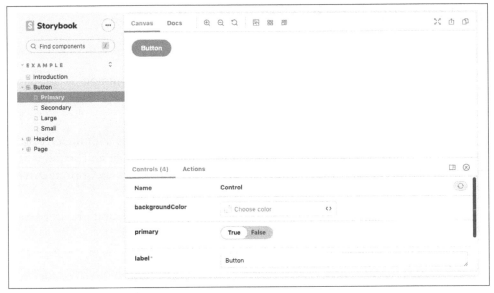

Figure 1-12. An example story

Discussion

Despite its simple appearance, Storybook is a productive development tool. It allows you to focus on one component at a time. Like a kind of visual unit test, it enables you to try a component in a series of possible scenarios to check that it behaves appropriately.

Storybook also has a large selection of additional add-ons (*https://oreil.ly/3kSVa*).

The add-ons allow you to:

- Check for accessibility problems (*addon-a11y*)
- Add interactive controls for setting properties (*Knobs*)
- Include inline documentation for each story (*Docs*)
- Record snapshots of the HTML to test the impact of changes (*Storyshots*)

And do much more.

For further information about Storybook, see the website (*https://storybook.js.org*).

You can download the source for this recipe from the GitHub site (*https://oreil.ly/GyxTX*).

1.10 Test Your Code in a Browser with Cypress

Problem

Most React projects include a testing library. The most common is probably `@testing-library/react`, which comes bundled with `create-react-app`, or Enzyme, which is used by Preact.

But nothing quite beats testing code in a real browser, with all the additional complications that entails. Traditionally, browser testing can be unstable and requires frequent maintenance as you need to upgrade browser drivers (such as ChromeDriver) every time you upgrade the browser.

Add to that the issue of generating test data on a backend server, and browser-based testing can be complex to set up and manage.

Solution

The Cypress testing framework (*https://www.cypress.io*) avoids many of the downsides of traditional browser testing. It runs in a browser but avoids the need for an external web-driver tool. Instead, it communicates directly with a browser, like Chrome or Electron, over a network port and then injects JavaScript to run much of the test code.

Let's create an application `create-react-app` to see how it works:

```
$ npx create-react-app --use-npm my-app
```

Now let's go into the app directory and install Cypress:

```
$ cd my-app
$ npm install cypress --save-dev
```

Before we run Cypress, we need to configure it so that it knows how to find our application. We can do this by creating a *cypress.json* file in the application directory and telling it the uniform resource locator (URL) of our app:

```
{
  "baseUrl": "http://localhost:3000/"
}
```

Once we have started the main application:

```
$ npm start
```

we can then open Cypress:

```
$ npx cypress open
```

The first time you run Cypress, it will install all the dependencies it needs. We'll now create a test in the *cypress/integration* directory called *screenshot.js*, which opens the home page and takes a screenshot:

```
describe('screenshot', () => {
    it('should be able to take a screenshot', () => {
        cy.visit('/');
        cy.screenshot('frontpage');
    });
});
```

You'll notice that we wrote the tests in Jest format. Once you save the test, it will appear in the main Cypress window, shown in Figure 1-13.

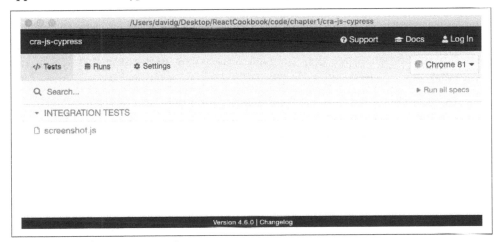

Figure 1-13. The Cypress window

If you double-click the test, Cypress will run it in a browser. The front page of the application will open, and the test will save a screenshot to *cypress/screenshots/screenshot.js/frontpage.png*.

Discussion

Here are some example commands you can perform with Cypress:

Command	Description
cy.contains('Fred')	Finds the element containing *Fred*
cy.get('.Norman').click()	Clicks the element with class *Norman*
cy.get('input').type('Hi!')	Types "Hi!" into the input field
cy.get('h1').scrollIntoView()	Scrolls the <h1/> into view

These are just some of the commands that interact with the web page. But Cypress has another trick up its sleeve. Cypress can also modify the code inside the browser to change the time (cy.clock()), the cookies (cy.setCookie()), the local storage (cy.clearLocalStorage()) and—most impressively—fake requests and responses to an API server.

It does this by modifying the networking functions that are built into the browser so that this code:

```
cy.route("/api/server?*", [{some: 'Data'}])
```

will intercept any requests to a server endpoint beginning */api/server?* and return the JSON array [{some: 'Data'}].

Simulating network responses can completely change the way teams develop applications because it decouples the frontend development from the backend. The browser tests can specify what data they need without having to create a real server and database.

To learn more about Cypress, visit the documentation site (*https://oreil.ly/eX09t*).

You can download the source for this recipe from the GitHub site (*https://oreil.ly/3j8vI*).

CHAPTER 2

Routing

This chapter looks at recipes using React routes and the `react-router-dom` library.

`react-router-dom` uses *declarative routing*, which means you treat routes as you would any other React component. Unlike buttons, text fields, and blocks of text, React routes have no visual appearance. But in most other ways, they are similar to buttons and blocks of text. Routes live in the virtual DOM tree of components. They listen for changes in the current browser location and allow you to switch on and switch off parts of the interface. They are what give SPAs the appearance of multipage applications.

Used well, they can make your application feel like any other website. Users will be able to bookmark sections of your application, as they might bookmark a page from Wikipedia. They can go backward and forward in their browser history, and your interface will behave properly. If you are new to React, then it is well worth your time to look deeply into the power of routing.

2.1 Create Interfaces with Responsive Routes

Problem

People use most applications on both mobile and laptop computers, which means you probably want your React application to work well across all screen sizes. Making your application responsive involves relatively simple CSS changes to adjust the sizing of text and screen layout, and more substantial changes, which can give mobile and desktop users very different experiences when navigating around your site.

Our example application shows the names and addresses of a list of people. In Figure 2-1, you can see the application running on a desktop machine.

Figure 2-1. The desktop view of the app

But this layout won't work very well on a mobile device, which might have space to display either the list of people or the details of one person, but not both.

What can we do in React to provide a custom navigation experience for both mobile and desktop users without creating two completely separate versions of the application?

Solution

We're going to use *responsive routes*. A responsive route changes according to the size of the user's display. Our existing application uses a single route for displaying the information for a person: */people/:id*.

When you navigate to this route, the browser shows the page in Figure 2-1. You can see the people listed down the left side. The page highlights the selected person and displays their details on the right.

We're going to modify our application to cope with an additional route at */people*. Then we will make the routes responsive so that the user will see different things on different devices:

Route	Mobile	Desktop
/people	Shows list of people	Redirects to *people*:someId
people:id	Shows details for :id	Shows list of people and details of :id

What ingredients will we need to do this? First, we need to install react-router-dom if our application does not already have it:

```
$ npm install react-router-dom
```

The `react-router-dom` library allows us to coordinate the browser's current location with the state of our application. Next, we will install the `react-media` library, which allows us to create React components that respond to changes in the display screen size:

```
$ npm install react-media
```

Now we're going to create a responsive `PeopleContainer` component that will manage the routes we want to create. On small screens, our component will display *either* a list of people or the details of a single person. On large screens, it will show a combined view of a list of people on the left and the details of a single person on the right.

The `PeopleContainer` will use the `Media` component from `react-media`. The `Media` component performs a similar job to the CSS `@media` rule: it allows you to generate output for a specified range of screen sizes. The `Media` component accepts a `queries` property that allows you to specify a set of screen sizes. We're going to define a single screen size—small—that we'll use as the break between mobile and desktop screens:

```
<Media queries={{
        small: "(max-width: 700px)"
    }}>
    ...
</Media>
```

The `Media` component takes a single child component, which it expects to be a function. This function is given a `size` object that can be used to tell what the current screen size is. In our example, the `size` object will have a `small` attribute, which we can use to decide what other components to display:

```
<Media queries={{
        small: "(max-width: 700px)"
    }}>
    {
      size => size.small ? [SMALL SCREEN COMPONENTS] : [BIG SCREEN COMPONENTS]
    }
</Media>
```

Before we look at the details of what code we are going to return for large and small screens, it's worth taking a look at how we will mount the `PeopleContainer` in our application. The following code is going to be our main `App` component:

```
import { BrowserRouter, Link, Route, Switch } from 'react-router-dom'
import PeopleContainer from './PeopleContainer'

function App() {
  return (
    <BrowserRouter>
      <Switch>
        <Route path="/people">
```

```
          <PeopleContainer />
        </Route>
        <Link to="/people">People</Link>
      </Switch>
    </BrowserRouter>
  )
}

export default App
```

We are using the BrowserRouter from react-router-dom, which links our code and the HTML5 history API in the browser. We need to wrap all of our routes in a Router to give them access to the browser's current address.

Inside the BrowserRouter, we have a Switch. The Switch looks at the components inside it, looking for a Route that matches the current location. Here we have a single Route matching paths that begin with /people. If that's true, we display the People Container. If no route matches, we fall through to the end of the Switch and render a Link to the /people path. So when someone goes to the front page of the application, they see only a link to the People page.

 The code will match routes beginning with the specified path, unless the exact attribute is specified, in which case a route will be displayed only if the entire path matches.

So we know if we're in the PeopleContainer, we're already on a route that begins with /people/.... If we're on a small screen, we need to either show a list of people or display the details of a single person, but not both. We can do this with Switch:

```
<Media queries={{
        small: "(max-width: 700px)"
    }}>
  {
    size => size.small ? [SMALL SCREEN COMPONENTS]
        <Switch>
          <Route path='/people/:id'>
            <Person/>
          </Route>
          <PeopleList/>
        </Switch>
        : [BIG SCREEN COMPONENTS]
  }
</Media>
```

On a small device, the Media component will call its child function with a value that means size.small is true. Our code will render a Switch that will show a Person component if the current path contains an `id`. Otherwise, the `Switch` will fail to match that `Route` and will instead render a `PeopleList`.

Ignoring the fact that we've yet to write the code for large screens, if we were to run this code right now on a mobile device and hit the `People` link on the front page, we would navigate to *people*, which could cause the application to render the `PeopleList` component. The `PeopleList` component displays a set of links to people with paths of the form */people/id*.[1] When someone selects a person from the list, our components are re-rendered, and this time `PeopleContainer` displays the details of a single person (see Figure 2-2).

Figure 2-2. In mobile view: the list of people (left) that links to a person's details (right)

So far, so good. Now we need to make sure that our application still works for larger screens. We need to generate responsive routes in `PeopleContainer` for when `size.small` is `false`. If the current route is of the form */people/id*, we can display the `PeopleList` component on the left and the `Person` component on the right:

```
<div style={{display: 'flex'}}>
  <PeopleList/>
  <Person/>
</div>
```

---

1 We won't show the code for the `PeopleList` here, but it is available on GitHub (*https://oreil.ly/tZzMD*).

Unfortunately, that doesn't handle the case where the current path is */people*. We need another Switch that either will display the details for a single person or will *redirect* to */people/first-person-id* for the first person in the list of people.

```
<div style={{display: 'flex'}}>
    <PeopleList/>
    <Switch>
        <Route path='/people/:id'>
            <Person/>
        </Route>
        <Redirect to={`/people/${people[0].id}`}/>
    </Switch>
</div>
```

The Redirect component doesn't perform an *actual* browser redirect. It simply updates the current path to */people/first-person-id*, which causes the PeopleContainer to re-render. It's similar to making a call to history.push() in JavaScript, except it doesn't add an extra page to the browser history. If a person navigates to */people*, the browser will simply change its location to */people/first-person-id*.

If we were now to go to */people* on a laptop or larger tablet, we would see the list of people next to the details for the first person (Figure 2-3).

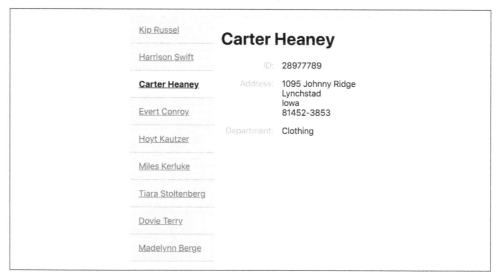

Figure 2-3. What you see at http://localhost:3000/people *on a large display*

Here is the final version of our PeopleContainer:

```
import Media from 'react-media'
import { Redirect, Route, Switch } from 'react-router-dom'
import Person from './Person'
import PeopleList from './PeopleList'
import people from './people'
```

```
const PeopleContainer = () => {
  return (
    <Media
      queries={{
        small: '(max-width: 700px)',
      }}
    >
      {(size) =>
        size.small ? (
          <Switch>
            <Route path="/people/:id">
              <Person />
            </Route>
            <PeopleList />
          </Switch>
        ) : (
          <div style={{ display: 'flex' }}>
            <PeopleList />
            <Switch>
              <Route path="/people/:id">
                <Person />
              </Route>
              <Redirect to={`/people/${people[0].id}`} />
            </Switch>
          </div>
        )
      }
    </Media>
  )
}

export default PeopleContainer
```

Discussion

Declarative routing inside components can seem an odd thing when you first meet it. Suppose you've used a centralized routing model before. In that case, declarative routes may at first seem messy because they spread the wiring of your application across several components rather than in a single file. Instead of creating clean components that know nothing of the outside world, you are suddenly giving the intimate knowledge of the paths used in the application, which might make them less portable.

However, responsive routes show the real power of declarative routing. If you're concerned about your components knowing too much about the paths in your application, consider extracting the path strings into a shared file. That way, you will have the best of both worlds: components that modify their behavior based upon the current path and a centralized set of path configurations.

You can download the source for this recipe from the GitHub site (*https://oreil.ly/tZzMD*).

2.2 Move State into Routes

Problem

It is often helpful to manage the internal state of a component using the route that displays it. For example, this is a React component that displays two tabs of information: one for */people* and one for */offices*:

```
import { useState } from 'react'
import People from './People'
import Offices from './Offices'

import './About.css'

const OldAbout = () => {
  const [tabId, setTabId] = useState('people')

  return (
    <div className="About">
      <div className="About-tabs">
        <div
          onClick={() => setTabId('people')}
          className={
            tabId === 'people' ? 'About-tab active' : 'About-tab'
          }
        >
          People
        </div>
        <div
          onClick={() => setTabId('offices')}
          className={
            tabId === 'offices' ? 'About-tab active' : 'About-tab'
          }
        >
          Offices
        </div>
      </div>
      {tabId === 'people' && <People />}
      {tabId === 'offices' && <Offices />}
    </div>
  )
}

export default OldAbout
```

When a user clicks a tab, an internal `tabId` variable is updated, and the `People` or `Offices` component is displayed (see Figure 2-4).

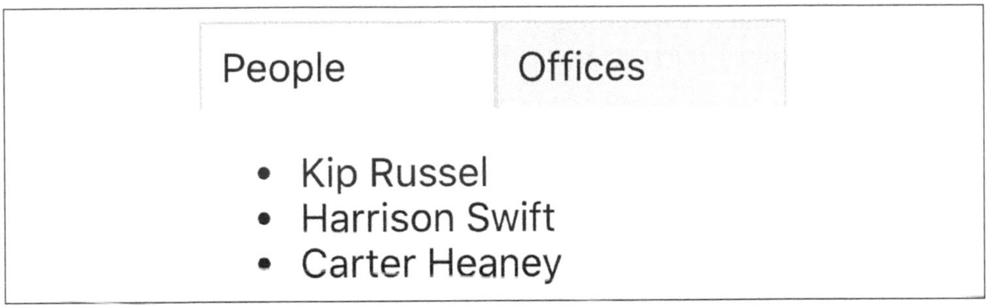

Figure 2-4. By default, the OldAbout component shows people's details

What's the problem? The component works, but if we select the Offices tab and then refresh the page, the component resets to the People tab. Likewise, we can't bookmark the page when it's on the Offices tab. We can't create a link anywhere else in the application, which takes us directly to Offices. Accessibility hardware is less likely to notice that the tabs are working as hyperlinks because they are not rendered in that way.

Solution

We are going to move the tabId state from the component into the current browser location. So instead of rendering the component at */about* and then using onClick events to change the internal state, we are instead going to have routes to */about/people* and */about/offices*, which display one tab or the other. The tab selection will survive a browser refresh. We can bookmark the page on a given tab or create a link to a given tab. And we make the tabs actual hyperlinks, which will be recognized as such by anyone navigating with a keyboard or screen reader.

What ingredients do we need? Just one: react-router-dom:

```
$ npm install react-router-dom
```

react-router-dom will allow us to synchronize the current browser URL with the components that we render on the screen.

Our existing application is already using react-router-dom to display the OldAbout component at path */oldabout* as you can see from this fragment of code from the *App.js* file:

```
<Switch>
    <Route path="/oldabout">
        <OldAbout/>
    </Route>
    <p>Choose an option</p>
</Switch>
```

You can see the complete code for this file at the GitHub repository (*https://oreil.ly/WmZ18*).

We're going to create a new version of the OldAbout component called About, and we're going to mount it at its own route:

```
<Switch>
    <Route path="/oldabout">
        <OldAbout/>
    </Route>
    <Route path="/about/:tabId?">
        <About/>
    </Route>
    <p>Choose an option</p>
</Switch>
```

This addition allows us to open both versions of the code in the example application.

Our new version is going to appear to be virtually identical to the old component. We'll extract the tabId from the component and move it into the current path.

Setting the path of the Route to */about/:tabId?* means that */about, /about/offices,* and */about/people* will all mount our component. The ? indicates that the tabId parameter is optional.

We've now done the first part: we've put the component's state into the path that displays it. We now need to update the component to interact with the route rather than an internal state variable.

In the OldAbout component, we had onClick listeners on each of the tabs:

```
<div onClick={() => setTabId("people")}
     className={tabId === "people" ? "About-tab active" : "About-tab"}
>
    People
</div>
<div onClick={() => setTabId("offices")}
     className={tabId === "offices" ? "About-tab active" : "About-tab"}
>
    Offices
</div>
```

We're going to convert these into Link components, going to */about/people* and */about/offices.* In fact, we're going to convert them into NavLink components. A NavLink is like a link, except it has the ability to set an additional class name, if the place it's linking to is the current location. This means we don't need the className logic in the original code:

```
<NavLink to="/about/people"
         className="About-tab"
         activeClassName="active">
    People
</NavLink>
<NavLink to="/about/offices"
         className="About-tab"
```

```
            activeClassName="active">
        Offices
    </NavLink>
```

We no longer set the value of a `tabId` variable. We instead go to a new location with a new `tabId` value in the path.

But what do we do to read the `tabId` value? The `OldAbout` code displays the current tab contents like this:

```
{tabId === "people" && <People/>}
{tabId === "offices" && <Offices/>}
```

This code can be replaced with a `Switch` and a couple of `Route` components:

```
<Switch>
    <Route path='/about/people'>
        <People/>
    </Route>
    <Route path='/about/offices'>
        <Offices/>
    </Route>
</Switch>
```

We're now *almost* finished. There's just one step remaining: deciding what to do if the path is */about* and contains no `tabId`.

The `OldAbout` sets a default value for `tabId` when it first creates the state:

```
const [tabId, setTabId] = useState("people")
```

We can achieve the same effect by adding a `Redirect` to the end of our `Switch`. The `Switch` will process its child components in order until it finds a matching `Route`. If no `Route` matches the current path, it will reach the `Redirect`, which will change the address to */about/people*. This will cause a re-render of the `About` component, and the People tab will be selected by default:

```
<Switch>
    <Route path='/about/people'>
        <People/>
    </Route>
    <Route path='/about/offices'>
        <Offices/>
    </Route>
    <Redirect to='/about/people'/>
</Switch>
```

 You can make `Redirect` conditional on the current path by giving it a `from` attribute. In this case, we could set `from` to `/about` so that only routes matching `/about` are redirected to `/about/people`.

This is our completed About component:

```
import { NavLink, Redirect, Route, Switch } from 'react-router-dom'
import './About.css'
import People from './People'
import Offices from './Offices'

const About = () => (
  <div className="About">
    <div className="About-tabs">
      <NavLink
        to="/about/people"
        className="About-tab"
        activeClassName="active"
      >
        People
      </NavLink>
      <NavLink
        to="/about/offices"
        className="About-tab"
        activeClassName="active"
      >
        Offices
      </NavLink>
    </div>
    <Switch>
      <Route path="/about/people">
        <People />
      </Route>
      <Route path="/about/offices">
        <Offices />
      </Route>
      <Redirect to="/about/people" />
    </Switch>
  </div>
)

export default About
```

We no longer need an internal `tabId` variable, and we now have a purely declarative component (see Figure 2-5).

People　　　Offices

South Dakota
　　18627 Sporer Mews
　　Maximechester
　　South Dakota
　　04691

Wisconsin
　　910 Lueilwitz Lake
　　Lake Troy
　　Wisconsin
　　25072

Figure 2-5. Going to http://localhost/about/offices *with the new component*

Discussion

Moving state out of your components and into the address bar can simplify your code, but this is merely a fortunate side effect. The real value is that your application starts to behave less like an application and more like a website. We can bookmark pages, and the browser's Back and Forward buttons work correctly. Managing more state in routes is not an abstract design decision; it's a way of making your application less surprising to users.

You can download the source for this recipe from the GitHub site (*https://oreil.ly/ myAGj*).

2.3 Use MemoryRouter for Unit Testing

Problem

We use routes in React applications so that we make more of the facilities of the browser. We can bookmark pages, create deep links into an app, and go backward and forward in history.

However, once we use routes, we make the component dependent upon something outside itself: the browser location. That might not seem like too big an issue, but it does have consequences.

Let's say we want to unit test a route-aware component. As an example, let's create a unit test for the About component we built in Recipe 2.2:[2]

```
describe('About component', () => {
  it('should show people', () => {
    render(<About />)
    expect(screen.getByText('Kip Russel')).toBeInTheDocument()
  })
})
```

This unit test renders the component and then checks that it can find the name "Kip Russel" appearing in the output. When we run this test, we get the following error:

```
console.error node_modules/jsdom/lib/jsdom/virtual-console.js:29
    Error: Uncaught [Error: Invariant failed: You should not use <NavLink>
        outside a <Router>]
```

The error occurred because a NavLink could not find a Router higher in the component tree. That means we need to wrap the component in a Router before we test it.

Also, we might want to write a unit test that checks that the About component works when we mount it on a specific route. Even if we provide a Router component, how will we fake a particular route?

It's not just an issue with unit tests. If we're using a library tool like Storybook,[3] we might want to show an example of how a component appears when we mount it on a given path.

We need something like an actual browser router but that allows us to specify its behavior.

Solution

The react-router-dom library provides just such a router: MemoryRouter. The MemoryRouter appears to the outside world just like BrowserRouter. The difference is that while the BrowserRouter is an interface to the underlying browser history API, the MemoryRouter has no such dependency. It can keep track of the current location, and it can go backward and forward in history, but it achieves this through simple memory structures.

---

2 We are using the React Testing Library in this example.

3 See Recipe 1.9.

Let's take another look at that failing unit test. Instead of just rendering the About component, let's wrap it in a MemoryRouter:

```
describe('About component', () => {
  it('should show people', () => {
    render(
      <MemoryRouter>
        <About />
      </MemoryRouter>
    )

    expect(screen.getByText('Kip Russel')).toBeInTheDocument()
  })
})
```

Now, when we run the test, it works. That's because the MemoryRouter injects a mocked-up version of the API into the context. That makes it available to all of its child components. The About component can now render a Link or Route because the history is available.

But the MemoryRouter has an additional advantage. Because it's faking the browser history API, it can be given a completely fake history, using the initialEntries property. The initialEntries property should be set to an array of history entries. If you pass a single value array, it will be interpreted as the current location. That allows you to write unit tests that check for component behavior when it's mounted on a given route.

```
describe('About component', () => {
  it('should show offices if in route', () => {
    render(
      <MemoryRouter initialEntries={[{ pathname: '/about/offices' }]}>
        <About />
      </MemoryRouter>
    )

    expect(screen.getByText('South Dakota')).toBeInTheDocument()
  })
})
```

We can use a real BrowserRouter inside Storybook because we're in a real browser, but the MemoryRouter also allows us to fake the current location, as we do in the ToAboutOffices Storybook story (see Figure 2-6).

Figure 2-6. Using MemoryRouter, we can fake the /about/offices route

Discussion

Routers let you separate the details of *where* you want to go from *how* you're going to get there. In this recipe, we see one advantage of this separation: we can create a fake browser location to examine component behavior on different routes. This separation allows you to change the way the application follows links without breaking. If you convert your SPA to an SSR application, you swap your `BrowserRouter` for a `StaticRouter`. The links used to make calls into the browser's history API will become native hyperlinks that cause the browser to make native page loads. Routers are an excellent example of the advantages of splitting policy (what you want to do) from mechanisms (how you're going to do it).

You can download the source for this recipe from the GitHub site (*https://oreil.ly/1NW8e*).

2.4 Use Prompt for Page Exit Confirmations

Problem

Sometimes you need to ask a user to confirm that they want to leave a page if they're in the middle of editing something. This seemingly simple task can be complicated because it relies on spotting when the user clicks the Back button and then finding a way to intercept the move back through history and potentially canceling it (see Figure 2-7).

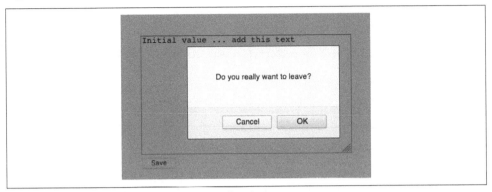

Figure 2-7. Asking for a confirmation before leaving

What if there are several pages in the application that need the same feature? Is there a simple way to create this feature across any component that needs it?

Solution

The `react-router-dom` library includes a component called `Prompt`, which asks users to confirm that they want to leave a page.

The only ingredient we need for this recipe is the `react-router-dom` library itself:

```
npm install react-router-dom
```

Let's say we have a component called `Important` mounted at */important*, which allows a user to edit a piece of text:

```
import React, { useEffect, useState } from 'react'

const Important = () => {
  const initialValue = 'Initial value'

  const [data, setData] = useState(initialValue)
  const [dirty, setDirty] = useState(false)

  useEffect(() => {
    if (data !== initialValue) {
      setDirty(true)
    }
  }, [data, initialValue])

  return (
    <div className="Important">
      <textarea
        onChange={(evt) => setData(evt.target.value)}
```

```
          cols={40}
          rows={12}
        >
          {data}
        </textarea>
        <br />
        <button onClick={() => setDirty(false)} disabled={!dirty}>
          Save
        </button>
      </div>
    )
  }

  export default Important
```

Important is already tracking whether the text in the textarea has changed from the original value. If the text is different, the value of dirty is true. How do we ask the user to confirm they want to leave the page if they click the Back button when dirty is true?

We add a Prompt component:

```
  return (
    <div className="Important">
      <textarea
        onChange={(evt) => setData(evt.target.value)}
        cols={40}
        rows={12}
      >
        {data}
      </textarea>
      <br />
      <button onClick={() => setDirty(false)} disabled={!dirty}>
        Save
      </button>
      <Prompt
        when={dirty}
        message={() => 'Do you really want to leave?'}
      />
    </div>
  )
```

If the user edits the text and then hits the Back button, the Prompt appears (see Figure 2-8).

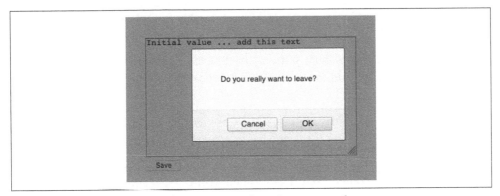

Figure 2-8. The Prompt *asks the user to confirm they want to leave*

Adding the confirmation is easy, but the default prompt interface is a simple Java-Script dialog. It would be helpful to decide for ourselves how we want the user to confirm they're leaving.

To demonstrate how we can do this, let's add the Material-UI component library to the application:

```
$ npm install '@material-ui/core'
```

The Material-UI library is a React implementation of Google's Material Design standard. We'll use it as an example of how to replace the standard Prompt interface with something more customized.

The Prompt component does not render any UI. Instead, the Prompt component asks the current Router to show the confirmation. By default, BrowserRouter shows the default JavaScript dialog, but you can replace this with your own code.

When the BrowserRouter is added to the component tree, we can pass it a property called getUserConfirmation:

```
<div className="App">
    <BrowserRouter
        getUserConfirmation={(message, callback) => {
          // Custom code goes here
        }}
    >
        <Switch>
            <Route path='/important'>
                <Important/>
            </Route>
        </Switch>
    </BrowserRouter>
</div>
```

The `getUserConfirmation` property is a function that accepts two parameters: the message it should display and a callback function.

When the user clicks the Back button, the `Prompt` component will run `getUser Confirmation` and then wait for the callback function to be called with the value `true` or `false`.

The callback function returns the user's response asynchronously. The `Prompt` component will wait while we ask the user what they want to do. That allows us to create a custom interface.

Let's create a custom Material-UI dialog called `Alert`. We'll show this instead of the default JavaScript modal:

```
import Button from '@material-ui/core/Button'
import Dialog from '@material-ui/core/Dialog'
import DialogActions from '@material-ui/core/DialogActions'
import DialogContent from '@material-ui/core/DialogContent'
import DialogContentText from '@material-ui/core/DialogContentText'
import DialogTitle from '@material-ui/core/DialogTitle'

const Alert = ({ open, title, message, onOK, onCancel }) => {
  return (
    <Dialog
      open={open}
      onClose={onCancel}
      aria-labelledby="alert-dialog-title"
      aria-describedby="alert-dialog-description"
    >
      <DialogTitle id="alert-dialog-title">{title}</DialogTitle>
      <DialogContent>
        <DialogContentText id="alert-dialog-description">
          {message}
        </DialogContentText>
      </DialogContent>
      <DialogActions>
        <Button onClick={onCancel} color="primary">
          Cancel
        </Button>
        <Button onClick={onOK} color="primary" autoFocus>
          OK
        </Button>
      </DialogActions>
    </Dialog>
  )
}

export default Alert
```

Of course, there is no reason why we need to display a dialog. We could show a countdown timer or a snackbar message or automatically save the user's changes. But we will display a custom `Alert` dialog.

How will we use the `Alert` component in our interface? The first thing we'll need to do is create our own `getUserConfirmation` function. We'll store the message and the callback function and then set a Boolean value saying that we want to open the `Alert` dialog:

```
const [confirmOpen, setConfirmOpen] = useState(false)
const [confirmMessage, setConfirmMessage] = useState()
const [confirmCallback, setConfirmCallback] = useState()

return (
  <div className="App">
    <BrowserRouter
      getUserConfirmation={(message, callback) => {
        setConfirmMessage(message)
        // Use this setter form because callback is a function
        setConfirmCallback(() => callback)
        setConfirmOpen(true)
      }}
    >
    .....
```

It's worth noting that when we store the callback function, we use `setConfirmCall back(() => callback)` instead of simply writing `setConfirmCallback(callback)`. That's because the setters returned by the `useState` hook will execute any function passed to them, rather than store them.

We can then use the values of `confirmMessage`, `confirmCallback`, and `confirmOpen` to render the `Alert` in the interface.

This is the complete *App.js* file:

```
import { useState } from 'react'
import './App.css'
import { BrowserRouter, Link, Route, Switch } from 'react-router-dom'
import Important from './Important'
import Alert from './Alert'

function App() {
  const [confirmOpen, setConfirmOpen] = useState(false)
  const [confirmMessage, setConfirmMessage] = useState()
  const [confirmCallback, setConfirmCallback] = useState()

  return (
    <div className="App">
      <BrowserRouter
        getUserConfirmation={(message, callback) => {
          setConfirmMessage(message)
```

```
          // Use this setter form because callback is a function
          setConfirmCallback(() => callback)
          setConfirmOpen(true)
        }}
    >
        <Alert
          open={confirmOpen}
          title="Leave page?"
          message={confirmMessage}
          onOK={() => {
            confirmCallback(true)
            setConfirmOpen(false)
          }}
          onCancel={() => {
            confirmCallback(false)
            setConfirmOpen(false)
          }}
        />
        <Switch>
          <Route path="/important">
            <Important />
          </Route>
          <div>
            <h1>Home page</h1>
            <Link to="/important">Go to important page</Link>
          </div>
        </Switch>
      </BrowserRouter>
    </div>
  )
}

export default App
```

Now when a user backs out of an edit, they see the custom dialog, as shown in Figure 2-9.

Figure 2-9. The custom Alert appears when the user clicks the Back button

Discussion

In this recipe, we have re-implemented the `Prompt` modal using a component library, but you don't need to be limited to just replacing one dialog box with another. There is no reason why, if someone leaves a page, that you couldn't do something else: such as store the work-in-progress somewhere so that they could return to it later. The asynchronous nature of the `getUserConfirmation` function allows this flexibility. It's another example of how `react-router-dom` abstracts away a cross-cutting concern.

You can download the source for this recipe from the GitHub site (*https://oreil.ly/ 1FyoE*).

2.5 Create Transitions with React Transition Group

Problem

Native and desktop applications often use animation to connect different elements visually. If you tap an item in a list, it expands to show you the details. Swiping left or right can be used to indicate whether a user accepts or rejects an option.

Animations, therefore, are often used to indicate a location change. They zoom in on the details. They take you to the next person on the list. We reflect a change in the URL with a matching animation.

But how do we create an animation when we move from one location to another?

Solution

For this recipe, we're going to need the `react-router-dom` library and the `react-transition-group` library:

```
$ npm install react-router-dom
$ npm install react-transition-group
```

We're going to animate the `About` component that we've used previously.[4] The `About` component has two tabs called People and Offices, which are displayed for the routes */about/people* and */about/offices*.

When someone clicks one of the tabs, we're going to fade out the old tab's content and then fade in the content of the new tab. Although we're using a fade, there's no reason why we couldn't use a more complex animation, such as sliding the tab contents left

---

4 See Recipes 2.2 and 2.3.

or right.[5] However, a simple fade animation will more clearly demonstrate how it works.

Inside the About component, the tab contents are rendered by People and Offices components within distinct routes:

```
import { NavLink, Redirect, Route, Switch } from 'react-router-dom'
import './About.css'
import People from './People'
import Offices from './Offices'

const About = () => (
  <div className="About">
    <div className="About-tabs">
      <NavLink
        to="/about/people"
        className="About-tab"
        activeClassName="active"
      >
        People
      </NavLink>
      <NavLink
        to="/about/offices"
        className="About-tab"
        activeClassName="active"
      >
        Offices
      </NavLink>
    </div>
    <Switch>
      <Route path="/about/people">
        <People />
      </Route>
      <Route path="/about/offices">
        <Offices />
      </Route>
      <Redirect to="/about/people" />
    </Switch>
  </div>
)

export default About
```

We need to animate the components inside the Switch component. We'll need two things to do this:

---

5 This is a common feature of third-party tabbed components. The animation reinforces in the user's mind that they are moving left and right through the tabs.

- Something to track when the location has changed
- Something to animate the tab contents when that happens

How do we know when the location has changed? We can get the current location from the useLocation hook from react-router-dom:

```
const location = useLocation()
```

Now on to the more complex task: the animation itself. What follows is quite a complex sequence of events, but taking time to understand it is worth it.

When we are animating from one component to another, we need to keep both components on the page. As the Offices component fades out, the People component fades in.[6] We can do this by keeping both components in a *transition group*. A transition group is a set of components, some of which are appearing and others are disappearing.

We can create a transition group by wrapping our animation in a TransitionGroup component. We also need a CSSTransition component to coordinate the details of the CSS animation.

Our updated code wraps the Switch in both a TransitionGroup and a CSSTransition:

```
import {
  NavLink,
  Redirect,
  Route,
  Switch,
  useLocation,
} from 'react-router-dom'
import People from './People'
import Offices from './Offices'
import {
  CSSTransition,
  TransitionGroup,
} from 'react-transition-group'

import './About.css'
import './fade.css'

const About = () => {
  const location = useLocation()

  return (
    <div className="About">
```

---

6 The code uses relative positioning to place both components in the same position during the fade.

```
        <div className="About-tabs">
          <NavLink
            to="/about/people"
            className="About-tab"
            activeClassName="active"
          >
            People
          </NavLink>
          <NavLink
            to="/about/offices"
            className="About-tab"
            activeClassName="active"
          >
            Offices
          </NavLink>
        </div>
        <TransitionGroup className="About-tabContent">
          <CSSTransition
            key={location.key}
            classNames="fade"
            timeout={500}
          >
            <Switch location={location}>
              <Route path="/about/people">
                <People />
              </Route>
              <Route path="/about/offices">
                <Offices />
              </Route>
              <Redirect to="/about/people" />
            </Switch>
          </CSSTransition>
        </TransitionGroup>
      </div>
    )
}

export default About
```

Notice that we pass the location.key to the key of the CSSTransition group, and we pass the location to the Switch component. The location.key is a hash value of the current location. Passing the location.key to the transition group will keep the CSSTransition in the virtual DOM until the animation is complete. When the user clicks one of the tabs, the location changes, which refreshes the About component. The TransitionGroup will keep the existing CSSTransition in the tree of components until its timeout occurs: in 500 milliseconds. But it will now also have a second CSSTransition component.

Each of these `CSSTransition` components will keep their child components alive (see Figure 2-10).

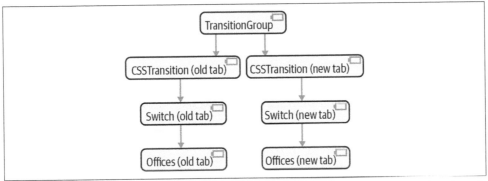

Figure 2-10. The TransitionGroup keeps both the old and new components in the virtual DOM

We need to pass the `location` value to the `Switch` components: we need the `Switch` for the old tab, and we need the `Switch` for the new tab to keep rendering their routes.

So now, on to the animation itself. The `CSSTransition` component accepts a property called `classNames`, which we have set to the value `fade`. Note that `classNames` is a plural to distinguish it from the standard `className` attribute.

`CSSTransition` will use `classNames` to generate four distinct class names:

- `fade-enter`
- `fade-enter-active`
- `fade-exit`
- `fade-exit-active`

The `fade-enter` class is for components that are about to start to animate into view. The `fade-enter-active` class is applied to components that are actually animating. `fade-exit` and `fade-exit-active` are for components that are beginning or animating their disappearance.

The `CSSTransition` component will add these class names to their immediate children. If we are animating from the Offices tab to the People tab, then the old `CSSTransition` will add the `fade-enter-active` class to the `People` HTML and will add the `fade-exit-active` to the `Offices` HTML.

All that's left to do is define the CSS animations themselves:

```
.fade-enter {
    opacity: 0;
}
.fade-enter-active {
    opacity: 1;
    transition: opacity 250ms ease-in;
}
.fade-exit {
    opacity: 1;
}
.fade-exit-active {
    opacity: 0;
    transition: opacity 250ms ease-in;
}
```

The fade-enter- classes use CSS transitions to change the opacity of the component from 0 to 1. The fade-exit- classes animate the opacity from 1 back to 0. It's generally a good idea to keep the animation class definitions in a separate CSS file. That way, we can reuse them for other animations.

The animation is complete. When the user clicks a tab, they see the contents cross-fade from the old data to the new data (Figure 2-11).

Figure 2-11. The contents of the tab fade from offices to people

Discussion

Animations can be pretty irritating when used poorly. Each animation you add should have some intent. If you find that you want to add an animation just because you think it will be attractive, you will almost certainly find users will dislike it. Generally, it is best to ask a few questions before adding an animation:

- Will this animation clarify the relationship between the two routes? Are you zooming in to see more detail or moving across to look at a related item?

- How short should the animation be? Any longer than half a second is probably too much.

- What is the impact on performance? CSS transitions usually have minimal effect if the browser hands the work off to the GPU. But what happens in an old browser on a mobile device?

You can download the source for this recipe from the GitHub site (*https://oreil.ly/ UCu75*).

2.6 Create Secured Routes

Problem

Most applications need to prevent access to particular routes until a person logs in. But how do you secure some routes and not others? Is it possible to separate the security mechanisms from the user interface elements for logging in and logging out? And how do you do it without writing a vast amount of code?

Solution

Let's look at one way to implement route-based security in a React application. This application contains a home page (*/*), it has a public page with no security (*/public*), and it also has two private pages (*/private1* and */private2*) that we need to secure:

```
import React from 'react'
import './App.css'
import { BrowserRouter, Route, Switch } from 'react-router-dom'
import Public from './Public'
import Private1 from './Private1'
import Private2 from './Private2'
import Home from './Home'

function App() {
  return (
    <div className="App">
      <BrowserRouter>
        <Switch>
          <Route exact path="/">
            <Home />
          </Route>
          <Route path="/private1">
            <Private1 />
          </Route>
          <Route path="/private2">
            <Private2 />
          </Route>
          <Route exact path="/public">
            <Public />
          </Route>
        </Switch>
```

```
        </BrowserRouter>
      </div>
    )
}

export default App
```

We're going to build the security system using a context. A context is where data can be stored by a component and made available to the component's children. A `Browser Router` uses a context to pass routing information to the `Route` components within it.

We're going to create a custom context called `SecurityContext`:

```
import React from 'react'

const SecurityContext = React.createContext({})

export default SecurityContext
```

The default value of our context is an empty object. We need something that will add functions into the context for logging in and logging out. We'll do that by creating a `SecurityProvider`:

```
import { useState } from 'react'
import SecurityContext from './SecurityContext'

const SecurityProvider = (props) => {
  const [loggedIn, setLoggedIn] = useState(false)

  return (
    <SecurityContext.Provider
      value={{
        login: (username, password) => {
          // Note to engineering team:
          // Maybe make this more secure...
          if (username === 'fred' && password === 'password') {
            setLoggedIn(true)
          }
        },
        logout: () => setLoggedIn(false),
        loggedIn,
      }}
    >
      {props.children}
    </SecurityContext.Provider>
  )
}

export default SecurityProvider
```

The code would be very different in a real system. You would probably create a component that logged in and logged out using a web service or third-party security system. But in our example, the `SecurityProvider` keeps track of whether we have logged in using a simple `loggedIn` Boolean value. The `SecurityProvider` puts three things into the context:

- A function for logging in (`login`)
- A function for logging out (`logout`)
- A Boolean value saying whether we have logged in or out (`loggedIn`)

These three things will be available to any components placed inside a `Security Provider` component. To allow any component inside a `SecurityProvider` to access these functions, we'll add a custom hook called `useSecurity`:

```
import SecurityContext from './SecurityContext'
import { useContext } from 'react'

const useSecurity = () => useContext(SecurityContext)

export default useSecurity
```

Now that we have a `SecurityProvider`, we need to use it to secure a subset of the routes. We'll create another component, called `SecureRoute`:

```
import Login from './Login'
import { Route } from 'react-router-dom'
import useSecurity from './useSecurity'

const SecureRoute = (props) => {
  const { loggedIn } = useSecurity()

  return (
    <Route {...props}>{loggedIn ? props.children : <Login />}</Route>
  )
}

export default SecureRoute
```

The `SecureRoute` component gets the current `loggedIn` status from the `Security Context` (using the `useSecurity` hook), and if the user is logged in, it renders the contents of the route. If the user is not logged in, it displays a login form.[7]

The `LoginForm` calls the `login` function, which—if successful—will re-render the `SecureRoute` and then show the secured data.

How do we use all of these new components? Here is an updated version of the *App.js* file:

---

7 We'll omit the contents of the `Login` component here, but the code is available on the GitHub repository.

```
import './App.css'
import { BrowserRouter, Route, Switch } from 'react-router-dom'
import Public from './Public'
import Private1 from './Private1'
import Private2 from './Private2'
import Home from './Home'
import SecurityProvider from './SecurityProvider'
import SecureRoute from './SecureRoute'

function App() {
  return (
    <div className="App">
      <BrowserRouter>
        <SecurityProvider>
          <Switch>
            <Route exact path="/">
              <Home />
            </Route>
            <SecureRoute path="/private1">
              <Private1 />
            </SecureRoute>
            <SecureRoute path="/private2">
              <Private2 />
            </SecureRoute>
            <Route exact path="/public">
              <Public />
            </Route>
          </Switch>
        </SecurityProvider>
      </BrowserRouter>
    </div>
  )
}

export default App
```

The SecurityProvider wraps our whole routing system, making login(), logout(), and loggedIn available to each SecureRoute.

You can see the application running in Figure 2-12.

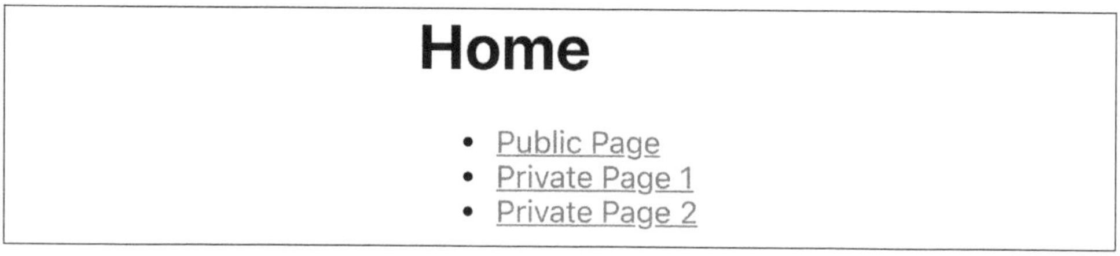

Home

- Public Page
- Private Page 1
- Private Page 2

Figure 2-12. The home page has links to the other pages

If we click the *Public Page* link, the page appears (see Figure 2-13).

Public Page

Anyone can see this page.

Figure 2-13. The public page is available without logging in

But if we click *Private Page 1*, we're presented with the login screen (Figure 2-14).

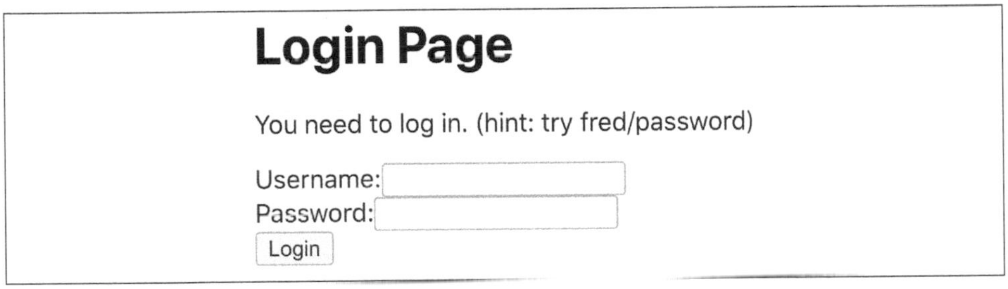

Login Page

You need to log in. (hint: try fred/password)

Username: [   ]
Password: [   ]
[Login]

Figure 2-14. You need to log in before you can see Private Page 1

If you log in with the username *fred* and password *password*, you will then see the private content (see Figure 2-15).

Private page 1

Highly secret information here.

[Logout]

Figure 2-15. The content of Private Page 1 after login

Discussion

Real security is only ever provided by secured backend services. However, secured routes prevent a user from stumbling into a page that can't read data from the server.

A better implementation of the `SecurityProvider` would defer to some third-party OAuth tool or other security services. But by splitting the `SecurityProvider` from the security UI (`Login` and `Logout`) and the main application, you can modify the security mechanisms over time without changing a lot of code in your application.

If you want to see how your components behave when people log in and out, you can always create a mocked version of the `SecurityProvider` for use in unit tests.

You can download the source for this recipe from the GitHub site (*https://oreil.ly/ Kut73*).

CHAPTER 3

Managing State

When we manage state in React, we have to store data, but we also record data dependencies. Dependencies are intrinsic to the way that React works. They allow React to update the page efficiently and only when necessary.

Managing data dependencies, then, is the key to managing state in React. You will see throughout this chapter that most of the tools and techniques we use are to ensure that we manage dependencies efficiently.

A key concept in the following recipes is a data reducer. A *reducer* is simply a function that receives a single object or an array and then returns a modified copy. This simple concept is what lies behind much of the state management in React. We'll look at how React uses reducer functions natively and how we can use the Redux library to manage data application-wide with reducers.

We'll also look at selector functions. These allow us to drill into the state returned by reducers. Selectors help us ignore the irrelevant data, and in doing so, they significantly improve the performance of our code.

Along the way, we'll look at simple ways of checking whether you're online, how to manage form data, and various other tips and tricks to keep your application ticking along.

3.1 Use Reducers to Manage Complex State

Problem

Many React components are straightforward. They do little more than render a section of HTML and perhaps show a few properties.

However, some components can be more complicated. They might need to manage several pieces of internal state. For example, consider the simple number game you can see in Figure 3-1.

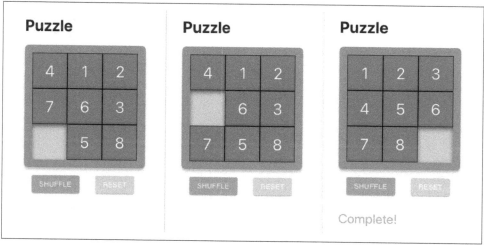

Figure 3-1. A simple number puzzle

The component displays a series of numeric tiles, in a grid, with a single space. If the user clicks a tile next to the space, they can move it. In this way, the user can rearrange the tiles until they are in the correct order from 1 to 8.

This component renders a small amount of HTML, but it will require some fairly complex logic and data. It will record the positions of the tiles. It will need to know whether a user can move a given tile. It will need to know how to move the tile. It will need to know whether the game is complete. It will also need to do other things, such as reset the game by shuffling the tiles.

It's entirely possible to write all this code inside the component, but it will be harder to test it. You could use the React Testing Library, but that is probably overkill, given that most of the code will have very little to do with rendering HTML.

Solution

If you have a component with some complex internal state or that needs to manipulate its state in complex ways, consider using a reducer.

A reducer is a function that accepts two parameters:

- An object or array that represents a given state
- An action that describes how you want to modify the state

The function returns a new copy of the state we pass to it.

The action parameter can be whatever you want, but typically it is an object with a string `type` attribute and a `payload` with additional information. You can think of the `type` as a command name and the `payload` as parameters to the command.

For example, if we number our tile positions from 0 (top-left) to 8 (bottom-right), we might tell the reducer to move whatever tile is in the top-left corner with:

```
{type: 'move', payload: 0}
```

We need an object or array that completely defines our game's internal state. We could use a simple array of strings:

```
['1', '2', '3', null, '5', '6', '7', '8', '4']
```

That would represent the tiles laid out like this:

```
1  2  3
   5  6
7  8  4
```

However, a slightly more flexible approach uses an object for our state and gives it an `items` attribute containing the current tile layout:

```
{
    items: ['1', '2', '3', null, '5', '6', '7', '8', '4']
}
```

Why would we do this? Because it will allow our reducer to return other state values, such as whether or not the game is complete:

```
{
    items: ['1', '2', '3', '4', '5', '6', '7', '8', null],
    complete: true
}
```

We've decided on an action (`move`) and know how the state will be structured, which means we've done enough design to create a test:

```
import reducer from './reducer'

describe('reducer', () => {
  it('should be able to move 1 down if gap below', () => {
    let state = {
      items: ['1', '2', '3', null, '5', '6', '7', '8', '4'],
    }

    state = reducer(state, { type: 'move', payload: 0 })

    expect(state.items).toEqual([
      null,
      '2',
```

```
          '3',
          '1',
          '5',
          '6',
          '7',
          '8',
          '4',
      ])
    })

    it('should say when it is complete', () => {
      let state = {
        items: ['1', '2', '3', '4', '5', '6', '7', null, '8'],
      }

      state = reducer(state, { type: 'move', payload: 8 })

      expect(state.complete).toBe(true)

      state = reducer(state, { type: 'move', payload: 5 })

      expect(state.complete).toBe(false)
    })
  })
```

In our first test scenario, we pass in the tiles' locations in one state. Then we check that the reducer returns the tiles in a new state.

In our second test, we perform two tile moves and then look for a `complete` attribute to tell us the game has ended.

OK, we've delayed looking at the actual reducer code long enough:

```
function trySwap(newItems, position, t) {
  if (newItems[t] === null) {
    const temp = newItems[position]
    newItems[position] = newItems[t]
    newItems[t] = temp
  }
}

function arraysEqual(a, b) {
  for (let i = 0; i < a.length; i++) {
    if (a[i] !== b[i]) {
      return false
    }
  }
  return true
}

const CORRECT = ['1', '2', '3', '4', '5', '6', '7', '8', null]

function reducer(state, action) {
```

```
    switch (action.type) {
      case 'move': {
        const position = action.payload
        const newItems = [...state.items]
        const col = position % 3

        if (position < 6) {
          trySwap(newItems, position, position + 3)
        }
        if (position > 2) {
          trySwap(newItems, position, position - 3)
        }
        if (col < 2) {
          trySwap(newItems, position, position + 1)
        }
        if (col > 0) {
          trySwap(newItems, position, position - 1)
        }

        return {
          ...state,
          items: newItems,
          complete: arraysEqual(newItems, CORRECT),
        }
      }
      default: {
        throw new Error('Unknown action: ' + action.type)
      }
    }
  }
}

export default reducer
```

Our reducer currently recognizes a single action: move. The code in our GitHub repository (*https://oreil.ly/q85H3*) also includes actions for shuffle and reset. The repository also has a more exhaustive set of tests (*https://oreil.ly/yRNyU*) that we used to create the previous code.

But *none* of this code includes any React components. It's pure JavaScript and so can be created and tested in isolation from the outside world.

 Be careful to generate a new object in the reducer to represent the new state. Doing so ensures each new state completely independent of those that came before it.

Now it's time to wire up our reducer into a React component, with the useReducer hook:

```
import { useReducer } from 'react'
import reducer from './reducer'

import './Puzzle.css'

const Puzzle = () => {
  const [state, dispatch] = useReducer(reducer, {
    items: ['4', '1', '2', '7', '6', '3', null, '5', '8'],
  })

  return (
    <div className="Puzzle">
      <div className="Puzzle-squares">
        {state.items.map((s, i) => (
          <div
            className={`Puzzle-square ${
              s ? '' : 'Puzzle-square-empty'
            }`}
            key={`square-${i}`}
            onClick={() => dispatch({ type: 'move', payload: i })}
          >
            {s}
          </div>
        ))}
      </div>
      <div className="Puzzle-controls">
        <button
          className="Puzzle-shuffle"
          onClick={() => dispatch({ type: 'shuffle' })}
        >
          Shuffle
        </button>
        <button
          className="Puzzle-reset"
          onClick={() => dispatch({ type: 'reset' })}
        >
          Reset
        </button>
      </div>
      {state.complete && (
        <div className="Puzzle-complete">Complete!</div>
      )}
    </div>
  )
}

export default Puzzle
```

Even though our puzzle component is doing something quite complicated, that actual
React code is relatively short.

The useReducer accepts a reducer function and a starting state, and it returns a two-element array:

- The first element in the array is the current state from the reducer
- The second element is a dispatch function that allows us to send actions to the reducer.

We display the tiles by looping through the strings in the array given by state.items.

If someone clicks a tile at position i, we send a move command to the reducer:

```
onClick={() => dispatch({type: 'move', payload: i})}
```

The React component has no idea what it takes to move the tile. It doesn't even know if it can move the tile at all. The component sends the action to the reducer.

If the move action moves a tile, the component will automatically re-render the component with the tiles in their new positions. If the game is complete, the component will know by the value of state.complete:

```
state.complete && <div className='Puzzle-complete'>Complete!</div>
```

We also added two buttons to run the shuffle and reset actions, which we omitted earlier but is in the GitHub repository (*https://oreil.ly/WmZ18*).

Now that we've created our component, let's try it. When we first load the component, we see it in its initial state, as shown in Figure 3-2.

Figure 3-2. The starting state of the game

If we click the tile labeled 7, it moves into the gap (see Figure 3-3).

Figure 3-3. After moving tile 7

If we click the Shuffle button, the reducer rearranges tiles randomly, as shown in Figure 3-4.

Figure 3-4. The Shuffle button moves tiles to random positions

And if we click Reset, the puzzle changes to the completed position, and the "Complete!" text appears (see Figure 3-5).

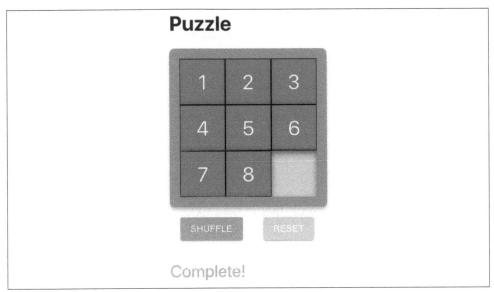

Figure 3-5. The Reset button moves the tiles to their correct positions

We bury all of the complexity inside the reducer function, where we can test it, and the component is simple and easy to maintain.

Discussion

Reducers are a way of managing complexity. You will typically use a reducer in either of these cases:

- You have a large amount of internal state to manage.
- You need complex logic to manage the internal state of your component.

If either of these things is correct, then a reducer can make your code significantly easier to manage.

However, be wary of using reducers for very small components. If your component has a simple state and little logic, you probably don't need the added complexity of a reducer.

Sometimes, even if you do have a complex state, there are alternative approaches. For example, if you are capturing and validating data in a form, it might be better to create a validating form component (see Recipe 3.3).

You need to ensure that your reducer does not have any side effects. Avoid, say, making network calls that update a server. If your reducer has side effects, there is every chance that it might break. React (sneakily) might sometimes make additional calls to your reducer in development mode to make sure that no side effects are happening. If you're using a reducer and notice that React calls your code twice when rendering a component, it means React is checking for bad behavior.

 With all of those provisos, reducers are an excellent tool at fighting complexity. They are integral to libraries such as Redux, can easily be reused and combined, simplify components, and make your React code significantly easier to test.

You can download the source for this recipe from the GitHub site (*https://oreil.ly/q85H3*).

3.2 Create an Undo Feature

Problem

Part of the promise of JavaScript-rich frameworks like React is that web applications can closely resemble desktop applications. One common feature in desktop applications is the ability to undo an action. Some native components within React applications automatically support an undo function. If you edit some text in a text area, and then press Cmd/Ctrl-Z, it will undo your edit. But what about extending undo into custom components? How is it possible to track state changes without a large amount of code?

Solution

If a reducer function manages the state in your component, you can implement a quite general undo function using an undo-reducer.

Consider this piece of code from the `Puzzle` example from Recipe 3.1:

```
const [state, dispatch] = useReducer(reducer, {
  items: ['4', '1', '2', '7', '6', '3', null, '5', '8'],
})
```

This code uses a reducer function (called `reducer`) and an initial state to manage the tiles in a number-puzzle game (see Figure 3-6).

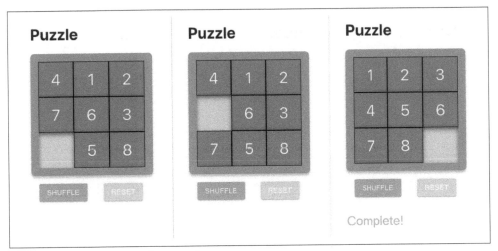

Figure 3-6. A simple number puzzle game

If the user clicks the Shuffle button, the component updates the tile state by sending a shuffle action to the reducer:

```
<button className='Puzzle-shuffle'
        onClick={() => dispatch({type: 'shuffle'})}>Shuffle</button>
```

(For more details on what reducers are and when you should use them, see Recipe 3.1.)

We will create a new hook called useUndoReducer, which is a drop-in replacement for useReducer:

```
const [state, dispatch] = useUndoReducer(reducer, {
  items: ['4', '1', '2', '7', '6', '3', null, '5', '8'],
})
```

The useUndoReducer hook will magically give our component the ability to go back in time:

```
<button
  className="Puzzle-undo"
  onClick={() => dispatch({ type: 'undo' })}
>
  Undo
</button>
```

If we add this button to the component, it undoes the last action the user performed, as shown in Figure 3-7.

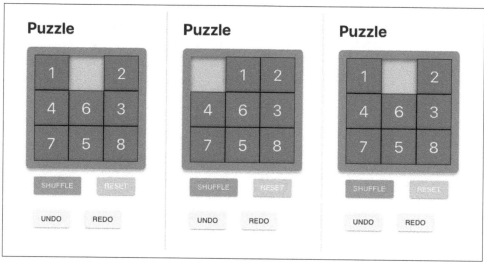

Figure 3-7. (1) Game in progress; (2) Make a move; (3) Click Undo to undo move

But how do we perform this magic? Although `useUndoReducer` is relatively easy to use, it's somewhat harder to understand. But it's worth doing so that you can adjust the recipe to your requirements.

We can take advantage of the fact that all reducers work in the same way:

- The action defines what you want to do.
- The reducer returns a fresh state after each action.
- No side effects are allowed when calling the reducer.

Also, reducers are just simple JavaScript functions that accept a state object and an action object.

Because reducers work in such a well-defined way, we can create a new reducer (an undo-reducer) that wraps around another reducer function. Our undo-reducer will work as an intermediary. It will pass most actions through to the underlying reducer while keeping a history of all previous states. If someone wants to undo an action, it will find the last state from its history and then return that without calling the underlying reducer.

We'll begin by creating a higher-order function that accepts one reducer and returns another:

```
import lodash from 'lodash'

const undo = (reducer) => (state, action) => {
  let {
    undoHistory = [],
```

```
        undoActions = [],
        ...innerState
      } = lodash.cloneDeep(state)
      switch (action.type) {
        case 'undo': {
          if (undoActions.length > 0) {
            undoActions.pop()
            innerState = undoHistory.pop()
          }
          break
        }

        case 'redo': {
          if (undoActions.length > 0) {
            undoHistory = [...undoHistory, { ...innerState }]
            undoActions = [
              ...undoActions,
              undoActions[undoActions.length - 1],
            ]
            innerState = reducer(
              innerState,
              undoActions[undoActions.length - 1]
            )
          }
          break
        }

        default: {
          undoHistory = [...undoHistory, { ...innerState }]
          undoActions = [...undoActions, action]
          innerState = reducer(innerState, action)
        }
      }
      return { ...innerState, undoHistory, undoActions }
    }

    export default undo
```

This reducer is quite a complex function, so it's worth taking some time to understand what it does.

It creates a reducer function that keeps track of the actions and states we pass to it. Let's say our game component sends an action to shuffle the tiles in the game. Our reducer will first check if the action has the type undo or redo. It doesn't. So it passes the shuffle action to the underlying reducer that manages the tiles in our game (see Figure 3-8).

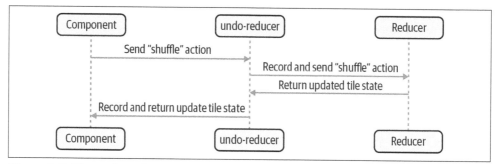

Figure 3-8. The undo-reducer passes most actions to the underlying reducer

As it passes the `shuffle` action through to the underlying reducer, the undo code keeps track of the existing state and the `shuffle` action by adding them to the undo History and undoActions. It then returns the state of the underlying game reducer and the undoHistory and undoActions.

If our puzzle component sends in an `undo` action, the undo-reducer returns the previous state from the undoHistory, completely bypassing the game's own reducer function (see Figure 3-9).

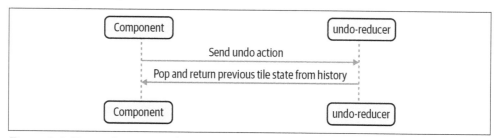

Figure 3-9. For undo actions, the undo-reducer returns the latest historic state

Now let's look at the `useUndoReducer` hook itself:

```
import { useReducer } from 'react'
import undo from './undo'

const useUndoReducer = (reducer, initialState) =>
  useReducer(undo(reducer), initialState)

export default useUndoReducer
```

This `useUndoReducer` hook is a concise piece of code. It's simply a call to the built-in useReducer hook, but instead of passing the reducer straight through, it passes undo(reducer). The result is that your component uses an enhanced version of the reducer you provide: one that can undo and redo actions.

Here is our updated `Puzzle` component (see Recipe 3.1 for the original version):

```
import reducer from './reducer'
import useUndoReducer from './useUndoReducer'

import './Puzzle.css'

const Puzzle = () => {
  const [state, dispatch] = useUndoReducer(reducer, {
    items: ['4', '1', '2', '7', '6', '3', null, '5', '8'],
  })

  return (
    <div className="Puzzle">
      <div className="Puzzle-squares">
        {state.items.map((s, i) => (
          <div
            className={`Puzzle-square ${
              s ? '' : 'Puzzle-square-empty'
            }`}
            key={`square-${i}`}
            onClick={() => dispatch({ type: 'move', payload: i })}
          >
            {s}
          </div>
        ))}
      </div>
      <div className="Puzzle-controls">
        <button
          className="Puzzle-shuffle"
          onClick={() => dispatch({ type: 'shuffle' })}
        >
          Shuffle
        </button>
        <button
          className="Puzzle-reset"
          onClick={() => dispatch({ type: 'reset' })}
        >
          Reset
        </button>
      </div>
      <div className="Puzzle-controls">
        <button
          className="Puzzle-undo"
          onClick={() => dispatch({ type: 'undo' })}
        >
          Undo
        </button>
        <button
          className="Puzzle-redo"
          onClick={() => dispatch({ type: 'redo' })}
        >
          Redo
        </button>
```

```
    </div>
    {state.complete && (
      <div className="Puzzle-complete">Complete!</div>
    )}
  </div>
  )
}

export default Puzzle
```

The only changes are that we use useUndoReducer instead of useReducer, and we've added a couple of buttons to call the "undo" and "redo" actions.

If you now load the component and makes some changes, you can undo the changes one at a time, as shown in Figure 3-10.

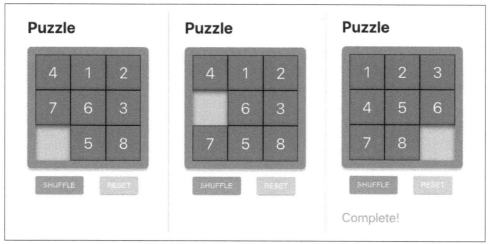

Figure 3-10. With useUndoReducer, you can now send undo and redo actions

Discussion

The undo-reducer shown here will work with reducers that accept and return state objects. If your reducer manages state using arrays, you will have to modify the undo function.

Because it keeps a history of all previous states, you probably want to avoid using it if your state data is extensive or if you're using it in circumstances where it might make a huge number of changes. Otherwise, you might want to limit the maximum size of the history.

Also, bear in mind that it maintains its history in memory. If a user reloads the entire page, then the history will disappear. It should be possible to resolve this issue by persisting the global state in local storage whenever it changes.

You can download the source for this recipe from the GitHub site (*https://oreil.ly/Oz27A*).

3.3 Create and Validate Forms

Problem

Most React applications use forms to some degree, and most applications take an ad-hoc approach to creating them. If a team is building your application, you might find that some developers manage individual fields in separate state variables. Others will choose to record form state in a single-value object, which is simpler to pass into and out of the form but can be tricky for each field to update. Field validation often leads to spaghetti code, with some forms validating at submit time and others validating dynamically as the user types. Some forms might show validation messages when the form first loads. In other forms, the messages might appear only after the user has touched the fields.

These variations in design can lead to poor user experience and an inconsistent approach to writing code. In our experience working with React teams, forms and form validation are common stumbling blocks for developers.

Solution

To apply some consistency to form development, we will create a SimpleForm component that we will wrap around one or more InputField components. This is an example of the use of SimpleForm and InputField:

```
import { useEffect, useState } from 'react'
import './App.css'
import SimpleForm from './SimpleForm'
import InputField from './InputField'

const FormExample0 = ({ onSubmit, onChange, initialValue = {} }) => {
  const [formFields, setFormFields] = useState(initialValue)

  const [valid, setValid] = useState(true)
  const [errors, setErrors] = useState({})

  useEffect(() => {
    if (onChange) {
      onChange(formFields, valid, errors)
    }
  }, [onChange, formFields, valid, errors])

  return (
    <div className="TheForm">
      <h1>Single field</h1>
```

```
        <SimpleForm
          value={formFields}
          onChange={setFormFields}
          onValid={(v, errs) => {
            setValid(v)
            setErrors(errs)
          }}
        >
          <InputField
            name="field1"
            onValidate={(v) =>
              !v || v.length < 3 ? 'Too short!' : null
            }
          />

          <button
            onClick={() => onSubmit && onSubmit(formFields)}
            disabled={!valid}
          >
            Submit!
          </button>
        </SimpleForm>
      </div>
    )
}

export default FormExample0
```

We track the state of the form in a single object, formFields. Whenever we change a field in the form, the field will call onChange on the SimpleForm. The field1 field is validated using the onValidate method, and whenever the validation state changes, the field calls the onValid method on the SimpleForm. Validation will occur only if the user has interacted with a field: making it *dirty*.

You can see the form running in Figure 3-11.

There is no need to track individual field values. The form value object records individual field values with attributes derived from the name of the field. The InputField handles the details of when to run the validation: it will update the form value and decide when to display errors.

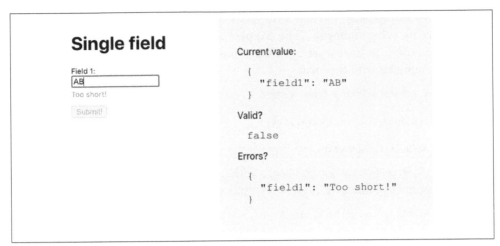

Figure 3-11. A simple form with field validation

Figure 3-12 shows a slightly more complex example that uses the `SimpleForm` with several fields.

Multiple fields

Address 1:
`AB`
Too short!

Address 2:
Required

Address 3:
Required

Address 4:
Required

Price:
`101`
Must be at least 102

Required By:
dd / mm / yyyy
Required

Submit!

Current value:

```
{
    "address1": "AB",
    "price": "101"
}
```

Valid?

```
false
```

Errors?

```
{
    "address1": "Too short!",
    "address2": "Required",
    "address3": "Required",
    "address4": "Required",
    "price": "Must be at least 102",
    "requiredBy": "Required"
}
```

Figure 3-12. A more complex form

To create the `SimpleForm` and `InputField` components, we must first look at how they will communicate with each other. An `InputField` component will need to tell the `SimpleForm` when its value has changed and whether or not the new value is valid. It will do this with a context.

A *context* is a storage scope. When a component stores values in a context, that value is visible to its subcomponents. The SimpleForm will create a context called Form Context and use it to store a set of callback functions that any child component can use to communicate with the form:

```
import { createContext } from 'react'

const FormContext = createContext({})

export default FormContext
```

To see how SimpleForm works, let's begin with a simplified version, which tracks only its subcomponents' values, without worrying about validation just yet:

```
import React, { useCallback, useEffect, useState } from 'react'

import './SimpleForm.css'
import FormContext from './FormContext'

function updateWith(oldValue, field, value) {
  const newValue = { ...oldValue }
  newValue[field] = value
  return newValue
}

const SimpleForm = ({ children, value, onChange, onValid }) => {
  const [values, setValues] = useState(value || {})

  useEffect(() => {
    setValues(value || {})
  }, [value])

  useEffect(() => {
    if (onChange) {
      onChange(values)
    }
  }, [onChange, values])

  let setValue = useCallback(
    (field, v) => setValues((vs) => updateWith(vs, field, v)),
    [setValues]
  )
  let getValue = useCallback((field) => values[field], [values])
  let form = {
    setValue: setValue,
    value: getValue,
  }

  return (
    <div className="SimpleForm-container">
      <FormContext.Provider value={form}>
        {children}
```

```
      </FormContext.Provider>
    </div>
  )
}
```

```
export default SimpleForm
```

The final version of `SimpleForm` will have additional code for tracking validation and errors, but this cut-down form is easier to understand.

The form is going to track all of its field values in the `values` object. The form creates two callback functions called `getValue` and `setValue` and puts them into the context (as the `form` object), where subcomponents will find them. We put the `form` into the context by wrapping a `<FormContext.Provider>` around the child components.

Notice that we have wrapped the `getValue` and `setValue` callbacks in `useCallback`, which prevents the component from creating a new version of each function every time we render the `SimpleForm`.

Whenever a child component calls the `form.value()` function, it will receive the current value of the specified field. If a child component calls `form.setValue()`, it will update that value.

Now let's look at a simplified version of the `InputField` component, again with any validation code removed to make it easier to understand:

```
import React, { useContext } from 'react'
import FormContext from './FormContext'

import './InputField.css'

const InputField = (props) => {
  const form = useContext(FormContext)

  if (!form.value) {
    return 'InputField should be wrapped in a form'
  }

  const { name, label, ...otherProps } = props

  const value = form.value(name)

  return (
    <div className="InputField">
      <label htmlFor={name}>{label || name}:</label>
      <input
        id={name}
        value={value || ''}
        onChange={(event) => {
          form.setValue(name, event.target.value)
        }}
```

```
        {...otherProps}
      />{' '}
      {}
    </div>
  )
}

export default InputField
```

The `InputField` extracts the `form` object from the `FormContext`. If it cannot find a form object, it knows that we have not wrapped it in a `SimpleForm` component. The `InputField` then renders an `input` field, setting its value to whatever is returned by `form.value(name)`. If the user changes the field's value, the `InputField` component sends the new value to `form.setValue(name, event.target.value)`.

If you need a form field other than an `input`, you can wrap it in some component similar to the `InputField` shown here.

The validation code is just more of the same. In the same way that the form tracks its current value in the `values` state, it also needs to track which fields are dirty and which are invalid. It then needs to pass callbacks for `setDirty`, `isDirty`, and `set Invalid`. These callbacks are used by the child fields when running their `onValidate` code.

Here is the final version of the `SimpleForm` component, including validation:

```
import { useCallback, useEffect, useState } from 'react'
import FormContext from './FormContext'
import './SimpleForm.css'

const SimpleForm = ({ children, value, onChange, onValid }) => {
  const [values, setValues] = useState(value || {})
  const [dirtyFields, setDirtyFields] = useState({})
  const [invalidFields, setInvalidFields] = useState({})

  useEffect(() => {
    setValues(value || {})
  }, [value])

  useEffect(() => {
    if (onChange) {
      onChange(values)
    }
  }, [onChange, values])

  useEffect(() => {
    if (onValid) {
      onValid(
        Object.keys(invalidFields).every((i) => !invalidFields[i]),
        invalidFields
      )
```

```
    }
  }, [onValid, invalidFields])

  const setValue = useCallback(
    (field, v) => setValues((vs) => ({ ...vs, [field]: v })),
    [setValues]
  )
  const getValue = useCallback((field) => values[field], [values])
  const setDirty = useCallback(
    (field) => setDirtyFields((df) => ({ ...df, [field]: true })),
    [setDirtyFields]
  )
  const getDirty = useCallback(
    (field) => Object.keys(dirtyFields).includes(field),
    [dirtyFields]
  )
  const setInvalid = useCallback(
    (field, error) => {
      setInvalidFields((i) => ({
        ...i,
        [field]: error ? error : undefined,
      }))
    },
    [setInvalidFields]
  )
  const form = {
    setValue: setValue,
    value: getValue,

    setDirty: setDirty,
    isDirty: getDirty,

    setInvalid: setInvalid,
  }

  return (
    <div className="SimpleForm-container">
      <FormContext.Provider value={form}>
        {children}
      </FormContext.Provider>
    </div>
  )
}

export default SimpleForm
```

And this is the final version of the InputField component. Notice that the field is counted as *dirty* once it loses focus or its value changes:

```
import { useContext, useEffect, useState } from 'react'
import FormContext from './FormContext'

import './InputField.css'
```

```
const splitCamelCase = (s) =>
  s
    .replace(/([a-z0-9])([A-Z0-9])/g, '$1 $2')
    .replace(/^([a-z])/, (x) => x.toUpperCase())

const InputField = (props) => {
  const form = useContext(FormContext)

  const [error, setError] = useState('')

  const { onValidate, name, label, ...otherProps } = props

  let value = form.value && form.value(name)

  useEffect(() => {
    if (onValidate) {
      setError(onValidate(value))
    }
  }, [onValidate, value])

  const setInvalid = form.setInvalid

  useEffect(() => {
    if (setInvalid) {
      setInvalid(name, error)
    }
  }, [setInvalid, name, error])

  if (!form.value) {
    return 'InputField should be wrapped in a form'
  }

  return (
    <div className="InputField">
      <label htmlFor={name}>{label || splitCamelCase(name)}:</label>
      <input
        id={name}
        onBlur={() => form.setDirty(name)}
        value={value || ''}
        onChange={(event) => {
          form.setDirty(name)
          form.setValue(name, event.target.value)
        }}
        {...otherProps}
      />{' '}
      {
        <div className="InputField-error">
          {form.isDirty(name) && error ? error : <> </>}
        </div>
      }
    </div>
```

```
    )
  }

  export default InputField
```

Discussion

You can use this recipe to create many simple forms, and you can extend it for use with any React component. For example, if you are using a third-party calendar or date picker, you would only need to wrap it in a component similar to InputField to use it inside a SimpleForm.

This recipe doesn't support forms within forms or arrays of forms. It should be possible to modify the SimpleForm component to behave like an InputField to place one form inside another.

You can download the source for this recipe from the GitHub site (*https://oreil.ly/gU03F*).

3.4 Measure Time with a Clock

Problem

Sometimes a React application needs to respond to the time of day. It might only need to display the current time, or it might need to poll a server at regular intervals or change its interface as day turns to night. But how do you cause your code to re-render as the result of a time change? How do you avoid rendering components too often? And how do you do all that without overcomplicating your code?

Solution

We're going to create a useClock hook. The useClock hook will give us access to a formatted version of the current date and time and automatically update the interface when the time changes. Here's an example of the code in use, and Figure 3-13 shows it running:

```
import { useEffect, useState } from 'react'
import useClock from './useClock'
import ClockFace from './ClockFace'

import './Ticker.css'

const SimpleTicker = () => {
  const [isTick, setTick] = useState(false)

  const time = useClock('HH:mm:ss')
```

```
  useEffect(() => {
    setTick((t) => !t)
  }, [time])

  return (
    <div className="Ticker">
      <div className="Ticker-clock">
        <h1>Time {isTick ? 'Tick!' : 'Tock!'}</h1>
        {time}
        <br />
        <ClockFace time={time} />
      </div>
    </div>
  )
}

export default SimpleTicker
```

Figure 3-13. The `SimpleTicker` *over three seconds*

The `time` variable contains the current time in the format `HH:mm:ss`. When the time changes, the value of the `isTick` state is toggled between true and false and then used to display the word *Tick!* or *Tock!* We show the current time and then also display the time with a `ClockFace` component.

As well as accepting a date and time format, `useClock` can take a number specifying the number of milliseconds between updates (see Figure 3-14):

```
import { useEffect, useState } from 'react'
import useClock from './useClock'

import './Ticker.css'

const IntervalTicker = () => {
  const [isTick3, setTick3] = useState(false)
```

```
  const tickThreeSeconds = useClock(3000)

  useEffect(() => {
    setTick3((t) => !t)
  }, [tickThreeSeconds])

  return (
    <div className="Ticker">
      <div className="Ticker-clock">
        <h1>{isTick3 ? '3 Second Tick!' : '3 Second Tock!'}</h1>
        {tickThreeSeconds}
      </div>
    </div>
  )
}

export default IntervalTicker
```

3 Second Tick!	**3 Second Tock!**
2021-05-15T23:49:12.472	2021-05-15T23:49:15.472

Figure 3-14. The `IntervalTicker` re-renders the component every three seconds

This version is more useful if you want to perform some task at regular intervals, such as polling a network service.

To poll a network service, consider using a clock with Recipe 5.1. If the current value of the clock is passed as a dependency to a hook that makes network calls, the network call will be repeated every time the clock changes.

If you pass a numeric parameter to `useClock`, it will return a time string in ISO format like `2021-06-11T14:50:34.706`.

To build this hook, we will use a third-party library called Moment.js (*https:// momentjs.com*) to handle date and time formatting. If you would prefer to use another library, such as Day.js (*https://day.js.org*), it should be straightforward to convert:

```
$ npm install moment
```

This is the code for `useClock`:

```
import { useEffect, useState } from 'react'
import moment from 'moment'

const useClock = (formatOrInterval) => {
  const format =
    typeof formatOrInterval === 'string'
      ? formatOrInterval
      : 'YYYY-MM-DDTHH:mm:ss.SSS'
  const interval =
    typeof formatOrInterval === 'number' ? formatOrInterval : 500
  const [response, setResponse] = useState(
    moment(new Date()).format(format)
  )

  useEffect(() => {
    const newTimer = setInterval(() => {
      setResponse(moment(new Date()).format(format))
    }, interval)

    return () => clearInterval(newTimer)
  }, [format, interval])

  return response
}

export default useClock
```

We derive the date and time `format` and the required *ticking* `interval` from the `formatOrInterval` parameter passed to the hook. Then we create a timer with `setInterval`. This time will set the `response` value every `interval` milliseconds. When we set the `response` string to a new time, any component that relies on `use Clock` will re-render.

We need to make sure that we cancel any timers that are no longer in use. We can do this using a feature of the `useEffect` hook. If we return a function at the end of our `useEffect` code, then that function will be called the next time `useEffect` needs to run. So, we can use it to clear the old timer before creating a new one.

If we pass a new format or interval to `useClock`, it will cancel its old timer and respond using a new timer.

Discussion

This recipe is an example of how you can use hooks to solve a simple problem simply. React code (the clue is in the name) reacts to dependency changes. Instead of thinking, "How can I run this piece of code every second?" the `useClock` hook allows you to write code that depends on the current time and hides away all of the gnarly details of creating timers, updating state, and clearing timers.

If you use the useClock hook several times in a component, then a time change can result in multiple renders. For example, if you have two clocks that format the current time in 12-hour format (04:45) and 24-hour format (16:45), then your component will render twice when the minute changes. An extra render once a minute is unlikely to have much of a performance impact.

You can also use the useClock hook inside other hooks. If you create a useMessages hook to retrieve messages from a server, you can call useClock inside it to poll the server at regular intervals.

You can download the source for this recipe from the GitHub site (*https://oreil.ly/hohKK*).

3.5 Monitor Online Status

Problem

Let's say someone is using your application on their cell phone, and then they head into a subway with no data connection. How can you check that the network connection has disappeared? What's a React-friendly way of updating your interface to either tell the user that there's a problem or disable some features that require network access?

Solution

We will create a hook called useOnline that will tell us whether we're connected to a network. We need code that runs when the browser loses or regains a connection to the network. Fortunately, there are window/body-level events called online and offline that do exactly that. When the online and offline events are triggered, the current network state will be given by navigator.onLine, which will be set to true or false:

```
import { useEffect, useState } from 'react'

const useOnline = () => {
  const [online, setOnline] = useState(navigator.onLine)

  useEffect(() => {
    if (window.addEventListener) {
      window.addEventListener('online', () => setOnline(true), false)
      window.addEventListener(
        'offline',
        () => setOnline(false),
        false
      )
    } else {
      document.body.ononline = () => setOnline(true)
```

```
      document.body.onoffline = () => setOnline(false)
    }
  }, [])

  return online
}

export default useOnline
```

This hook manages its connection state in the `online` variable. When the hook is first run (notice the empty dependency array), we register listeners to the browser's online/offline events. When either of these events occurs, we can set the value of `online` to `true` or `false`. If this is a change to the current value, then any component using this hook will re-render.

Here's an example of the hook in action:

```
import useOnline from './useOnline'
import './App.css'

function App() {
  const online = useOnline()

  return (
    <div className="App">
      <h1>Network Checker</h1>
      <span>
        You are now....
        {online ? (
          <div className="App-indicator-online">ONLINE</div>
        ) : (
          <div className="App-indicator-offline">OFFLINE</div>
        )}
      </span>
    </div>
  )
}

export default App
```

If you run the app, the page will currently show as online. If you disconnect/reconnect your network, the message will switch to OFFLINE and then back to ONLINE (see Figure 3-15).

Figure 3-15. The code re-renders when the network is switched off and back on again

Discussion

It's important to note that this hook checks your browser's connection to a network, not whether it connects to the broader Internet or your server. If you would like to check that your server is running and available, you would have to write additional code.

You can download the source for this recipe from the GitHub site (*https://oreil.ly/9hkSA*).

3.6 Manage Global State with Redux

Problem

In other recipes in this chapter, we've seen that you can manage complex component state with a pure JavaScript function called a reducer. *Reducers* simplify components and make business logic more testable.

But what if you have some data, such as a shopping basket, that needs to be accessed everywhere?

Solution

We will use the Redux library to manage the global application state. Redux uses the same reducers we can give to the React useReducer function, but they are used to manage a single state object for the entire application. Plus, there are many extensions to Redux that solve common programming problems and develop and manage your application more quickly.

First, we need to install the Redux library:

```
$ npm install redux
```

We will also install the React Redux library, which will make Redux far easier to use with React:

```
$ npm install react-redux
```

We're going to use Redux to build an application containing a shopping basket (see Figure 3-16).

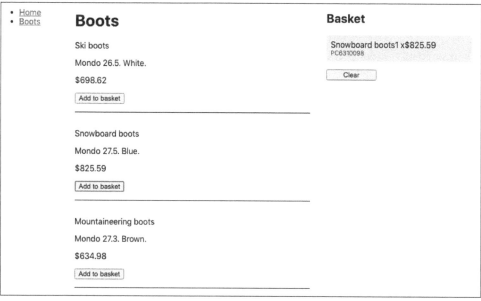

Figure 3-16. When a customer buys a product, the application adds it to the basket

If a customer clicks a Buy button, the application adds the product to the basket. If they click the Buy button again, the quantity in the basket is updated. The basket will appear in several places across the application, so it's a good candidate for moving to Redux. Here is the reducer function that we will use to manage the basket:

```
const reducer = (state = {}, action = {}) => {
  switch (action.type) {
    case 'buy': {
      const basket = state.basket ? [...state.basket] : []
      const existing = basket.findIndex(
        (item) => item.productId === action.payload.productId
      )
      if (existing !== -1) {
        basket[existing].quantity = basket[existing].quantity + 1
      } else {
        basket.push({ quantity: 1, ...action.payload })
      }
      return {
        ...state,
        basket,
      }
    }
    case 'clearBasket': {
      return {
        ...state,
        basket: [],
      }
    }
  }
```

```
    default:
      return { ...state }
  }
}

export default reducer
```

 We are creating a single reducer here. Once your application grows in size, you will probably want to split your reducer into smaller reducers, which you can combine with the Redux combine Reducers function (*https://oreil.ly/IVh7x*).

The reducer function responds to buy and clearBasket actions. The buy action will either add a new item to the basket or update the quantity of an existing item if one has a matching productId. The clearBasket action will set the basket back to an empty array.

Now that we have a reducer function, we will use it to create a Redux *store*. The store is going to be our central repository for the shared application state. To create a store, add these two lines to some top-level component such as *App.js*:

```
import { createStore } from 'redux'
import reducer from './reducer'

const store = createStore(reducer)
```

The store needs to be available globally in the app, and to do that, we need to inject it into the context of the components that might need it. The React Redux library provides a component to inject the store in a component context called Provider:

```
<Provider store={store}>
  All the components inside here can access the store
</Provider>
```

Here is the *reducer.js* component from the example application, which you can find in the GitHub repository (*https://oreil.ly/j90xI*) for this book:

```
const reducer = (state = {}, action = {}) => {
  switch (action.type) {
    case 'buy': {
      const basket = state.basket ? [...state.basket] : []
      const existing = basket.findIndex(
        (item) => item.productId === action.payload.productId
      )
      if (existing !== -1) {
        basket[existing].quantity = basket[existing].quantity + 1
      } else {
        basket.push({ quantity: 1, ...action.payload })
      }
      return {
```

```
      ...state,
      basket,
    }
  }
  case 'clearBasket': {
    return {
      ...state,
      basket: [],
    }
  }
  default:
    return { ...state }
  }
}

export default reducer
```

Now that the store is available to our components, how do we use it? React Redux allows you to access the store through hooks. If you want to read the contents of the global state, you can use useSelector:

```
const basket = useSelector((state) => state.basket)
```

The useSelector hook accepts a function to extract part of the central state. Selectors are pretty efficient and will cause your component to re-render only if the particular part of the state you are interested in changes.

If you need to submit an action to the central store, you can do it with the useDispatch hook:

```
const dispatch = useDispatch()
```

This returns a dispatch function that you can use to send actions to the store:

```
dispatch({ type: 'clearBasket' })
```

These hooks work by extracting the store from the current context. If you forget to add a Provider to your application or try to run useSelector or useDispatch outside of a Provider context, you will get an error, as shown in Figure 3-17.

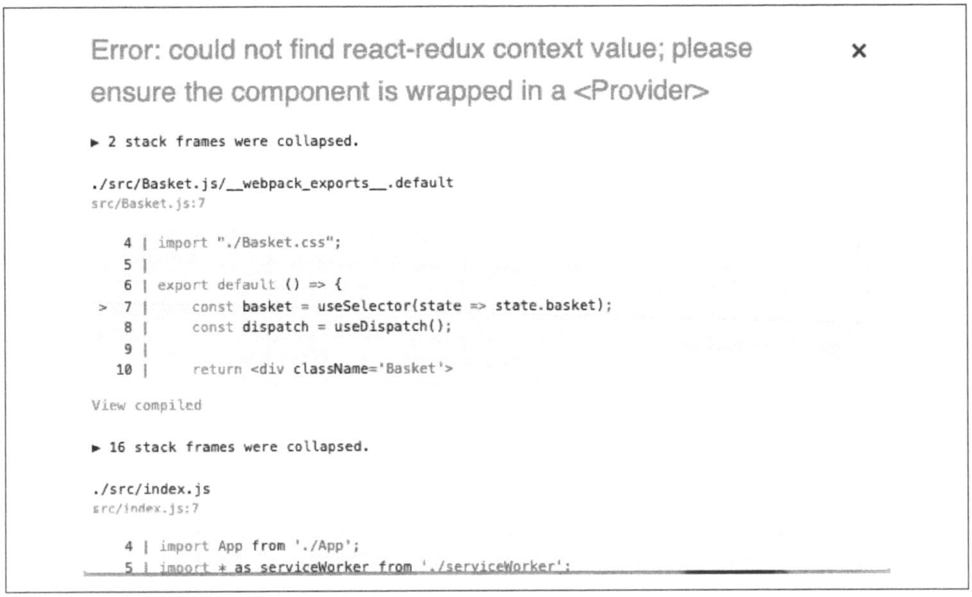

Figure 3-17. If you forget to include a Provider, *you will get this error*

The completed Basket component reads and clears the app-wide shopping basket:

```javascript
import { useDispatch, useSelector } from 'react-redux'

import './Basket.css'

const Basket = () => {
  const basket = useSelector((state) => state.basket)
  const dispatch = useDispatch()

  return (
    <div className="Basket">
      <h2>Basket</h2>
      {basket && basket.length ? (
        <>
          {basket.map((item) => (
            <div className="Basket-item">
              <div className="Basket-itemName">{item.name}</div>
              <div className="Basket-itemProductId">
                {item.productId}
              </div>
              <div className="Basket-itemPricing">
                <div className="Basket-itemQuantity">
                  {item.quantity}
                </div>
                <div className="Basket-itemPrice">{item.price}</div>
              </div>
            </div>
          ))}
```

```
        ))}
        <button onClick={() => dispatch({ type: 'clearBasket' })}>
          Clear
        </button>
      </>
    ) : (
      'Empty'
    )}
  </div>
  )
}

export default Basket
```

To demonstrate some code adding items to the basket, here's a Basket component that allows a customer to buy a selection of products:

```
import { useDispatch } from 'react-redux'

import './Boots.css'

const products = [
  {
    productId: 'BE8290004',
    name: 'Ski boots',
    description: 'Mondo 26.5. White.',
    price: 698.62,
  },
  {
    productId: 'PC6310098',
    name: 'Snowboard boots',
    description: 'Mondo 27.5. Blue.',
    price: 825.59,
  },
  {
    productId: 'RR5430103',
    name: 'Mountaineering boots',
    description: 'Mondo 27.3. Brown.',
    price: 634.98,
  },
]

const Boots = () => {
  const dispatch = useDispatch()

  return (
    <div className="Boots">
      <h1>Boots</h1>

      <dl className="Boots-products">
        {products.map((product) => (
          <>
            <dt>{product.name}</dt>
```

```
        <dd>
          <p>{product.description}</p>
          <p>${product.price}</p>
          <button
            onClick={() =>
              dispatch({ type: 'buy', payload: product })
            }
          >
            Add to basket
          </button>
        </dd>
      </>
    ))}
    </dl>
  </div>
  )
}

export default Boots
```

These two components may appear at very different locations in the component tree, but they share the same Redux store. As soon as a customer adds a product to the basket, the `Basket` component will automatically update with the change (see Figure 3-18).

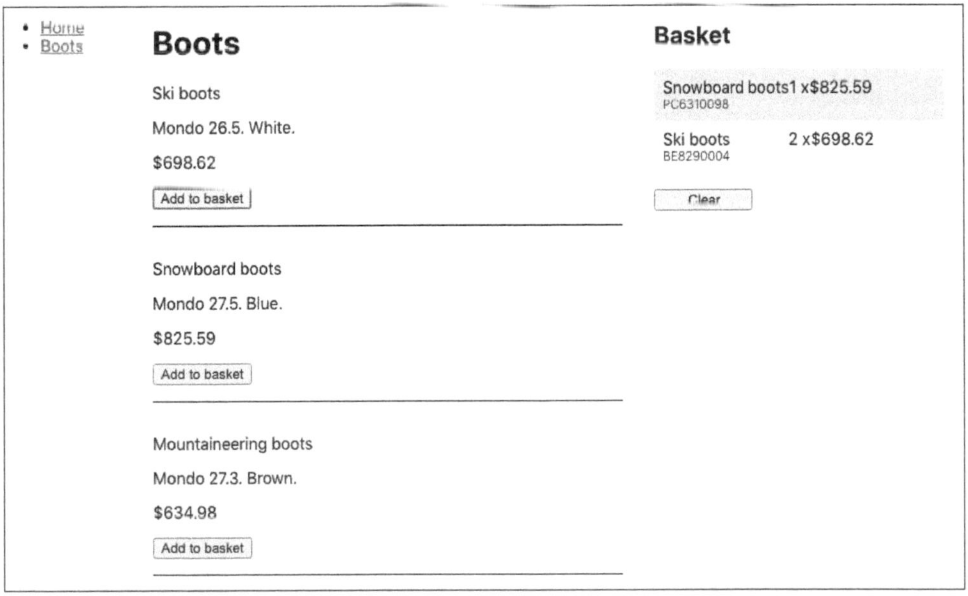

Figure 3-18. The Redux-React hooks make sure that when a user buys a product, the Basket is re-rendered

Discussion

Developers often use the Redux library with the React framework. For a long time, it seemed, almost every React application included Redux by default. It's probably true that Redux was often overused or used inappropriately. We have seen projects that have even banned local state in favor of using Redux for *all* state. We believe this approach is a mistake. Redux is intended for central application state management, not for simple component state. If you are storing data that is of concern to only one component, or its subcomponents, you should probably not store it in Redux.

However, if your application manages some global application state, then Redux is still the tool of choice.

You can download the source for this recipe from the GitHub site (*https://oreil.ly/j90xI*).

3.7 Survive Page Reloads with Redux Persist

Problem

Redux is an excellent way of managing the application state centrally. However, it does have a small problem: when you reload the page, the entire state disappears (see Figure 3-19).

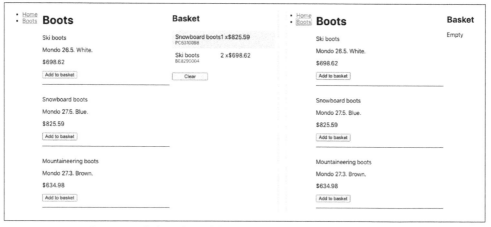

Figure 3-19. Redux state (left) is lost if the page is reloaded (right)

The state disappears because Redux keeps its state in memory. How do we prevent the state from disappearing?

Solution

We will use the Redux Persist library to keep a copy of the Redux state in local storage. To install Redux Persist, type the following:

```
$ npm install redux-persist
```

The first thing we need to do is create a *persisted reducer,* wrapped around our existing reducer:

```
import storage from 'redux-persist/lib/storage'

const persistConfig = {
  key: 'root',
  storage,
}

const persistedReducer = persistReducer(persistConfig, reducer)
```

The `storage` specifies where we will persist the Redux state: it will be in `local Storage` by default. The `persistConfig` says that we want to keep our state in a `localStorage` item called `persist:root`. When the Redux state changes, the `persis tedReducer` will write a copy with `localStorage.setItem('persist:root', ...)`. We now need to create our Redux store with `persistedReducer`:

```
const store = createStore(persistedReducer)
```

We need to interject the Redux Persist code between the Redux store and the code that's accessing the Redux store. We do that with a component called `PersistGate`:

```
import { PersistGate } from 'redux-persist/integration/react'
import { persistStore } from 'redux-persist'

const persistor = persistStore(store)
...
<Provider store={store}>
  <PersistGate loading={<div>Loading...</div>} persistor={persistor}>
    Components live in here
  </PersistGate>
</Provider>
```

The `PersistGate` must be *inside* the Redux `Provider` and *outside* the components that are going to use Redux. The `PersistGate` will watch for when the Redux state is lost and then reload it from `localStorage`. It might take a moment to reload the data, and if you want to show that the UI is briefly busy, you can pass a `loading` component to the `PersistGate`: for example, an animated spinner. The loading component will be displayed in place of its child components when Redux is reloading. If you don't want a loading component, you can set it to `null`.

Here is the final version of the modified *App.js* from the example app:

```
import { BrowserRouter, Route, Switch } from 'react-router-dom'
import { Provider } from 'react-redux'
import { createStore } from 'redux'

import Menu from './Menu'
import Home from './Home'
import Boots from './Boots'
import Basket from './Basket'

import './App.css'
import reducer from './reducer'

import { persistStore, persistReducer } from 'redux-persist'
import { PersistGate } from 'redux-persist/integration/react'
import storage from 'redux-persist/lib/storage'

const persistConfig = {
  key: 'root',
  storage,
}

const persistedReducer = persistReducer(persistConfig, reducer)

const store = createStore(persistedReducer)

const persistor = persistStore(store)

function App() {
  return (
    <div className="App">
      <Provider store={store}>
        <PersistGate
          loading={<div>Loading...</div>}
          persistor={persistor}
        >
          <BrowserRouter>
            <Menu />
            <Switch>
              <Route exact path="/">
                <Home />
              </Route>
              <Route path="/boots">
                <Boots />
              </Route>
            </Switch>
            <Basket />
          </BrowserRouter>
        </PersistGate>
      </Provider>
    </div>
  )
```

```
}

export default App
```

Now, when the user reloads the page, the Redux state survives, as shown in Figure 3-20.

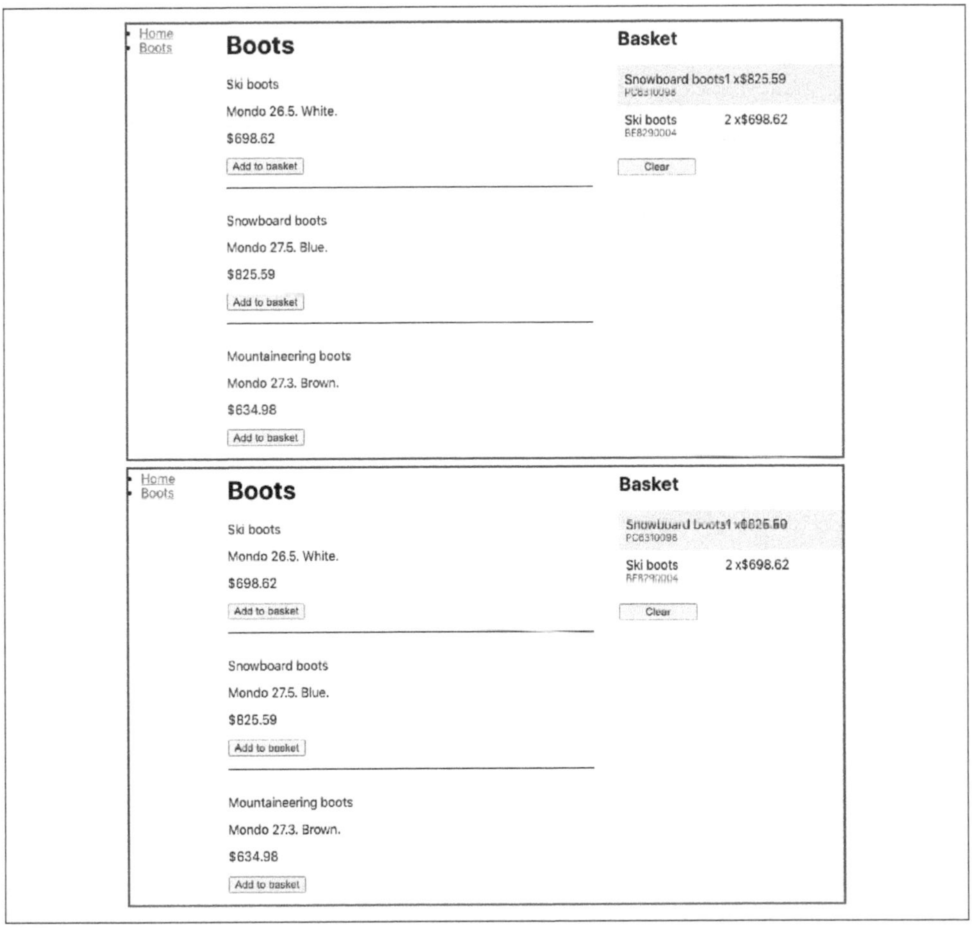

Figure 3-20. Redux state before the reload (top) and after (bottom)

Discussion

The Redux Persist library is a simple way of persisting Redux state through page reloads. If you have a substantial amount of Redux data, you will need to be careful not to break the `localStorage` limit, which will vary from browser to browser but is typically around 10 MB. However, if your Redux data is that size, you should consider offloading some of it to a server.

You can download the source for this recipe from the GitHub site (*https://oreil.ly/K8U5J*).

3.8 Calculate Derived State with Reselect

Problem

When you extract your application state into an external object with a tool like Redux, you often need to process the data in some way before displaying it. For example, Figure 3-21 shows an application we have used in a few recipes in this chapter.

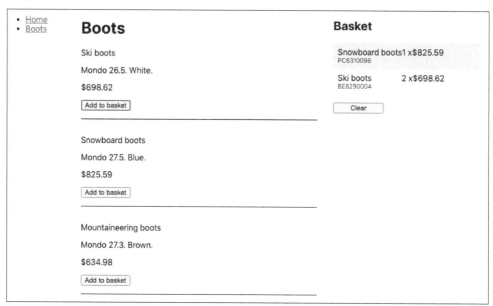

Figure 3-21. What's the best method for calculating the total cost and tax of the basket?

What if we want to calculate the total cost of the items in the basket and then calculate the amount of sales tax to pay? We could create a JavaScript function that reads through the basket items and calculates both, but that function would have to recalculate the values every time the basket renders. Is there a way of calculating derived values from the state that updates only when the state changes?

Solution

The Redux developers have created a library specifically designed to derive values efficiently from state objects, called reselect.

The reselect library creates selector functions. A *selector function* takes a single parameter—a state object—and returns a processed version.

We've already seen one selector in Recipe 3.6. We used it to return the current basket from the central Redux state:

```
const basket = useSelector((state) => state.basket)
```

The state => state.basket is a selector function; it derives some value from a state object. The reselect library creates highly efficient selector functions that can cache their results if the state they depend upon has not changed.

To install reselect, enter this command:

```
$ npm install reselect
```

Let's begin by creating a selector function that will do the following:

- Count the total number of items in a basket
- Calculate the total cost of all of the items

We'll call this function summarizer. Before we go into the details of how we'll write it, we'll begin by writing a test that will show what it will need to do:

```
it('should be able to handle multiple products', () => {
  const actual = summarizer({
    basket: [
      { productId: '1234', quantity: 2, price: 1.23 },
      { productId: '5678', quantity: 1, price: 1.5 },
    ],
  })
  expect(actual).toEqual({ itemCount: 3, cost: 3.96 })
})
```

So if we give it a state object, it will add up the quantities and costs and return an object containing the itemCount and cost.

We can create a selector function called summarizer with the Reselect library like this:

```
import { createSelector } from 'reselect'

const summarizer = createSelector(
  (state) => state.basket || [],
  (basket) => ({
    itemCount: basket.reduce((i, j) => i + j.quantity, 0),
    cost: basket.reduce((i, j) => i + j.quantity * j.price, 0),
  })
)

export default summarizer
```

The `createSelector` function creates a selector function *based* on other selector functions. Each of the parameters passed to it—except the last parameter—should be selector functions. We are passing just one:

```
(state) => state.basket || []
```

This code extracts the basket from the state.

The final parameter passed to `createSelector` (the *combiner*) is a function that derives a new value, based on the results of the preceding selectors:

```
(basket) => ({
  itemCount: basket.reduce((i, j) => i + j.quantity, 0),
  cost: basket.reduce((i, j) => i + j.quantity * j.price, 0),
})
```

The `basket` value is the result of running the state through the first selector.

Why on Earth would anyone create functions this way? Isn't it *way* more complicated than just creating a JavaScript function manually, without the need to pass all of these functions to functions?

The answer is *efficiency*. Selectors will recalculate their values only when they need to. State objects can be complex and might have dozens of attributes. But we are interested only in the contents of the `basket` attribute, and we don't want to have to recalculate our costs if anything else changes.

What `reselect` does is work out when the value it returns is likely to have changed. Let's say we call it one time, and it calculates the `itemCount` and `value` like this:

```
{itemCount: 3, cost: 3.96}
```

Then the user runs a bunch of commands that update personal preferences, posts a message to somebody, adds several things to their wish list, and so on.

Each of the events might update the global application state. But the next time we run the `summarizer` function, it will return the cached value that it produced before:

```
{itemCount: 3, cost: 3.96}
```

Why? Because it knows that this value is dependent *only* upon the `basket` value in the global state. And if that hasn't changed, then it doesn't need to recalculate the return value.

Because `reselect` allows us to build selector functions from other selector functions, we could build another selector called `taxer` to calculate the basket's sales tax:

```
import { createSelector } from 'reselect'
import summarizer from './summarizer'

const taxer = createSelector(
  summarizer,
```

```
      (summary) => summary.cost * 0.07
)

export default taxer
```

The `taxer` selector uses the value returned by the `summarizer` function. It takes the `cost` of the `summarizer` result and multiplies it by 7%. If the basket's summarized total doesn't change, then the `taxer` function will not need to update its result.

Now that we have the `summarizer` and `taxer` selectors, we can use them inside a component, just as we would any other selector function:

```
import { useDispatch, useSelector } from 'react-redux'

import './Basket.css'
import summarizer from './summarizer'
import taxer from './taxer'

const Basket = () => {
  const basket = useSelector((state) => state.basket)
  const { itemCount, cost } = useSelector(summarizer)
  const tax = useSelector(taxer)
  const dispatch = useDispatch()

  return (
    <div className="Basket">
      <h2>Basket</h2>
      {basket && basket.length ? (
        <>
          {basket.map((item) => (
            <div className="Basket-item">
              <div className="Basket-itemName">{item.name}</div>
              <div className="Basket-itemProductId">
                {item.productId}
              </div>
              <div className="Basket-itemPricing">
                <div className="Basket-itemQuantity">
                  {item.quantity}
                </div>
                <div className="Basket-itemPrice">{item.price}</div>
              </div>
            </div>
          ))}
          <p>{itemCount} items</p>
          <p>Total: ${cost.toFixed(2)}</p>
          <p>Sales tax: ${tax.toFixed(2)}</p>
          <button onClick={() => dispatch({ type: 'clearBasket' })}>
            Clear
          </button>
        </>
      ) : (
        'Empty'
```

```
        )}
      </div>
    )
  }

export default Basket
```

When we run the code now, we see a summary at the bottom of the shopping basket, which will update whenever we buy a new product (see Figure 3-22).

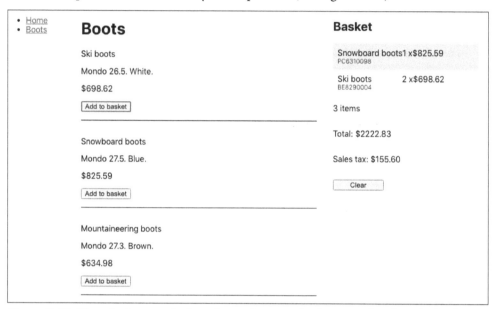

Figure 3-22. The selectors recalculate the total cost and sales tax only when the basket changes

Discussion

The first time you meet selector functions, they can seem complicated and hard to understand. But it is worth taking the time to understand them. There is nothing Redux-specific about them. There is no reason why you can't also use them with non-Redux reducers. Because they have no dependencies beyond the `reselect` library itself, they are easy to unit test. We include example tests in the code for this chapter.

You can download the source for this recipe from the GitHub site (*https://oreil.ly/ U7SLr*).

CHAPTER 4

Interaction Design

In this chapter, we look at some recipes that address a bunch of typical interface problems. How do you deal with errors? How do you help people use your system? How do you create complex input sequences without writing a bunch of spaghetti code?

This is a collection of tips that we've found useful, time and again. At the end of the chapter, we look at various ways of adding animation to your application. We take a low-tech approach where possible, and ideally, the recipes we include will add meaning to your interface designs with a minimum of fuss.

4.1 Build a Centralized Error Handler

Problem

It's hard to define precisely what makes good software good. But one thing that most excellent software has in common is how it responds to errors and exceptions. There will always be exceptional, unexpected situations when people are running your code: the network can disappear, the server can crash, the storage can become corrupted. It's important to consider how you should deal with these situations when they occur.

One approach that is almost certain to fail is to ignore the fact that error conditions occur and to hide the gory details of what went wrong. Somewhere, somehow, you need to leave a trail of evidence that you can use to prevent that error from happening again.

When we're writing server code, we might log the error details and return an appropriate message to a request. But if we're writing client code, we need a plan for how we'll deal with local errors. We might choose to display the crash's details to the user and ask them to file an error report. We might use a third-party service like Sentry.io (*https://sentry.io*) to log the details remotely.

Whatever our code does, it should be consistent. But how can we handle exceptions consistently in a React application?

Solution

In this recipe, we're going to look at one way of creating a centralized error handler. To be clear: this code won't automatically capture all exceptions. It still needs to be added explicitly to JavaScript `catch` blocks. It's also not a replacement for dealing with any error from which we can otherwise recover. If an order fails because the server is down for maintenance, it is much better to ask the user to try again later.

But this technique helps catch any errors for which we have not previously planned.

As a general principle, when something goes wrong, there are three things that you should tell the user:

- What happened
- Why it happened
- What they should do about it

In the example we show here, we're going to handle errors by displaying a dialog box that shows the details of a JavaScript `Error` object and asks the user to email the contents to systems support. We want a simple error-handler function that we can call when an error happens:

```
setVisibleError('Cannot do that thing', errorObject)
```

If we want to make the function readily available across the entire application, the usual way is by using a *context*. A context is a kind of scope that we can wrap around a set of React components. Anything we put into that context is available to all the child components. We will use our context to store the error-handler function that we can run when an error occurs.

We'll call our context `ErrorHandlerContext`:

```
import React from 'react'

const ErrorHandlerContext = React.createContext(() => {})

export default ErrorHandlerContext
```

To allow us to make the context available to a set of components, let's create an `ErrorHandlerProvider` component that will create an instance of the context and make it available to any child components we pass to it:

```
import ErrorHandlerContext from './ErrorHandlerContext'

let setError = () => {}
```

```
const ErrorHandlerProvider = (props) => {
  if (props.callback) {
    setError = props.callback
  }

  return (
    <ErrorHandlerContext.Provider value={setError}>
      {props.children}
    </ErrorHandlerContext.Provider>
  )
}

export default ErrorHandlerProvider
```

Now we need some code that says what to do when we call the error-handler function. In our case, we need some code that will respond to an error report by displaying a dialog box containing all of the error details. If you want to handle errors differently, this is the code you need to modify:

```
import { useCallback, useState } from 'react'
import ErrorHandlerProvider from './ErrorHandlerProvider'
import ErrorDialog from './ErrorDialog'

const ErrorContainer = (props) => {
  const [error, setError] = useState()
  const [errorTitle, setErrorTitle] = useState()
  const [action, setAction] = useState()

  if (error) {
    console.error(
      'An error has been thrown',
      errorTitle,
      JSON.stringify(error)
    )
  }

  const callback = useCallback((title, err, action) => {
    console.error('ERROR RAISED ')
    console.error('Error title: ', title)
    console.error('Error content', JSON.stringify(err))
    setError(err)
    setErrorTitle(title)
    setAction(action)
  }, [])
  return (
    <ErrorHandlerProvider callback={callback}>
      {props.children}

      {error && (
        <ErrorDialog
          title={errorTitle}
```

```
                onClose={() => {
                    setError(null)
                    setErrorTitle('')
                }}
                action={action}
                error={error}
            />
        )}
    </ErrorHandlerProvider>
    )
}

export default ErrorContainer
```

The `ErrorContainer` displays the details using an `ErrorDialog`. We won't go into the details of the code for `ErrorDialog` here as this is the code that you are most likely to replace with your implementation.[1]

We need to wrap the bulk of our application in an `ErrorContainer`. Any components inside the `ErrorContainer` will be able to call the error handler:

```
import './App.css'
import ErrorContainer from './ErrorContainer'
import ClockIn from './ClockIn'

function App() {
  return (
    <div className="App">
      <ErrorContainer>
        <ClockIn />
      </ErrorContainer>
    </div>
  )
}

export default App
```

How does a component use the error handler? We'll create a custom hook called `useErrorHandler()`, which will get the error-handler function out of the context and return it:

```
import ErrorHandlerContext from './ErrorHandlerContext'
import { useContext } from 'react'

const useErrorHandler = () => useContext(ErrorHandlerContext)

export default useErrorHandler
```

---

1 You can download all source code for this recipe on the GitHub repository (*https://oreil.ly/wUM7Q*).

That's quite a complex set of code, but now we come to use the error handler; it's very simple. This example code makes a network request when a user clicks a button. If the network request fails, then the details of the error are passed to the error handler:

```
import useErrorHandler from './useErrorHandler'
import axios from 'axios'

const ClockIn = () => {
  const setVisibleError = useErrorHandler()

  const doClockIn = async () => {
    try {
      await axios.put('/clockTime')
    } catch (err) {
      setVisibleError('Unable to record work start time', err)
    }
  }

  return (
    <>
      <h1>Click Button to Record Start Time</h1>
      <button onClick={doClockIn}>Start work</button>
    </>
  )
}

export default ClockIn
```

You can see what the app looks like in Figure 4-1.

Figure 4-1. The time-recording app

When you click the button, the network request fails because the server code doesn't exist. Figure 4-2 shows the error dialog that appears. Notice that it shows what went wrong, why it went wrong, and what the user should do about it.

Figure 4-2. When the network request throws an exception, we pass it to the error handler

Discussion

Of all the recipes that we've created over the years, this one has saved the most time. During development, code often breaks, and if the only evidence of a failure is a stack trace hidden away inside the JavaScript console, you are likely to miss it.

Significantly, when some piece of infrastructure (networks, gateways, servers, data-bases) fails, this small amount of code can save you untold hours tracking down the cause.

You can download the source for this recipe from the GitHub site (*https://oreil.ly/ wUM7Q*).

4.2 Create an Interactive Help Guide

Problem

Tim Berners-Lee deliberately designed the web to have very few features. It has a sim-ple protocol (HTTP), and it originally had a straightforward markup language

(HTML). The lack of complexity meant that new users of websites immediately knew how to use them. If you saw something that looked like a hyperlink, you could click on it and go to another page.

But rich JavaScript applications have changed all that. No longer are web applications a collection of hyperlinked web pages. Instead, they resemble old desktop applications; they are more powerful and feature-rich, but the downside is that they are now far more complex to use.

How do you build an interactive guide into your application?

Solution

We're going to build a simple help system that you can overlay onto an existing application. When the user opens the help, they will see a series of pop-up notes that describe how to use the various features they can see on the page, as shown in Figure 4-3.

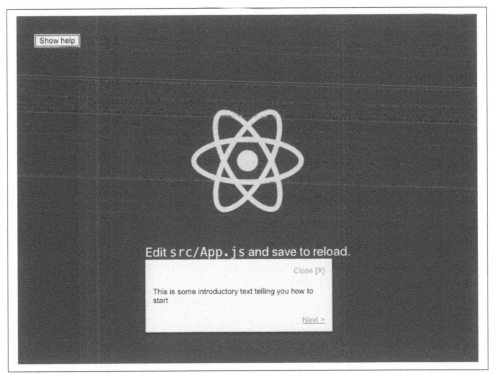

Figure 4-3. Show a sequence of help messages when the user asks

We want something that will be easy to maintain and will provide help only for visible components. That sounds like quite a big task, so let's begin by first constructing a component that will display a pop-up help message:

```
import { Popper } from '@material-ui/core'
import './HelpBubble.css'

const HelpBubble = (props) => {
  const element = props.forElement
    ? document.querySelector(props.forElement)
    : null

  return element ? (
    <Popper
      className="HelpBubble-container"
      open={props.open}
      anchorEl={element}
      placement={props.placement || 'bottom-start'}
    >
      <div className="HelpBubble-close" onClick={props.onClose}>
        Close [X]
      </div>
      {props.content}
      <div className="HelpBubble-controls">
        {props.previousLabel ? (
          <div
            className="HelpBubble-control HelpBubble-previous"
            onClick={props.onPrevious}
          >
            &lt; {props.previousLabel}
          </div>
        ) : (
          <div> </div>
        )}
        {props.nextLabel ? (
          <div
            className="HelpBubble-control HelpBubble-next"
            onClick={props.onNext}
          >
            {props.nextLabel} &gt;
          </div>
        ) : (
          <div> </div>
        )}
      </div>
    </Popper>
  ) : null
}

export default HelpBubble
```

We're using the Popper component from the @material-ui library. The Popper component can be anchored on the page, next to some other component. Our Help Bubble takes a forElement string, which will represent a CSS selector such as `.class-name` or `#some-id`. We will use selectors to associate things on the screen with pop-up messages.

Now that we have a pop-up message component, we'll need something that coordinates a sequence of HelpBubbles. We'll call this the HelpSequence:

```
import { useEffect, useState } from 'react'

import HelpBubble from './HelpBubble'

function isVisible(e) {
  return !!(
    e.offsetWidth ||
    e.offsetHeight ||
    e.getClientRects().length
  )
}

const HelpSequence = (props) => {
  const [position, setPosition] = useState(0)
  const [sequence, setSequence] = useState()

  useEffect(() => {
    if (props.sequence) {
      const filter = props.sequence.filter((i) => {
        if (!i.forElement) {
          return false
        }
        const element = document.querySelector(i.forElement)
        if (!element) {
          return false
        }
        return isVisible(element)
      })
      setSequence(filter)
    } else {
      setSequence(null)
    }
  }, [props.sequence, props.open])

  const data = sequence && sequence[position]

  useEffect(() => {
    setPosition(0)
  }, [props.open])

  const onNext = () =>
    setPosition((p) => {
      if (p === sequence.length - 1) {
        props.onClose && props.onClose()
      }
      return p + 1
```

```
    })

    const onPrevious = () =>
      setPosition((p) => {
        if (p === 0) {
          props.onClose && props.onClose()
        }
        return p - 1
      })

    return (
      <div className="HelpSequence-container">
        {data && (
          <HelpBubble
            open={props.open}
            forElement={data.forElement}
            placement={data.placement}
            onClose={props.onClose}
            previousLabel={position > 0 && 'Previous'}
            nextLabel={
              position < sequence.length - 1 ? 'Next' : 'Finish'
            }
            onPrevious={onPrevious}
            onNext={onNext}
            content={data.text}
          />
        )}
      </div>
    )
  }

  export default HelpSequence
```

The HelpSequence takes an array of JavaScript objects like this:

```
[
    {forElement: "p",
        text: "This is some introductory text telling you how to start"},
    {forElement: ".App-link", text: "This will show you how to use React"},
    {forElement: ".App-nowhere", text: "This help text will never appear"},
]
```

and converts it into a dynamic sequence of HelpBubbles. It will show a HelpBubble only if it can find an element that matches the forElement selector. It then places the HelpBubble next to the element and shows the help text.

Let's add a HelpSequence to the default *App.js* code generated by create-react-app:

```
import { useState } from 'react'
import logo from './logo.svg'
import HelpSequence from './HelpSequence'
import './App.css'
```

```
function App() {
  const [showHelp, setShowHelp] = useState(false)

  return (
    <div className="App">
      <header className="App-header">
        <img src={logo} className="App-logo" alt="logo" />
        <p>
          Edit <code>src/App.js</code> and save to reload.
        </p>
        <a
          className="App-link"
          href="https://reactjs.org"
          target="_blank"
          rel="noopener noreferrer"
        >
          Learn React
        </a>
      </header>
      <button onClick={() => setShowHelp(true)}>Show help</button>
      <HelpSequence
        sequence={[
          {
            forElement: 'p',
            text: 'This is some introductory text telling you how to start',
          },
          {
            forElement: '.App-link',
            text: 'This will show you how to use React',
          },
          {
            forElement: '.App-nowhere',
            text: 'This help text will never appear',
          },
        ]}
        open={showHelp}
        onClose={() => setShowHelp(false)}
      />
    </div>
  )
}

export default App
```

To begin with, we cannot see anything different other than a help button (see Figure 4-4).

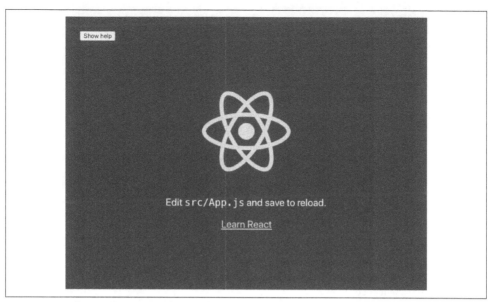

Figure 4-4. The application, when it first loads

When the user clicks the help button, the first help topic appears, as shown in Figure 4-5.

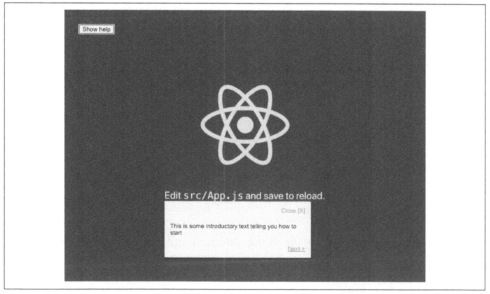

Figure 4-5. When the user clicks the help button, the help bubble appears for the first match

Figure 4-6 shows the help moving to the next element when the user clicks Next. The user can continue to move from item to item until there are no more matching elements visible.

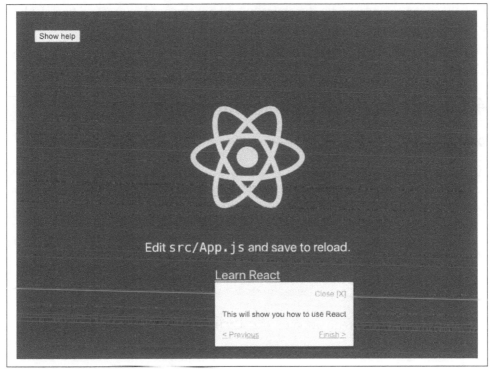

Figure 4-6. The final element has a Finish button

Discussion

Adding interactive help to your application makes your user interface *discoverable*. Developers spend a lot of their time adding functionality to applications that people might never use, simply because they don't know that it's there.

The implementation in this recipe displays the help as simple plain text. You might consider using Markdown, as that will allow for a richer experience, and help topics can then include links to other more expansive help pages.[2]

The help topics are automatically limited to just those elements that are visible on the page. You could choose to create either a separate help sequence for each page or a

---

2 See Recipe 4.5 for details on how to use Markdown in your application.

single large help sequence that will automatically adapt to the user's current view of the interface.

Finally, a help system like this is ideally suited for storage in a headless CMS, which will allow you to update help dynamically, without the need to create a new deployment each time.

You can download the source for this recipe from the GitHub site (*https://oreil.ly/CsiMN*).

4.3 Use Reducers for Complex Interactions

Problem

Applications frequently need users to follow a sequence of actions. They might be completing the steps in a wizard, or they might need to log in and confirm some dangerous operation (see Figure 4-7).

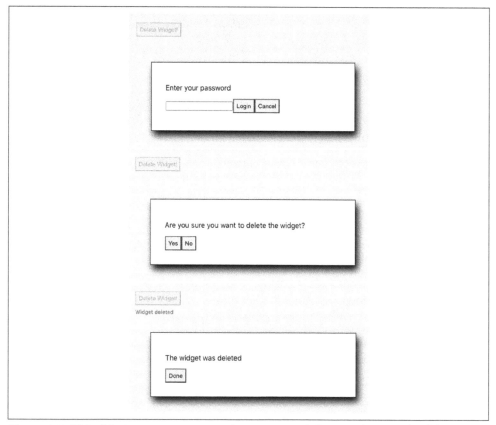

Figure 4-7. This deletion process requires logging in and then confirming the deletion

Not only will the user need to perform a sequence of steps, but the steps might be conditional. If the user has logged in recently, they perhaps don't need to log in again. They might want to cancel partway through the sequence.

If you model the complex sequences inside your components, you can soon find your application is full of spaghetti code.

Solution

We are going to use a reducer to manage a complex sequence of operations. We introduced reducers for managing state in Chapter 3. A *reducer* is a function that accepts a state object and an action. The reducer uses the action to decide how to change the state, and it must have no side effects.

Because reducers have no user-interface code, they are perfect for managing gnarly pieces of interrelated state without worrying about the visual appearance. They are particularly amenable to unit testing.

For example, let's say we implement the deletion sequence mentioned at the start of this recipe. We can begin in classic test-driven style by writing a unit test:

```
import deletionReducer from './deletionReducer'

describe('deletionReducer', () => {
  it('should show the login dialog if we are not logged in', () => {
    const actual = deletionReducer({}, { type: 'START_DELETION' })
    expect(actual.showLogin).toBe(true)
    expect(actual.message).toBe('')
    expect(actual.deleteButtonDisabled).toBe(true)
    expect(actual.loginError).toBe('')
    expect(actual.showConfirmation).toBe(false)
  })
})
```

Here our reducer function is going to be called `deletionReducer`. We pass it an empty object (`{}`) and an action that says we want to start the deletion process (`{type: 'START_DELETION'}`). We then say that we expect the new version of the state to have a `showLogin` value of `true`, a `showConfirmation` value of `false`, and so on.

We can then implement the code for a reducer to do just that:

```
function deletionReducer(state, action) {
  switch (action.type) {
    case 'START_DELETION':
      return {
        ...state,
        showLogin: true,
        message: '',
        deleteButtonDisabled: true,
```

```
        loginError: '',
        showConfirmation: false,
      }
    default:
      return null // Or anything
  }
}
```

At first, we are merely setting the state attributes to values that pass the test. As we add more and more tests, our reducer improves as it handles more situations.

Eventually, we get something that looks like this:[3]

```
function deletionReducer(state, action) {
  switch (action.type) {
    case 'START_DELETION':
      return {
        ...state,
        showLogin: !state.loggedIn,
        message: '',
        deleteButtonDisabled: true,
        loginError: '',
        showConfirmation: !!state.loggedIn,
      }
    case 'CANCEL_DELETION':
      return {
        ...state,
        showLogin: false,
        showConfirmation: false,
        showResult: false,
        message: 'Deletion canceled',
        deleteButtonDisabled: false,
      }
    case 'LOGIN':
      const passwordCorrect = action.payload === 'swordfish'
      return {
        ...state,
        showLogin: !passwordCorrect,
        showConfirmation: passwordCorrect,
        loginError: passwordCorrect ? '' : 'Invalid password',
        loggedIn: true,
      }
    case 'CONFIRM_DELETION':
      return {
        ...state,
        showConfirmation: false,
        showResult: true,
        message: 'Widget deleted',
      }
```

---

3 See the GitHub repository (*https://oreil.ly/DCGIv*) for the tests we used to drive out this code.

```
      case 'FINISH':
        return {
          ...state,
          showLogin: false,
          showConfirmation: false,
          showResult: false,
          deleteButtonDisabled: false,
        }
      default:
        throw new Error('Unknown action: ' + action.type)
  }
}

export default deletionReducer
```

Although this code is complicated, you can write it quickly if you create the tests first.

Now that we have the reducer, we can use it in our application:

```
import { useReducer, useState } from 'react'
import './App.css'
import deletionReducer from './deletionReducer'

function App() {
  const [state, dispatch] = useReducer(deletionReducer, {})
  const [password, setPassword] = useState()

  return (
    <div className="App">
      <button
        onClick={() => {
          dispatch({ type: 'START_DELETION' })
        }}
        disabled={state.deleteButtonDisabled}
      >
        Delete Widget!
      </button>
      <div className="App-message">{state.message}</div>
      {state.showLogin && (
        <div className="App-dialog">
          <p>Enter your password</p>
          <input
            type="password"
            value={password}
            onChange={(evt) => setPassword(evt.target.value)}
          />
          <button
            onClick={() =>
              dispatch({ type: 'LOGIN', payload: password })
            }
          >
            Login
          </button>
```

```
          <button
            onClick={() => dispatch({ type: 'CANCEL_DELETION' })}
          >
            Cancel
          </button>
          <div className="App-error">{state.loginError}</div>
        </div>
      )}
      {state.showConfirmation && (
        <div className="App-dialog">
          <p>Are you sure you want to delete the widget?</p>
          <button
            onClick={() =>
              dispatch({
                type: 'CONFIRM_DELETION',
              })
            }
          >
            Yes
          </button>
          <button
            onClick={() =>
              dispatch({
                type: 'CANCEL_DELETION',
              })
            }
          >
            No
          </button>
        </div>
      )}
      {state.showResult && (
        <div className="App-dialog">
          <p>The widget was deleted</p>
          <button
            onClick={() =>
              dispatch({
                type: 'FINISH',
              })
            }
          >
            Done
          </button>
        </div>
      )}
    </div>
  )
}

export default App
```

Most of this code is purely creating the user interface for each of the dialogs in the sequence. There is virtually no logic in this component. It just does what the reducer tells it. It will take the user through the *happy path* of logging in and confirming the deletion (see Figure 4-8).

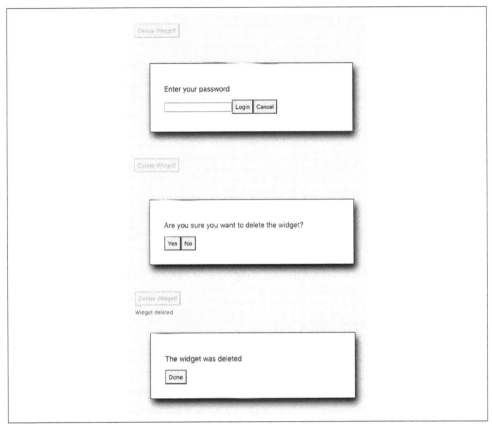

Figure 4-8. The final result

But Figure 4-9 shows it also handles all of the edge cases, such as invalid passwords and cancellation.

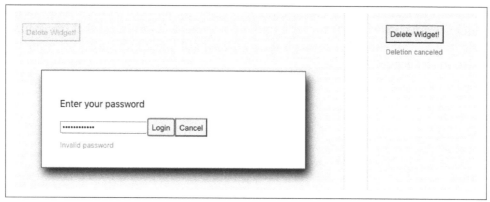

Figure 4-9. The edge cases are all handled by the reducer

Discussion

There are times when reducers can make your code convoluted; if you have few pieces of state with few interactions between them, you probably don't need a reducer. But if you find yourself drawing a flowchart or a state diagram to describe a sequence of user interactions, that's a sign that you might need a reducer.

You can download the source for this recipe from the GitHub site (*https://oreil.ly/hfqLn*).

4.4 Add Keyboard Interaction

Problem

Power users like to use keyboards for frequently used operations. React components can respond to keyboard events, but only when they (or their children) have focus. What do you do if you want your component to respond to events at the document level?

Solution

We're going to create a key-listener hook to listen for keydown events at the document level. Still, it could be easily modified to listen for any other JavaScript event in the DOM. This is the hook:

```
import { useEffect } from 'react'

const useKeyListener = (callback) => {
  useEffect(() => {
    const listener = (e) => {
      e = e || window.event
      const tagName = e.target.localName || e.target.tagName
```

```
      // Only accept key-events that originated at the body level
      // to avoid key-strokes in e.g. text-fields being included
      if (tagName.toUpperCase() === 'BODY') {
        callback(e)
      }
    }
    document.addEventListener('keydown', listener, true)
    return () => {
      document.removeEventListener('keydown', listener, true)
    }
  }, [callback])
}

export default useKeyListener
```

The hook accepts a callback function and registers it for keydown events on the document object. At the end of the useEffect, it returns a function that will unregister the callback. If the callback function we pass in changes, we will first unregister the old function before registering the new one.

How do we use the hook? Here is an example. See if you notice the little coding wrinkle we have to deal with:

```
import { useCallback, useState } from 'react'
import './App.css'
import useKeyListener from './useKeyListener'

const RIGHT_ARROW = 39
const LEFT_ARROW = 37
const ESCAPE = 27

function App() {
  const [angle, setAngle] = useState(0)
  const [lastKey, setLastKey] = useState('')

  let onKeyDown = useCallback(
    (evt) => {
      if (evt.keyCode === LEFT_ARROW) {
        setAngle((c) => Math.max(-360, c - 10))
        setLastKey('Left')
      } else if (evt.keyCode === RIGHT_ARROW) {
        setAngle((c) => Math.min(360, c + 10))
        setLastKey('Right')
      } else if (evt.keyCode === ESCAPE) {
        setAngle(0)
        setLastKey('Escape')
      }
    },
    [setAngle]
  )
  useKeyListener(onKeyDown)
```

```
    return (
      <div className="App">
        <p>
          Angle: {angle} Last key: {lastKey}
        </p>
        <svg
          width="400px"
          height="400px"
          title="arrow"
          fill="none"
          strokeWidth="10"
          stroke="black"
          style={{
            transform: `rotate(${angle}deg)`,
          }}
        >
          <polyline points="100,200 200,0 300,200" />
          <polyline points="200,0 200,400" />
        </svg>
      </div>
    )
}

export default App
```

This code listens for the user pressing the left/right cursor keys. Our onKeyDown function says what should happen when those key clicks occur, but notice that we've wrapped it in a useCallback. If we *didn't* do that, the browser would re-create the onKeyDown function each time it rendered the App component. The new function would do the same as the old onKeyDown function, but it would live in a different place in memory, and the useKeyListener would keep unregistering and re-registering it.

 If you forget to wrap your callback function in a useCallback, it may result in a blizzard of render calls, which might slow your application down.

By using useCallback, we can ensure that we only create the function if setAngle changes.

If you run the application, you will see an arrow on the screen. If you press the left/right cursor keys (Figure 4-10), you can rotate the image. If you press the Escape key, you can reset it to vertical.

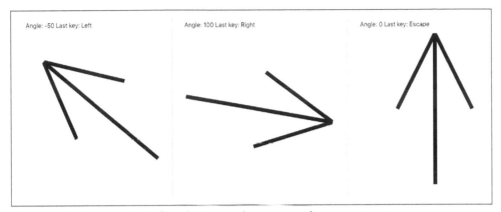

| Angle: -50 Last key: Left | Angle: 100 Last key: Right | Angle: 0 Last key: Escape |

Figure 4-10. Pressing the left/right/Escape keys causes the arrow to rotate

Discussion

We are careful in the `useKeyListener` function to only listen to events that originated at the body level. If the user clicks the arrow keys in a text field, the browser won't send those events to your code.

You can download the source for this recipe from the GitHub site (*https://oreil.ly/ VIY1O*).

4.5 Use Markdown for Rich Content

Problem

If your application allows users to provide large blocks of text content, it would be helpful if that content could also include formatted text, links, and so forth. However, allowing users to pass in such horrors as raw HTML can lead to security flaws and untold misery for developers.

How do you allow users to post rich content without undermining the security of your application?

Solution

Markdown is an excellent way of allowing users to post rich content into your application safely. To see how to use Markdown in your application, let's consider this simple application, which allows a user to post a timestamped series of messages into a list:

```
import { useState } from 'react'
import './Forum.css'
```

```
const Forum = () => {
  const [text, setText] = useState('')
  const [messages, setMessages] = useState([])

  return (
    <section className="Forum">
      <textarea
        cols={80}
        rows={20}
        value={text}
        onChange={(evt) => setText(evt.target.value)}
      />
      <button
        onClick={() => {
          setMessages((msgs) => [
            {
              body: text,
              timestamp: new Date().toISOString(),
            },
            ...msgs,
          ])
          setText('')
        }}
      >
        Post
      </button>
      {messages.map((msg) => {
        return (
          <dl>
            <dt>{msg.timestamp}</dt>
            <dd>{msg.body}</dd>
          </dl>
        )
      })}
    </section>
  )
}

export default Forum
```

When you run the application (Figure 4-11), you see a large text area. When you post a plain-text message, the app preserves white space and line breaks.

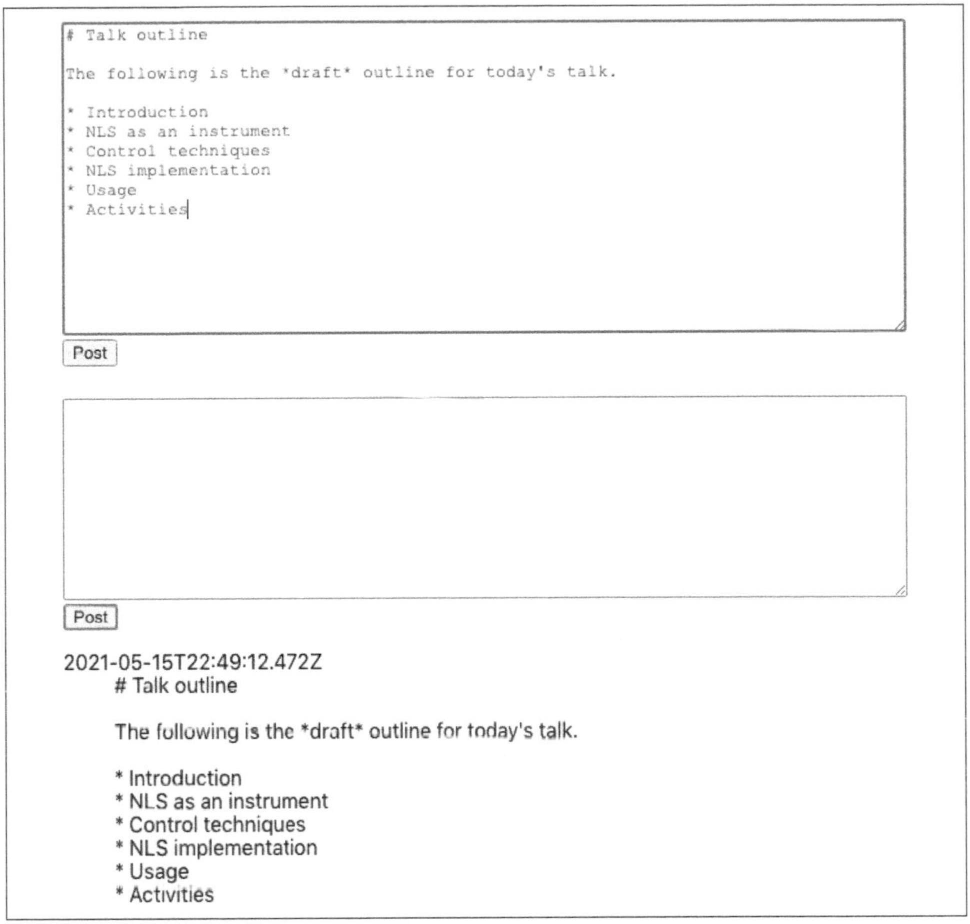

```
# Talk outline

The following is the *draft* outline for today's talk.

* Introduction
* NLS as an instrument
* Control techniques
* NLS implementation
* Usage
* Activities
```

Post

Post

```
2021-05-15T22:49:12.472Z
    # Talk outline

    The following is the *draft* outline for today's talk.

    * Introduction
    * NLS as an instrument
    * Control techniques
    * NLS implementation
    * Usage
    * Activities
```

Figure 4-11. A user enters text into a text area, and it gets posted as a plain-text message

If your application contains a text area, it's worth considering allowing the user to enter Markdown content.

There are many, many Markdown libraries available, but most of them are wrappers for react-markdown or a syntax highlighter like PrismJS (*https://prismjs.com*) or CodeMirror (*https://codemirror.net*).

We'll look at a library called react-md-editor that adds extra features to react-markdown and allows you to display Markdown and edit it. We will begin by installing the library:

```
$ npm install @uiw/react-md-editor
```

We'll now convert our plain-text area to a Markdown editor and convert the posted messages from Markdown to HTML:

```
import { useState } from 'react'
import MDEditor from '@uiw/react-md-editor'

const MarkdownForum = () => {
  const [text, setText] = useState('')
  const [messages, setMessages] = useState([])

  return (
    <section className="Forum">
      <MDEditor height={300} value={text} onChange={setText} />
      <button
        onClick={() => {
          setMessages((msgs) => [
            {
              body: text,
              timestamp: new Date().toISOString(),
            },
            ...msgs,
          ])
          setText('')
        }}
      >
        Post
      </button>
      {messages.map((msg) => {
        return (
          <dl>
            <dt>{msg.timestamp}</dt>
            <dd>
              <MDEditor.Markdown source={msg.body} />
            </dd>
          </dl>
        )
      })}
    </section>
  )
}

export default MarkdownForum
```

Converting plain text to Markdown is a small change with a significant return. As you can see in Figure 4-12, the user can apply rich formatting to a message and choose to edit it full-screen before posting it.

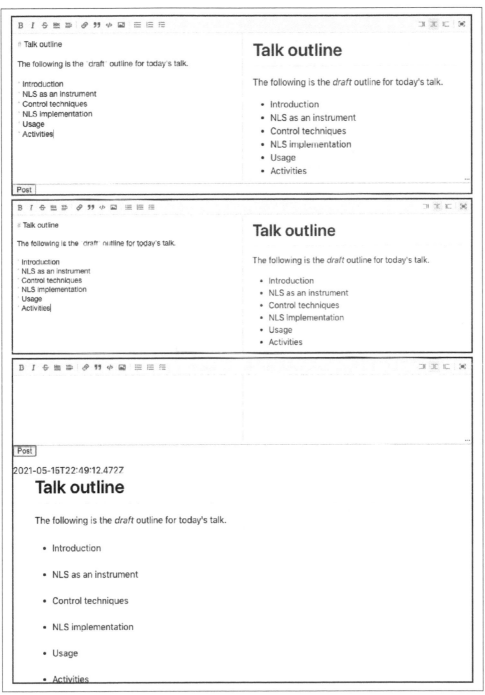

Figure 4-12. The Markdown editor shows a preview as you type and also allows you to work full-screen

Discussion

Adding Markdown to an application is quick and improves the user's experience with minimal effort. For more details on Markdown, see John Gruber's original guide (*https://oreil.ly/2EE9x*).

You can download the source for this recipe from the GitHub site (*https://oreil.ly/S0n7x*).

4.6 Animate with CSS Classes

Problem

You want to add a small amount of simple animation to your application, but you don't want to increase your application size by installing a third-party library.

Solution

Most of the animation you are ever likely to need in a React application will probably not require a third-party animation library. That's because CSS animation now gives browsers the native ability to animate CSS properties with minimal effort. It takes very little code, and the animation is smooth because the graphics hardware will generate it. GPU animation uses less power, making it more appropriate for mobile devices.

 If you are looking to add animation to your React application, begin with CSS animation before looking elsewhere.

How does CSS animation work? It uses a CSS property called `transition`. Let's say we want to create an expandable information panel. When the user clicks the button, the panel opens smoothly. When they click it again, it closes smoothly, as shown in Figure 4-13.

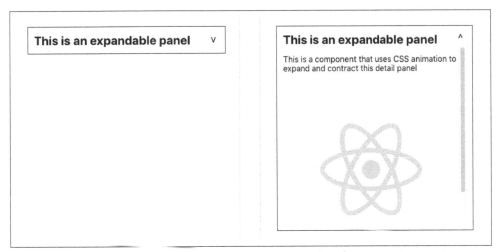

Figure 4-13. Simple CSS animation will smoothly expand and contract the panel

We can create this effect using the CSS `transition` property:

```
.InfoPanel-details {
    height: 350px;
    transition: height 0.5s;
}
```

This CSS specifies a height, as well as a `transition` property. This combination translates to "Whatever your current height, animate to my preferred height during the next half-second."

The animation will occur whenever the `height` of the element changes, such as when an additional CSS rule becomes valid. For example, if we have an extra CSS class-name with a different height, the transition property will animate the height change when an element switches to a different class:

```
.InfoPanel-details {
    height: 350px;
    transition: height 0.5s;
}
.InfoPanel-details.InfoPanel-details-closed {
    height: 0;
}
```

 This class name structure is an example of block element modifier (BEM) naming. The *block* is the component (`InfoPanel`), the *element* is a thing inside the block (`details`), and the *modifier* says something about the element's current state (`closed`). The BEM convention reduces the chances of name clashes in your code.

If an `InfoPanel-details` element suddenly acquires an additional `.InfoPanel-details-closed` class, the `height` will change from 350px to 0, and the `transition` property will smoothly shrink the element. Conversely, if the component *loses* the `.InfoPanel-details-closed` class, the element will expand again.

That means that we can defer the hard work to CSS, and all we need to do in our React code is add or remove the class to an element:

```
import { useState } from 'react'

import './InfoPanel.css'

const InfoPanel = ({ title, children }) => {
  const [open, setOpen] = useState(false)

  return (
    <section className="InfoPanel">
      <h1>
        {title}
        <button onClick={() => setOpen((v) => !v)}>
          {open ? '^' : 'v'}
        </button>
      </h1>
      <div
        className={`InfoPanel-details ${
          open ? '' : 'InfoPanel-details-closed'
        }`}
      >
        {children}
      </div>
    </section>
  )
}

export default InfoPanel
```

Discussion

We have frequently seen many projects bundle in third-party component libraries to use some small widget that expands or contracts its contents. As you can see, such animation is trivial to include.

You can download the source for this recipe from the GitHub site (*https://oreil.ly/FKnIc*).

4.7 Animate with React Animation

Problem

CSS animations are very low-tech and will be appropriate for most animations that you are likely to need.

However, they require you to understand a lot about the various CSS properties and the effects of animating them. If you want to illustrate an item being deleted by it rapidly expanding and becoming transparent, how do you do that?

Libraries such as Animate.css (*https://animate.style*) contain a whole host of precanned CSS animations, but they often require more advanced CSS animation concepts like keyframes and are not particularly tuned for React. How can we add CSS library animations to a React application?

Solution

The React Animations library is a React wrapper for the Animate.css library. It will efficiently add animated styling to your components without generating unnecessary renders or significantly increasing the size of the generated DOM.

It's able to work so efficiently because React Animations works with a CSS-in-JS library. CSS-in-JS is a technique for coding your style information directly in your JavaScript code. React will let you add your style attributes as React components, but CSS-in-JS does this more efficiently, dynamically creating shared style elements in the head of the page.

There are several CSS-in-JS libraries to choose from, but in this recipe, we're going to use one called Radium (*https://oreil.ly/oNBEl*).

Let's begin by installing Radium and React Animations:

```
$ npm install radium
$ npm install react-animations
```

Our example application (Figure 4-14) will run an animation each time we add an image item to the collection.

Figure 4-14. Clicking the Add button will load a new image from picsum.photos

Likewise, when a user clicks an image, it shows a fade-out animation before removing the images from the list, as shown in Figure 4-15.[4]

Figure 4-15. If we click the fifth image, it will fade out from the list and disappear

---

4 Paper books are beautiful things, but to fully experience the animation effect, see the complete code on GitHub (*https://oreil.ly/OcAqo*).

We'll begin by importing some animations and helper code from Radium:

```
import { pulse, zoomOut, shake, merge } from 'react-animations'
import Radium, { StyleRoot } from 'radium'

const styles = {
  created: {
    animation: 'x 0.5s',
    animationName: Radium.keyframes(pulse, 'pulse'),
  },
  deleted: {
    animation: 'x 0.5s',
    animationName: Radium.keyframes(merge(zoomOut, shake), 'zoomOut'),
  },
}
```

From React Animations we get `pulse`, `zoomOut`, and `shake` animations. We are going to use the `pulse` animation when we add an image. We'll use a *combined* animation of `zoomOut` and `shake` when we remove an image. We can combine animations using React Animations' `merge` function.

The `styles` generate all of the CSS styles needed to run each of these half-second animations. The call to `Radium.keyframes()` handles all of the animation details for us.

We must know when an animation has completely ended. If we delete an image before the deletion-animation completes, there would be no image to animate.

We can keep track of CSS animations by passing an `onAnimationEnd` callback to any element we are going to animate. For each item in our image collection, we are going to track three things:

- The URL of the image it represents
- A Boolean value that will be true while the "created" animation is running
- A Boolean value that will be true while the "deleted" animation is running

Here is the example code to animate images into and out of the collection:

```
import { useState } from 'react'
import { pulse, zoomOut, shake, merge } from 'react-animations'
import Radium, { StyleRoot } from 'radium'

import './App.css'

const styles = {
  created: {
    animation: 'x 0.5s',
    animationName: Radium.keyframes(pulse, 'pulse'),
  },
  deleted: {
    animation: 'x 0.5s',
```

```
      animationName: Radium.keyframes(merge(zoomOut, shake), 'zoomOut'),
  },
}

function getStyleForItem(item) {
  return item.deleting
    ? styles.deleted
    : item.creating
    ? styles.created
    : null
}

function App() {
  const [data, setData] = useState([])

  let deleteItem = (i) =>
    setData((d) => {
      const result = [...d]
      result[i].deleting = true
      return result
    })
  let createItem = () => {
    setData((d) => [
      ...d,
      {
        url: `https://picsum.photos/id/${d.length * 3}/200`,
        creating: true,
      },
    ])
  }
  let completeAnimation = (d, i) => {
    if (d.deleting) {
      setData((d) => {
        const result = [...d]
        result.splice(i, 1)
        return result
      })
    } else if (d.creating) {
      setData((d) => {
        const result = [...d]
        result[i].creating = false
        return result
      })
    }
  }
  return (
    <div className="App">
      <StyleRoot>
        <p>
          Images from 
          <a href="https://picsum.photos/">Lorem Picsum</a>
        </p>
```

```
      <button onClick={createItem}>Add</button>
      {data.map((d, i) => (
        <div
          style={getStyleForItem(d)}
          onAnimationEnd={() => completeAnimation(d, i)}
        >
          <img
            id={`image${i}`}
            src={d.url}
            width={200}
            height={200}
            alt="Random"
            title="Click to delete"
            onClick={() => deleteItem(i)}
          />
        </div>
      ))}
    </StyleRoot>
  </div>
  )
}

export default App
```

Discussion

When choosing which animation to use, we should first ask: what will this animation mean?

All animation should have meaning. It can show something existential (creation or deletion). It might indicate a change of state (becoming enabled or disabled). It might zoom in to show detail or zoom out to reveal a broader context. Or it might illustrate a limit or boundary (a spring-back animation at the end of a long list) or allow a user to express a preference (swiping left or right).

Animation should also be short. Most animations should probably be over in half a second so that the user can experience the meaning of the animation without being consciously aware of its appearance.

An animation should never be merely *attractive*.

You can download the source for this recipe from the GitHub site (*https://oreil.ly/rRK8F*).

4.8 Animate Infographics with TweenOne

Problem

CSS animations are smooth and highly efficient. Browsers might defer CSS animations to the graphics hardware at the compositing stage, which means that not only are the animations running at machine-code speeds, but the machine-code itself is not running on the CPU.

However, the downside to running CSS animations on graphics hardware is that your application code won't know what's happening *during* an animation. You can track when an animation has started, ended, or is repeated (onAnimationStart, on AnimationEnd, onAnimationIteration), but everything that happens in between is a mystery.

If you are animating an infographic, you may want to animate the numbers on a bar chart as the bars grow or shrink. Or, if you are writing an application to track cyclists, you might want to show the current altitude as the bicycle animates its way up and down the terrain.

But how do you create animations that you can *listen* to while they are happening?

Solution

The TweenOne library creates animations with JavaScript, which means you can track them as they happen, frame by frame.

Let's begin by installing the TweenOne library:

```
$ npm install rc-tween-one
```

TweenOne works with CSS, but it doesn't use CSS animations. Instead, it generates CSS transforms, which it updates many times each second.

You need to wrap the thing you want to animate in a <TweenOne/> element. For example, let's say we want to animate a rect inside an SVG:

```
<TweenOne component='g' animation={...details here}>
    <rect width="2" height="6" x="3" y="-3" fill="white"/>
</TweenOne>
```

TweenOne takes an element name and an object that will describe the animation to perform. We'll come to what that animation object looks like shortly.

TweenOne will use the element name (g in this case) to generate a wrapper around the animated thing. This wrapper will have a style attribute that will include a set of CSS transforms to move and rotate the contents somewhere.

So in our example, at some point in the animation, the DOM might look like this:

```
<g style="transform: translate(881.555px, 489.614px) rotate(136.174deg);">
  <rect width="2" height="6" x="3" y="-3" fill="white"/>
</g>
```

Although you can create similar effects to CSS animations, the TweenOne library works differently. Instead of handing the animation to the hardware, the TweenOne library uses JavaScript to create each frame, which has two consequences. First, it uses more CPU power (bad), and second, we can track the animation while it's happening (good).

If we pass TweenOne an onUpdate callback, we will be sent information about the animation on every single frame:

```
<TweenOne component='g' animation={...details here} onUpdate={info=>{...}}>
    <rect width="2" height="6" x="3" y="-3" fill="white"/>
</TweenOne>
```

The info object passed to onUpdate has a ratio value between 0 and 1, representing the proportion of the way the TweenOne element is through an animation. We can use the ratio to animate text that is associated with the graphics.

For example, if we build an animated dashboard that shows vehicles on a race track, we can use onUpdate to show each car's speed and distance as it animates.

We'll create the visuals for this example in SVG. First, let's create a string containing an SVG path, which represents the track:

```
export default 'm 723.72379,404.71306 ...  -8.30851,-3.00521 z'
```

This is a greatly truncated version of the actual path that we'll use. We can import the path string from *track.js* like this:

```
import path from './track'
```

To display the track inside a React component, we can render an svg element:

```
<svg height="600" width="1000" viewBox="0 0 1000 600"
    style={{backgroundColor: 'black'}}>
  <path stroke='#444' strokeWidth={10}
      fill='none' d={path}/>
</svg>
```

We can add a couple of rectangles for the vehicle—a red one for the body and a white one for the windshield:

```
<svg height="600" width="1000" viewBox="0 0 1000 600"
    style={{backgroundColor: 'black'}}>
  <path stroke='#444' strokeWidth={10}
      fill='none' d={path}/>
  <rect width={24} height={16} x={-12} y={-8} fill='red'/>
  <rect width={2} height={6} x={3} y={-3} fill='white'/>
</svg>
```

Figure 4-16 shows the track with the vehicle at the top-left corner.

Figure 4-16. The static image with a tiny vehicle at the top left

But how do we animate the vehicle around the track? TweenOne makes this easy because it contains a plugin to generate animations that follow SVG path strings.

```
import PathPlugin from 'rc-tween-one/lib/plugin/PathPlugin'

TweenOne.plugins.push(PathPlugin)
```

We've configured TweenOne for use with SVG path animations. That means we can look at how to describe an animation for TweenOne. We do it with a simple Java-Script object:

```
import path from './track'

const followAnimation = {
  path: { x: path, y: path, rotate: path },
  repeat: -1,
}
```

We tell TweenOne two things with this object: first, we're telling it to generate translates and rotations that follow the `path` string that we've imported from *track.js*. Second, we're saying that we want the animation to loop infinitely by setting the `repeat` count to −1.

We can use this as the basis of animation for our vehicle:

```
<svg height="600" width="1000" viewBox="0 0 1000 600"
    style={{backgroundColor: 'black'}}>
  <path stroke='#444' strokeWidth={10}
      fill='none' d={path}/>
  <TweenOne component='g' animation={{...followAnimation, duration: 16000}}>
    <rect width={24} height={16} x={-12} y={-8} fill='red'/>
    <rect width={2} height={6} x={3} y={-3} fill='white'/>
  </TweenOne>
</svg>
```

Notice that we're using the spread operator to provide an additional animation parameter: duration. A value of 16000 means we want the animation to take 16 seconds.

We can add a second vehicle and use the onUpdate callback method to create a very rudimentary set of faked telemetry statistics for each one as they move around the track. Here is the completed code:

```
import { useState } from 'react'
import TweenOne from 'rc-tween-one'
import Details from './Details'
import path from './track'
import PathPlugin from 'rc-tween-one/lib/plugin/PathPlugin'
import grid from './grid.svg'

import './App.css'

TweenOne.plugins.push(PathPlugin)

const followAnimation = {
  path: { x: path, y: path, rotate: path },
  repeat: -1,
}

function App() {
  const [redTelemetry, setRedTelemetry] = useState({
    dist: 0,
    speed: 0,
    lap: 0,
  })
  const [blueTelemetry, setBlueTelemetry] = useState({
    dist: 0,
    speed: 0,
    lap: 0,
  })

  const trackVehicle = (info, telemetry) => ({
    dist: info.ratio,
    speed: info.ratio - telemetry.dist,
    lap:
```

```
        info.ratio < telemetry.dist ? telemetry.lap + 1 : telemetry.lap,
  })

  return (
    <div className="App">
      <h1>Nürburgring</h1>
      <Details
        redTelemetry={redTelemetry}
        blueTelemetry={blueTelemetry}
      />
      <svg
        height="600"
        width="1000"
        viewBox="0 0 1000 600"
        style={{ backgroundColor: 'black' }}
      >
        <image href={grid} width={1000} height={600} />
        <path stroke="#444" strokeWidth={10} fill="none" d={path} />
        <path
          stroke="#c0c0c0"
          strokeWidth={2}
          strokeDasharray="3 4"
          fill="none"
          d={path}
        />

        <TweenOne
          component="g"
          animation={{
            ...followAnimation,
            duration: 16000,
            onUpdate: (info) =>
              setRedTelemetry((telemetry) =>
                trackVehicle(info, telemetry)
              ),
          }}
        >
          <rect width={24} height={16} x={-12} y={-8} fill="red" />
          <rect width={2} height={6} x={3} y={-3} fill="white" />
        </TweenOne>

        <TweenOne
          component="g"
          animation={{
            ...followAnimation,
            delay: 3000,
            duration: 15500,
            onUpdate: (info) =>
              setBlueTelemetry((telemetry) =>
                trackVehicle(info, telemetry)
              ),
          }}
```

```
      >
        <rect width={24} height={16} x={-12} y={-8} fill="blue" />
        <rect width={2} height={6} x={3} y={-3} fill="white" />
      </TweenOne>
    </svg>
  </div>
  )
}

export default App
```

Figure 4-17 shows the animation. The vehicles follow the path of the race track, rotating to face the direction of travel.

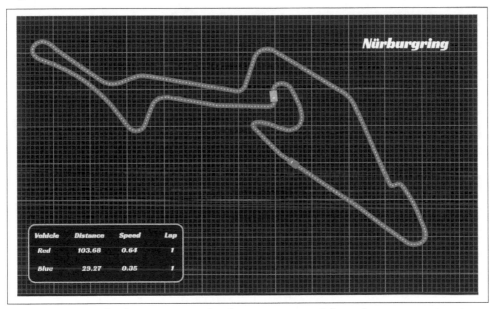

Figure 4-17. Our final animation with telemetry generated from the current animation state

Discussion

CSS animations are what you should use for most UI animation. However, in the case of infographics, you often need to synchronize the text and the graphics. TweenOne makes that possible, at the cost of greater CPU usage.

You can download the source for this recipe from the GitHub site (*https://oreil.ly/ 8l7Vp*).

CHAPTER 5

Connecting to Services

React, unlike frameworks such as Angular, does not include everything you might need for an application. In particular, it does not provide a standard way to get data from network services into your application. That freedom is excellent because it means that React applications can use the latest technology. The downside is that developers just starting with React are left to struggle on their own.

In this chapter, we will look at a few ways to attach network services to your application. We will see some common themes through each of these recipes, and we'll try to keep the network code separate from the components that use it. That way, when a new web service technology comes along, we can switch to it without changing a lot of code.

5.1 Convert Network Calls to Hooks

Problem

One of the advantages of component-based development is that it breaks the code down into small manageable chunks, each of which performs a distinct, identifiable action. In some ways, the best kind of component is one that you can see on a large screen without scrolling. One of the great features of React is that it has, in many ways, gotten simpler over time. React hooks and the move away from class-based components have removed boilerplate and reduced the amount of code.

However, one way to inflate the size of a component is by filling it with networking code. If you aim to create simple code, you should try to strip out networking code from your components. The components will become smaller, and the network code will be more reusable.

But how should we split out the networking code?

Solution

In this recipe, we will look at a way of moving your network requests into React hooks to track whether a network request is still underway or if there has been some error that prevented it from succeeding.

Before we look at the details, we need to think about what is important to us when making an asynchronous network request. There are three things that we need to track:

- The data returned by the request
- Whether the request is still loading the data from the server
- Any errors that might have occurred when running the request

You will see these three things appearing in each of the recipes in this chapter. It doesn't matter whether we are making the requests with fetch or axios commands, via Redux middleware, or through an API query layer like *GraphQL*; our component will always care about data, loading state, and errors.

As an example, let's build a simple message board that contains several forums. The messages on each forum contain an author field and a text field. Figure 5-1 shows a screenshot of the example application, which you can download from the GitHub site.

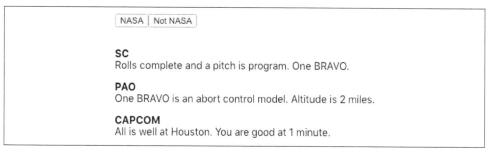

Figure 5-1. The buttons select the NASA or Not NASA forums

The buttons at the top of the page select the "NASA" or "Not NASA" forums. A small Node server provides the backend for our example application, which has pre-populated some messages into the NASA forum. Once you have downloaded the source code, you can run the backend server by running the *server.js* script in the application's main directory:

```
$ node ./server.js
```

The backend server runs at *http://localhost:5000*. We can start the React application itself in the usual way:

```
$ npm run start
```

The React application will run on port 3000.

 When in development mode, we proxy all backend requests through the React server. If you're using `create-react-app`, you can do this by adding a `proxy` property to *package.json* and setting it to *http://localhost:5000*. The React server will pass API calls to our *server.js* backend. For example, *http://localhost:3000/messages/nasa* (which returns an array of messages for the NASA forum) will be proxied to *http://localhost:5000/messages/nasa*.

We'll make the network request to read the messages using a simple `fetch` command:

```
const response = await fetch(`/messages/${forum}`)
if (!response.ok) {
  const text = await response.text()
  throw new Error(`Unable to read messages for ${forum}: ${text}`)
}
const body = await response.json()
```

Here, the `forum` value will contain the string ID of the forum. The `fetch` command is asynchronous and returns a promise, so we will `await` it. Then we can check whether the call failed with any bad HTTP status, and if so, we will throw an error. We will extract the JSON object out of the response and store it in the `body` variable. If the response body is not a correctly formatted JSON object, we will also throw an error.

We need to keep track of three things in this call: the data, the loading state, and any errors. We're going to bundle this whole thing up inside a custom hook, so let's have three states called `data`, `loading`, and `error`:

```
const useMessages = (forum) => {
  const [data, setData] = useState([])
  const [loading, setLoading] = useState(false)
  const [error, setError] = useState()
  ....
  return { data, loading, error }
}
```

We'll pass in the forum name as a parameter to the `useMessages` hook, which will return an object containing the `data`, `loading`, and `error` states. We can use object destructuring to extract and rename the values in any component that uses the hook, like this:

```
const {
  data: messages,
  loading: messagesLoading,
  error: messagesError,
} = useMessages('nasa')
```

Renaming the variables in a spread operator helps avoid naming conflicts. For example, if you want to read messages from more than one forum, you could make a second call to the useMessages hook and choose a variable other than messages for the second hook response.

Let's get back to the useMessages hook. The network request depends upon the forum value that we pass in, so we need to make sure that we run the fetch request inside a useEffect:

```
useEffect(() => {
  setError(null)
  if (forum) {
    ....
  } else {
    setData([])
    setLoading(false)
  }
}, [forum])
```

We're omitting for the moment the code that makes the actual request. The code inside the useEffect will run the first time the hook is called. If the client component is re-rendered and passes in the same value for forum, the useEffect will not run because the [forum] dependency will not have changed. It will run again only if the forum value changes.

Now let's look at how we can drop in the fetch request to this hook:

```
import { useEffect, useState } from 'react'

const useMessages = (forum) => {
  const [data, setData] = useState([])
  const [loading, setLoading] = useState(false)
  const [error, setError] = useState()

  useEffect(() => {
    let didCancel = false
    setError(null)
    if (forum) {
      ;(async () => {
        try {
          setLoading(true)
          const response = await fetch(`/messages/${forum}`)
          if (!response.ok) {
            const text = await response.text()
            throw new Error(
              `Unable to read messages for ${forum}: ${text}`
            )
          }
          const body = await response.json()
```

```
          if (!didCancel) {
            setData(body)
          }
        } catch (err) {
          setError(err)
        } finally {
          setLoading(false)
        }
      })()
    } else {
      setData([])
      setLoading(false)
    }
    return () => {
      didCancel = true
    }
  }, [forum])

  return { data, loading, error }
}

export default useMessages
```

Because we're using await to handle the promises correctly, we need to wrap the code in a rather ugly (async () => {...}) call. Inside there, we're able to set values for data, loading, and error as the request runs, finishes, and (possibly) fails. All of this will happen asynchronously after the call to the hook has been completed. When the data, loading, and error states change, the hook will cause the component to be re-rendered with the new values.

 A consequence of having asynchronous code inside a hook is that the hook will return before the network response has been received. This means there's a chance that the hook might be called again, before the previous network response has been received. To avoid the network responses being resolved in the wrong order, the example code tracks if the current request was overridden by a later request using the didCancel variable. This variable will control whether the hook returns the data from the hook. It won't cancel the network request itself. To do that, see Recipe 5.3.

Let's take a look at *App.js* in the example application to see what it looks like to use this hook:

```
import './App.css'
import { useState } from 'react'
import useMessages from './useMessages'

function App() {
  const [forum, setForum] = useState('nasa')
```

```
const {
  data: messages,
  loading: messagesLoading,
  error: messagesError,
} = useMessages(forum)

return (
  <div className="App">
    <button onClick={() => setForum('nasa')}>NASA</button>
    <button onClick={() => setForum('notNasa')}>Not NASA</button>
    {messagesError ? (
      <div className="error">
        Something went wrong:
        <div className="error-contents">
          {messagesError.message}
        </div>
      </div>
    ) : messagesLoading ? (
      <div className="loading">Loading...</div>
    ) : messages && messages.length ? (
      <dl>
        {messages.map((m) => (
          <>
            <dt>{m.author}</dt>
            <dd>{m.text}</dd>
          </>
        ))}
      </dl>
    ) : (
      'No messages'
    )}
  </div>
)
}

export default App
```

Our example application changes which forum is loaded when you click either the NASA or Not NASA button. The example server returns a 404-status for the "Not NASA" forum, which causes an error to appear on-screen. In Figure 5-2, we can see the example application showing the loading state, the messages from the NASA forum, and an error when we try to load data from the missing "Not NASA" forum.

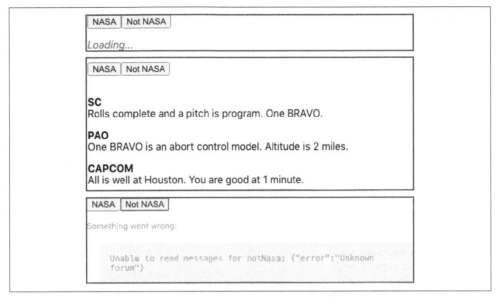

Figure 5-2. The application showing loading, messages, and errors

The `useMessages` hook will also cope if the server throws an error, as shown in Figure 5-3.

Figure 5-3. The component can display errors from the server

Discussion

When you're creating an application, it's tempting to spend your time building features that assume everything works. But it is worth investing the time to handle errors and make an effort to show when data is still loading. Your application will be pleasant to use, and you will have an easier time tracking down slow services and errors.

You might also consider combining this recipe with Recipe 4.1, which will make it easier for users to describe what happened.

You can download the source for this recipe from the GitHub site (*https://oreil.ly/ T6M6q*).

5.2 Refresh Automatically with State Counters

Problem

Network services often need to interact with each other. Take, for example, the forum application we used in the previous recipe. If we add a form to post a new message, we want the message list to update automatically every time a person posts something.

In the previous version of this application, we created a custom hook called useMessages, which contained all of the code needed to read a forum's messages.

We'll add a form to the application to post new messages to the server:

```
const {
  data: messages,
  loading: messagesLoading,
  error: messagesError,
} = useMessages('nasa')
const [text, setText] = useState()
const [author, setAuthor] = useState()
const [createMessageError, setCreateMessageError] = useState()
// Other code here...
<input
  type="text"
  value={author}
  placeholder="Author"
  onChange={(evt) => setAuthor(evt.target.value)}
/>
<textarea
  value={text}
  placeholder="Message"
  onChange={(evt) => setText(evt.target.value)}
/>
<button
  onClick={async () => {
    try {
      await [code to post message here]
      setText('')
      setAuthor('')
    } catch (err) {
      setCreateMessageError(err)
    }
  }}
>
  Post
</button>
```

Here's the problem: when you post a new message, it doesn't appear on the list unless you refresh the page manually (see Figure 5-4).

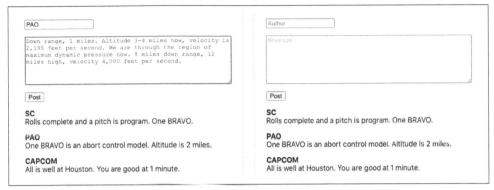

Figure 5-4. Posting a message does not refresh the message list

How do we automatically reload the messages from the server each time we post a new one?

Solution

We're going to trigger data refreshes by using a thing called a *state counter*. A state counter is just an increasing number. It doesn't matter what the counter's current value is; it just matters that we change it every time we want to reload the data:

```
const [stateVersion, setStateVersion] = useState(0)
```

You can think of a state counter as representing our perceived version of the data on the server. When we do something that we suspect will change the server state, we update the state counter to reflect the change:

```
// code to post a new message here
setStateVersion((v) => v + 1)
```

 Notice that we're increasing the `stateVersion` value using a function, rather than saying `setStateVersion(stateVersion + 1)`. You should always use a function to update a state value if the new value depends upon the old value. That's because React sets states asynchronously. If we ran `setStateVersion(stateVersion + 1)` twice in rapid succession, the value of `stateVersion` might not change in between the two calls, and we would miss an increment.

The code that reads the current set of messages is wrapped inside a `useEffect`, which we can force to rerun by making it dependent upon the `stateVersion` value:

```
useEffect(() => {
  setError(null)
  if (forum) {
    // Code to read /messages/:forum
```

```
    } else {
      setData([])
      setLoading(false)
    }
  }, [forum, stateVersion])
```

If the value of the `forum` variable changes or if the `stateVersion` changes, it will auto-matically reload the messages (see Figure 5-5).

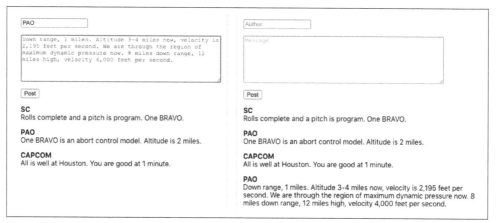

Figure 5-5. Posting a new message causes the message list to reload

So that's our approach. Now we need to look at where we're going to put the code. Here is the previous version of the component, which is only reading messages:

```
import './App.css'
import { useState } from 'react'
import useMessages from './useMessages'

function App() {
  const [forum, setForum] = useState('nasa')
  const {
    data: messages,
    loading: messagesLoading,
    error: messagesError,
  } = useMessages(forum)

  return (
    <div className="App">
      <button onClick={() => setForum('nasa')}>NASA</button>
      <button onClick={() => setForum('notNasa')}>Not NASA</button>
      {messagesError ? (
        <div className="error">
          Something went wrong:
          <div className="error-contents">
            {messagesError.message}
          </div>
```

```
        </div>
      ) : messagesLoading ? (
        <div className="loading">Loading...</div>
      ) : messages && messages.length ? (
        <dl>
          {messages.map((m) => (
            <>
              <dt>{m.author}</dt>
              <dd>{m.text}</dd>
            </>
          ))}
        </dl>
      ) : (
        'No messages'
      )}
    </div>
  )
}
```

```
export default App
```

We're going to add the new form to this component. We could also include the networking code and the state counter code right here, inside the component. However, that would put the posting code in the component and the reading code in the useMessages hook. It's better to keep all the networking code together in the hook. Not only will the component be cleaner, but the networking code will be more reusable.

This is code we'll use for a new version of the useMessages hook, which we will rename useForum:[1]

```
import { useCallback, useEffect, useState } from 'react'

const useForum = (forum) => {
  const [data, setData] = useState([])
  const [loading, setLoading] = useState(false)
  const [error, setError] = useState()
  const [creating, setCreating] = useState(false)
  const [stateVersion, setStateVersion] = useState(0)

  const create = useCallback(
    async (message) => {
      try {
        setCreating(true)
        const response = await fetch(`/messages/${forum}`, {
          method: 'POST',
          body: JSON.stringify(message),
```

---

1 We're renaming it because it is no longer just a way to read a list of messages but the forum as a whole. We could eventually add functions to delete, edit, or flag messages.

```
            headers: {
              'Content-type': 'application/json; charset=UTF-8',
            },
          })
          if (!response.ok) {
            const text = await response.text()
            throw new Error(
              `Unable to create a ${forum} message: ${text}`
            )
          }
          setStateVersion((v) => v + 1)
        } finally {
          setCreating(false)
        }
      },
      [forum]
  )

  useEffect(() => {
    let didCancel = false
    setError(null)
    if (forum) {
      ;(async () => {
        try {
          setLoading(true)
          const response = await fetch(`/messages/${forum}`)
          if (!response.ok) {
            const text = await response.text()
            throw new Error(
              `Unable to read messages for ${forum}: ${text}`
            )
          }
          const body = await response.json()
          if (!didCancel) {
            setData(body)
          }
        } catch (err) {
          setError(err)
        } finally {
          setLoading(false)
        }
      })()
    } else {
      setData([])
      setLoading(false)
    }
    return () => {
      didCancel = true
    }
  }, [forum, stateVersion])

  return { data, loading, error, create, creating }
```

```
  }
```

```
export default useForum
```

We now construct a `create` function inside the `useForum` hook and then return it with various other pieces of state to the component. Notice that we are wrapping the `create` function inside a `useCallback`, which means that we won't create a new version of the function unless we need to do it to create data for a different `forum` value.

Be careful when creating functions inside hooks and components. React will often trigger a re-render if a new function object is created, even if that function does the same thing as the previous version.

When we call the `create` function, it posts a new message to the forum and then updates the `stateVersion` value, which will automatically cause the hook to re-read the messages from the server. Notice that we also have a `creating` value, which is true when the network code is sending the message to the server. We can use the `creating` value to disable the POST button.

However, we don't track any errors inside the `create`. Why don't we? After all, we do when we're *reading* data from the server. It's because you often want more control over exception handling when changing data on the server than you do when you are simply reading it. In the example application, we clear out the message form when sending a message to the server. If there's an error, we want to leave the text in the message form.

Now let's look at the code that calls the hook:

```
import './App.css'
import { useState } from 'react'
import useForum from './useForum'

function App() {
  const {
    data: messages,
    loading: messagesLoading,
    error: messagesError,
    create: createMessage,
    creating: creatingMessage,
  } = useForum('nasa')
  const [text, setText] = useState()
  const [author, setAuthor] = useState()
  const [createMessageError, setCreateMessageError] = useState()

  return (
    <div className="App">
      <input
```

```
      type="text"
      value={author}
      placeholder="Author"
      onChange={(evt) => setAuthor(evt.target.value)}
    />
    <textarea
      value={text}
      placeholder="Message"
      onChange={(evt) => setText(evt.target.value)}
    />
    <button
      onClick={async () => {
        try {
          await createMessage({ author, text })
          setText('')
          setAuthor('')
        } catch (err) {
          setCreateMessageError(err)
        }
      }}
      disabled={creatingMessage}
    >
      Post
    </button>
    {createMessageError ? (
      <div className="error">
        Unable to create message
        <div className="error-contents">
          {createMessageError.message}
        </div>
      </div>
    ) : null}
    {messagesError ? (
      <div className="error">
        Something went wrong:
        <div className="error-contents">
          {messagesError.message}
        </div>
      </div>
    ) : messagesLoading ? (
      <div className="loading">Loading...</div>
    ) : messages && messages.length ? (
      <dl>
        {messages.map((m) => (
          <>
            <dt>{m.author}</dt>
            <dd>{m.text}</dd>
          </>
        ))}
      </dl>
    ) : (
      'No messages'
```

```
        )}
      </div>
    )
  }

  export default App
```

The details of how we read and write messages are hidden inside the `useForum` hook. We use object destructuring to assign the `create` function to the `createMessage` variable. If we call `createMessage`, it will not only post the message but also automatically re-read the new messages from the forum and update the screen (see Figure 5-6).

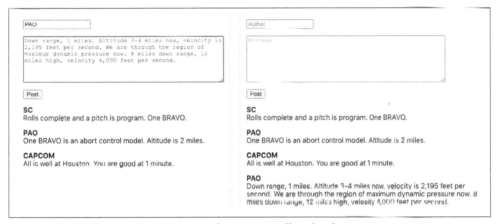

Figure 5-6. Posting a new message and automatically reloading

Our hook is no longer just a way to read data from the server. It's becoming a *service* for managing the forum itself.

Discussion

Be careful using this approach if you intend to post data to the server in one component and then read data in a *different* component. Separate hook instances will have separate state counters, and posting data from one component will not automatically re-read the data in another component. If you want to split code to post and read across separate components, call the custom hook in some common parent component, pass the data, and post functions to the child components that need them.

If you want to make your code poll a network service at a regular interval, then consider creating a clock and making your network code depend upon the current clock value, much as the preceding code depends upon the state counter.[2]

---

2 See Recipe 3.4.

You can download the source for this recipe from the GitHub site (*https://oreil.ly/knyC5*).

5.3 Cancel Network Requests with Tokens

Problem

Let's consider a buggy application that can search for cities. When a user starts to type a name in the search field, a list of matching cities appears. As the user types "C... H... I... G..." the matching cities appear in the table of results. But then, after a moment, a longer list of cities appears, which includes erroneous results, such as Wichita Falls (see Figure 5-7).

Figure 5-7. The search works initially; then the wrong cities appear

The problem is that the application is sending a new network request each time the user types a character. But not all network requests take the same amount of time. In the example you can see here, the network request searching for "CHI" took a couple of seconds longer than the search for "CHIG." That meant that the "CHI" results returned after the results for "CHIG."

How can you prevent a series of asynchronous network calls from returning out of sequence?

Solution

If you are making multiple GET calls to a network server, you can cancel old calls before sending new ones, which means that you will never get results back out of order because you will have only one network request calling the service at a time.

For this recipe, we are going to use the Axios network library. That means that we have to install it:

```
$ npm install axios
```

The Axios library is a wrapper for the native `fetch` function and allows you to cancel network requests using tokens. The Axios implementation is based on the cancelable promises proposal (*https://oreil.ly/jd4LF*) from ECMA.

Let's begin by looking at our problem code. The network code is wrapped in a custom hook:[3]

```
import { useEffect, useState } from 'react'
import axios from 'axios'

const useSearch = (terms) => {
  const [data, setData] = useState([])
  const [loading, setLoading] = useState(false)
  const [error, setError] = useState()

  useEffect(() => {
    setError(null)
    if (terms) {
      ;(async () => {
        try {
          setLoading(true)
          const response = await axios.get('/search', {
            params: { terms },
          })
          setData(response.data)
        } catch (err) {
          setError(err)
        } finally {
          setLoading(false)
        }
      })()
    } else {
      setData([])
      setLoading(false)
    }
  }, [terms])

  return { data, loading, error }
}

export default useSearch
```

---

3 Compare this code with Recipe 5.1, which uses `fetch`.

The `terms` parameter contains the search string. The problem occurred because the code made a network request to *search* for the string `"CHI"`.

While that was in progress, we made another call with the string `"CHIG"`. The earlier request took longer, which caused the bug.

We're going to avoid this problem by using an Axios cancel token. If we attach a token to a request, we can then later use the token to cancel the request. The browser will terminate the request, and we'll never hear back from it.

To use the token, we need to first create a source for it:

```
const source = axios.CancelToken.source()
```

The `source` is like a remote control for the network request. Once a network request is connected to a source, we can tell the source to cancel it. We associate a source with a request using `source.token`:

```
const response = await axios.get('/search', {
  params: { terms },
  cancelToken: source.token,
})
```

Axios will remember which token is attached to which network request. If we want to cancel the request, we can call this:

```
source.cancel('axios request canceled')
```

We need to make sure that we cancel a request only when we make a new request. Fortunately, our network call is inside a `useEffect`, which has a handy feature. If we return a function that cancels the current request, this function will be run *just before* the `useEffect` runs again. So if we return a function that cancels the current network request, we will automatically cancel the old network request each time we run a new one.[4] Here is the updated version of the custom hook:

```
import { useEffect, useState } from 'react'
import axios from 'axios'

const useCancelableSearch = (terms) => {
  const [data, setData] = useState([])
  const [loading, setLoading] = useState(false)
  const [error, setError] = useState()

  useEffect(() => {
    setError(null)
    if (terms) {
      const source = axios.CancelToken.source()
      ;(async () => {
```

---

4 If the previous network request has completed, canceling it will have no effect.

```
      try {
        setLoading(true)
        const response = await axios.get('/search', {
          params: { terms },
          cancelToken: source.token,
        })
        setData(response.data)
      } catch (err) {
        setError(err)
      } finally {
        setLoading(false)
      }
    })()

    return () => {
      source.cancel('axios request cancelled')
    }
  } else {
    setData([])
    setLoading(false)
  }
}, [terms])

  return { data, loading, error }
}

export default useCancelableSearch
```

Discussion

You should use this approach only if you are accessing idempotent services. In practice, this means that you should use it for GET requests where you are interested only in the latest results.

You can download the source for this recipe from the GitHub site (*https://oreil.ly/aQj5g*).

5.4 Make Network Calls with Redux Middleware

Problem

Redux is a library that allows you to manage application state centrally.[5] When you want to change the application state, you do it by dispatching commands (called *actions*) that are captured and processed by JavaScript functions called *reducers*. Redux is popular with React developers because it provides a way to separate

---

5 It can also be quite confusing when you first use it. See Chapter 3 for more Redux recipes.

state-management logic from component code. Redux performs actions asynchronously but in strict order. So, you can create large, complex applications in Redux that are both efficient and stable.

It would be great if we could leverage the power of Redux to orchestrate all of our network requests. We could dispatch actions that say things like "Go and read the latest search results," and Redux could make the network request and then update the central state.

However, to ensure that Redux code is stable, reducer functions have to meet several quite strict criteria: and one of them is that *no reducer function can have side effects*. That means that you should never make network requests inside a reducer.

But if we cannot make network requests inside reducer functions, how can we configure Redux to talk to the network for us?

Solution

In a React Redux application, components publish (*dispatch*) actions, and reducers respond to actions by updating the central state (see Figure 5-8).

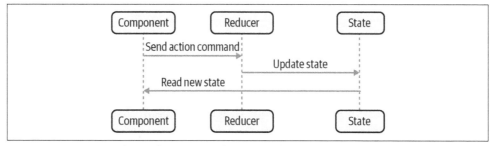

Figure 5-8. Using Redux reducers to update central state

If we want to create actions with side effects, we will have to use Redux *middleware*. Middleware receives actions before Redux sends them to the reducers, and middleware can transform actions, cancel them, or create new actions. Most importantly, Redux middleware code is allowed to have side effects. That means that if a component dispatches an action that says "Go and search for this string," we can write middleware that receives that action, generates a network call, and then converts the response into a new "Store these search results" action. You can see how Redux middleware works in Figure 5-9.

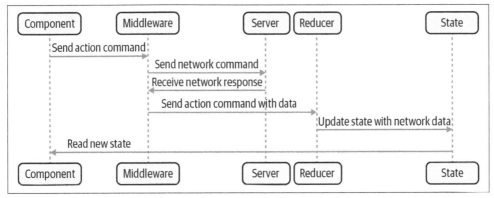

Figure 5-9. Middleware can make network calls

Let's create some middleware that intercepts an action of type "SEARCH" and uses it to generate a network service.

When we get the results back from the network, we will then create a new action of type "SEARCH_RESULTS", which we can then use to store the search results in the central Redux state. Our action object will look something like this:

```
{
  "type": "SEARCH",
  "payload": "Some search text"
}
```

This is the *axiosMiddleware.js* code that we'll use to intercept SEARCH actions:

```
import axios from 'axios'

const axiosMiddleware = (store) => (next) => (action) => {
  if (action.type === 'SEARCH') {
    const terms = action.payload
    if (terms) {
      ;(async () => {
        try {
          store.dispatch({
            type: 'SEARCH_RESULTS',
            payload: {
              loading: true,
              data: null,
              error: null,
            },
          })
          const response = await axios.get('/search', {
            params: { terms },
          })
          store.dispatch({
            type: 'SEARCH_RESULTS',
            payload: {
```

```
          loading: false,
          error: null,
          data: response.data,
        },
      })
    } catch (err) {
      store.dispatch({
        type: 'SEARCH_RESULTS',
        payload: {
          loading: false,
          error: err,
          data: null,
        },
      })
    }
  })()
  }
}
  return next(action)
}
export default axiosMiddleware
```

The function signature for Redux middleware can be confusing. You can think of it as a function that receives a store, an action, and another function called `next` that can forward actions on to the rest of Redux.

In the preceding code, we check to see if the action is of type `SEARCH`. If it is, we will make a network call. If it isn't, we run `next(action)`, which will pass it on to any other code interested in it.

When we start the network call, receive data, or capture any errors, then we can generate a new `SEARCH_RESULTS` action:

```
store.dispatch({
  type: 'SEARCH_RESULTS',
  payload: {
    loading: ...,
    error: ...,
    data: ...
  },
})
```

The payload for our new action has the following:

- A Boolean flag called `loading`, which is `true` while the network request is running

- A `data` object that contains the response from the server

- An `error` object containing the details of any error that has occurred[6]

We can then create a reducer that will store SEARCH_RESULTS in the central state:

```
const reducer = (state, action) => {
  if (action.type === 'SEARCH_RESULTS') {
    return {
      ...state,
      searchResults: { ...action.payload },
    }
  }
  return { ...state }
}

export default reducer
```

We also need to register our middleware using the Redux `applyMiddleware` function when we create the Redux store. In the example code, we do this in the *App.js* file:

```
import { Provider } from 'react-redux'
import { createStore, applyMiddleware } from 'redux'
import './App.css'

import reducer from './reducer'
import Search from './Search'
import axiosMiddleware from './axiosMiddleware'

const store = createStore(reducer, applyMiddleware(axiosMiddleware))

function App() {
  return (
    <div className="App">
      <Provider store={store}>
        <Search />
      </Provider>
    </div>
  )
}

export default App
```

Finally, we can wire everything up in a `Search` component, which will dispatch a search request, and then read the results through a Redux selector:

```
import './App.css'
import { useState } from 'react'
import { useDispatch, useSelector } from 'react-redux'
```

---

6 To simplify things, we are simply storing the entire object. In reality, you would want to ensure that the error contained only serializable text.

```
const Search = () => {
  const [terms, setTerms] = useState()
  const {
    data: results,
    error,
    loading,
  } = useSelector((state) => state.searchResults || {})
  const dispatch = useDispatch()

  return (
    <div className="App">
      <input
        placeholder="Search..."
        type="text"
        value={terms}
        onChange={(e) => {
          setTerms(e.target.value)
          dispatch({
            type: 'SEARCH',
            payload: e.target.value,
          })
        }}
      />
      {error ? (
        <p>Error: {error.message}</p>
      ) : loading ? (
        <p>Loading...</p>
      ) : results && results.length ? (
        <table>
          <thead>
            <tr>
              <th>City</th>
              <th>State</th>
            </tr>
          </thead>
          {results.map((r) => (
            <tr>
              <td>{r.name}</td>
              <td>{r.state}</td>
            </tr>
          ))}
        </table>
      ) : (
        <p>No results</p>
      )}
    </div>
  )
}
export default Search
```

You can see the demo application running in Figure 5-10.

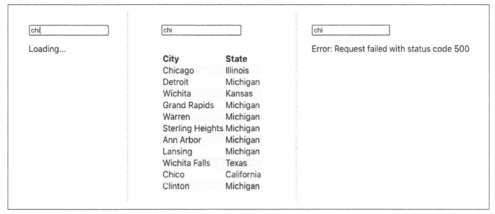

City	State
Chicago	Illinois
Detroit	Michigan
Wichita	Kansas
Grand Rapids	Michigan
Warren	Michigan
Sterling Heights	Michigan
Ann Arbor	Michigan
Lansing	Michigan
Wichita Falls	Texas
Chico	California
Clinton	Michigan

Figure 5-10. The application when data is loading, loaded, or errored

Discussion

Redux reducers always process actions in strict dispatch order. The same is not true for network requests generated by middleware. If you are making many network requests in quick succession, you might find that responses return in a different order. If this is likely to lead to bugs, then consider using cancellation tokens.[7]

You might also consider moving all Redux useDispatch()/useSelector() code out of components and into custom hooks, which will give you a more flexible architecture by separating your service layer from your component code.

You can download the source for this recipe from the GitHub site (*https://oreil.ly/YlqEF*).

5.5 Connect to GraphQL

Problem

GraphQL is an excellent way of creating APIs. If you've used REST services for a while, then some features of GraphQL will seem odd (or even heretical), but having worked on a few GraphQL projects, we would certainly recommend that you consider it for your next development project.

When people refer to GraphQL, they can mean several things. They might be referring to the GraphQL language, which is managed and maintained by the GraphQL Foundation. GraphQL allows you to specify APIs and to create queries to access and mutate the data stored behind those APIs. They might be referring to a GraphQL

---

7 See Recipe 5.3.

server, which stitches together multiple low-level data access methods into a rich web service. Or they might be talking about a GraphQL client, which allows you to rapidly create new client requests with very little code and transfer just the data you need across the network.

But how do you integrate GraphQL with your React application?

Solution

Before we look at how to use GraphQL from React, we will begin by creating a small GraphQL server. The first thing we need is a GraphQL *schema*. The schema is a formal definition of the data and services that our GraphQL server will provide.

Here is the *schema.graphql* schema we'll use. It's a GraphQL specification of the forum message example we've used previously in this chapter:

```
type Query {
    messages: [Message]
}

type Message {
    id: ID!
    author: String!
    text: String!
}

type Mutation {
    addMessage(
        author: String!
        text: String!
    ): Message
}
```

This schema defines a single *query* (method for reading data) called messages, which returns an array of Message objects. Each Message has an id, a non-null string called author, and a non-null string called text. We also have a single *mutation* (method for changing data) called addMessage, which will store a message based on an author string and a text string.

Before we create our sample server, we'll install a few libraries:

```
$ npm install apollo-server
$ npm install graphql
$ npm install require-text
```

The apollo-server is a framework for creating GraphQL servers. The require-text library will allows us to read the schema.graphql file. This is *server.js*, our example server:

```
const { ApolloServer } = require('apollo-server')
const requireText = require('require-text')
```

```
const typeDefs = requireText('./schema.graphql', require)

const messages = [
  {
    id: 0,
    author: 'SC',
    text: 'Rolls complete and a pitch is program. One BRAVO.',
  },
  {
    id: 1,
    author: 'PAO',
    text: 'One BRAVO is an abort control model. Altitude is 2 miles.',
  },
  {
    id: 2,
    author: 'CAPCOM',
    text: 'All is well at Houston. You are good at 1 minute.',
  },
]

const resolvers = {
  Query: {
    messages: () => messages,
  },
  Mutation: {
    addMessage: (parent, message) => {
      const item = { id: messages.length + 1, ...message }
      messages.push(item)
      return item
    },
  },
}

const server = new ApolloServer({
  typeDefs,
  resolvers,
})

server.listen({ port: 5000 }).then(({ url }) => {
  console.log(Launched at ${url}!)
})
```

The server stores messages in an array, which is prepopulated with a few messages. You can start the server with:

```
$ node ./server.js
```

This command will start the server on port 5000. If you open a browser to *http:// localhost:5000*, you will see the GraphQL Playground client. The Playground client is a tool that allows you to try out queries and mutations interactively before adding them to your code (see Figure 5-11).

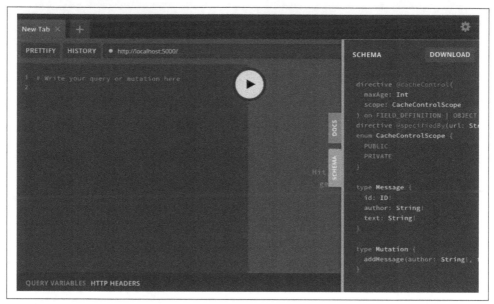

Figure 5-11. The GraphQL Playground should be running at http://localhost:5000

Now we can start to look at the React client code. We'll install the Apollo client:

```
$ npm install @apollo/client
```

GraphQL supports both GET and POST requests, but the Apollo client sends queries and mutations to the GraphQL server as POST requests, which avoids any cross-domain issues and means you can connect to a third-party GraphQL server without having to proxy. As a consequence, it means that a GraphQL client has to handle its own caching, so we will need to provide a cache and the address of the server when we configure the client in *App.js*:

```
import './App.css'
import {
  ApolloClient,
  ApolloProvider,
  InMemoryCache,
} from '@apollo/client'
import Forum from './Forum'

const client = new ApolloClient({
  uri: 'http://localhost:5000',
  cache: new InMemoryCache(),
})

function App() {
  return (
    <div className="App">
      <ApolloProvider client={client}>
```

```
      <Forum />
    </ApolloProvider>
  </div>
 )
}

export default App
```

The `ApolloProvider` makes the client available to any child component. If you forget to add the `ApolloProvider`, you will find that all of your GraphQL client code will fail.

We're going to make the calls to GraphQL from inside the `Forum` component. We'll be performing two actions:

- A *query* called `Messages` that reads all of the messages
- A *mutation* called `AddMessage` that will post a new message

The query and the mutation are written in the GraphQL language. Here's the `Messages` query:

```
query Messages {
  messages {
    author text
  }
}
```

This query means that we want to read all of the messages, but we only want to return the `author` and `text` strings. Because we're not asking for the message `id`, the GraphQL server won't return it. This is part of the flexibility of GraphQL: you specify what you want at query time rather than by crafting a particular API call for each variation.

The `AddMessage` mutation is a little more complex, because it needs to be parameterized so that we can specify the `author` and `text` values each time we call it:

```
mutation AddMessage(
  $author: String!
  $text: String!
) {
  addMessage(
    author: $author
    text: $text
  ) {
    author
    text
  }
}
```

We're going to use the useQuery and useMutation hooks provided by the Apollo GraphQL client. The useQuery hook returns an object with data, loading, and error attributes.[8] The useMutation hook returns an array with two values: a function and an object representing the result.

In Recipe 5.2, we looked at how to automatically reload data after some mutation has changed it on the server. Thankfully, the Apollo client has a ready-made solution. When you call a mutation, you can specify an array of other queries that should be rerun if the mutation is successful:

```
await addMessage({
  variables: { author, text },
  refetchQueries: ['Messages'],
})
```

The 'Messages' string refers to the name of the GraphQL query, which means we can be running multiple queries against the GraphQL service and specify which of them are likely to need refreshing after a change.

Finally, here is the complete Forum component:

```
import { gql, useMutation, useQuery } from '@apollo/client'
import { useState } from 'react'

const MESSAGES = gql`
  query Messages {
    messages {
      author
      text
    }
  }
`

const ADD_MESSAGE = gql`
  mutation AddMessage($author: String!, $text: String!) {
    addMessage(author: $author, text: $text) {
      author
      text
    }
  }
`

const Forum = () => {
  const {
    loading: messagesLoading,
    error: messagesError,
    data,
  } = useQuery(MESSAGES)
```

---

8 This is a standard set of values for an asynchronous service. We've used them in other recipes in this chapter.

```jsx
const [addMessage] = useMutation(ADD_MESSAGE)
const [text, setText] = useState()
const [author, setAuthor] = useState()

const messages = data && data.messages

return (
  <div className="App">
    <input
      type="text"
      value={author}
      placeholder="Author"
      onChange={(evt) => setAuthor(evt.target.value)}
    />
    <textarea
      value={text}
      placeholder="Message"
      onChange={(evt) => setText(evt.target.value)}
    />
    <button
      onClick={async () => {
        try {
          await addMessage({
            variables: { author, text },
            refetchQueries: ['Messages'],
          })
          setText('')
          setAuthor('')
        } catch (err) {}
      }}
    >
      Post
    </button>
    {messagesError ? (
      <div className="error">
        Something went wrong:
        <div className="error-contents">
          {messagesError.message}
        </div>
      </div>
    ) : messagesLoading ? (
      <div className="loading">Loading...</div>
    ) : messages && messages.length ? (
      <dl>
        {messages.map((m) => (
          <>
            <dt>{m.author}</dt>
            <dd>{m.text}</dd>
          </>
        ))}
      </dl>
    ) : (
```

```
          'No messages'
      )}
    </div>
  )
}
export default Forum
```

When you run the application and post a new message, the messages list automatically updates with the new message added to the end, as shown in Figure 5-12.

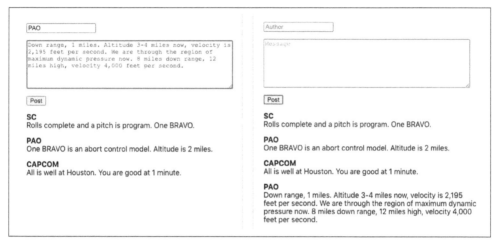

Figure 5-12. After we post a message, it appears on the list

Discussion

GraphQL is particularly useful if you have a team split between frontend and backend developers. Unlike REST, a GraphQL system does not require the backend developers to handcraft every API call made by the client. Instead, the backend team can provide a solid and consistent API structure and leave it to the frontend team to decide precisely *how* they will use it.

If you are creating a React application using GraphQL, you might consider extracting all of the `useQuery` and `useMutation` calls into a custom hooks.[9] In this way, you will create a more flexible architecture in which the components are less bound to the details of the service layer.

You can download the source for this recipe from the GitHub site (*https://oreil.ly/xTcAK*).

---

9 Much as we do with HTTP network calls in Recipe 5.2.

5.6 Reduce Network Load with Debounced Requests

Problem

It is easy to forget about performance when you're working in a development system. That's probably a good thing because it's more important that code does the right thing rather than do the wrong thing quickly.

But when your application gets deployed to its first realistic environment—such as one used for user acceptance testing—then performance will become more important. The kind of dynamic interfaces associated with React often make a lot of network calls, and the cost of these calls will be noticeable only once the server has to cope with lots of concurrent clients.

We've used an example search application a few times in this chapter. In the search app, a user can look for a city by name or state. The search happens immediately—while they are typing. If you open the developer tools and look at the network requests (see Figure 5-13), you will see that it generates network requests for each character typed.

Name	Status	Type
search?terms=c	200	xhr
search?terms=ch	200	xhr
search?terms=chi	200	xhr
search?terms=chic	200	xhr
search?terms=chica	200	xhr
search?terms=chicag	200	xhr
search?terms=chicago	200	xhr

Figure 5-13. The demo search application runs a network request for each character

Most of these network requests will provide almost no value. The average typist will probably hit a key every half-second, and if they are looking at their keyboard, they probably won't even see the results for each of those searches. Of the seven requests they send to the server, they will likely read the results from only one of them: the last. That means the server is doing seven times more work than was needed.

What can we do to avoid sending so many wasted requests?

Solution

We're going to *debounce* the network requests for the search calls. Debouncing means that we will delay sending a network request for a very short period, say a half-second. If another request comes in while we're waiting, we'll forget about the first request and then create another delayed request. In this way, we defer sending any request until we receive no new requests for half a second.

To see how to do this, look at our example search hook, *useSearch.js*:

```
import { useEffect, useState } from 'react'
import axios from 'axios'

const useSearch = (terms) => {
  const [data, setData] = useState([])
  const [loading, setLoading] = useState(false)
  const [error, setError] = useState()

  useEffect(() => {
    let didCancel = false
    setError(null)
    if (terms) {
      ;(async () => {
        try {
          setLoading(true)
          const response = await axios.get('/search', {
            params: { terms },
          })
          if (!didCancel) {
            setData(response.data)
          }
        } catch (err) {
          setError(err)
        } finally {
          setLoading(false)
        }
      })()
    } else {
      setData([])
      setLoading(false)
    }
    return () => {
      didCancel = true
    }
  }, [terms])

  return { data, loading, error }
}
export default useSearch
```

The code that sends the network request is inside the (async ()....)() block of code. We need to delay this code until we get a half-second to spare.

The JavaScript function setTimeout will run the code after a delay. This will be key to how we implement the debounce feature:

```
const newTimer = setTimeout(SOMEFUNCTION, 500)
```

We can use the `newTimer` value to clear the timeout, which might mean that our function never gets called if we do it quickly enough. To see how we can use this to debounce the network requests, look at *useDebouncedSearch.js*, a debounced version of *useSearch.js*:

```js
import { useEffect, useState } from 'react'
import axios from 'axios'

const useDebouncedSearch = (terms) => {
  const [data, setData] = useState([])
  const [loading, setLoading] = useState(false)
  const [error, setError] = useState()

  useEffect(() => {
    setError(null)
    if (terms) {
      const newTimer = setTimeout(() => {
        ;(async () => {
          try {
            setLoading(true)
            const response = await axios.get('/search', {
              params: { terms },
            })
            setData(response.data)
          } catch (err) {
            setError(err)
          } finally {
            setLoading(false)
          }
        })()
      }, 500)
      return () => clearTimeout(newTimer)
    } else {
      setData([])
      setLoading(false)
    }
  }, [terms])

  return { data, loading, error }
}

export default useDebouncedSearch
```

We pass the network code into the `setTimeout` function and then return the following:

```js
() => clearTimeout(newTimer)
```

If you return a function from useEffect, this code is called just before the next time useEffect triggers, which means if the user keeps typing quickly, we will keep deferring the network request. Only when the user stops typing for half a second will the code submit a network request.

The original version of the useSearch hook ran a network request for every single character. With the debounced version of the hook, typing at an average speed will result in just a single network request (see Figure 5-14).

Name	Status	Type
☐ search?terms=chicago	200	xhr

Figure 5-14. The debounced search hook will send fewer requests

Discussion

Debouncing requests will reduce your network traffic and the load on the server. It's important to remember that debouncing reduces the number of unnecessary network requests. It does *not* avoid the problem of network responses returning in a different order. For more details on how to avoid the response order problem, see Recipe 5.3.

You can download the source for this recipe from the GitHub site (*https://oreil.ly/5nciD*).

CHAPTER 6

Component Libraries

If you are building an application of any size, you are likely to need a component library. The data types that native HTML supports are somewhat limited, and the implementations can vary from browser to browser. For example, a date input field looks very different on Chrome, Firefox, and Edge browsers.

Component libraries allow you to create a consistent feel for your application. They will often adapt well when switching between desktop and mobile clients. Most importantly, component libraries often give your application a usability boost. They have been either generated from design standards that have been thoroughly tested (such as Material Design) or developed over several years. Any rough corners have generally been smoothed out.

Be aware: there is no such thing as the *perfect* component library. They all have strengths and weaknesses, and you need to choose a library that best meets your needs. If you have a large UX team and a robust set of preexisting design standards, you will likely want a library that allows for a lot of *tweaking* to adapt the library to match your corporate themes. An example would be Material-UI, which allows you to modify its components quite significantly. If you have a small UX team or no UX team at all, you would probably want to consider something like Semantic UI, which is clean and functional and gets you up and running quickly.

Whichever library you choose, always remember that the essential thing in UX is not how your application looks but how it behaves. Users will soon ignore whatever flashy graphics you add to the interface, but they will never forget (or forgive) some part of the interface that irritates them each time they use it.

6.1 Use Material Design with Material-UI

Problem

Many applications are now available on both the web and as native applications on mobile devices. Google created Material Design to provide a seamless experience across all platforms. Material Design will seem familiar to your users if they also use Android phones or anything created by Google. Material Design is just a specification, and there are several implementations available. One such is the Material-UI library for React. But what are the steps involved in using Material-UI, and how do you install it?

Solution

Let's begin by installing the core Material-UI library:

```
$ npm install @material-ui/core
```

The core library includes the main components, but it omits one notable feature: the standard typeface. To make Material-UI feel the same as it does in a native mobile application, you should also install Google's Roboto typeface:

```
$ npm install fontsource-roboto
```

Material Design also specifies a large set of standard icons. These provide a common visual language for standard tasks such as editing tasks, creating new items, sharing content, etc. To use high-quality versions of these icons, you should also install the Material-UI icon library:

```
$ npm install @material-ui/icons
```

Now that we have Material-UI up and running, what can we do with it? We can't look in detail at all of the available components here, but we will look at some of the more popular features.[1]

We'll begin by looking at the basics of styling within Material-UI. To ensure that Material-UI components look the same across different browsers, they have included a CssBaseline component, which will normalize the basic styling of your application. It will remove margins and apply standard background colors. You should add a CssBaseline component somewhere near the start of your application. For example, if you are using create-react-app, you should probably add it to your *App.js*:

```
import CssBaseline from '@material-ui/core/CssBaseline'
...
```

---

[1] For full details of the entire component set, see the Material-UI site (*https://material-ui.com*).

```
function App() {
  // ...

  return (
    <div className="App">
      <CssBaseline />
      ...
    </div>
  )
}

export default App
```

Next, we'll take a look at the Material Design `AppBar` and `Toolbar` components. These provide the standard heading you see in most Material Design applications and are where other features such as hamburger menus and drawer panels will appear.

We'll place an `AppBar` at the top of the screen and put a `Toolbar` inside. This will give us a chance to look at the way that typography is handled inside Material-UI:

```
<div className="App">
    <CssBaseline/>
    <AppBar position='relative'>
        <Toolbar>
            <Typography component='h1' variant='h6' color='inherit' noWrap>
                Material-UI Gallery
            </Typography>
        </Toolbar>
    </AppBar>
    <main>
        {/* Main content goes here...*/}
    </main>
</div>
```

Although you can insert ordinary textual content inside Material-UI applications, it is generally better to display it inside `Typography`. A `Typography` component will ensure that the text matches the Material Design standards. We can also use it to display text inside the appropriate markup elements. In this case, we're going to display the text in the `Toolbar` as an `h1` element. That's what the `Typography` component attribute specifies: the HTML element that should be used to wrap the text. However, we can also tell Material-UI to *style* the text as if it's an `h6` heading. That will make it a little smaller and less overpowering as a page heading.

Next, let's look at how Material-UI styles the output. It uses *themes*. A theme is a JavaScript object that defines a hierarchy of CSS styles. You can define themes centrally, and this allows you to control the overall appearance of your application.

Themes are extensible. We'll import a function called `makeStyles`, which will allow us to create a modified version of the default theme:

```
import { makeStyles } from '@material-ui/core/styles'
```

We're going to make our example application display a gallery of images, so we will want to create styles for gallery items, descriptions, and so on. We can create styles for these different screen elements with `makeStyles`:

```
const useStyles = makeStyles((theme) => ({
  galleryGrid: {
    paddingTop: theme.spacing(4),
  },
  galleryItemDescription: {
    overflow: 'hidden',
    textOverflow: 'ellipsis',
    whiteSpace: 'nowrap',
  },
}))
```

In this simplified example, we extend the base theme to include styles for the classes `galleryGrid` and `galleryItemDescription`. Either we can add CSS attributes literally or (in the case of `paddingTop` in the `galleryGrid`) we can reference some value in the current theme: in this case `theme.spacing(4)`. So, we can defer parts of the styling to a centralized theme, where we can change it later.

The `useStyles` returned by `makeStyles` is a hook that will generate a set of CSS classes and then return their names so we can refer to them inside our component.

For example, we will want to display a grid of images, using `Container` and `Grid` components.[2] We can attach the styles to them from the theme like this:

```
const classes = useStyles()

return (
  <div className="App">
    ...
    <main>
      <Container className={classes.galleryGrid}>
        <Grid container spacing="4">
          <Grid item>...</Grid>
          <Grid item>...</Grid>
          ...
        </Grid>
      </Container>
    </main>
  </div>
)
```

Each `Grid` component is either a *container* or an *item*. We will display a gallery image within each item.

---

2 For more information on these components, see the Material-UI site (*https://material-ui.com*).

In Material Design, we show significant items inside cards. A *card* is a rectangular panel that appears to float slightly above the background. If you've ever used the Google Play Store, you will have seen cards used to display applications, music tracks, or other things you might want to download. We will place a card inside each `Grid` item and use it to display a preview, a text description, and a button that can show a more detailed version of the image. You can see the cards in the example application in Figure 6-1.

Figure 6-1. Cards are inside grid items, which are inside a container

Material-UI also has extensive support for dialog windows. Here is an example of a custom dialog:

```
import Dialog from '@material-ui/core/Dialog'
import DialogTitle from '@material-ui/core/DialogTitle'
import Typography from '@material-ui/core/Typography'
import DialogContent from '@material-ui/core/DialogContent'
import DialogActions from '@material-ui/core/DialogActions'
import Button from '@material-ui/core/Button'
import CloseIcon from '@material-ui/icons/Close'

const MyDialog = ({ onClose, open, title, children }) => {
  return (
    <Dialog open={open} onClose={onClose}>
      <DialogTitle>
        <Typography
          component="h1"
          variant="h5"
          color="inherit"
```

```
        noWrap
      >
        {title}
      </Typography>
    </DialogTitle>
    <DialogContent>{children}</DialogContent>
    <DialogActions>
      <Button
        variant="outlined"
        startIcon={<CloseIcon />}
        onClick={onClose}
      >
        Close
      </Button>
    </DialogActions>
  </Dialog>
  )
}

export default MyDialog
```

Notice that we are importing an SVG icon from the Material-UI icons library that we installed earlier. The `DialogTitle` appears at the top of the dialog. The `DialogActions` are the buttons that appear at the base of the dialog. You define the main body of the dialog in the `DialogContent`.

Here is the complete code for *App.js*:

```
import './App.css'
import CssBaseline from '@material-ui/core/CssBaseline'
import AppBar from '@material-ui/core/AppBar'
import { Toolbar } from '@material-ui/core'
import Container from '@material-ui/core/Container'
import Grid from '@material-ui/core/Grid'
import Card from '@material-ui/core/Card'
import CardMedia from '@material-ui/core/CardMedia'
import CardContent from '@material-ui/core/CardContent'
import CardActions from '@material-ui/core/CardActions'
import Typography from '@material-ui/core/Typography'
import { makeStyles } from '@material-ui/core/styles'
import { useState } from 'react'
import MyDialog from './MyDialog'
import ImageSearchIcon from '@material-ui/icons/ImageSearch'

import gallery from './gallery.json'
import IconButton from '@material-ui/core/IconButton'

const useStyles = makeStyles((theme) => ({
  galleryGrid: {
    paddingTop: theme.spacing(4),
  },
  galleryItem: {
```

```
      height: '100%',
      display: 'flex',
      flexDirection: 'column',
      // maxWidth: '200px'
    },
    galleryImage: {
      paddingTop: '54%',
    },
    galleryItemDescription: {
      overflow: 'hidden',
      textOverflow: 'ellipsis',
      whiteSpace: 'nowrap',
    },
}))

function App() {
  const [showDetails, setShowDetails] = useState(false)
  const [selectedImage, setSelectedImage] = useState()
  const classes = useStyles()

  return (
    <div className="App">
      <CssBaseline />
      <AppBar position="relative">
        <Toolbar>
          <Typography
            component="h1"
            variant="h6"
            color="inherit"
            noWrap
          >
            Material-UI Gallery
          </Typography>
        </Toolbar>
      </AppBar>
      <main>
        <Container className={classes.galleryGrid}>
          <Grid container spacing="4">
            {gallery.map((item, i) => {
              return (
                <Grid item key={`photo-${i}`} xs={12} sm={3} lg={2}>
                  <Card className={classes.galleryItem}>
                    <CardMedia
                      image={item.image}
                      className={classes.galleryImage}
                      title="A photo"
                    />
                    <CardContent>
                      <Typography
                        gutterBottom
                        variant="h6"
                        component="h2"
```

```
                        >
                          Image
                        </Typography>
                        <Typography
                          className={classes.galleryItemDescription}
                        >
                          {item.description}
                        </Typography>
                      </CardContent>
                      <CardActions>
                        <IconButton
                          aria-label="delete"
                          onClick={() => {
                            setSelectedImage(item)
                            setShowDetails(true)
                          }}
                          color="primary"
                        >
                          <ImageSearchIcon />
                        </IconButton>
                      </CardActions>
                    </Card>
                  </Grid>
                )
              })}
            </Grid>
          </Container>
        </main>
        <MyDialog
          open={showDetails}
          title="Details"
          onClose={() => setShowDetails(false)}
        >
          <img
            src={selectedImage && selectedImage.image}
            alt="From PicSum"
          />
          <Typography>
            {selectedImage && selectedImage.description}
          </Typography>
        </MyDialog>
      </div>
    )
}

export default App
```

Discussion

Material-UI is a great library to use and is one of the most popular libraries currently used with React. Users coming to your application will almost certainly have used it elsewhere, which will increase your application's usability. Before launching into using Material-UI in your application, it is worth spending some time understanding the Material Design principles (*https://oreil.ly/Jlk7w*). That way, you will create an application that is not only attractive but also easy to use and accessible (*https://oreil.ly/RJiW1*) to users.

You can download the source for this recipe from the GitHub site (*https://oreil.ly/TqVFz*).

6.2 Create a Simple UI with React Bootstrap

Problem

The most popular CSS library of the last 10 years is probably Twitter's Bootstrap library. It's also a good choice if you are creating a new application and have very little time to worry about creating a custom UI and simply want something easy-to-use and familiar to the vast number of users.

But Bootstrap comes from a time before frameworks like React existed. Bootstrap includes CSS resources and a set of JavaScript libraries designed for web pages containing a small amount of handcrafted client code. The base Bootstrap library doesn't play well with a framework like React.

How do you use Bootstrap when you're creating a React application?

Solution

There are several ports of the Bootstrap library for use with React. In this recipe, we will look at React Bootstrap. React Bootstrap works alongside the standard Bootstrap CSS libraries, but it extends the Bootstrap JavaScript to make it more React-friendly.

Let's begin by first installing the React Bootstrap components and the Bootstrap Java-Script libraries:

```
$ npm install react-bootstrap bootstrap
```

The React Bootstrap library does not include any CSS styling of its own. You will need to include a copy of that yourself. The most common way of doing this is by downloading it from a content distribution network (CDN) in your HTML. For example, if you are using `create-react-app`, you should include something like this in your *public/index.html* file:

```
<link
  rel="stylesheet"
  href="https://maxcdn.bootstrapcdn.com/bootstrap/4.5.0/css/bootstrap.min.css"
  integrity="sha384-9aIt2nRpC12Uk9gS9baDl411NQApFmC26EwAOH8WgZl5MYYxFfc+NcPb1dKG"
  crossorigin="anonymous"
/>
```

It would be best if you replaced this with the latest stable version of Bootstrap that's available. You will need to manage the version of Bootstrap manually; it will not update when you upgrade your JavaScript libraries.

Bootstrap is a good, general-purpose library, but its support for forms is particularly strong. Good form layout can take time and can be tedious. Bootstrap handles all of the hard work for you and allows you to focus on the functionality of your form. For example, the React Bootstrap Form component contains almost everything you need to create a form. The Form.Control component will generate an input by default. The Form.Label will generate a label, and a Form.Group will associate the two together and lay them out appropriately:

```
<Form.Group controlId="startupName">
    <Form.Label>Startup name</Form.Label>
    <Form.Control placeholder="No names ending in ...ly, please"/>
</Form.Group>
```

Form fields are normally displayed on a single line and take up the available width. If you want more than one field to appear on a line, then you can use a Form.Row:

```
<Form.Row>
    <Form.Group as={Col} controlId="startupName">
        <Form.Label>Startup name</Form.Label>
        <Form.Control placeholder="No names ending in ...ly, please"/>
    </Form.Group>
    <Form.Group as={Col} controlId="market">
        <Form.Label>Market</Form.Label>
        <Form.Control placeholder="e.g. seniors on Tik-Tok"/>
    </Form.Group>
</Form.Row>
```

The Col component ensures that the labels and fields are sized appropriately. If you want a form field that's something other than an input, you can use the as attribute:

```
<Form.Control as="select" defaultValue="Choose...">
    <option>Progressive web application</option>
    <option>Conservative web application</option>
    <option>Android native</option>
    <option>iOS native</option>
    <option>New Jersey native</option>
    <option>VT220</option>
</Form.Control>
```

This will generate a Bootstrap-styled select element.

Putting the whole thing together leads to the form you can see in Figure 6-2:

```
import Form from 'react-bootstrap/Form'
import Col from 'react-bootstrap/Col'
import Button from 'react-bootstrap/Button'
import Alert from 'react-bootstrap/Alert'
import { useState } from 'react'
import './App.css'

function App() {
  const [submitted, setSubmitted] = useState(false)

  return (
    <div className="App">
      <h1>VC Funding Registration</h1>
      <Form>
        <Form.Row>
          <Form.Group as={Col} controlId="startupName">
            <Form.Label>Startup name</Form.Label>
            <Form.Control placeholder="No names ending in ...ly, please" />
          </Form.Group>
          <Form.Group as={Col} controlId="market">
            <Form.Label>Market</Form.Label>
            <Form.Control placeholder="e.g. seniors on Tik-Tok" />
          </Form.Group>
          <Form.Group as={Col} controlId="appType">
            <Form.Label>Type of application</Form.Label>
            <Form.Control as="select" defaultValue="Choose...">
              <option>Progressive web application</option>
              <option>Conservative web application</option>
              <option>Android native</option>
              <option>iOS native</option>
              <option>New Jersey native</option>
              <option>VT220</option>
            </Form.Control>
          </Form.Group>
        </Form.Row>

        <Form.Row>
          <Form.Group as={Col} controlId="description">
            <Form.Label>Description</Form.Label>
            <Form.Control as="textarea" />
          </Form.Group>
        </Form.Row>

        <Form.Group id="technologiesUsed">
          <Form.Label>
            Technologies used (check at least 3)
          </Form.Label>
          <Form.Control as="select" multiple>
            <option>Blockchain</option>
            <option>Machine learning</option>
            <option>Quantum computing</option>
```

```
          <option>Autonomous vehicles</option>
          <option>For-loops</option>
        </Form.Control>
      </Form.Group>

      <Button variant="primary" onClick={() => setSubmitted(true)}>
        Submit
      </Button>
    </Form>
    <Alert
      show={submitted}
      variant="success"
      onClose={() => setSubmitted(false)}
      dismissible
    >
      <Alert.Heading>We'll be in touch!</Alert.Heading>
      <p>One of our partners will be in touch shortly.</p>
    </Alert>
  </div>
 )
}

export default App
```

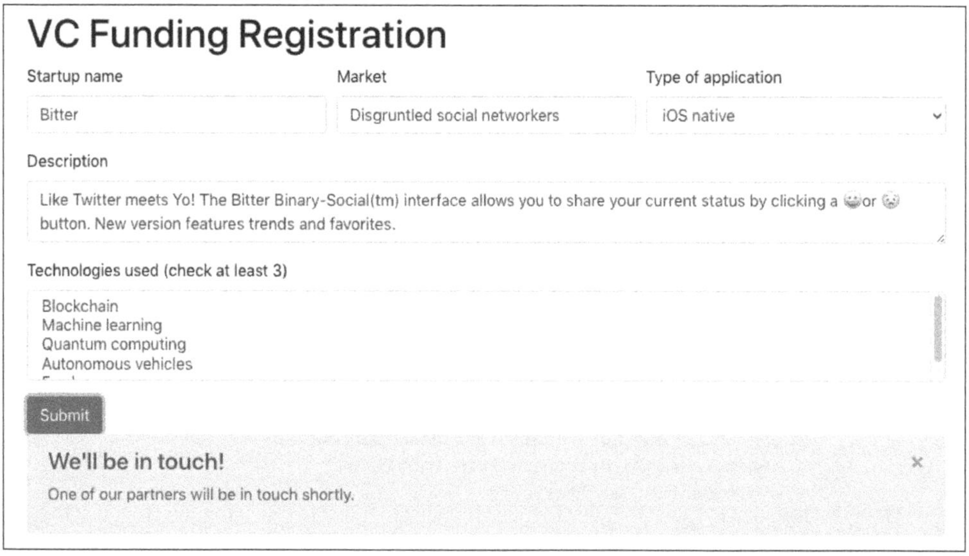

Figure 6-2. A React bootstrap form and alert box

Discussion

Bootstrap is a much older UI toolkit than Material Design, but there are still markets where it feels more appropriate. If you're building an application that has to feel more like a traditional website, then Bootstrap will give it that more traditional feel. If you want to build something that feels more like a cross-platform application, you should consider Material-UI.[3]

You can download the source for this recipe from the GitHub site (*https://oreil.ly/ZpzF3*).

6.3 View Data Sets with React Window

Problem

Some applications need to display a seemingly endless quantity of data. If you are writing an application like Twitter, you don't want to download all of the tweets in the user's timeline because it would probably take several hours, days, or months. The solution is to *window* the data. When you window a list of items, you keep only the items in memory that are currently on display. As you scroll up or down, the application downloads the data needed for the current view.

But creating this windowing logic is quite complex. Not only does it involve meticulous tracking of what's currently visible,[4] but if you're not careful, you can quickly run into memory issues if you fail to cache the windowing data efficiently.

How do you implement windowing code inside a React application?

Solution

The React Window library is a set of components for applications that need to scroll a large amount of data. We'll look at how to create a large, fixed-size list.[5]

To start, we need to create a component that will show the details for a single item. In our example application, we're going to create a set of 10,000 date strings. We will render each date with a component called DateRow, which will be our item-renderer. React Window works by rendering only the items that are visible in the current viewport. As the user scrolls up or down the list, it will create new items as they come into view and remove them as they disappear.

When React Window calls an item renderer, it passes it two properties: an item number, which begins at 0, and a style object.

---

3 See Recipe 5.1 for more information.

4 Including dealing with all the nasty edge cases that occur if the viewport changes size.

5 You can use the library for variable and fixed-sized lists and grids. See the documentation (*https://oreil.ly/pCYaq*) for more details.

This is our DateRow item-renderer:

```
import moment from 'moment'

const DateRow = ({ index, style }) => (
  <div className={`aDate ${index % 2 && 'aDate-odd'}`} style={style}>
    {moment().add(index, 'd').format('dddd, MMMM Do YYYY')}
  </div>
)

export default DateRow
```

This component calculates a date index days in the future. In a more realistic application, this component would probably download an item of data from a backend server.

To generate the list itself, we will use a FixedSizeList. We need to give the list a fixed width and height. React Window calculates how many items are visible using the height of the list and the height of each item, using the value from the itemSize attribute. If the height is 400 and the itemHeight is 40, then the list will only need to display 10 or 11 DateRow components (see Figure 6-3).

Here is the final version of the code. Notice that the FixedSizeList does not include an instance of the DateRow component. That's because it wants to use the DateRow function to create multiple items dynamically as we scroll the list. So instead of using <DateRow/>, the list uses the {DateRow} function itself:

```
import { FixedSizeList } from 'react-window'
import DateRow from './DateRow'
import './App.css'

function App() {
  return (
    <div className="App">
      <FixedSizeList
        height={400}
        itemCount={10000}
        itemSize={40}
        width={300}
      >
        {DateRow}
      </FixedSizeList>
    </div>
  )
}

export default App
```

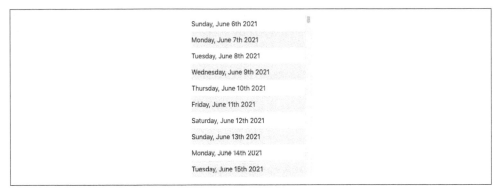

Figure 6-3. The list contains only visible items

One final point to note is that because the items are dynamically added to and removed from the list, you have to be careful using the `nth-child` selector in CSS:

```
.aDate:nth-child(even) { /* This won't work */
    background-color: #eee;
}
```

Instead, you need to dynamically check the current index for an item and check if it's odd using a little modulo-2 math, as we do in the example:

```
<div className={`aDate ${index % 2 && 'aDate-odd'}`} ...>
```

Discussion

React Window is a narrowly focused component library but valuable if you need to present a vast data set. You are still responsible for downloading and caching the data that appears in the list, but this is a relatively simple task compared to the windowing magic that React Window performs.

You can download the source for this recipe from the GitHub site (*https://oreil.ly/lXxv3*).

6.4 Create Responsive Dialogs with Material-UI

Problem

If you're using a component library, there's a good chance that at some point you will display a dialog window. Dialogs allow you to add UI detail without making the user feel they are traveling to another page. They work well for content creation or as a quick way of displaying more detail about an item.

However, dialogs don't play well with mobile devices. Mobiles have a small display screen, and dialogs frequently waste a lot of space around the edges to display the background page.

How can you create responsive dialogs, which act like floating windows when you are using a desktop machine but look like separate full-screen pages on a mobile device?

Solution

The Material-UI library includes a higher-order function that can tell when you are on a mobile device and display dialogs as full-screen windows:

```
import { withMobileDialog } from '@material-ui/core'
...

const ResponsiveDialog = withMobileDialog()(
  ({ fullScreen }) => {
    // Return some component using the fullScreen (true/false) property
  }
)
```

The withMobileDialog gives any component it wraps an extra property called full Screen, which is set to true or false. A Dialog component can use this property to change its behavior. If you pass fullScreen to a Dialog like this:

```
import { withMobileDialog } from '@material-ui/core'
import Dialog from '@material-ui/core/Dialog'
import DialogTitle from '@material-ui/core/DialogTitle'
import Typography from '@material-ui/core/Typography'
import DialogContent from '@material-ui/core/DialogContent'
import DialogActions from '@material-ui/core/DialogActions'
import Button from '@material-ui/core/Button'
import CloseIcon from '@material-ui/icons/Close'

const ResponsiveDialog = withMobileDialog()(
  ({ onClose, open, title, fullScreen, children }) => {
    return (
      <Dialog open={open} fullScreen={fullScreen} onClose={onClose}>
        <DialogTitle>
          <Typography
            component="h1"
            variant="h5"
            color="inherit"
            noWrap
          >
            {title}
          </Typography>
        </DialogTitle>
        <DialogContent>{children}</DialogContent>
        <DialogActions>
          <Button
```

```
          variant="outlined"
          startIcon={<CloseIcon />}
          onClick={onClose}
        >
          Close
        </Button>
      </DialogActions>
    </Dialog>
  )
 }
)

export default ResponsiveDialog
```

the dialog will change its behavior when running on a mobile or desktop device.

Let's say we modify the application we created in Recipe 5.1. In our original application, a dialog appears when the user clicked an image in a gallery. The dialog is shown on a mobile device in Figure 6-4.

Figure 6-4. By default, a dialog on a mobile device has space around the edge

If you replace this dialog with a ResponsiveDialog, it will look the same on a large screen. But on a small screen, the dialog will fill the display, as you can see in

Figure 6-5. This not only gives you more space for the contents of the dialog, but it will simplify the experience of mobile users. Instead of it working like a pop-up window, it will feel more like a separate page.

Figure 6-5. On a mobile device, the responsive dialog fills the screen

Discussion

For more ideas on how to deal with responsive interfaces, see Recipe 2.1.

You can download the source for this recipe from the GitHub site (*https://oreil.ly/ 836i2*).

6.5 Build an Admin Console with React Admin

Problem

Developers can spend so long creating and maintaining end-user applications that one important task is often left neglected: admin consoles. Customers don't use admin consoles; they are used by back-office staff and administrators to look at the current data set and to investigate and resolve data issues in an application. Some data storage systems like Firebase (*https://oreil.ly/ugvEI*) have quite advanced admin consoles built-in. But that's not the case for most backend services. Instead, developers often have to dig into data problems by directly accessing the databases, which live behind several layers of cloud infrastructure.

How can we create an admin console for almost any React application?

Solution

We're going to look at the React Admin, and although this chapter is about component libraries, React Admin contains far more than components. It's an application framework that makes it easy to build interfaces to allow administrators to examine and maintain the data in your application.

Different applications will use different network service layers. They might use REST, GraphQL, or one of many other systems. But in most cases, data is accessed as a set of *resources* held on the server. React Admin has most of the pieces in place for creating an admin application that will allow you to browse through each resource. It lets you create, maintain, and search data. It can also export the data to an external application.

To show how `react-admin` works, we're going to create an admin console for the message board application we created in Chapter 5 (see Figure 6-6).

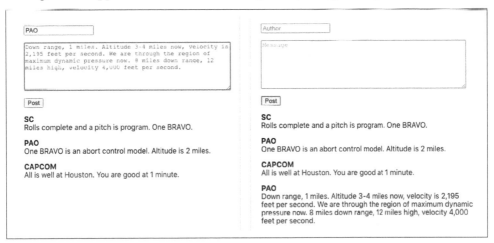

Figure 6-6. The original message board application

The backend for the application is a simple GraphQL server. The GraphQL server has a relatively simple schema, which defines messages in the schema language like this:

```
type Message {
    id: ID!
```

```
      author: String!
      text: String!
  }
```

Each message had a unique `id`. Strings record the text of the message and the name of the author.

There was only one type of change that a user could make to the data: they could add a message. There was one type of query they could run: they could read all of the messages.

To create a `react-admin` application, you first need to create a new React application and then install the `react-admin` library:

```
$ npm install react-admin
```

The main component of the library is called `Admin`. This will form the shell of our entire application:

```
<Admin dataProvider={...}>
  ...UI for separate resources goes here...
</Admin>
```

An `Admin` component needs a *data provider*. A data provider is an adapter that will connect the application to the backend service. Our backend service uses GraphQL, so we need a GraphQL data provider:

```
$ npm install graphql
$ npm install ra-data-graphql-simple
```

There are data providers available for most backend services. See the React Admin website (*https://oreil.ly/2qtVY*) for more details. We'll need to initialize our data provider before we can use it. GraphQL is configured with a `buildGraphQLProvider` function that is asynchronous, so we need to be careful that it's ready before we use it:

```
import { Admin } from 'react-admin'
import buildGraphQLProvider from 'ra-data-graphql-simple'
import { useEffect, useState } from 'react'

function App() {
  const [dataProvider, setDataProvider] = useState()

  useEffect(() => {
    let didCancel = false
    ;(async () => {
      const dp = await buildGraphQLProvider({
        clientOptions: { uri: 'http://localhost:5000' },
      })
      if (!didCancel) {
        setDataProvider(() => dp)
      }
    })()
```

```
      return () => {
        didCancel = true
      }
    }, [])

    return (
      <div className="App">
        {dataProvider && (
          <Admin dataProvider={dataProvider}>
            ...resource UI here...
          </Admin>
        )}
      </div>
    )
  }

  export default App
```

The data provider connects to our GraphQL server running on port 5000.[6] The data provider will first download the schema for the application, which will tell it what resources (just a single resource, Messages, in our case) are available and what operations it can perform on them.

If we try to run the application now, it won't do anything. That's because even though it knows that there's a Messages resource on the server, it doesn't know that we want to do anything with it. So, let's add the Messages resource to the application.

If we want the application to list all the messages on the server, we will need to create a simple component called ListMessages. This will use some of the ready-made components in react-admin to build its interface:

```
  const ListMessages = (props) => {
    return (
      <List {...props}>
        <Datagrid>
          <TextField source="id" />
          <TextField source="author" />
          <TextField source="text" />
        </Datagrid>
      </List>
    )
  }
```

This will create a table with columns for message id, author, and text. We can now tell the admin system about the new component by passing a Resource to the Admin component:

---

6 You will find the server in the source code for this chapter. You can run the server by typing **node ./ server.js**.

```
<Admin dataProvider={dataProvider}>
    <Resource name="Message" list={ListMessages}/>
</Admin>
```

The Admin component will see the new Resource, contact the server to read the messages, and then render them with a ListMessages component (see Figure 6-7).

Figure 6-7. Displaying the messages from the server

The screen update appears to work by magic, but it's because the server has to follow certain conventions so that the GraphQL adapter knows which service to call. In this case, it will find a query called allMessages, which returns messages:

```
type Query {
    Message(id: ID!): Message
    allMessages(page: Int, perPage: Int,
        sortField: String, sortOrder: String,
        filter: MessageFilter): [Message]
}
```

As a result, you might need to change your backend API to meet the requirements of your data provider. However, the services that you add will probably be useful in your main application.

The allMessages query allows the admin interface to page through the data from your server. It can accept a property called filter, which it uses to search for the data. The MessageFilter in the example schema will allow the admin console to find messages containing strings for author and text. It will also allow the admin console to send a general search string (q), which it will use to find messages that contain a string in any field.

Here is the GraphQL schema definition of the MessageFilter object. You will need to create something similar for each resource in your application:

```
input MessageFilter {
    q: String
```

```
    author: String
    text: String
}
```

To enable filtering and searching in the frontend, we will first need to create some filtering fields in a React component we'll call `MessageFilter`. This is quite distinct from the `MessageFilter` in the schema, although you will notice it contains matching fields:

```
const MessageFilter = (props) => (
  <Filter {...props}>
    <TextInput label="Author" source="author" />
    <TextInput label="Text" source="text" />
    <TextInput label="Search" source="q" alwaysOn />
  </Filter>
)
```

We can now add the `MessageFilter` to the `ListMessages` component, and we will suddenly find that we can page, search, and filter messages in the admin console (see Figure 6-8):

```
const ListMessages = (props) => {
  return (
    <List {...props} filters={<MessageFilter />}>
      <Datagrid>
        <TextField source="id" />
        <TextField source="author" />
        <TextField source="text" />
      </Datagrid>
    </List>
  )
}
```

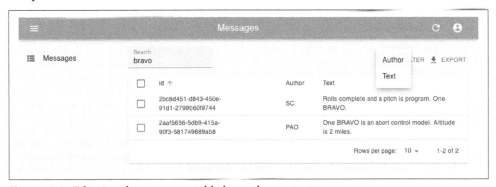

Figure 6-8. Filtering the messages table by author or text

We can also add the ability to create new messages by adding a `CreateMessage` component:

```
const CreateMessage = (props) => {
  return (
    <Create title="Create a Message" {...props}>
      <SimpleForm>
        <TextInput source="author" />
        <TextInput multiline source="text" />
      </SimpleForm>
    </Create>
  )
}
```

and then adding the `CreateMessage` component to the `Resource` (see Figure 6-9):

```
<Resource name="Message" list={ListMessages} create={CreateMessage}/>
```

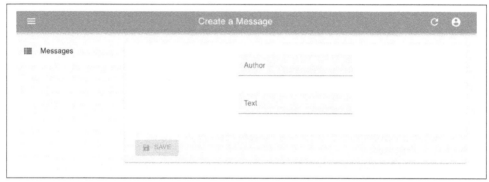

Figure 6-9. Creating messages on the console

The GraphQL data provider will create messages by passing the contents of the `CreateMessage` form to a mutation called `CreateMessage`:

```
type Mutation {
    createMessage(
        author: String!
        text: String!
    ): Message
}
```

Similarly, you can add the ability to update or delete messages. If you have a complex schema with subresources, `react-admin` can display subitems within a table. It can also handle different display types. It can show images and links. There are components available that can display resources on calendars or in charts (see Figure 6-10 for examples from the online demo application (*https://oreil.ly/fmFwR*)).[7] Admin consoles can also work with your existing security system.

---

7 Some of them are available only if you subscribe to the Enterprise edition.

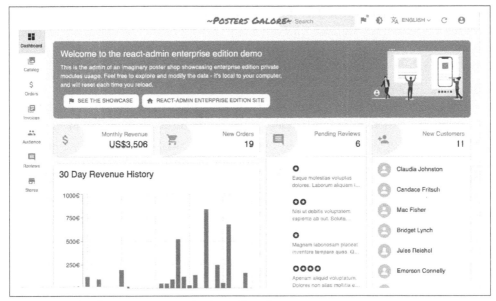

Figure 6-10. Different view types in the online demo

Discussion

Although you will have to make some additional changes to your backend services to make `react-admin` work for you, there is an excellent chance that these additional services will also be helpful for your main application. Even if they aren't, the building blocks that `react-admin` provides will likely slash the development time needed to create a back-office system.

You can download the source for this recipe from the GitHub site (*https://oreil.ly/2sUhp*).

6.6 No Designer? Use Semantic UI

Problem

Well-designed styling can add a lot of visual appeal to an application. But poor styling can make even a good application appear cheap and amateurish. Many developers have a limited sense of design.[8] In cases where you have little or no access to professional design help, a simple, clear UI component library can allow you to focus on the application's functionality without spending endless hours tweaking the location of buttons and borders.

---

8 Including at least one of the authors…

Tried-and-tested frameworks like Bootstrap can provide a good, no-gloss foundation for most applications.[9] But even they often require a lot of focus on visual appearance. If you want to focus on the functionality of an application and want to get a clear functional visual appearance, then the Semantic UI library is a good choice.

But the Semantic UI library is old, coming from the days when jQuery ruled the roost. At the time of writing, it has not been updated in more than two years. What do you do if you want to use a reliable and well-established library like Semantic UI with React?

Solution

The Semantic UI React library is a wrapper that makes the Semantic UI library available for React users.

As the name suggests, Semantic UI focuses on the meaning of the interface. You manage its visual appearance with CSS rather than components. Instead, Semantic UI components focus on functionality. When you create a form, for example, you say which fields to include, rather than saying anything about their layout. That leads to a clean, consistent appearance, which needs little or no visual adjustment.

To get started, let's install the Semantic library and its styling support:

```
$ npm install semantic-ui-react semantic-ui-css
```

In addition, we also need to include a reference to the stylesheet in the *index.js* file of the application:

```
import React from 'react'
import ReactDOM from 'react-dom'
import './index.css'
import App from './App'
import reportWebVitals from './reportWebVitals'
import 'semantic-ui-css/semantic.min.css'

ReactDOM.render(
  <React.StrictMode>
    <App />
  </React.StrictMode>,
  document.getElementById('root')
)

// If you want to start measuring performance in your app, pass a function
// to log results (for example: reportWebVitals(console.log))
// or send to an analytics endpoint. Learn more: https://bit.ly/CRA-vitals
reportWebVitals()
```

---

9 See Recipe 6.2 for guidance on how to use Bootstrap with your application.

We're going to re-create our message posting application. We'll need a form with a text field for the author's name and a text area for posting a message. Semantic components are designed to be as similar to simple HTML elements as possible. So if we're building a form, we'll import a Form, Input, TextArea, and Button to post the message:

```
import { Button, Form, Input, TextArea } from 'semantic-ui-react'
import './App.css'
import { useState } from 'react'

function App() {
  const [author, setAuthor] = useState('')
  const [text, setText] = useState('')
  const [messages, setMessages] = useState([])

  return (
    <div className="App">
      <Form>
        <Form.Field>
          <label htmlFor="author">Author</label>
          <Input
            value={author}
            id="author"
            onChange={(evt) => setAuthor(evt.target.value)}
          />
        </Form.Field>
        <Form.Field>
          <label htmlFor="text">Message</label>
          <TextArea
            value={text}
            id="text"
            onChange={(evt) => setText(evt.target.value)}
          />
        </Form.Field>
        <Button
          basic
          onClick={() => {
            setMessages((m) => [
              {
                icon: 'pencil',
                date: new Date().toString(),
                summary: author,
                extraText: text,
              },
              ...m,
            ])
            setAuthor('')
            setText('')
          }}
        >
          Post
        </Button>
```

```
          </Form>
        </div>
      )
    }

    export default App
```

This code should feel familiar. The Form component does have a Field helper, which makes it a little easier to group labels and fields, but beyond that, the code looks similar to an elementary HTML form.

In the example application, we're "posting" messages by adding them to an array called messages. You may have noticed that we're adding messages to the array in a particular object structure:

```
setMessages((m) => [
  {
    icon: 'pencil',
    date: new Date().toString(),
    summary: author,
    extraText: text,
  },
  ...m,
])
```

We did not choose these attributes by accident. Although most of the components in Semantic are simple, there are some more complex components, which are there to support some common use cases. One such example is the Feed component. The Feed component is there to render a social message stream, such as you might see on Twitter or Instagram. It will render a clean series of messages, with date stamps, headlines, icons, and so on. Here's what our final code looks like with the Feed included:

```
import {
  Button,
  Form,
  Input,
  TextArea,
  Feed,
} from 'semantic-ui-react'
import './App.css'
import { useState } from 'react'

function App() {
  const [author, setAuthor] = useState('')
  const [text, setText] = useState('')
  const [messages, setMessages] = useState([])

  return (
    <div className="App">
      <Form>
        <Form.Field>
```

```
          <label htmlFor="author">Author</label>
          <Input
            value={author}
            id="author"
            onChange={(evt) => setAuthor(evt.target.value)}
          />
        </Form.Field>
        <Form.Field>
          <label htmlFor="text">Message</label>
          <TextArea
            value={text}
            id="text"
            onChange={(evt) => setText(evt.target.value)}
          />
        </Form.Field>
        <Button
          basic
          onClick={() => {
            setMessages((m) => [
              {
                icon: 'pencil',
                date: new Date().toString(),
                summary: author,
                extraText: text,
              },
              ...m,
            ])
            setAuthor('')
            setText('')
          }}
        >
          Post
        </Button>
      </Form>
      <Feed events={messages} />
    </div>
  )
}

export default App
```

When you run the application, the interface is clean and unfussy (see Figure 6-11).

Figure 6-11. The Semantic UI interface in action

Discussion

Semantic UI is an old library. But that's not a bad thing. Its battle-tested interface is clean and functional and is one of the best ways of getting your application up and running without the support of a visual designer. It's particularly useful if you're creating a Lean Startup and want to throw something together quickly to test if there is a market for your product.[10]

You can download the source for this recipe from the GitHub site (*https://oreil.ly/qeNqy*).

---

10 For more details, see *The Lean Startup* by Eric Ries (Crown Business).

CHAPTER 7

Security

In this chapter, we look at various ways of securing your application. We'll look at common patterns for integrating your application with standard security systems. We'll look at how you can audit your code for several common security flaws. In several recipes in this chapter, we will use the WebAuthn API to integrate an application with security devices, such as fingerprint sensors and physical tokens. WebAuthn is an exciting and underused technology that can increase your application's security and enhance the user's experience.

7.1 Secure Requests, Not Routes

Problem

Recipe 2.6 showed how you could use React Router to create secured routes. That means if the user tries to get to specific paths within your application, you can force them to submit a login form before seeing the contents of that page.

The secured routes approach is a good, reasonably general approach when you are first building an application. However, some applications don't fall so easily into this static model of security. Some pages will be secure, and some will be insecure. But in many applications, it's easier to secure data services rather than pages. What matters is not which page you are on but the data you are viewing.

All of these complexities are usually straightforward to define at the API level. But it's the kind of complexity that you don't want to reproduce in the logic of your frontend client. For these reasons, the simple approach of marking some routes secure and others as insecure is not good enough.

Solution

If defining routes as secure or insecure is not sufficient for your client's security, you might want to consider controlling access to your application by using the security responses you receive from the backend server.

With this approach, you begin by assuming the user can go anywhere in your app. You don't worry about secure routes and insecure routes. You just have routes. If a user visits a path that contains private data, the API server will return an error, typically an HTTP status 401 (Unauthorized). When the error occurs, the security redirects the user to a login form.

With this approach, the API server drives the policy of what is private and what is public. If the security policies change, you only need to modify the code on the API server without changing the client code.

Let's take a look at the code for the original secured-routes recipe again. In our application, we inject a `SecurityProvider`, which controls the security of all of its child components. In the example application, we do this in the *App.js* file:

```
import './App.css'
import { BrowserRouter, Route, Switch } from 'react-router-dom'
import Public from './Public'
import Private1 from './Private1'
import Private2 from './Private2'
import Home from './Home'
import SecurityProvider from './SecurityProvider'
import SecureRoute from './SecureRoute'

function App() {
  return (
    <div className="App">
      <BrowserRouter>
        <SecurityProvider>
          <Switch>
            <Route exact path="/">
              <Home />
            </Route>
            <SecureRoute path="/private1">
              <Private1 />
            </SecureRoute>
            <SecureRoute path="/private2">
              <Private2 />
            </SecureRoute>
            <Route exact path="/public">
              <Public />
            </Route>
          </Switch>
        </SecurityProvider>
      </BrowserRouter>
    </div>
```

```
  )
}

export default App
```

You can see that the application has simple `Routes` and `SecuredRoutes`. If an unauthenticated user tries to access a secured route, they are redirected to the login form, as you can see in Figure 7-1.

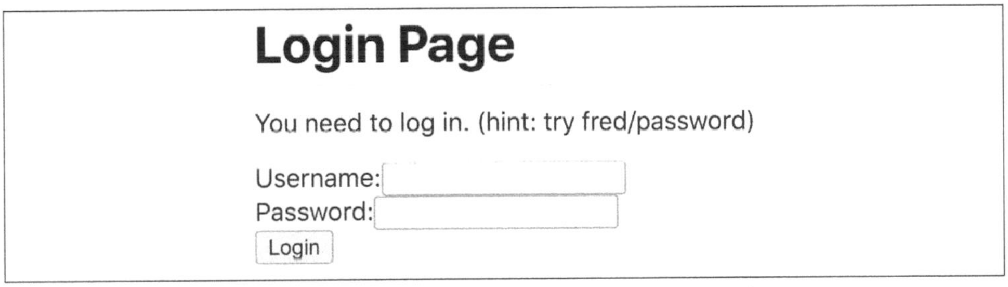

Figure 7-1. When you first access a secured route, you see a login form

Once they are logged in (see Figure 7-2), they can access the secured content.

Figure 7-2. Once you are logged in, secured routes are visible

If we want to base our security upon the security of the backend API, we'll begin by replacing all of the `SecuredRoutes` with simple `Routes`. The application simply doesn't know, until the API server tells it, which data is private and public. For the example app in this recipe, we'll have two pages on the application that contain a mix of public and private data. The Transactions page will read secure data from the server. The Offers page will read insecure data from the server. Here is the new version of our *App.js* file:

```
import './App.css'
import { BrowserRouter, Route, Switch } from 'react-router-dom'
import Transactions from './Transactions'
import Offers from './Offers'
import Home from './Home'
import SecurityProvider from './SecurityProvider'

function App() {
```

```
    return (
      <div className="App">
        <BrowserRouter>
          <SecurityProvider>
            <Switch>
              <Route exact path="/">
                <Home />
              </Route>
              <Route exact path="/transactions">
                <Transactions />
              </Route>
              <Route exact path="/offers">
                <Offers />
              </Route>
            </Switch>
          </SecurityProvider>
        </BrowserRouter>
      </div>
    )
}

export default App
```

We'll also need to make a change to our `SecurityProvider`. In an API security model, the client begins by assuming that all data is public, which is the opposite of the secured-routes approach, which assumes you don't have access until you prove that you do by logging in.

This means our new `SecurityProvider` has to default its initial logged-in state to `true`:

```
import { useState } from 'react'
import SecurityContext from './SecurityContext'
import Login from './Login'
import axios from 'axios'

const SecurityProvider = (props) => {
  const [loggedIn, setLoggedIn] = useState(true)

  return (
    <SecurityContext.Provider
      value={{
        login: async (username, password) => {
          await axios.post('/api/login', { username, password })
          setLoggedIn(true)
        },
        logout: async () => {
          await axios.post('/api/logout')
          return setLoggedIn(false)
        },
        onFailure() {
          return setLoggedIn(false)
```

```
      },
      loggedIn,
    }}
  >
    {loggedIn ? props.children : <Login />}
  </SecurityContext.Provider>
  )
}

export default SecurityProvider
```

We've also made several other changes:

- The code that decides whether the user should see the `Login` form is now in the `SecurityProvider`. This code used to live inside the `SecuredRoute` component, but now we display it centrally.

- We've replaced the dummy username/password checks with calls to the backend services called *_/api/login_* and *_/api/logout_*. It would be best if you replaced these with whatever security code applies to your system.

- The `SecurityProvider` now provides a new function called `onFailure`, which simply marks the person as logged out.

When you call this function, it forces the user to log in. If we no longer have secured routes, at what point do we perform the security checks? We do them in the API calls themselves.

 In a real application, you would want to add code that deals with an invalid login attempt. To keep the code short, we've omitted any special handling here. A failed login will simply leave you in the login form without any error messages.

Let's look at our new Transactions page, as defined in *src/Transactions.js*. This component reads the transactions data and displays it on the screen:

```
import useTransactions from './useTransactions'

const Transactions = () => {
  const { data: transactions } = useTransactions()

  return (
    <div>
      <h1>Transactions</h1>
      <main>
        <table>
          <thead>
            <tr>
              <th>Date</th>
```

```
          <th>Amount</th>
          <th>Description</th>
        </tr>
      </thead>
      <tbody>
        {transactions &&
          transactions.map((trx) => (
            <tr>
              <td>{trx.date}</td>
              <td>{trx.amount}</td>
              <td>{trx.description}</td>
            </tr>
          ))}
      </tbody>
    </table>
  </main>
</div>
  )
}

export default Transactions
```

The useTransactions hook contains the network code to read data from the server.
It's inside this hook that we need to add our check for a 401 (Unauthorized) response
from the server:

```
import { useEffect, useState } from 'react'
import axios from 'axios'
import useSecurity from './useSecurity'

const useTransactions = () => {
  const security = useSecurity()
  const [transactions, setTransactions] = useState([])

  useEffect(() => {
    ;(async () => {
      try {
        const result = await axios.get('/api/transactions')
        setTransactions(result.data)
      } catch (err) {
        const status = err.response && err.response.status
        if (status === 401) {
          security.onFailure()
        }
        // Handle other exceptions here (consider a shared
        // error handler -- see elsewhere in the book)
      }
    })()
  }, [])

  return { data: transactions }
}
```

```
export default useTransactions
```

In the example application, we're using the axios library to contact the server. axios handles HTTP errors such as 401 (the HTTP status for Unauthorized) as exceptions. That makes it a little clearer which code is dealing with an unexpected response. If you were using a different API standard, like GraphQL, you would be able to deal with security errors in an analogous way by examining the contents of the error objcct that GraphQL returns.

In the event that there's an unauthorized response from the server, the use Transactions hook makes a call to the onFailure function in the Security Provider.

We'll build the Offers page in the same way. The *src/Offers.js* component will format the offers data from the server:

```
import useOffers from './useOffers'

const Offers = () => {
  const { data: offers } = useOffers()

  return (
    <div>
      <h1>Offers</h1>
      <main>
        <ul>
          {offers &&
            offers.map((offer) => <li className="offer">{offer}</li>)}
        </ul>
      </main>
    </div>
  )
}

export default Offers
```

And the code that reads the data is inside the *src/useOffers.js* hook:

```
import { useEffect, useState } from 'react'
import axios from 'axios'
import useSecurity from './useSecurity'

const useOffers = () => {
  const security = useSecurity()
  const [offers, setOffers] = useState([])

  useEffect(() => {
    ;(async () => {
      try {
        const result = await axios.get('/api/offers')
        setOffers(result.data)
```

```
      } catch (err) {
        const status = err.response && err.response.status
        if (status === 401) {
          security.onFailure()
        }
        // Handle other exceptions here (consider a shared
        // error handler -- see elsewhere in the book)
      }
    })()
  }, [])

  return { data: offers }
}

export default useOffers
```

 Even though the */api/offers* endpoint is not secured, we still have code that checks for security errors. One consequence of the API security approach is that you have to treat all endpoints as secure, just in case they become secure in the future.

Let's try our example application. We'll begin by opening the front page (see Figure 7-3).

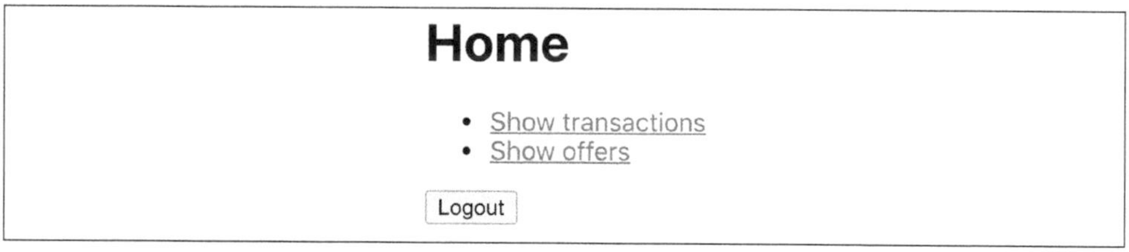

Home

- Show transactions
- Show offers

Logout

Figure 7-3. The front page of the application

If we click the Offers link, we see the offers read from the server (see Figure 7-4). This data is unsecured, and the application doesn't ask us to log in.

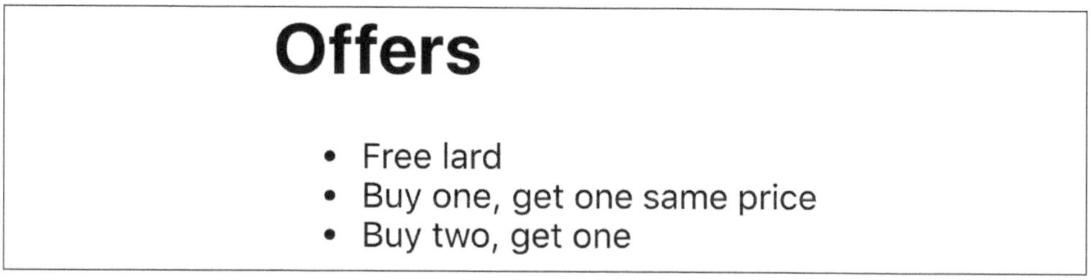

Offers

- Free lard
- Buy one, get one same price
- Buy two, get one

Figure 7-4. If we click the Offers link, we can see the contents

If we now go back to the home page and click the Transactions link, the application asks us to log in (see Figure 7-5). The transactions page has attempted to download transaction data from the server, which resulted in a 401 (Unauthorized) response. The code catches this as an exception and calls the `onFailure` function in the SecurityProvider, which then displays the login form (see Figure 7-5).

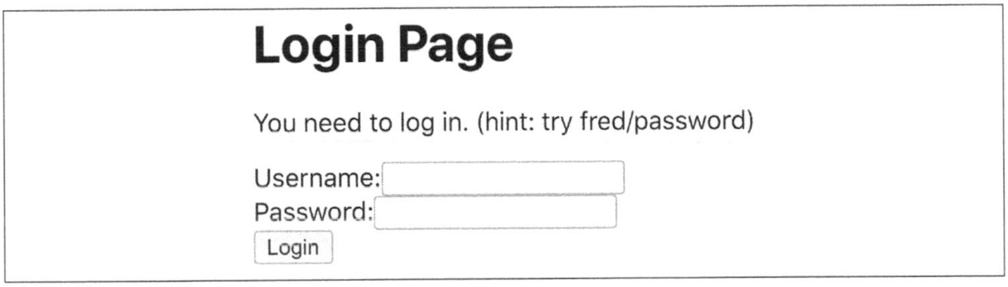

Login Page

You need to log in. (hint: try fred/password)

Username: [_____]
Password: [_____]
[Login]

Figure 7-5. If we try to access the Transactions page, we are asked to log in

If we log in, the application sends our username and password to the server. Assuming that doesn't result in an error, the `SecurityProvider` hides the login form, the Transactions page is re-rendered, and the data is now able to be read as we've logged in (see Figure 7-6).

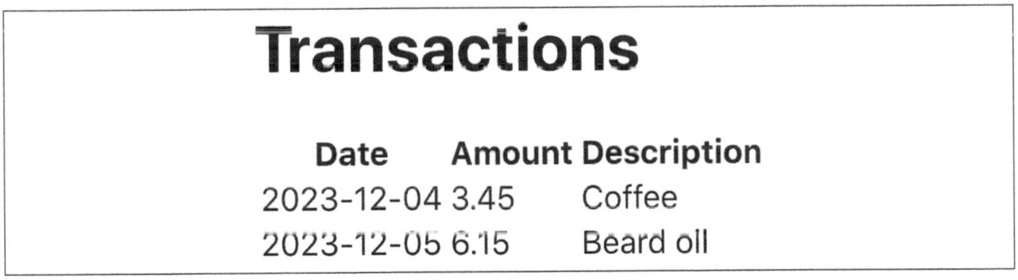

Transactions

Date	Amount	Description
2023-12-04	3.45	Coffee
2023-12-05	6.15	Beard oil

Figure 7-6. Once we log in, we can see the Transactions page

Discussion

Our example app now contains nothing to indicate which APIs are secured and which are unsecured. The server now handles all of that work. The API endpoints are entirely in charge of the security of the application.

Using this approach, you should apply the same security handling to all API calls. One of the benefits of extracting API calls into custom hooks is that the hooks can share the security code. Hooks can call other hooks, and a common approach is to create hooks that act as general-purpose `GET` and `POST` calls.[1] A general-purpose `GET`

---

1 Or, in the case of GraphQL, accessors and mutators.

hook could not only handle access failures but also include request cancellations, debouncing (Recipes 5.3 and 5.6), and shared error handling (Recipe 4.1).

Another advantage to the secured API approach is that it's possible to disable security in some circumstances entirely. For example, during development, you can do away with the need for developers to have an identity provider configured. You can also choose to have different security configurations in different deployments.

Finally, for automated testing systems, like Cypress, which can simulate network responses, you can split the testing of application functionality from nonfunctional security testing. It's a good idea to have additional server-only security tests that are separate from the UI tests to ensure that the server is secure in its own right.

You can download the source for this recipe from the GitHub site (*https://oreil.ly/ByWVZ*).

7.2 Authenticate with Physical Tokens

Problem

Usernames and passwords are not always enough; they might be stolen or guessed. So some users might only use applications that provide additional security.

An increasing number of systems now provide *two-factor authentication*. A two-factor system requires the user to log in with a form and then provide some additional information. The additional information might be a code sent to them by an SMS text message. Or it might be an application on their phone that generates a one-time password. Or, perhaps most securely, it might involve the use of a physical hardware device, like a YubiKey (*https://www.yubico.com*), which is attached to the computer when required and pressed.

These physical tokens work using public-key cryptography, which generates a public key for use with a given application and encrypts strings using a private key. An application can send a random "challenge" string to the device, generating a signature using the private key. The application can then use the public key to check that the string was signed correctly.

But how do you integrate them with your React application?

Solution

Web Authentication (also known as *WebAuthn*) is a widely supported[2] W3C standard that allows a browser to communicate with a physical device, like a YubiKey.

---

2 With the notable exception of Internet Explorer.

There are two *flows* in web authentication. The first is called *attestation*. During attestation, a user registers a security device with an application. During *assertion*, the user can verify their identity to log in to a system.

First, let's look at attestation. During this flow, the user registers a physical device against their account. That means that the user should always be logged in during attestation.

The code for this recipe includes a dummy Node server, which you can run from the *server* directory within the application:

```
$ cd server
$ npm install
$ npm run start
```

There are three steps to attestation:

1. The server generates an attestation request, saying what kind of device is acceptable.
2. The user connects the device and activates it, probably by pressing a button on it.
3. A response is generated from the device, which includes the public key, and is then returned to the server, where it can be stored against the user's account.

We can tell if the browser supports WebAuthn by checking for the existence of `window.PublicKeyCredential`. If it exists, you're good to go.

There is an endpoint at */startRegister*, which will create the attestation request on the server. So we'll begin by calling that:

```
import axios from 'axios'
...
// Ask to start registering a physical token for the current user
const response = await axios.post('/startRegister')
```

This is what an attestation request looks like:

```
{
    "rpName": "Physical Token Server",
    "rpID": "localhost",
    "userID": "1234",
    "userName": "freda",
    "excludeCredentials": [
        {"id": "existingKey1", "type": "public-key"}
    ],
    "authenticatorSelection": {
        "userVerification": "discouraged"
    },
    "extensions": {
        "credProps": true
```

```
        }
    }
```

Some of the attributes begin with the letters `rp...`, which stands for *relying party*. The relying party is the application that generated the request.

The `rpName` is a free-form text string that describes the application. You should set the `rpId` to the current domain name. Here it's `localhost` because we're running on a development server. The `userID` is a string that uniquely identifies the user. The `userName` is the name of the user.

`excludeCredentials` is an interesting attribute. Users might record multiple devices against their accounts. This value lists the devices that are already recorded to avoid the user registering the same device twice. If you attempt to register the same device more than once, the browser will immediately throw an exception saying that the device has been registered elsewhere.

The `authenticatorSelection` allows you to set various options about what the user needs to do when they activate their device. Here we're setting `userVerification` to `false` to prevent the user from performing any additional steps (such as entering a PIN) when activating their device. Consequently, when asked to plug in their device, the user will insert it into the USB socket and press the button, with nothing else needed.

The `credProps` extension asks the device to return additional credential properties, which might be helpful to the server.

Once the server has generated the attestation request, we need to ask the user to connect their security device. We do this with a browser function called:

```
navigator.credentials.create()
```

The `create` function accepts an attestation request object. Unfortunately, the data within the object needs to be in a variety of low-level binary forms, such as byte arrays. We can make our life significantly easier by installing a library from GitHub called `webauthn-json`, which lets you use JSON to specify the request:

```
$ npm install "@github/webauthn-json"
```

We can then pass the contents of the WebAuthn request to the GitHub version of the `create` function:

```
import { create } from '@github/webauthn-json'
import axios from 'axios'
...
// Ask to start registering a physical token for the current user
const response = await axios.post('/startRegister')
// Pass the WebAuthn config to webauthn-json 'create' function
const attestation = await create({ publicKey: response.data })
```

This is the point where the browser asks the user to insert and activate their security device (see Figure 7-7).

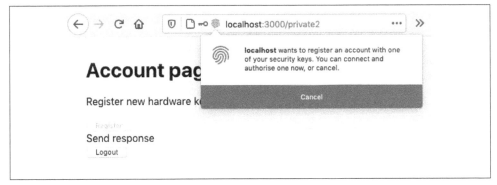

Figure 7-7. The browser asks for the token when create *is called*

The create function resolves to an *attestation object*, which you can think of as the registration information for the device. The server can use the attestation object to verify the user's identity when they log in. We need to record the attestation object against the user's account. We'll do that by posting it back to an endpoint on the example server at */register*:

```
import { create } from '@github/webauthn-json'
import axios from 'axios'
...
// Ask to start registering a physical token for the current user
const response = await axios.post('/startRegister')
// Pass the WebAuthn config to webauthn-json 'create' function
const attestation = await create({ publicKey: response.data })
// Send the details of the physical YubiKey to be stored against the user
const attestationResponse = await axios.post('/register', {
  attestation,
})
```

That's the overview of how we register a new device for a user. But where do we put that in the code?

The example application has an Account page (see Figure 7-8), and we'll add a button in there to register a new key.

Figure 7-8. We'll add a button to the account page to register a new device

Here is the registration code in place:

```
import { useState } from 'react'
import Logout from './Logout'
import axios from 'axios'
import { create } from '@github/webauthn-json'

const Private2 = () => {
  const [busy, setBusy] = useState(false)
  const [message, setMessage] = useState()

  return (
    <div className="Private2">
      <h1>Account page</h1>

      {window.PublicKeyCredential && (
        <>
          <p>Register new hardware key</p>
          <button
            onClick={async () => {
              setBusy(true)
              try {
                const response = await axios.post('/startRegister')
                setMessage('Send response')
                const attestation = await create({
                  publicKey: response.data,
                })
                setMessage('Create attestation')
                const attestationResponse = await axios.post(
                  '/register',
                  {
                    attestation,
                  }
                )
                setMessage('registered!')
                if (
                  attestationResponse.data &&
                  attestationResponse.data.verified
                ) {
                  alert('New key registered')
                }
              } catch (err) {
                setMessage('' + err)
              } finally {
                setBusy(false)
              }
            }}
            disabled={busy}
          >
            Register
          </button>
        </>
      )}
```

```
        <div className="Account-message">{message}</div>

        <Logout />
      </div>
    )
  }

  export default Private2
```

If we click the registration button on the account page, the browser asks us to connect the security device (see Figure 7-9). Once we do that, the application sends the device's credentials to the server and then tells us it has recorded a new device against our account (see Figure 7-10).

Figure 7-9. When you choose to register a new device, you are asked to activate it

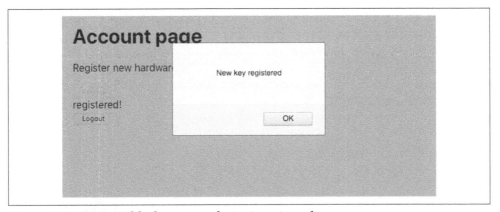

Figure 7-10. We are told when a new device is registered

The next flow we need to think about is assertion. Assertion happens when a user verifies their identity when logging in.

The steps are pretty similar to attestation:

1. The application asks the server to create an assertion request.

2. The user converts that request into an assertion object by activating their security device.

3. The server checks the assertion against its stored credentials to prove the person is who they say they are.

Let's begin with the first stage when we create an assertion request. This is what an assertion request looks like:

```
{
    "allowCredentials": [
        {"id": "existingTokenID", "type": "public-key"}
    ],
    "attestation": "direct",
    "extensions": {
        "credProps": true,
    },
    "rpID": "localhost",
    "timeout": 60000,
    "challenge": "someRandomString"
}
```

The `allowCredentials` attribute is an array of registered devices that will be acceptable. The browser will use this array to check that the user has connected the correct device.

The assertion request also includes a `challenge` string: a randomly generated string the device will need to create a signature with its private key. The server will check this signature with the public key to ensure that we used the correct device.

The `timeout` specifies how long the user will have to prove their identity.

The example server generates an assertion request when you call the */startVerify* endpoint with a specified user ID:

```
import axios from 'axios'
...
// Ask for a challenge to verify user userID
const response = await axios.post('/startVerify', { userID })
```

We can then pass the assertion request to the `get` webauthn-json function, which will ask the user to verify their identity by connecting an acceptable device (see Figure 7-11):

```
import { get } from '@github/webauthn-json'
import axios from 'axios'
...
const response = await axios.post('/startVerify', { userID })
const assertion = await get({ publicKey: response.data })
```

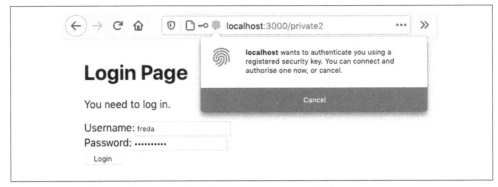

Figure 7-11. The get function asks the user to connect the device

The `get` function returns an assertion object, which contains a signature for the challenge string sent back to the server's */verify* endpoint to check the signature. The response to that call will tell us if the user has correctly verified their identity:

```
import { get } from '@github/webauthn-json'
import axios from 'axios'
...
const response = await axios.post('/startVerify', { userID })
const assertion = await get({ publicKey: response.data })
const resp2 = await axios.post('/verify', { userID, assertion })
if (resp2.data && resp2.data.verified) {
  // User is verified
}
```

Where do we put this code in the application?

The example application is based on the secured-routes recipe.[3] It contains a `SecurityProvider`, which manages the security for all of its child components. The `SecurityProvider` provides a `login` function, which is called with the username and password when the user submits a login form. We'll put the verification code in here:

```
import { useState } from 'react'
import SecurityContext from './SecurityContext'
import { get } from '@github/webauthn-json'
import axios from 'axios'

const SecurityProvider = (props) => {
  const [loggedIn, setLoggedIn] = useState(false)

  return (
    <SecurityContext.Provider
      value={{
        login: async (username, password) => {
```

_____

3 See Recipe 2.6.

```
            const response = await axios.post('/login', {
              username,
              password,
            })
            const { data } = response
            if (data.twoFactorNeeded) {
              const userID = data.userID
              const response = await axios.post('/startVerify', {
                userID,
              })
              const assertion = await get({ publicKey: response.data })
              const resp2 = await axios.post('/verify', {
                userID,
                assertion,
              })
              if (resp2.data && resp2.data.verified) {
                setLoggedIn(true)
              }
            } else {
              setLoggedIn(true)
            }
          },
          logout: async () => {
            await axios.post('/logout')
            setLoggedIn(false)
          },
          loggedIn,
        }}
      >
        {props.children}
      </SecurityContext.Provider>
    )
  }
  export default SecurityProvider
```

We first send the username and password to the */login* endpoint. If the user has registered a security device, the response to the */login* will have a twoFactorNeeded attribute set to true. We can call the */startVerify* endpoint with the user's ID and use the resulting assertion request to ask the user to activate their device. We can send the assertion back to the server. And if all is well, we set loggedIn to true, and the user will then see the page.

Let's look at it in action. We'll assume we've already registered the device against our account. We open the application and click the Account page (see Figure 7-12).

Home

- Public Page
- Private Page 1
- Account page

Figure 7-12. When the application opens, click the Account link

The Account page is secured, so we're asked for a username and password (see Figure 7-13.) In the example application, you can enter **freda** as the username and **mypassword** as the password.

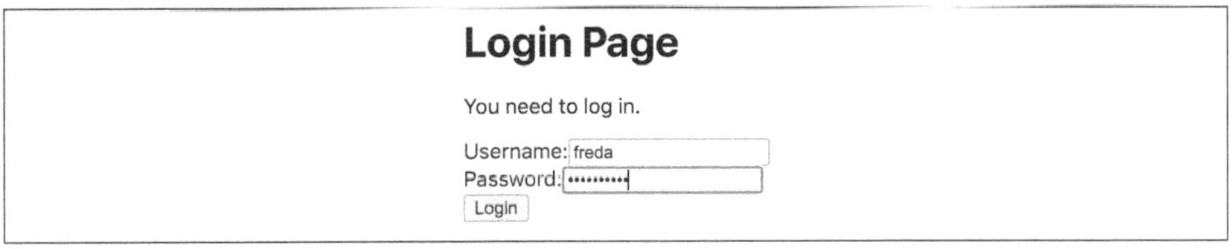

Login Page

You need to log in.

Username: freda
Password: ••••••••••

Login

Figure 7-13. The login form appears

Once we've entered the username and password, the browser asks us to connect the security device (see Figure 7-14).

Figure 7-14. The browser asks the user to activate their security device

If they connect their device and activate it, the user can see the secured page (see Figure 7-15).

Figure 7-15. The Account page is visible once the user has verified their identity

Discussion

As you can probably tell, WebAuthn is quite a complex API. It uses quite obscure language (*attestation* for *registration*, and *assertion* for *verification*) and uses some low-level data types, which fortunately the GitHub webauthn-json allows us to avoid.

The complexity lives on the server. The example server in the downloadable source code uses a library called SimpleWebAuthn to handle most of the cryptological *stuff* for us. If you are planning on using SimpleWebAuthn for the server side of your application, be aware that there is also a client SimpleWebAuthn library that works with it. We've avoided using it in the example client source to avoid making our code too SimpleWebAuthn-specific.

If you implement two-factor authentication, you will need to think about what you will do if a user loses their security device. Technically, all you will have to do to re-enable their account is remove the device that's registered against their name. But it would be best to be extremely careful. A typical attack against two-factor authentication is to call the service desk and pretend to be a user who has lost their token.

Instead, you will need to create a sufficiently rigorous process that will check the identity of any person asking for an account reset.

You can download the source for this recipe from the GitHub site (*https://oreil.ly/Diy5D*).

7.3 Enable HTTPS

Problem

HTTPS is often used in production environments, but there are circumstances where it can be helpful to use HTTPS during development. Some networked services will only work from within pages secured with HTTPS. WebAuthn will only work remotely with HTTPS.[4] Numerous bugs and other issues can creep into your code if your application uses a proxy server with HTTPS.

Enabling HTTPS on production servers is now relatively straightforward,[5] but how do you enable HTTPS on a development server?

Solution

If you've created your application with `create-react-app`, you can enable HTTPS by:

- Generating a self-signed SSL certificate
- Registering the certificate with your development server

To generate a self-signed certificate, we need to understand a little about how HTTPS works.

HTTPS is just HTTP that is tunneled through an encrypted Secure Sockets Layer (SSL) connection. When a browser connects to an HTTPS address, it opens a connection to a secure socket on the server.[6] The server has to provide a certificate from an organization the browser trusts. If the browser accepts the certificate, it will then send encrypted data to the secure socket on the server, which will then be decrypted on the server and forwarded to an HTTP server.

The main difficulty setting up an HTTPS server is getting a certificate that a web browser will trust. Browsers maintain a set of *root certificates*. These are certificates that large, trustworthy organizations issue. When an HTTPS server presents a certificate to a browser, that certificate must be signed by one of the browser's root certificates.

If we want to generate an SSL certificate, we will first need to create a root certificate and tell the browser to trust it. Then we must generate a certificate for our development server that has been signed by the root certificate.

If this sounds complicated, it's because it is.

Let's begin by creating a root certificate. To do this, you will need a tool called OpenSSL installed on your machine.

---

4 It is possible to get around this problem on Android devices by proxying your phone through your development machine. See Recipe 7.7.

5 See the Let's Encrypt site (*https://letsencrypt.org*).

6 By default, this will be on port 443.

We'll use the `openssl` command to create a key file. It will ask you for a passphrase, which you will have to enter twice:

```
$ openssl genrsa -des3 -out mykey.key 2048
Generating RSA private key, 2048 bit long modulus
....................................................+++
.............................+++
e is 65537 (0x10001)
Enter pass phrase for mykey.key:
Verifying - Enter pass phrase for mykey.key:
$
```

The *mykey.key* file now contains a private key, which can be used for encrypting data. We can use the key file to create a certificate file. A certificate file contains information about an organization and an end date after which it is no longer valid.

You can create a certificate using the following command:

```
$ openssl req -x509 -new -nodes -key mykey.key -sha256 -days 2048 -out mypem.pem
Enter pass phrase for mykey.key:
You are about to be asked to enter information that will be incorporated
into your certificate request.
What you are about to enter is what is called a Distinguished Name or a DN.
There are quite a few fields but you can leave some blank
For some fields there will be a default value,
If you enter '.', the field will be left blank.
-----
Country Name (2 letter code) []:US
State or Province Name (full name) []:Massachusetts
Locality Name (eg, city) []:Cambridge
Organization Name (eg, company) []:O'Reilly Media
Organizational Unit Name (eg, section) []:Harmless scribes
Common Name (eg, fully qualified host name) []:Local
Email Address []:me@example.com
$
```

Here we are creating a certificate that will be valid for the next 2,048 days. The passphrase you are asked for is the one you set when you created the *mykey.key* file. It doesn't matter what you enter for the organization details, as you will be using it only on your local machine.

The certificate is stored in a file called *mypem.pem*, and we need to install this file as a root certificate on our machine.[7] There are several ways to install root certificates on your machine.[8] You can use a root certificate to sign website certificates, which is what we'll do next.

---

7 The *.pem* extension stands for Privacy-Enhanced Mail. The PEM format was initially designed for use with email but is now used as a general certificate storage format.

8 For a detailed guide, see this tutorial from BounCA (*https://oreil.ly/9NN1H*).

We'll create a local key file, and a certificate signing request (CSR) file, with the following command:

```
$ openssl req -new -sha256 -nodes -out myprivate.csr -newkey rsa:2048 \
-keyout myprivate.key \
-subj "/C=US/ST=Massachusetts/L=Cambridge/O=O'Reilly \
Media/OU=Harmless scribes/CN=Local/emailAddress=me@example.com"
Generating a 2048 bit RSA private key
...................+++
..+++
writing new private key to 'myprivate.key'
-----
$
```

Next, create a file called `extfile.txt`, containing the following:

```
authorityKeyIdentifier=keyid,issuer
basicConstraints=CA:FALSE
keyUsage=digitalSignature,nonRepudiation,keyEncipherment,dataEncipherment
subjectAltName=DNS:localhost
```

We can now run a command that will generate an SSL certificate for our application:

```
$ openssl x509 -req -in myprivate.csr -CA mypem.pem -CAkey mykey.key \
-CAcreateserial -out \
myprivate.crt -days 500 -sha256 -extfile ./extfile.txt
Signature ok
subject=/C=US/ST=Massachusetts/L=Cambridge/O=O'Reilly
Media/OU=Harmless scribes/CN=Local/
emailAddress=me@example.com
Getting CA Private Key
Enter pass phrase for mykey.key:
$
```

Remember, the passphrase is the one you created when you first created the *mykey.key* file.

The result of going through all of those steps is that we have two files that we can use to secure our development server:

- The *myprivate.crt* file is a certificate signed by the root certificate, which is the file that reassures the browser that it can trust our application
- The *myprivate.key* file will be used to encrypt connections between the development server and the browser.

If you created your application with `create-react-app`, you could enable HTTPS by putting this in a `.env` file in your application directory:

```
HTTPS=true
SSL_CRT_FILE=myprivate.crt
SSL_KEY_FILE=myprivate.key
```

If you restart your server, you should be able to access your application at *https://localhost:3000* instead of *http://localhost:3000*.

Discussion

Self-signed certificates are pretty complex things to create, but there are circumstances when they are required. However, even if you don't need to run HTTPS in your development environment, it can still be worth understanding what HTTPS is, how it works, and why you should trust it.

You can download the source for this recipe from the GitHub site (*https://oreil.ly/BAKAE*).

7.4 Authenticate with Fingerprints

Problem

Recipe 7.2 looked at how physical tokens, such as YubiKeys, can be used for two-factor authentication. But physical tokens are still relatively rare and can be pretty expensive. Most people already have mobile devices, such as cell phones and tablets. Many of those have built-in fingerprint sensors. But how can we get a React application to use a fingerprint sensor for two-factor authentication?

Solution

We can use fingerprint sensors as WebAuthn authentication tokens. They connect to the API in the same way, although several configuration changes are required.

This recipe is based on Recipe 7.2 for using removable tokens for two-factor authentication. We saw in Recipe 7.2 that there are two main flows in WebAuthn authentication:

Attestation
> In this flow, the user registers a device or token against their account. One way to do this is by pressing the fingerprint sensor on their phone.

Assertion
> In this flow, the user activates the device or token, and the server checks that it matches the device or token that was previously registered.

Both attestation and assertion have three stages:

1. The server generates a request.
2. The user uses the token, which generates a response.

3. The response is sent to the server.

If we want to switch from using a removable physical token to using the built-in fingerprint sensor in a device, we will only need to change the attestation request stage. The attestation request says what kind of token the browser can register for a user. For removable physical tokens, like YubiKeys, we generated an attestation request that looked like this:

```
{
    "rpName": "Physical Token Server",
    "rpID": "localhost",
    "userID": "1234",
    "userName": "freda",
    "excludeCredentials": [
        {"id": "existingKey1", "type": "public-key"}
    ],
    "authenticatorSelection": {
        "userVerification": "discouraged"
    },
    "extensions": {
        "credProps": true,
    },
}
```

We need to change this slightly to allow the user to use a fingerprint sensor:

```
{
    "rpName": "Physical Token Server",
    "rpID": "localhost",
    "userID": "1234",
    "userName": "freda",
    "excludeCredentials": [
        {"id": "existingKey1", "type": "public-key"}
    ],
    "authenticatorSelection": {
        "authenticatorAttachment": "platform",
        "userVerification": "required"
    },
    "attestation": "direct",
    "extensions": {
        "credProps": true,
    },
}
```

The two requests are almost the same. The first change is in the authenticator selection. We now want to use a `platform` authenticator because fingerprint sensors are built into the device and not removable, which means we effectively limit the user to their current physical device. In contrast, a YubiKey can be disconnected from one machine and then connected to another.

We're also saying that we want to use direct attestation, which means we won't require any additional verification. For example, we won't be asking the user to press the fingerprint sensor and then enter a PIN.

Beyond changing this initial attestation request object, all of the other code remains the same. Once a user responds to the attestation request by pressing the fingerprint sensor, it will generate a public key that we can store against the user. When the user logs back in and confirms their identity by pressing the fingerprint sensor, it will sign the challenge string in the same way that a YubiKey would.

Therefore, if you're going to support one type of authenticator, it's worth allowing the user to use both fingerprint sensors and removable tokens.

Unless a user has a removable token that also works on mobile devices—for example, by using Near-Field Communication (NFC)—it's unlikely that any user will register both removable tokens and fingerprints. As soon as they have registered a fingerprint, they won't be able to log in and register a removable token, and vice versa.

Here is the updated component that allows a user to register a token:

```
import { useState } from 'react'
import Logout from './Logout'
import axios from 'axios'
import { create } from '@github/webauthn-json'

const Private2 = () => {
  const [busy, setBusy] = useState(false)
  const [message, setMessage] = useState()

  const registerToken = async (startRegistrationEndpoint) => {
    setBusy(true)
    try {
      const response = await axios.post(startRegistrationEndpoint)
      setMessage('Send response')
      const attestation = await create({ publicKey: response.data })
      setMessage('Create attestation')
      const attestationResponse = await axios.post('/register', {
        attestation,
      })
      setMessage('registered!')
      if (
        attestationResponse.data &&
        attestationResponse.data.verified
      ) {
        alert('New key registered')
      }
    } catch (err) {
```

```
      setMessage('' + err)
    } finally {
      setBusy(false)
    }
  }
}
  return (
    <div className="Private2">
      <h1>Account page</h1>

      {window.PublicKeyCredential && (
        <>
          <p>Register new hardware key</p>
          <button
            onClick={() => registerToken('/startRegister')}
            disabled={busy}
          >
            Register Removable Token
          </button>
          <button
            onClick={() => registerToken('/startFingerprint')}
            disabled={busy}
          >
            Register Fingerprint
          </button>
        </>
      )}
      <div className="Account-message">{message}</div>

      <Logout />
    </div>
  )
}
```

```
export default Private2
```

We're calling a slightly different endpoint when we want to register a fingerprint. Otherwise, the rest of the code remains the same.

To try it, you'll need to use a device with a fingerprint sensor. We can only use WebAuthn if we run the application on *localhost* or a remote server using HTTPS. To test this code from a mobile device, you will need to configure HTTPS on your development server (see Recipe 7.3), or you will need to configure your device to proxy *localhost* connections to your development machine (see Recipe 7.7).

To run the example application, you will need to change into the application directory and start the development server with the following:

```
$ npm run start
```

You will also need to run the API server. Open a separate terminal for this and then run it from the *server* subdirectory:

```
$ cd server
$ npm run start
```

The development server will run on port 3000 and the API server on port 5000. The development server will proxy API requests to the API server.

When you open the application, you should click the "Account page" link (see Figure 7-16).

Figure 7-16. Click the "Account page" link on the home page

The application will ask you to sign in. Enter the username **freda** and the password **mypassword** (see Figure 7-17). These values have been hardcoded in the example server.

*Figure 7-17. Enter **freda/mypassword** into the login form*

You will now see two buttons for registering tokens against your account: one for removable tokens, the other for fingerprints (see Figure 7-18).

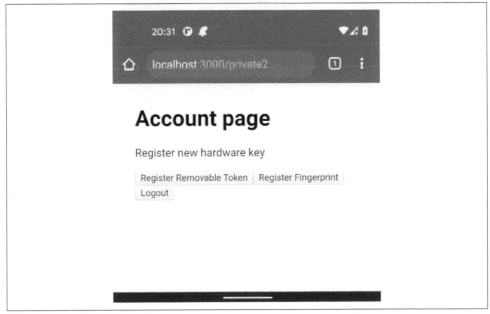

Figure 7-18. There are buttons to register removable tokens and fingerprints

---

Press the button to register a fingerprint. Your mobile device will ask you to press the fingerprint sensor. Your fingerprint sensor will generate a public key that the application can store against the *freda* account. A message box will appear to tell you when this has been done, as shown in Figure 7-19.

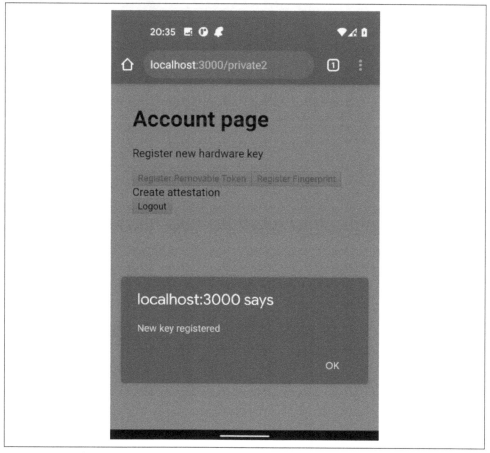

Figure 7-19. The application will confirm when the token is registered

Now log out. When you log back in again, enter **freda** and **mypassword** in the form. The application will now ask you to confirm your identity by pressing the fingerprint sensor, and it will then log you back in.

Discussion

Built-in fingerprint sensors are much more common than removable tokens like YubiKeys. There is a difference in the usage pattern of the two devices. YubiKeys can be moved from device to device, whereas fingerprints are typically limited to a single device.[9] Removable tokens, therefore, have additional flexibility for users who might want to connect from several devices. The downside to removable devices is that they are far easier to lose than a cell phone. In most cases, it is worth supporting both types of devices and leaving it to the users to decide which option is best for them.

You can download the source for this recipe from the GitHub site (*https://oreil.ly/ m8hs6*).

7.5 Use Confirmation Logins

Problem

Sometimes a user might want to perform operations that are more dangerous or are not easily reversible. They might want to delete data, remove a user account, or do something that will send an email. How do you prevent a malicious third party from carrying out these operations if they find a logged-in but unattended machine?

Solution

Many systems force users to confirm their login credentials before being able to perform sensitive operations. You will most likely want to do this for several operations, so it would be helpful if there was a way of doing the confirmation centrally.

We'll base this recipe on the code for the secured routes in Recipe 2.6. In that recipe, we built a `SecurityProvider` component that provided `login` and `logout` functions to its child components:

```
import { useState } from 'react'
import SecurityContext from './SecurityContext'

const SecurityProvider = (props) => {
  const [loggedIn, setLoggedIn] = useState(false)

  return (
    <SecurityContext.Provider
      value={{
        login: (username, password) => {
          // Note to engineering team:
          // Maybe make this more secure...
          if (username === 'fred' && password === 'password') {
            setLoggedIn(true)
          }
        },
        logout: () => setLoggedIn(false),
        loggedIn,
```

---

9 An exception would be if the user has connected an external fingerprint sensor.

```
      }}
    >
      {props.children}
    </SecurityContext.Provider>
  )
}

export default SecurityProvider
```

Components that needed to use the `login` and `logout` functions could access them from the `useSecurity` hook:

```
const security = useSecurity()
...
// Anywhere that we need to logout...
security.logout()
```

For this recipe, we'll add an extra function to `SecurityProvider` that will allow a child component to confirm that the user is logged in. Once they've provided the username and password, we allow them to perform the dangerous operation.

We could do this by creating a function that accepts a callback function containing the dangerous operation, which the application calls after the user confirms their login details. This function will be easier to implement in the `SecurityProvider` but will have some issues when we call it from a component. We could return a success/failure flag:

```
// We WON'T do it like this
confirmLogin((success) => {
    if (success) {
        // Do dangerous thing here
    } else {
        // Handle the user canceling the login
    }
})
```

This approach has the disadvantage that if you forget to check the value of the `suc cess` flag, the code will perform the dangerous operation, even if the user cancels the login form.

Alternatively, we will have to pass two separate callbacks: one for success and one for cancellation:

```
// We WON'T do it like this either
confirmLogin(
    () => {
        // Do dangerous thing here
    },
    () => {
        // Handle the user canceling the login
    });
```

However, this code is a little ugly.

Instead, we'll implement the code with a promise, which will make the implementation more complex, but it will simplify any code that calls it.

This is a version of `SecurityProvider`, complete with the new `confirmLogin` function:

```
import { useRef, useState } from 'react'
import SecurityContext from './SecurityContext'
import LoginForm from './LoginForm'

export default (props) => {
  const [showLogin, setShowLogin] = useState(false)
  const [loggedIn, setLoggedIn] = useState(false)
  const resolver = useRef()
  const rejecter = useRef()

  const onLogin = async (username, password) => {
    // Note to engineering team:
    // Maybe make this more secure...
    if (username === 'fred' && password === 'password') {
      setLoggedIn(true)
    }
  }
  const onConfirmLogin = async (username, password) => {
    // Note to engineering team:
    // Same here...
    return username === 'fred' && password === 'password'
  }

  return (
    <SecurityContext.Provider
      value={{
        login: onLogin,
        confirmLogin: async (callback) => {
          setShowLogin(true)
          return new Promise((res, rej) => {
            resolver.current = res
            rejecter.current = rej
          })
        },
        logout: () => setLoggedIn(false),
        loggedIn,
      }}
    >
      {showLogin ? (
        <LoginForm
          onLogin={async (username, password) => {
            const valid = await onConfirmLogin(username, password)
            if (valid) {
              setShowLogin(false)
```

```
              resolver.current()
            }
          }}
          onCancel={() => {
            setShowLogin(false)
            rejecter.current()
          }}
        />
      ) : null}
      {props.children}
    </SecurityContext.Provider>
  )
}
```

If the user calls the `confirmLogin` function, the `SecurityProvider` will display a login form to allow the user to confirm their username and password. The `confirm Login` function returns a promise that will resolve only if the user types in the username and password correctly. If the user cancels the login form, the promise will be rejected.

We're not showing the details of the `LoginForm` component here, but you can find it in the downloadable source for this recipe.

Our example code here checks the username and password against static strings to see if they're correct. In your version of the code, you will replace this with a call to some security service.

 When we call the `confirmLogin`, we're storing the promise in a *ref*. Refs commonly point to elements in the DOM, but you can use them to store any piece of state. Unlike `useState`, refs will update immediately. In general, it's not good practice to use a lot of refs in your code, and we're only using them here so we can record the promise immediately, without waiting for a `useState` operation to finish.

How would you use the `confirmLogin` function in practice? Let's say we have a component that contains a button that performs some dangerous operation:

```
import { useState } from 'react'
import Logout from './Logout'

const Private1 = () => {
  const [message, setMessage] = useState()

  const doDangerousThing = () => {
    setMessage('DANGEROUS ACTION!')
  }

  return (
```

```
  <div className="Private1">
    <h1>Private page 1</h1>

    <button
      onClick={() => {
        doDangerousThing()
      }}
    >
      Do dangerous thing
    </button>

    <p className="message">{message}</p>

    <Logout />
  </div>
  )
}

export default Private1
```

If we want the user to confirm their login details before performing this operation, we can first get hold of the context provided by the `SecurityProvider`:

```
const security = useSecurity()
```

In the code that performs the dangerous operation, we can then `await` the promise returned by `confirmLogin`:

```
const security = useSecurity()
...
await security.confirmLogin()
setMessage('DANGEROUS ACTION!')
```

The code following the call to `confirmLogin` will run only if the user provides the correct username and password.

If the user cancels the login dialog, the promise will be rejected, and we can handle the cancellation in a `catch` block.

Here is a modified version of the component performing dangerous code that now confirms the user's login before proceeding:

```
import { useState } from 'react'
import Logout from './Logout'
import useSecurity from './useSecurity'

export default () => {
  const security = useSecurity()
  const [message, setMessage] = useState()

  const doDangerousThing = async () => {
    try {
      await security.confirmLogin()
```

```
        setMessage('DANGEROUS ACTION!')
      } catch (err) {
        setMessage('DANGEROUS ACTION CANCELLED!')
      }
    }

    return (
      <div className="Private1">
        <h1>Private page 1</h1>

        <button
          onClick={() => {
            doDangerousThing()
          }}
        >
          Do dangerous thing
        </button>

        <p className="message">{message}</p>

        <Logout />
      </div>
    )
  }
```

If we try the code, we will first need to run the application from the app directory:

```
$ npm run start
```

When the application opens (see Figure 7-20), you will need to click Private Page 1.

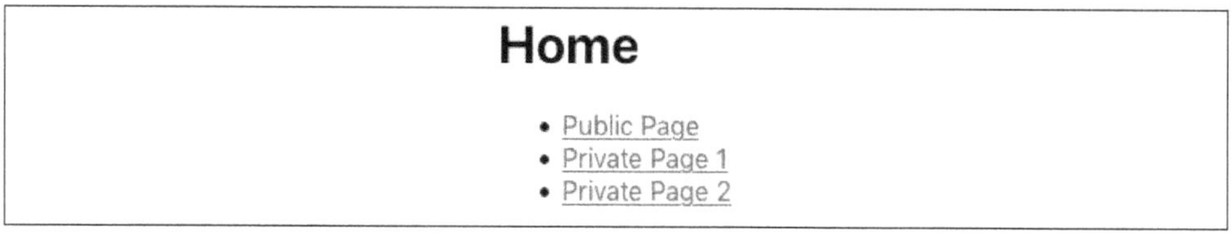

Home

- Public Page
- Private Page 1
- Private Page 2

Figure 7-20. Begin by clicking the Private Page 1 link

The application will then ask you to log in (see Figure 7-21.) You should log in with *fred/password*.

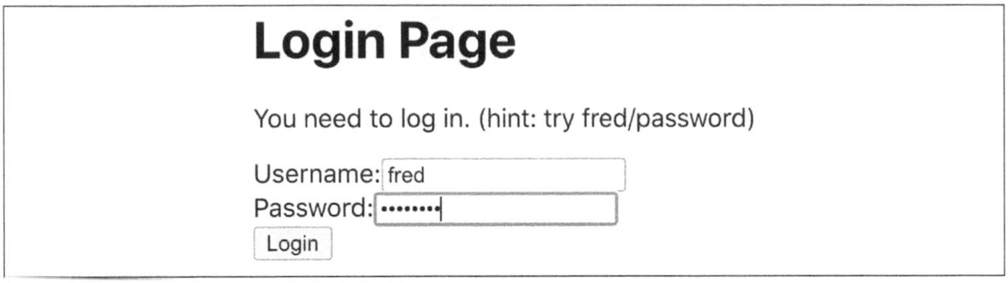

Login Page

You need to log in. (hint: try fred/password)

Username: fred
Password: ••••••••
[Login]

Figure 7-21. The page is secured, so you will need to log in

If you now click the button to perform the dangerous operation, you will need to confirm your credentials before continuing (as shown in Figure 7-22).

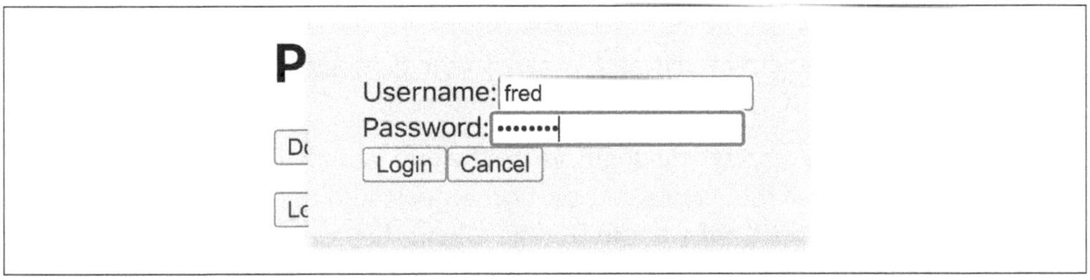

P

Username: fred
Password: ••••••••
[Login] [Cancel]

D(

L(

Figure 7-22. You must confirm your login details before continuing

Discussion

This recipe centralizes your confirmation code in the `SecurityProvider`, which has an advantage: not only does this lighten the code in our components, but it means that user confirmation can take place inside custom hooks. If you abstract a set of operations into some hook-based service,[10] you can also include the confirmation logic in that service. As a result, your components will be completely unaware of which operations are dangerous and which are not.

You can download the source for this recipe from the GitHub site (*https://oreil.ly/zP75q*).

7.6 Use Single-Factor Authentication

Problem

We've already seen that removable tokens and fingerprints can be used in a two-factor authentication system to provide additional security to a user's account.

---

10 For an example of such a service, see the `useForum` hook in Recipe 5.2.

However, you can also use them as a simple login convenience. Many mobile applications allow a user to log in by pressing the fingerprint sensor without entering a username or password.

How do you enable single-factor authentication for a React application?

Solution

Security tokens, such as fingerprint sensors and USB devices like YubiKeys, need to be recorded against a user account on the server. The problem with single-factor authentication is that we don't know who the user is supposed to be when they tap the fingerprint sensor. In a two-factor system, they have just typed their username into a form. But in a single-factor system, we need to know who the user is supposed to be when we create the assertion request.[11]

We can avoid this problem by setting a cookie in the browser containing the user ID whenever a person with a token-enabled account logs in.[12]

When the application displays the login form, the app can check for the existence of the cookie and then use it to create an assertion request and ask the user for the security token. If the user does not want to use the token, they can cancel the request and simply use the login form.[13]

 User IDs are often machine-generated internal keys, which contain no secure information. However, if your user IDs are more easily identifiable, such as an email address, you should not use this approach.

We're basing the code for this recipe on the secured routes code from Recipe 2.6. We manage all of our security through a wrapper component called `SecurityProvider`. This provides child components with `login` and `logout` functions. We'll add another functions called `loginWithToken`:

```
import { useState } from 'react'
import SecurityContext from './SecurityContext'
import { get } from '@github/webauthn-json'
```

---

11 The assertion request is needed when the browser asks the user to scan their fingerprint or activate their token. It includes a list of all acceptable devices and so will be unique to a given user.

12 A consequence of this approach is that the user will perform single-factor authentication on the browser only where they registered the token. If they use a different browser or have recently cleared their cookies, they will have to fall back to using the login form.

13 This assumes that you are using a cookie that is readable by JavaScript. It's also possible to use an HTTP-only cookie, which only the server (or service workers) can read. If you use an HTTP-only cookie, you will need code on the server to check whether the user should provide a token.

```
import axios from 'axios'

const SecurityProvider = (props) => {
  const [loggedIn, setLoggedIn] = useState(false)

  return (
    <SecurityContext.Provider
      value={{
        login: async (username, password) => {
          const response = await axios.post('/login', {
            username,
            password,
          })
          setLoggedIn(true)
        },
        loginWithToken: async (userID) => {
          const response = await axios.post('/startVerify', {
            userID,
          })
          const assertion = await get({ publicKey: response.data })
          await axios.post('/verify', { userID, assertion })
          setLoggedIn(true)
        },
        logout: async () => {
          await axios.post('/logout')
          setLoggedIn(false)
        },
        loggedIn,
      }}
    >
      {props.children}
    </SecurityContext.Provider>
  )
}
export default SecurityProvider
```

The `loginWithToken` accepts a user ID and then asks the user to verify their identity with a token by:

1. Calling a `startVerify` function on the server to create an assertion request
2. Passing the request to WebAuthn to ask the user to press the fingerprint sensor
3. Passing the generated assertion back to an endpoint called `verify` to check that the token is valid

You will need to replace the `startVerify` and `verify` endpoints in your implementation.

To call the `loginWithToken` function in `SecurityProvider`, we will need to find the current user's ID from the cookies. We'll do this by installing the `js-cookie` library:

```
$ npm install js-cookie
```

This will allow us to read a `userID` cookie like this:

```
import Cookies from 'js-cookie'
...
const userIDCookie = Cookies.get('userID')
```

We can now use this code in a `Login` component, which will check for a `userID` cookie. If one exists, it will ask to log in by token. Otherwise, it will allow the user to log in using a username and password:

```
import { useEffect, useState } from 'react'
import useSecurity from './useSecurity'
import Cookies from 'js-cookie'

const Login = () => {
  const { login, loginWithToken } = useSecurity()
  const [username, setUsername] = useState()
  const [password, setPassword] = useState()
  const userIDCookie = Cookies.get('userID')

  useEffect(() => {
    ;(async () => {
      if (userIDCookie) {
        loginWithToken(userIDCookie)
      }
    })()
  }, [userIDCookie])

  return (
    <div>
      <h1>Login Page</h1>

      <p>You need to log in.</p>

      <label htmlFor="username">Username:</label>
      <input
        id="username"
        name="username"
        type="text"
        value={username}
        onChange={(evt) => setUsername(evt.target.value)}
      />

      <br />
      <label htmlFor="password">Password:</label>
      <input
        id="password"
        name="password"
        type="password"
        value={password}
        onChange={(evt) => setPassword(evt.target.value)}
```

```
      />

      <br />
      <button onClick={() => login(username, password)}>Login</button>
    </div>
  )
}
```

```
export default Login
```

Let's try the example application. We must first start the development server from the application directory:

```
$ npm run start
```

Then in a separate terminal, we can start the example API server:

```
$ cd server
$ npm run start
```

The development server runs on port 3000; the API server runs on port 5000.

When the application starts, click the link to the Account page (as shown in Figure 7-23).

Home

- Public Page
- Private Page 1
- Private Page 2

Figure 7-23. When the app opens, click the link to the Account page

The application asks us to log in (see Figure 7-24). Use the username **freda** and the password **mypassword**.

Login Page

You need to log in.

Username: freda
Password: •••••••••••
Login

*Figure 7-24. Log in with **freda/mypassword***

The account page asks if we want to enable login with a fingerprint sensor or physical token (see Figure 7-25). You can register a token and then log out.

Figure 7-25. Choose to enable login with a physical token or fingerprint

The next time we log in, we will immediately see the request to activate a token (see Figure 7-26).

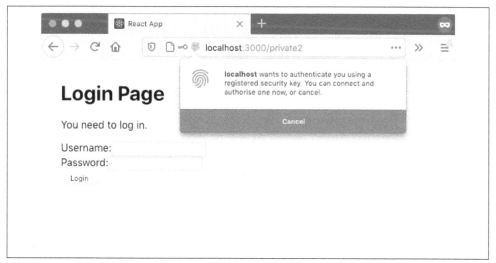

Figure 7-26. Once enabled, you can log in with just the token

If we activate the token, we will log in without providing a username and password.

Discussion

It's important to note that single-factor authentication is about increasing convenience rather than security. Fingerprint sensors are particularly convenient, as logging in literally involves moving one finger.

You should always provide the ability to fall back to using the login form. Doing so will not reduce the security of your application, as a wily hacker could delete the cookie and fall back to using the form anyway.

You can download the source for this recipe from the GitHub site (*https://oreil.ly/ 4ZDh6*).

7.7 Test on an Android Device

Problem

You can perform most mobile browser testing with a desktop browser simulating the appearance of a mobile device (see Figure 7-27).

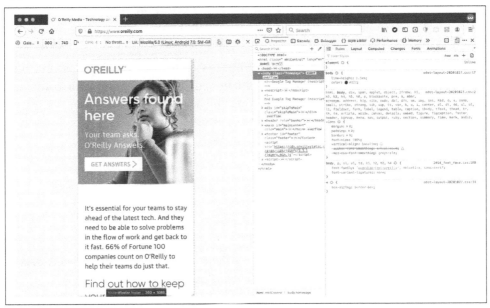

Figure 7-27. You can use a desktop browser for most mobile testing

But there are times when it is best to test a React application on a physical mobile device, which is usually not a problem; the mobile device can access the React application remotely using the IP address of the development machine.

There are, however, circumstances where that is not true:

- Your mobile device might not be able to connect to the same network as your development machine.
- You might be using a technology, such as WebAuthn, that requires HTTPS for domains other than *localhost*.

Is it possible to configure a mobile device to access a React app as if it is running on *localhost*, even though it is running on a separate machine?

Solution

This recipe will look at how we can proxy the network on an Android-based device so that connections to *localhost* will go to the server on your development machine.

The first thing you'll need is an Android device that has USB debugging enabled (*https://oreil.ly/fc5Fv*). You will also need a copy of the Android SDK (*https://oreil.ly/BFeXr*) installed, which will allow you to use a tool called the *Android Debug Bridge* (ADB). The ADB opens a communication channel between your development machine and an Android device.

You will then need to connect your Android device to your development machine with a USB cable and ensure that the `adb` command is available on your command path.[14] You can then list the Android devices connected to your machine:

```
$ adb devices
* daemon not running; starting now at tcp:5037
* daemon started successfully
List of devices attached
25PRIFFEJZWWDFWO        device
$
```

Here you can see there is a single device connected, with a device ID of `25PRIF FEJZWWDFWO`.

You can now use the `adb` command to configure a proxy on the Android device, which will redirect all HTTP traffic to its internal port 3000:

```
$ adb shell settings put global http_proxy localhost:3000
```

 If you have more than one Android device connected to your machine, you will need to specify its device ID with the `adb` option `-s <device-id>`.

You will next need to tell `adb` to run a proxy service on the Android device, which will forward any traffic from port 3000 on the device to port 3000 on the development machine:

```
$ adb reverse tcp:3000 tcp:3000
```

If you now open a browser on the Android device and tell it to go to *http://localhost:3000*, it will display the app running on your development machine, as if it's running inside the device (see Figure 7-28).

---

14 You will need to locate the Android SDK installed on your machine. You can find the `adb` command in a subdirectory within this installation.

Figure 7-28. If you open a mobile browser to localhost, it will connect to the development machine

Once you have finished using the app, you will need to disable the proxy setting on the Android device.

 If you fail to disable the proxy on the Android device, it will no longer access the network.

You can do this by resetting the proxy back to :0:

```
$ adb shell settings put global http_proxy :0
```

Discussion

This recipe requires a lot of work the first time you use it because it involves installing an entire Android SDK on your development machine. But then it will be straightforward to connect and disconnect real Android devices to your machine.

7.8 Check Security with ESlint

Problem

Just a few common coding issues frequently cause security threats in JavaScript. You can decide to create a set of coding standards that will avoid those errors. However, you will need to frequently review the standards to keep them up-to-date with the latest changes in technology, and you will also need to introduce slow and expensive code review processes.

Is there a way to check for poor security practices in code that will not slow down your development processes?

Solution

One way to introduce security reviews is to try to automate them. One tool that will allow you to do this is `eslint`. If you've created your application with a tool like `create-react-app`, you have probably already got `eslint` installed. In fact, `create-react-app` runs `eslint` each time it restarts its development server. If you've ever seen coding issues highlighted in the terminal, that output has come from `eslint`:

```
Compiled with warnings.

src/App.js
  Line 5:9:  'x' is assigned a value but never used  no-unused-vars

Search for the keywords to learn more about each warning.
To ignore, add // eslint-disable-next-line to the line before.
```

If you don't have `eslint` installed, you can install it through npm:

```
$ npm install --save-dev eslint
```

Once installed, you can initialize it like this:

```
$ node_modules/.bin/eslint --init
- How would you like to use ESLint? · problems
- What type of modules does your project use? · esm
- Which framework does your project use? · react
- Does your project use TypeScript? · No / Yes
- Where does your code run? · browser
- What format do you want your config file to be in? · JavaScript
Local ESLint installation not found.
The config that you've selected requires the following dependencies:

eslint-plugin-react@latest eslint@latest
- Would you like to install them now with npm? · No / Yes
$
```

Remember: you don't need to initialize `eslint` if you're using `create-react-app`; it's already done for you.

At this point, you could choose to write your own set of `eslint` rules to check for breaches of any security practices. However, it's far easier to install an `eslint` plugin with a set of security rules already written for you.

For example, let's install the `eslint-plugin-react-security` package, which is created and managed by Slyk (*https://slyk.io*):

```
$ npm install --save-dev eslint-plugin-react-security
```

Once installed, we can enable this plugin by editing the `eslintConfig` section of *package.json* (if you're using `create-react-app`) or the *eslintrc** file in your app directory.

You should change it from this:

```
"eslintConfig": {
  "extends": [
    "react-app",
    "react-app/jest"
  ]
},
```

to this:

```
"eslintConfig": {
  "extends": [
    "react-app",
    "react-app/jest"
  ],
  "plugins": [
    "react-security"
  ],
  "rules": {
    "react-security/no-javascript-urls": "warn",
    "react-security/no-dangerously-set-innerhtml": "warn",
    "react-security/no-find-dom-node": "warn",
    "react-security/no-refs": "warn"
  }
},
```

This change will enable four rules from the React Security plugin.

To check that they work, let's add some code to an application that will contravene the *no-dangerously-set-innerhtml* rule:

```
import logo from './logo.svg'
import './App.css'

function App() {
  return (
```

```
      <div className="App">
        <header className="App-header">
          <img src={logo} className="App-logo" alt="logo" />
          <p>
            Edit <code>src/App.js</code> and save to reload.
          </p>
          <div
            dangerouslySetInnerHTML={{
              __html: '<p>This is a bad idea</p>',
            }}
          />
          <a
            className="App-link"
            href="https://reactjs.org"
            target="_blank"
            rel="noopener noreferrer"
          >
            Learn React
          </a>
        </header>
      </div>
    )
  }

export default App
```

If you've installed eslint manually, you can now scan this file with:

```
$ node_modules/.bin/eslint src/App.js
```

If you're using create-react-app, you just need to restart the server to ensure that it reloads the eslint config:

```
Compiled with warnings.

src/App.js
  Line 12:16:  dangerouslySetInnerHTML prop usage detected
               react-security/no-dangerously-set-innerhtml

Search for the keywords to learn more about each warning.
To ignore, add // eslint-disable-next-line to the line before.
```

Discussion

If you have a team of developers, you might also want to run the eslint checks using a Git *pre-commit* hook to prevent developers from ever checking in code that fails the audit. A Git hook will give faster feedback to the developer and prevent them from failing the build for everyone else.

If you want to configure pre-commit hooks through your *package.json* file, consider installing Husky code hooks (*https://oreil.ly/uEjix*).

Another advantage of automating your security checks is that you can add them to your build-and-deploy pipeline. If you run the checks at the start of the pipeline, you can reject a commit immediately and notify the developer.

You can download the source for this recipe from the GitHub site (*https://oreil.ly/ kvBcS*).

7.9 Make Login Forms Browser Friendly

Problem

Many security solutions rely on username/password forms, but several usability traps are easy to fall into when creating them. On some devices, automated capitalization and autocorrect can corrupt usernames and passwords in an attempt to be helpful. Some browsers will attempt to autocomplete username fields, but it is often unclear what rules they use, so autocomplete works on some sites but not others.

What practices should you follow when building login forms so that they will work with the browser rather than against it?

Solution

Several HTML attributes can significantly improve the usability of your login forms.

First, it can be useful to disable autocorrect for username fields. Autocorrect is frequently applied on mobile devices to compensate for the small keyboards and the spelling mistakes that inevitably occur. But autocorrect is of little use when typing usernames. You can disable autocorrect using the `autoCorrect` attribute:

```
<input autoCorrect="off"/>
```

Next, if your username is an email address, consider setting the `type` to `email`, which might launch an email-specific keyboard on mobile devices. Some browsers may even show recent email addresses in an autocomplete window or in the header of an email-specific keyboard:

```
<input type="email"/>
```

You might also consider using `j_username` as the `id` and `name` of the username field. Why? It's because Java-based applications commonly have fields named `j_username`, and so the user is likely to have provided a `j_username` value in the past. This increases the likelihood that the browser might offer the email address in an autocomplete window:

```
<input id="j_username" name="j_username"/>
```

You can explicitly say that a field represents a username field, making it *very* likely that you will trigger an autocomplete response from the browser:

```
<input autoComplete="username"/>
```

Now, what to do about passwords?

First, always set the type to password:

```
<input type="password"/>
```

Never be tempted to reproduce the visual appearance of a password field in some other way, for example, by custom CSS styling. Doing so will prevent the browser from applying standard security features to the password field, such as disabling the copy function inside it. Also, if you don't set the type to password, the browser will not offer to store the value in its password manager.

There are two types of password fields: for current passwords (when logging in) and for new passwords (when signing up or changing a password).

Why is this relevant? It's because the HTML autoComplete attribute can indicate to the browser how you intend to use the password field.

If it's a login form, you will want to say that the password is a current-password:

```
<input type="password" autoComplete="current-password"/>
```

If it's a registration or change password form, you should set it to new-password:

```
<input type="password" autoComplete="new-password"/>
```

This value will encourage the browser to autocomplete stored passwords in a login form. It will also trigger any built-in or third-party password generation tools.

Finally, avoid using wizard-style login screens (see Figure 7-29 for an example from the *Washington Post*).

Browsers are less likely to recognize a single username field as a login form and so are less likely to offer to complete the details for you.

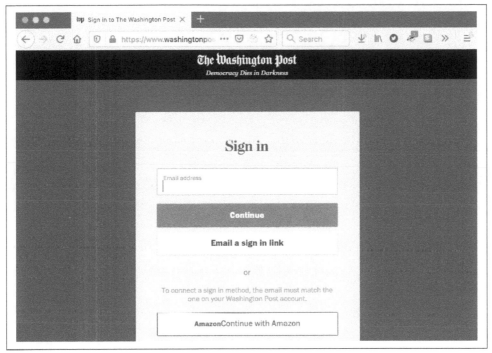

Figure 7-29. Multistep forms can prevent a browser from using autocomplete

Discussion

The `autocomplete` attribute has many other seldom-used values for several types of form fields, from address details and phone numbers to credit card numbers. For further information, see the Mozilla development site (*https://oreil.ly/TLHLF*).

CHAPTER 8

Testing

In this chapter, we'll look at various techniques for testing your React applications. In general, we've found that it is a bad idea to be too prescriptive about the precise mix of tests you should have. A good guiding principle is to follow these two rules:

- Never write code unless you have a failing test.
- If a test passes the first time you run it, delete it.

These two rules will help you build code that works while avoiding creating redundant tests that provide little value.

We have found that early in a project, it is easier to write more browser-based tests. These tests tend to be higher-level and help capture the principal business requirements for an application. Later, when the application's architecture starts to emerge and stabilize, it becomes easier to write more unit tests of individual components. They are faster to write and quicker to run, and once you have a stable structure to your code, you will not need to update them continuously.

Sometimes it's worth loosening the definition of what a test *is*. When you are working on layout code, whose primary value is visual, you might consider a Storybook story to be a "test." The assertion is done by your eye, looking at the component as you create. Of course, this kind of test will not automatically pick up regression failures, but we present a technique in a recipe that will allow you to turn these visual checks into actual automated tests.

If you write tests *before* you write code, you will find that tests are tools for design. They will become executable examples of how you would like your application to work.

Instead, if you write tests *after* you write the code, they will be simply artifacts. Pieces of code that you must slavishly create because they feel like the sorts of things a professional developer should write.

We focus on four tools in this chapter: the React Testing Library, Storybook, the Selenium library, and Cypress.

The React Testing Library is an excellent way of creating very detailed unit tests.

Storybook is a gallery tool that we have looked at previously. We include it in this chapter because a gallery is a set of code examples, which is also what tests are. You will find ways of using Storybook as part of your testing/development process.

Selenium is one of the most established libraries for testing your application in a real browser.

Finally, what is quickly becoming our favorite tool for testing: Cypress. Cypress is similar to Selenium in that it runs inside a browser. But it includes a whole host of additional features, such as test replays, generated videos of test runnings, and a significantly simpler programming model. If you use only one tool from this chapter, let it be Cypress.

8.1 Use the React Testing Library

Problem

There are many ways that you can test a React application. Early on in a project, when you are still defining an application's essential purpose and function, you might choose to create tests in some very high-level form, such as Cucumber tests (*https://cucumber.io*). If you are looking at some isolated piece of the system (such as creating and maintaining a data item), you might want to create functional tests using a tool like Cypress.

But if you are deep into the detail of creating a single component, then you will probably want to create unit tests. *Unit tests* are so-called because they attempt to test a single piece of code as an isolated unit. While it's debatable whether *unit test* is the correct term for testing components (which often contain subcomponents and so are not isolated), it's the name usually applied to tests of components that you can test outside of a browser.

But how do you unit test React components? There have historically been several approaches. Early unit tests relied on rendering the component into an HTML string, which required minimal testing infrastructure, but there were multiple downsides:

- Handling re-renders when the component state changed.
- Making assertions on HTML elements that the test must parse from the string.

- To test UI interactions, you need to mock the event model.

It was not long before developers created libraries to take care of the details of each of these problems.

However, tests created in this way lacked the reality of tests created in browsers. The subtleties of the interaction between the virtual *Document Object Model* (DOM) and the browser DOM were lost. Often subcomponents were not rendered to reduce the complexity of the tests.

The result was that React applications often had few unit tests. Developers would refactor their code to move complex logic into easily testable JavaScript functions. Developers would have to test anything more complex with a real browser, leading to slower tests. Because they were slow, developers would be discouraged from testing too many scenarios.

So how can you unit test React components realistically without the overhead of launching the entire app and running the tests in a real browser?

Solution

The Testing Library by Kent C. Dodds attempts to avoid the issues with previous unit testing libraries by providing a standalone implementation of the DOM. As a result, tests can render a React component to a virtual DOM, which can then be synchronized with the Testing Library's DOM and create a tree of HTML elements that behave like they would in a real browser.

You can inspect the elements in the same way that you would within a browser. They have the same attributes and properties. You can even pass keystrokes to input fields and have them behave the same way as fields in the browser.

If you created your application with `create-react-app`, you should already have the Testing Library installed. If not, you can install it from the command line:

```
$ npm install --save-dev "@testing-library/react"
$ npm install --save-dev "@testing-library/jest-dom"
$ npm install --save-dev "@testing-library/user-event"
```

These three libraries will allow us to unit test components.

The Testing Library allows us to render components using the DOM implementation in `@testing-library/jest-dom`. The User Event library (`@testing-library/user-event`) simplifies interacting with the generated DOM elements. This User Event library allows us to click the buttons and type into the fields of our components.

To show how to unit test components, we will need an application to test. We'll be using the same application through much of this chapter. When the application opens, it asks the user to perform a simple calculation. The application will say if the user's answer is right or wrong (see Figure 8-1).

Figure 8-1. The application under test

The main component of the application is called App. We can create a unit test for this component by writing a new file called *App.test.js*:

```
describe('App', () => {
  it('should tell you when you win', () => {
    // Given we've rendered the app
    // When we enter the correct answer
    // Then we are told that we've won
  })
})
```

The preceding code is a Jest test, with a single scenario that tests that the App component will tell us we've won if we enter the correct answer. We've put placeholder comments for the structure of the test.

We will begin by rendering the App component. We can do this by importing the component and passing it to the Testing Library's render function:

```
import { render } from '@testing-library/react'
import App from './App'

describe('App', () => {
  it('should tell you when you win', () => {
    // Given we've rendered the app
    render(<App />)

    // When we enter the correct answer
```

```
        // Then we are told that we've won
    })
  })
```

Notice that we pass actual *JSX* to the render function, which means that we could, if we wanted, test the component's behavior when passed different sets of properties.

For the next part of the test, we'll need to enter the correct answer. To do that, we must first know what the correct answer is. The puzzle is always a randomly generated multiplication, so we can capture the numbers from the page and then type the product into the Guess field.[1]

We will need to look at the elements generated by the App component. The render function returns an object that contains the elements and a set of functions for filtering them. Instead of using this returned value, we'll instead use the Testing Library's screen object.

You can think of the screen object as the contents of the browser window. It allows us to find elements within the page so that we can interact with them. For example, if we want to find the input field labeled Guess, we can do it like this:

```
const input = screen.getByLabelText(/guess:/i)
```

The filter methods in the screen object typically begin with:

getBy...
    If you know that the DOM contains a single instance of the matching element

queryBy...
    If you know there are zero or one elements that match

getAllBy...
    If you know there are one or more matching elements (returns an array)

queryAllBy...
    To find zero or more elements (returns an array)

These methods will throw an exception if they find more or fewer elements than they were expecting. There are also findBy... and findAllBy... methods that are asynchronous versions of getBy... and getAllBy... that return promises.

---

1 You will see in other recipes in this chapter that it's possible to dynamically remove the randomness from a test and fix the correct answer without capturing the question from the page.

For each of these filter method types, you can search the following:

Function name ends	Description
`...ByLabelText`	Finds field by label
`...ByPlaceHolderText`	Finds field with placeholder text
`...ByText`	With matching text content
`...ByDisplayValue`	Finds by value
`...ByAltText`	Matching the alt attribute
`...ByTitle`	Matching the title attribute
`...ByRole`	Finds by aria role
`...ByTestId`	Finds by data-testid attribute

There are nearly 50 ways to find elements within the page. However, you might have noticed that *none* of them use a CSS selector to track an element down, which is deliberate. The Testing Library restricts the number of ways that you can find elements within the DOM. It doesn't allow you to, for example, find elements by class name to reduce the fragility of the test. Class names are frequently used for cosmetic styling and are subject to frequent change.

It is still possible to track down elements with selectors, by using the `container` returned by the render method:

```
const { container } = render(<App />)
const theInput = container.querySelector('#guess')
```

But this approach is considered poor practice. If you use the Testing Library, it's probably best to follow the standard approach and find elements based upon their content or role.

There is one small concession to this approach made by the filter functions: the `...ByTestId` functions. If you have no practical way of finding an element by its content, you can always add a `data-testid` attribute to the relevant tag. That is useful for the test we are currently writing because we need to find two numbers displayed on the page. And these numbers are randomly generated, so we don't know their content (Figure 8-2).

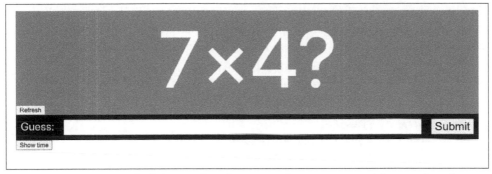

Figure 8-2. We cannot find the numbers by content because we won't know what they are

So, we make a small amendment to the code and add test IDs:

```
<div className="Question-detail">
  <div data-testid="number1" className="number1">
    {pair && pair[0]}
  </div>
  &times;
  <div data-testid="number2" className="number2">
    {pair && pair[1]}
  </div>
  ?
</div>
```

This means we can start to implement the next part of our test:

```
import { render, screen } from '@testing-library/react'
import App from './App'

describe('App', () => {
  it('should tell you when you win', () => {
    // Given we've rendered the app
    render(<App />)

    // When we enter the correct answer
    const number1 = screen.getByTestId('number1').textContent
    const number2 = screen.getByTestId('number2').textContent
    const input = screen.getByLabelText(/guess:/i)
    const submitButton = screen.getByText('Submit')
    // Err...

    // Then we are told that we've won
  })
})
```

We have the text for each of the numbers, and we have the input element. We now need to type the correct number into the field and then submit the answer. We'll do this with the @testing-library/user-event library. The User Event library simplifies the process of generating JavaScript events for HTML elements. You will often see the User Event library imported with the alias user, which is because you can think of the calls to the User Event library as the actions a user is making:

```
import { render, screen } from '@testing-library/react'
import user from '@testing-library/user-event'
import App from './App'

describe('App', () => {
  it('should tell you when you win', () => {
    // Given we've rendered the app
    render(<App />)

    // When we enter the correct answer
    const number1 = screen.getByTestId('number1').textContent
    const number2 = screen.getByTestId('number2').textContent
    const input = screen.getByLabelText(/guess:/i)
    const submitButton = screen.getByText('Submit')
    user.type(input, '' + parseFloat(number1) * parseFloat(number2))
    user.click(submitButton)

    // Then we are told that we've won
  })
})
```

Finally, we need to assert that we have won. We can write this simply by looking for some element containing the word *won*:[2]

```
// Then we are told that we've won
screen.getByText(/won/i)
```

This assertion will work because getByText throws an exception if it does not find precisely one matching element.

If you are unsure about the current HTML state at some point in a test, try adding screen.getByTestId('NONEXISTENT') into the code. The exception that's thrown will show you the current HTML.

However, the test is liable to break if your application is running slowly. This is because the get... and query... functions look at the existing state of the DOM. If the result takes a couple of seconds to appear, the assertion will fail. For this reason, it's a good idea to make some assertions asynchronous. It makes the code a little more complex, but the test will be more stable when running against slow-moving code.

---

2 Notice that many tests make text comparisons using regular expressions, which allows, as in this example, for case-insensitive matches of substrings. Regular expressions can prevent tests from breaking frequently.

The find... methods are asynchronous versions of the get... methods, and the Testing Library's waitFor will allow you to rerun code for a period of time. By combining the two functions, we can create the final part of our test:

```
import { render, screen, waitFor } from '@testing-library/react'
import user from '@testing-library/user-event'
import App from './App'

describe('App', () => {
  it('should tell you when you win', async () => {
    // Given we've rendered the app
    render(<App />)

    // When we enter the correct answer
    const number1 = screen.getByTestId('number1').textContent
    const number2 = screen.getByTestId('number2').textContent
    const input = screen.getByLabelText(/guess:/i)
    const submitButton = screen.getByText('Submit')
    user.type(input, '' + parseFloat(number1) * parseFloat(number2))
    user.click(submitButton)

    // Then we are told that we've won
    await waitFor(() => screen.findByText(/won/i), { timeout: 4000 })
  })
})
```

 Unit tests should run quickly, but if for some reason your test takes longer than five seconds, you will need to pass a second timeout value in milliseconds to the it function.

Discussion

Working with different teams, we found that early on in a project, the developers would write unit tests for each component. But over time, they would write fewer and fewer unit tests. Eventually, they might even delete unit tests if they required too much maintenance.

This happens partly because unit tests are more abstract than browser tests. They are doing the same kinds of things as browser tests, but they do them invisibly. When they are interacting with components, you don't *see* them.

A second reason is that teams often see tests as deliverable artifacts within a project. The team might even have builds that fail if unit tests don't cover a certain percentage of the code.

These issues generally disappear if developers write tests *before* they write code. If you write the tests first, a line at a time, you will have a much better grasp of the current state of HTML. If you stop seeing tests as development artifacts and start to look at them as tools for designing your code, they stop becoming a time-consuming burden and become tools that make your work easier.

The important thing when writing code is that you begin with a failing test. In the early days of a project, that might be a failing browser test. As the project matures and the architecture stabilizes, you should create more and more unit tests.

You can download the source for this recipe from the GitHub site (*https://oreil.ly/ P1Tqj*).

8.2 Use Storybook for Render Tests

Problem

Tests are simply examples that you can execute. Consequently, tests have a lot in common with component gallery systems like Storybook. Both tests and galleries are examples of components running in particular circumstances. Whereas a test will make assertions with code, a developer will make an *assertion* of a library example by looking at it and checking that it appears as expected. In both galleries and tests, exceptions will be easily visible.

There are differences. Tests can automatically interact with components; gallery components require a person to press buttons and type text. Developers can run tests with a single command; galleries have to be manually viewed, one example at a time. Gallery components are visual and easy to understand; tests are abstract and less fun to create.

Is there some way to combine galleries like Storybook with automated tests to get the best of both worlds?

Solution

We're going to look at how you can reuse your Storybook stories inside tests. You can install Storybook into your application with this command:

```
$ npx sb init
```

The example application in this chapter is a simple mathematical game in which the user needs to calculate the answer to a multiplication problem (see Figure 8-3).

Figure 8-3. The example application

One of the components in the game is called `Question`, and it displays a randomly generated multiplication question (Figure 8-4).

Figure 8-4. The Question component

Let's say we don't worry too much about tests for this component. Let's just build it by creating some Storybook stories. We'll write a new *Question.stories.js* file:

```
import Question from './Question'

const Info = {
  title: 'Question',
}

export default Info

export const Basic = () => <Question />
```

And then we'll create an initial version of the component that we can look at in Storybook and be happy with:

```
import { useEffect, useState } from 'react'
import './Question.css'

const RANGE = 10

function rand() {
  return Math.floor(Math.random() * RANGE + 1)
```

```
  }

const Question = ({ refreshTime }) => {
  const [pair, setPair] = useState()

  const refresh = () => {
    setPair((pair) => {
      return [rand(), rand()]
    })
  }

  useEffect(refresh, [refreshTime])

  return (
    <div className="Question">
      <div className="Question-detail">
        <div data-testid="number1" className="number1">
          {pair && pair[0]}
        </div>
        &times;
        <div data-testid="number2" className="number2">
          {pair && pair[1]}
        </div>
        ?
      </div>
      <button onClick={refresh}>Refresh</button>
    </div>
  )
}

export default Question
```

This component displays a randomly generated question if the user clicks the Refresh button or if a parent component passes in a new `refreshTime` value.

We display the component in Storybook, and it looks like it works fine. We can click the Refresh button, and it refreshes. So at that point, we start to use the component in the main application. After a while, we add a few extra features, but none of them are visual changes, so we don't look at the Storybook stories for it again. After all, it will still look the same. Right?

This is a modified version of the component, after we've wired it into the rest of the application:

```
import { useEffect, useState } from 'react'
import './Question.css'

const RANGE = 10

function rand() {
  return Math.floor(Math.random() * RANGE + 1)
}
```

```
const Question = ({ onAnswer, refreshTime }) => {
  const [pair, setPair] = useState()
  const result = pair && pair[0] * pair[1]

  useEffect(() => {
    onAnswer(result)
  }, [onAnswer, result])

  const refresh = () => {
    setPair((pair) => {
      return [rand(), rand()]
    })
  }

  useEffect(refresh, [refreshTime])

  return (
    <div className="Question">
      <div className="Question-detail">
        <div data-testid="number1" className="number1">
          {pair && pair[0]}
        </div>
        &times;
        <div data-testid="number2" className="number2">
          {pair && pair[1]}
        </div>
        ?
      </div>
      <button onClick={refresh}>Refresh</button>
    </div>
  )
}

export default Question
```

This version is only *slightly* longer than before. We've added an onAnswer callback function that will return the correct answer to the parent component each time the application generates a new question.

The new component appears to work well in the application, but then an odd thing occurs. The next time someone looks at Storybook, they notice an error, as shown in Figure 8-5.

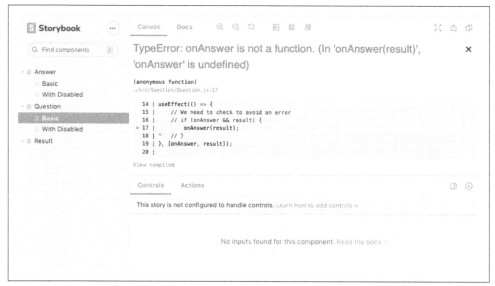

Figure 8-5. An error occurs when we look at the new version of the component

What happened? We've added an implicit assumption into the code that the parent component will always pass an onAnswer callback into the component. Because the Storybook stories rendered Basic story without an onAnswer, we got the error:

```
<Question/>
```

Does this matter? Not for a simple component like this. After all, the application itself still worked. But failure to cope with missing properties, such as the missing callback here or, more frequently, missing data, is one of the most typical causes of errors in React.

Applications frequently generate React properties using data from the network, and that means the initial properties you pass to components will often be null or undefined. It's generally a good idea to either use a type-safe language, like TypeScript, to avoid these issues or write tests that check that your components can cope with missing properties.

We created this component without any tests, but we did create it with a Storybook story—and that story *did* catch the issue. So is there some way to write a test that will automatically check that Storybook can render all the stories?

We're going to create a test for this component in a file called *Question.test.js*.

Consider creating a folder for each component. Instead of simply having a file called *Question.js* in the *src* directory, create a folder called *src/Question*, and inside there you can place *Question.js*, *Question.stories.js*, and *Question.test.js*. If you then add an *src/Question/index.js* file, which does a default export of the `Question` component, the rest of your code will be unaffected, and you will reduce the number of files other developers have to deal with.[3]

In the test file, we can then create a Jest test that loads each of the stories and then passes them to the Testing Library's render function:[4]

```
import { render } from '@testing-library/react'
import Question from './Question'

const stories = require('./Question.stories')

describe('Question', () => {
  it('should render all storybook stories without error', () => {
    for (let story in stories) {
      if (story !== 'default') {
        let C = stories[story]
        render(<C />)
      }
    }
  })
})
```

If your stories are using *decorators* to provide such things as routers or styling, this technique will not pick them up automatically. You should add them into the `render` method within the test.

When you run this test, you will get a failure:

```
onAnswer is not a function
TypeError: onAnswer is not a function
```

We can fix the error by checking if there is a callback before calling it:

```
useEffect(() => {
  // We need to check to avoid an error
  if (onAnswer && result) {
    onAnswer(result)
```

---

3 See the source code in the GitHub repository (*https://oreil.ly/P1Tqj*) to see how we've structured the code in the example application.

4 If you don't have the Testing Library installed, see Recipe 8.1.

```
    }
}, [onAnswer, result])
```

This technique allows you to create some elementary tests for a component with minimal effort. It's worth creating a story for the component, which includes no properties whatsoever. Then, before you add a new property, create a story that uses it and think about how you will expect the component to behave.

Even though the test will perform only a simple render of each story, there is no reason why you can't import a single story and create a test using that story:

```
import { render, screen } from '@testing-library/react'
import user from '@testing-library/user-event'
import Question from './Question'
import { Basic, WithDisabled } from './Question.stories'
...
it('should disable the button when asked', () => {
  render(<WithDisabled />)
  const refreshButton = screen.getByRole('button')
  expect(refreshButton.disabled).toEqual(true)
})
```

Discussion

Storybook render tests introduce rudimentary unit testing into your application, and it can find a surprising number of regression bugs. It also helps you think of tests as examples, which are there to help you design your code rather than coding artifacts that you must create to keep the team lead happy. Creating render tests for stories is also helpful if you have a team that is new to unit testing. By creating visual examples, it avoids the problems that can arise from nonvisual tests feeling abstract. It can also get developers into the habit of having a test file for each component in the system. When you need to make a minor change to the component, it will then be much easier to add a small unit test function before adding the change.

You can download the source for this recipe from the GitHub site (*https://oreil.ly/ P1Tqj*).

8.3 Test Without a Server Using Cypress

Problem

One of the principal features of high-quality code is the way it responds to errors. The first of Peter Deutsch's Eight Fallacies of Distributed Computing (*https://oreil.ly/ eDtKG*) is: *the network is reliable*. Not only is the network *not* reliable, but neither are the servers or databases that connect to it. At some point, your application is going to have to deal with some network failure. It might be that the phone loses its connection, or the server goes down, or the database crashes, or someone else has deleted the data you are trying to update. Whatever the causes, you will need to decide what your application will do when terrible things happen.

Network issues can be challenging to simulate in testing environments. If you write code that puts the server into some error state, that is likely to cause problems for other tests or users who connect to the server.

How can you create automated tests for network failure cases?

Solution

For this recipe, we are going to use Cypress. We mentioned the Cypress testing system in Chapter 1. It's a genuinely remarkable testing system that is rapidly becoming our go-to tool in many development projects.

To install Cypress into your project, type the following:

```
$ npm install --save-dev cypress
```

Cypress works by automating a web browser. In that sense, it is similar to other systems like Selenium. Still, the difference is that Cypress does not require you to install a separate driver, and it can both control the browser remotely and inject itself into the browser's JavaScript engine.

Cypress can therefore actively replace core parts of the JavaScript infrastructure with faked versions that it can control. For example, Cypress can replace the JavaScript fetch function used to make network calls to the server.[5] Cypress tests can therefore spoof the behavior of a network server and allow a client-side developer to artificially craft responses from the server.

We will use the example game application that we use for other recipes in this chapter. We will add a network call to store the result each time a user answers a question. We can do this without creating the actual server code by faking the responses in Cypress.

To show how this works, we will first create a test that simulates the server responding correctly. Then we will create a test to simulate a server failure.

---

5 Either directly or indirectly via libraries such as Axios.

Once Cypress is installed, create a file in *cypress/integration/* called *0001-basic-game-functions.js*:[6]

```
describe('Basic game functions', () => {
  it('should notify the server if I lose', () => {
    // Given I started the application
    // When I enter an incorrect answer
    // Then the server will be told that I have lost
  })
})
```

We've put placeholder comments for each of the steps we will need to write.

Each command and assertion in Cypress begins with cy. If we want to open the browser at location *http://localhost:3000*, we can do it with the following:

```
describe('Basic game functions', () => {
  it('should notify the server if I lose', () => {
    // Given I started the application
    cy.visit('http://localhost:3000')

    // When I enter an incorrect answer
    // Then the server will be told that I have lost
  })
})
```

To run the test, we can type:

```
$ npx cypress run
```

That command will run all tests without showing the browser.[7] We can also type the following:

```
$ npx cypress open
```

This command will open the Cypress application window (as you can see in Figure 8-6). If we double-click the test file, the test will open in a browser (as you can see in Figure 8-7).

---

6 It doesn't matter what you call the file, but we follow the convention of prefixing high-level tests such as this with story numbers. Doing so reduces the likelihood of test merge conflicts and makes it much easier to track the intent of individual changes.

7 This will run the tests more quickly and record a video for each one, which is helpful if your tests run on an integration server.

Figure 8-6. The test will appear in the Cypress window when you type **npx cypress open**

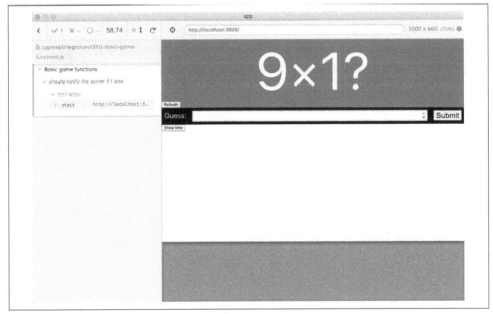

Figure 8-7. A Cypress test running in a browser

The example application asks the user to multiply two random numbers (see Figure 8-8). The numbers will be in the range 1–10, so if we enter the value **101**, we can be sure that the answer will be incorrect.

 Cypress does not allow you to capture textual content from the screen directly. So we cannot simply read the values of the two numbers and store them in variables because the commands in Cypress don't immediately perform the actions in the browser. Instead, when you run a command, Cypress adds it to a *chain* of instructions, which it performs at the end of the test. This approach might seem a little odd, but these *chainable* instructions allow Cypress to cope with most of the problems caused by asynchronous interfaces.[8] The downside is that no command can return the page's contents as the page will not exist when the command runs.

We will see elsewhere in this chapter how we can remove randomness in test scenarios and make this test deterministic, which will remove the need to capture data from the page.

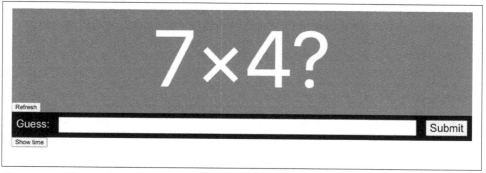

Figure 8-8. The application asks the user to calculate the product of two random numbers

We can use the `cy.get` command to find the input field by a CSS selector. We can also use the `cy.contains` command to find the Submit button:

```
describe('Basic game functions', () => {
  it('should notify the server if I lose', () => {
    // Given I started the application
    cy.visit('http://localhost:3000')

    // When I enter an incorrect answer
```

---

8 Cypress commands are similar in many ways to promises, although they are not promises. You can think of each one as a "prom-ish."

```
        cy.get('input').type('101')
        cy.contains('Submit').click()

        // Then the server will be told that I have lost
    })
})
```

Now we just need to test that the application contacts the server with the result of the game.

We will use the `cy.intercept()` command to do this. The `cy.intercept()` command will change the behavior of network requests in the application so that we can fake responses for a given request. If the result is going to be POSTed to the endpoint */api/result*, we generate a faked response like this:

```
cy.intercept('POST', '/api/result', {
  statusCode: 200,
  body: '',
})
```

Once this command takes effect, network requests to */api/result* will receive the faked response. That means we need to run the command *before* the network request is made. We will do it at the start of the test:

```
describe('Basic game functions', () => {
  it('should notify the server if I lose', () => {
    // Given I started the application
    cy.intercept('POST', '/api/result', {
      statusCode: 200,
      body: '',
    })
    cy.visit('http://localhost:3000')

    // When I enter an incorrect answer
    cy.get('input').type('101')
    cy.contains('Submit').click()

    // Then the server will be told that I have lost
  })
})
```

We've now specified the network response. But how do we assert that the application has made the network call, and how do we know that it has sent the correct data to the */api/result* endpoint?

We will need to give the network request an *alias*. This will allow us to refer to the request later in the test:[9]

```
cy.intercept('POST', '/api/result', {
  statusCode: 200,
  body: '',
}).as('postResult')
```

We can then make an assertion at the end of the test, which will wait for the network call to be made and will check the contents of the data sent in the request body:

```
describe('Basic game functions', () => {
  it('should notify the server if I lose', () => {
    // Given I started the application
    cy.intercept('POST', '/api/result', {
      statusCode: 200,
      body: '',
    }).as('postResult')
    cy.visit('http://localhost:3000')

    // When I enter an incorrect answer
    cy.get('input').type('101')
    cy.contains('Submit').click()

    // Then the server will be told that I have lost
    cy.wait('@postResult').then((xhr) => {
      expect(xhr.request.body.guess).equal(101)
      expect(xhr.request.body.result).equal('LOSE')
    })
  })
})
```

This assertion is checking two of the attributes of the request body for the expected values.

If we run the test now, it will pass (as you can see in Figure 8-9).

---

[9] The cy.intercept command cannot simply return a reference to the faked network request because of the chainable nature of Cypress commands.

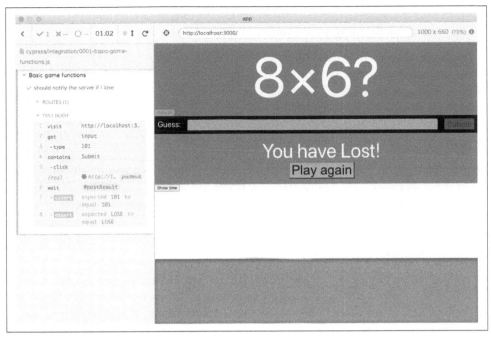

Figure 8-9. The completed test passes

Now that we've created a test for the successful case, we can write a test for the failure case. The application should display a message on-screen if the network call fails. We don't actually care what details are sent to the server in this test, but we still need to wait for the network request to complete before checking for the existence of the error message:

```
it('should display a message if I cannot post the result', () => {
  // Given I started the application
  cy.intercept('POST', '/api/result', {
    statusCode: 500,
    body: { message: 'Bad thing happened!' },
  }).as('postResult')
  cy.visit('http://localhost:3000')

  // When I enter an answer
  cy.get('input').type('16')
  cy.contains('We are unable to save the result').should('not.exist')
  cy.contains('Submit').click()

  // Then I will see an error message
  cy.wait('@postResult')
  cy.contains('We are unable to save the result')
})
```

Notice that we check for the error message *not* existing before we make the network call to ensure that the network call *causes* the error.

In addition to generating stubbed responses and status codes, cy.intercept can perform other tricks, such as slowing response times, throttling network speed, or generating responses from test functions. For further details, see the cy.intercept documentation (*https://oreil.ly/tcZR8*).

Discussion

Cypress testing can transform how a development team works, specifically in its ability to mock network calls. Teams frequently develop APIs at a different cadence than frontend code. Also, some teams have developers who specialize in frontend or server code. Cypress can help in these situations because it allows frontend developers to write code against endpoints that don't currently exist. Cypress can also simulate all of the pathological failure cases.

Network performance can introduce intermittent bugs. Development environments use local servers with little or no data, which means that API performance is far better at development time than in a production environment. It is straightforward to write code that assumes that data is immediately available, but this code will break in a production environment where the data may take a second or so to arrive.

It is therefore worth having at least one test for each API call where the response is slowed by a second or so:

```
cy.intercept('GET', '/api/widgets', {
  statusCode: 200,
  body: [{ id: 1, name: 'Flange' }],
  delay: 1000,
}).as('getWidgets')
```

Simulating slow network responses will often flush out a whole plethora of asynchronous bugs that might otherwise creep into your code.

Almost as importantly, creating artificially slow network responses will give you a sense of the overall impact of each API call on performance.

You can download the source for this recipe from the GitHub site (*https://oreil.ly/ P1Tqj*).

8.4 Use Cypress for Offline Testing

Problem

This recipe uses a custom Cypress command invented by Etienne Bruines (*https:// oreil.ly/oOMHP*).

Applications need to cope with being disconnected from the network. We've seen elsewhere how to create a hook to detect if we are currently offline.[10] But how are we test for offline behavior?

Solution

We can simulate offline working using Cypress. Cypress tests can inject code that modifies the internal behavior of the browser under test. We should therefore be able to modify the network code to simulate offline conditions.

For this recipe, you will need to install Cypress in your application. If you don't already have Cypress, you can install it by running this command in your application directory:

```
$ npm install --save-dev cypress
```

You can then add a *0002-offline-working.js* file to the *cypress/integration* directory:

```
describe('Offline working', () => {
  it(
    'should tell us when we are offline',
    { browser: '!firefox' },
    () => {
      // Given we have started the application
      // When the application is offline
      // Then we will see a warning
      // When the application is back online
      // Then we will not see a warning
    }
  )
})
```

 We will ignore this test on Firefox. The offline simulation code relies upon the Chrome DevTools remote debugging protocol, which is not currently available in the Firefox browser.

We have marked out the structure of the test as a series of comments. Cypress commands all begin with cy, so we can open the application like this:

```
describe('Offline working', () => {
  it(
    'should tell us when we are offline',
    { browser: '!firefox' },
    () => {
      // Given we have started the application
```

---

10 See Recipe 3.5.

```
            cy.visit('http://localhost:3000')

            // When the application is offline
            // Then we will see a warning
            // When the application is back online
            // Then we will not see a warning
        }
    )
})
```

The question is, how do we force the browser to simulate offline working?

We can do it because Cypress is designed to be extensible. We can add a custom Cypress command that will allow us to go offline and back online:

```
cy.network({ offline: true })
cy.network({ offline: false })
```

To add a custom command, open the *cypress/support/commands.js* file, and add the following code:

```
Cypress.Commands.add('network', (options = {}) => {
  Cypress.automation('remote:debugger:protocol', {
    command: 'Network.enable',
  })

  Cypress.automation('remote:debugger:protocol', {
    command: 'Network.emulateNetworkConditions',
    params: {
      offline: options.offline,
      latency: 0,
      downloadThroughput: 0,
      uploadThroughput: 0,
      connectionType: 'none',
    },
  })
})
```

This command uses the remote debugging protocol in DevTools to emulate offline network conditions. Once you have saved this file, you can then implement the rest of the test:

```
describe('Offline working', () => {
  it(
    'should tell us when we are offline',
    { browser: '!firefox' },
    () => {
      // Given we have started the application
      cy.visit('http://localhost:3000')
      cy.contains(/you are currently offline/i).should('not.exist')

      // When the application is offline
      cy.network({ offline: true })
```

```
    // Then we will see a warning
    cy.contains(/you are currently offline/i).should('be.visible')

    // When the application is back online
    cy.network({ offline: false })

    // Then we will not see a warning
    cy.contains(/you are currently offline/i).should('not.exist')
  }
 )
})
```

If you run the test now, in Electron, it will pass (see Figure 8-10).

Figure 8-10. You can view each stage of the online/offline test by clicking on the left panel

Discussion

It should be possible to create similar commands that simulate various network conditions and speeds.

For more information on how the network command works, see this blog post from Cypress.io (*https://oreil.ly/PB4zO*).

You can download the source for this recipe from the GitHub site (*https://oreil.ly/P1Tqj*).

8.5 Test in a Browser with Selenium

Problem

Nothing beats running your code inside a real browser, and the most common way of writing automated browser-based tests is by using a *web driver*. You can control most browsers by sending a command to a network port. Different browsers have different commands, and a web driver is a command-line tool that simplifies controlling the browser.

But how can we write a test for a React application that uses a web driver?

Solution

We are going to use the Selenium library. Selenium is a framework that provides a consistent API for a whole set of different web drivers, which means that you can write a test for Firefox and the same code should work in the same way for Chrome, Safari, and Edge.[11]

We will use the same example application that we are using for all recipes in this chapter. It's a game that asks the user for the answer to a simple multiplication problem.

The Selenium library is available for a whole set of different languages, such as Python, Java, and C#. We will be using the JavaScript version: Selenium WebDriver.

We'll begin by installing Selenium:

```
$ npm install --save-dev selenium-webdriver
```

We will also need to install at least one web driver. You can install web drivers globally, but it is more manageable to install them in your application. We could install a driver like `geckodriver` for Firefox, but for now, we will install `chromedriver` for Chrome:

```
$ npm install --save-dev chromedriver
```

We can now start to create a test. It's useful to include Selenium tests inside the *src* folder of the application, because it will make it easier to use an IDE to run the tests manually. So we'll create a folder called *src/selenium* and then add a file inside it called *0001-basic-game-functions.spec.js*:[12]

---

11 This doesn't mean that the tests will work against every browser, just that they will all run across every browser.

12 We are following a convention where we prefix the test with its associated story number. Selenium does not require this.

```
describe('Basic game functions', () => {
  it('should tell me if I won', () => {
    // Given I have started the application
    // When I enter the correct answer
    // Then I will be told that I have won
  })
})
```

We have outlined the test in the comments.

 While it's convenient to include Selenium tests in the *src* tree, it can mean that a tool like Jest will run it as if it were a unit test, which is a problem if you run unit tests continually in the background. For example, if you created your application with `create-react-app` and leave an `npm run test` command running, you will find that a browser will suddenly appear on your screen each time you save the Selenium test. To avoid this, adopt some naming convention to distinguish between Selenium and unit tests. If you name all your Selenium tests **.spec.js*, you can modify your test script to avoid them by setting it to *react-scripts test '.*.test.js'*.

Selenium uses a web driver to automate the web browser. We can create an instance of the driver at the start of each test:

```
import { Builder } from 'selenium-webdriver'
let driver

describe('Basic game functions', () => {
  beforeEach(() => {
    driver = new Builder().forBrowser('chrome').build()
  })

  afterEach(() => {
    driver.quit()
  })

  it('should tell me if I won', () => {
    // Given I have started the application
    // When I enter the correct answer
    // Then I will be told that I have won
  })
})
```

In this example, we are creating a Chrome driver.

By creating a driver for each test, we will also create a fresh instance of the browser for each test, ensuring that no browser state is carried between tests. If we carry no state between tests, it will allow us to run the tests in any order. We have no such guarantee on shared server state. If your tests are reliant upon, for example, database data, you should ensure that each test initializes the server correctly when it starts.

For Selenium to create an instance of the driver, we should also explicitly *require* the driver:

```
import { Builder } from 'selenium-webdriver'
require('chromedriver')

let driver

describe('Basic game functions', () => {
  beforeEach(() => {
    driver = new Builder().forBrowser('chrome').build()
  })

  afterEach(() => {
    driver.quit()
  })

  it('should tell me if I won', () => {
    // Given I have started the application
    // When I enter the correct answer
    // Then I will be told that I have won
  })
})
```

We can now start to fill out the test. The JavaScript version of Selenium is highly asynchronous. Virtually all commands return promises, which means that it is very efficient, but it is also far too easy to introduce testing bugs.

Let's begin our test by opening the application:

```
import { Builder } from 'selenium-webdriver'
require('chromedriver')

let driver

describe('Basic game functions', async () => {
  beforeEach(() => {
    driver = new Builder().forBrowser('chrome').build()
  })

  afterEach(() => {
    driver.quit()
  })
```

```
it('should tell me if I won', () => {
  // Given I have started the application
  await driver.get('http://localhost:3000')
  // When I enter the correct answer
  // Then I will be told that I have won
}, 60000)
})
```

The `driver.get` command tells the browser to open the given URL. For this to work, we've also had to make two other changes. First, we've had to mark the test function with `async`, which will allow us to `await` the promise returned by `driver.get`.

Second, we've added a timeout value of 60,000 milliseconds to the test, overriding the implicit five-second limit of Jest tests. If you don't increase the default timeout, you will find your test fails before the browser starts. We've set it to 60,000 milliseconds here to ensure the test works on any machine. You should adjust this value to match your expected hardware.

To enter the correct value into the game, we will need to read the two numbers that appear in the question (as shown in Figure 8-11).

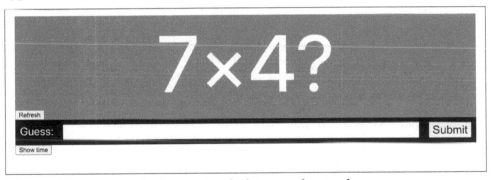

Figure 8-11. The game asks the user to calculate a random product

We can find the two numbers on the page and the `input` and `submit` buttons using a command called `findElement`:

```
const number1 = await driver.findElement(By.css('.number1')).getText()
const number2 = await driver.findElement(By.css('.number2')).getText()
const input = await driver.findElement(By.css('input'))
const submit = await driver.findElement(
  By.xpath("//button[text()='Submit']")
)
```

If you are ever reading a set of elements from the page and don't care about resolving them in a strict order, you can use the `Promise.all` function to combine them into a single promise that you can then await:

```
const [number1, number2, input, submit] = await Promise.all([
  driver.findElement(By.css('.number1')).getText(),
  driver.findElement(By.css('.number2')).getText(),
  driver.findElement(By.css('input')),
  driver.findElement(By.xpath("//button[text()='Submit']")),
])
```

In the example application, this optimization will save virtually no time, but if you have a page that renders different components in uncertain orders, combining the promises can improve test performance.

This means we can now complete the next part of our test:

```
import { Builder, By } from 'selenium-webdriver'
require('chromedriver')

let driver

describe('Basic game functions', async () => {
  beforeEach(() => {
    driver = new Builder().forBrowser('chrome').build()
  })

  afterEach(() => {
    driver.quit()
  })

  it('should tell me if I won', () => {
    // Given I have started the application
    await driver.get('http://localhost:3000')
    // When I enter the correct answer
    const [number1, number2, input, submit] = await Promise.all([
      driver.findElement(By.css('.number1')).getText(),
      driver.findElement(By.css('.number2')).getText(),
      driver.findElement(By.css('input')),
      driver.findElement(By.xpath("//button[text()='Submit']")),
    ])
    await input.sendKeys('' + number1 * number2)
    await submit.click()
    // Then I will be told that I have won
  }, 60000)
})
```

Notice that we are not combining the promises returned by sendKeys and click because we care that the test enters the answer into the input field *before* we submit it.

Finally, we want to assert that a *You have won!* message appears on the screen (see Figure 8-12).

Figure 8-12. The app tells the user they got the correct answer

Now we could write our assertion like this:

```
const resultText = await driver
  .findElement(By.css('.Result'))
  .getText()
expect(resultText).toMatch(/won/i)
```

This code will almost certainly work because the result is displayed quickly after the user submits an answer. React applications will often display dynamic results slowly, particularly if they rely upon data from the network. If we modify the application code to simulate a two-second delay before the result appears,[13] our test will produce the following error:

```
no such element: Unable to locate element: {"method":"css selector",
    "selector":".Result"}
  (Session info: chrome=88.0.4324.192)
NoSuchElementError: no such element: Unable to locate element: {
    "method":"css selector","selector":".Result"}
  (Session info: chrome=88.0.4324.192)
```

We can avoid this problem by waiting until the element appears on the screen and then waiting until the text matches the expected result. We can do both of those things with the driver.wait function:

```
await driver.wait(until.elementLocated(By.css('.Result')))
const resultElement = driver.findElement(By.css('.Result'))
await driver.wait(until.elementTextMatches(resultElement, /won/i))
```

---

13 You will find the code to do this in the downloadable source for this chapter from GitHub (*https://oreil.ly/P1Tqj*).

This gives us the final version of our test:

```
import { Builder, By } from 'selenium-webdriver'
require('chromedriver')

let driver

describe('Basic game functions', async () => {
  beforeEach(() => {
    driver = new Builder().forBrowser('chrome').build()
  })

  afterEach(() => {
    driver.quit()
  })

  it('should tell me if I won', () => {
    // Given I have started the application
    await driver.get('http://localhost:3000')
    // When I enter the correct answer
    const [number1, number2, input, submit] = await Promise.all([
      driver.findElement(By.css('.number1')).getText(),
      driver.findElement(By.css('.number2')).getText(),
      driver.findElement(By.css('input')),
      driver.findElement(By.xpath("//button[text()='Submit']")),
    ])
    await input.sendKeys('' + number1 * number2)
    await submit.click()
    // Then I will be told that I have won
    await driver.wait(until.elementLocated(By.css('.Result')))
    const resultElement = driver.findElement(By.css('.Result'))
    await driver.wait(until.elementTextMatches(resultElement, /won/i))
  }, 60000)
})
```

Discussion

In our experience, web driver tests are the most popular form of automated tests for web applications—*popular* that is, in the sense of *frequently used*. They are inevitably dependent upon matching versions of browsers and web drivers, and they do have a reputation for failing intermittently. Timing issues usually cause these failures, and those timing issues occur more in Single-Page Applications, which can update their contents asynchronously.

Although it is possible to avoid these problems by carefully adding timing delays and retries into the code, this can make your tests sensitive to environmental changes, such as running your application on a different testing server. Another option, if you experience a lot of intermittent failures, is to move more of your tests to a system like Cypress, which is generally more tolerant (*https://oreil.ly/IZJ2T*) of timing failures.

You can download the source for this recipe from the GitHub site (*https://oreil.ly/ P1Tqj*).

8.6 Test Cross-Browser Visuals with ImageMagick

Problem

Applications can look very different when viewed on different browsers. Applications can even look different if viewed on the same browser but on a different operating system. One example of this would be Chrome, which tends to hide scrollbars when viewed on a Mac but display them on Windows. Thankfully, old browsers like Internet Explorer are finally disappearing, but even modern browsers can apply CSS in subtly different ways, radically changing the appearance of a page.

It can be time-consuming to constantly check an application manually across a range of browsers and platforms.

What can we do to automate this compatibility process?

Solution

In this recipe, we're going to combine three tools to check for visual consistency across different browsers and platforms:

Storybook
This will give us a basic gallery of all of the components, in all relevant configurations, that we need to check.

Selenium
This will allow us to capture the visual appearance of all of the components in Storybook. The Selenium Grid will also allow us to remotely connect to browsers on different operating systems to make comparisons between operating systems.

ImageMagick
Specifically, we'll use ImageMagick's `compare` tool to generate visual differences between two screenshots and provide a numerical measure of how far apart the two images are.

We'll begin by installing Storybook. You can do this in your application with this command:

```
$ npx sb init
```

You will then need to create *stories* for each of the components and configurations you are interested in tracking. You can find out how to do this from other recipes in this book or the Storybook tutorials (*https://oreil.ly/ak7VW*).

Next, we will need Selenium to automate the capture of screenshots. You can install Selenium with this command:

```
$ npm install --save-dev selenium-webdriver
```

You will also need to install the relevant web drivers. For example, to automate Firefox and Chrome, you will need the following:

```
$ npm install --save-dev geckodriver
$ npm install --save-dev chromedriver
```

Finally, you will need to install ImageMagick, a set of command-line image manipulation tools. For details on how to install ImageMagick, see the ImageMagick download page (*https://oreil.ly/NIQ0A*).

We are going to use the same example game application that we've used previously in this chapter. You can see the components from the application displayed in Storybook in Figure 8-13.

Figure 8-13. Components from the application displayed in Storybook

You can run the Storybook server on your application by typing:

```
$ npm run storybook
```

Next, we will create a test that will just be a script for capturing screenshots of each of the components inside Storybook. In a folder called *src/selenium*, create a script called *shots.spec.js*:[14]

---

14 You could put this script anywhere, but this is the location we used in the example code on the GitHub site.

```
import { Builder, By, until } from 'selenium-webdriver'

require('chromedriver')
let fs = require('fs')

describe('shots', () => {
  it('should take screenshots of storybook components', async () => {
    const browserEnv = process.env.SELENIUM_BROWSER || 'chrome'
    const url = process.env.START_URL || 'http://localhost:6006'
    const driver = new Builder().forBrowser('chrome').build()
    driver.manage().window().setRect({
      width: 1200,
      height: 900,
      x: 0,
      y: 0,
    })

    const outputDir = './screenshots/' + browserEnv
    fs.mkdirSync(outputDir, { recursive: true })

    await driver.get(url)

    await driver.wait(
      until.elementLocated(By.className('sidebar-item')),
      60000
    )
    let elements = await driver.findElements(
      By.css('button.sidebar-item')
    )
    for (let e of elements) {
      const expanded = await e.getAttribute('aria-expanded')
      if (expanded !== 'true') {
        await e.click()
      }
    }
    let links = await driver.findElements(By.css('a.sidebar-item'))
    for (let link of links) {
      await link.click()
      const s = await link.getAttribute('id')
      let encodedString = await driver
        .findElement(By.css('#storybook-preview-wrapper'))
        .takeScreenshot()
      await fs.writeFileSync(
        `${outputDir}/${s}.png`,
        encodedString,
        'base64'
      )
    }

    driver.quit()
  }, 60000)
})
```

This script opens a browser to the Storybook server, opens each of the components, and takes a screenshot of each story, which it stores in a subdirectory within *screenshots*.

We could use a different testing system to take screenshots of each component, such as Cypress. The advantage of using Selenium is that we can remotely open a browser session on a remote machine.

By default, the *shots.spec.js* test will take screenshots of Storybook at address *http://localhost:6006* using the Chrome browser. Let's say we are running the *shots* test on a Mac. If we have a Windows machine on the same network, we can install a Selenium Grid server, which is a proxy server (*https://oreil.ly/gYLds*) that allows remote machines to start a web driver session.

If the Windows machine has address 192.168.1.16, we can set this environment variable on the command line before running the *shots.spec.js* test:

```
$ export SELENIUM_REMOTE_URL=http://192.168.1.16:4444/wd/hub
```

Because the Windows machine will be accessing the Storybook server back on the Mac, for example, with an IP address of 192.168.1.14, we will also need to set an environment variable for that on the command line:

```
$ export START_URL=http://192.168.1.14:6006
```

We can also choose which browser we want the Windows machine to use:[15]

```
$ export SELENIUM_BROWSER=firefox
```

If we create a script to run *shots.spec.js* in *package.json*:

```
"scripts": {
  ...
  "testShots": "CI=true react-scripts test --detectOpenHandles \
              'selenium/shots.spec.js'"
}
```

we can run the test and capture the screenshots of each component:

```
$ npm run testShots
```

The test will use the environment variables we created to contact the Selenium Grid server on the remote machine. It will ask Selenium Grid to open a Firefox browser to our local Storybook server. It will then send a screenshot of each of the components over the network, where the test will store them in a folder called *screenshots/firefox*.

Once we've run it for Firefox, we can then run it for Chrome:

---

15 The remote machine must have the appropriate browser and web driver installed for this to work.

```
$ export SELENIUM_BROWSER=chrome
$ npm run testShots
```

The test will write the Chrome screenshots to *screenshots/chrome*.

 A fuller implementation of this technique would also record the operating system and type of client (e.g., screen size) used.

We now need to check for visual differences between the screenshots from Chrome and the screenshots from Firefox, and this is where ImageMagick is useful. The compare command in ImageMagick can generate an image that highlights the visual differences between two other images. For example, consider the two screenshots from Firefox and Chrome in Figure 8-14.

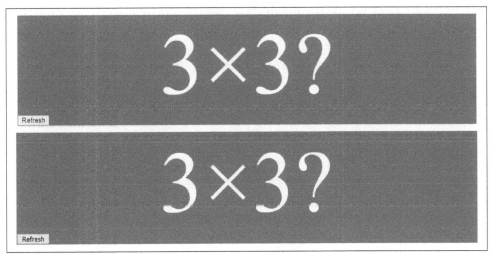

Figure 8-14. The same component in Chrome and Firefox

These two images appear to be identical. If we type in this command from the application directory:

```
$ compare -fuzz 15% screenshots/firefox/question--basic.png \
    screenshots/chrome/question--basic.png difference.png
```

we will generate a new image that shows the differences between the two screenshots, which you can see in Figure 8-15.

Figure 8-15. The generated image showing the differences between two screen captures

The generated image shows pixels that are more than 15% visually different between the two images. And you can see that the screenshots are virtually identical.

That's good, but it still requires a human being to look at the images and assess whether the differences are significant. What else can we do?

The `compare` command also has the ability to display a numerical measure of the difference between two images:

```
$ compare -metric AE -fuzz 15% screenshots/firefox/question--basic.png
  screenshots/chrome/question--basic.png difference.png
6774
```

The value `6774` is a numerical measure (based on the absolute error count, or *AE*) of the visual difference between the two images. For another example, consider the two screenshots in Figure 8-16, which show the `Answer` component when given a `disabled` property.

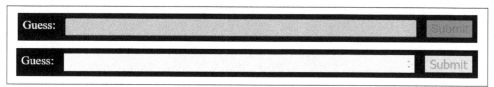

Figure 8-16. Disabled form rendered by Chrome and Firefox

Comparing these two images returns a much larger number:

```
$ compare -metric AE -fuzz 15% screenshots/firefox/answer--with-disabled.png
  screenshots/chrome/answer--with-disabled.png difference3.png
28713
```

Indeed, the generated image (see Figure 8-17) shows precisely where the difference lies: the disabled input field.

Figure 8-17. The visual difference between the Chrome and Firefox forms

Figure 8-18 shows a similarly significant difference (21,131) for a component that displays different font styling between the browsers, resulting from some Mozilla-specific CSS attributes.

Figure 8-18. A component with different text styling in Chrome and Firefox

In fact, it's possible to write a shell script to run through each of the images and generate a small web report showing the visual differences alongside their metrics:

```
#!/bin/bash
mkdir -p screenshots/diff
export HTML=screenshots/compare.html
echo '<body><ul>' > $HTML
for file in screenshots/chrome/*.png
do
    FROM=$file
    TO=$(echo $file | sed 's/chrome/firefox/')
    DIFF=$(echo $file | sed 's/chrome/diff/')
    echo "FROM $FROM TO $TO"
    ls -l $FROM
    ls -l $TO
    METRIC=$(compare -metric AE -fuzz 15% $FROM $TO $DIFF 2>&1)
    echo "<li>$FROM $METRIC<br/><img src=../$DIFF/></li>" >> $HTML
done
echo "</li></body>" >> $HTML
```

This script creates the *screenshots/compare.html* report you can see in Figure 8-19.

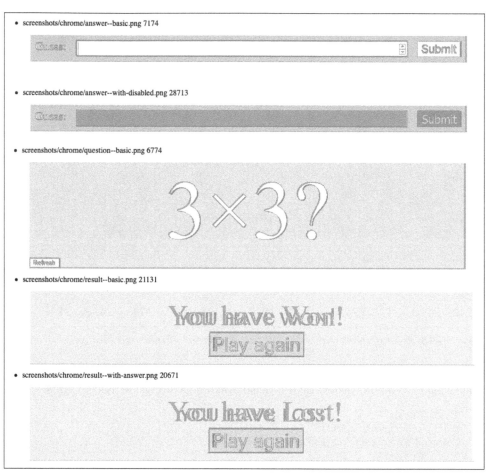

Figure 8-19. An example of the generated comparison report

Discussion

To save space, we have shown only a simplistic implementation of this technique. It would be possible to create a ranked report that showed visual differences from largest to smallest. Such a report would highlight the most significant visual differences between platforms.

You can also use automated visual tests to prevent regressions. You need to avoid false positives caused by minor variations, such as anti-aliasing. A continuous integration job could set some visual threshold between images and fail if any components vary by more than that threshold.

You can download the source for this recipe from the GitHub site (*https://oreil.ly/ P1Tqj*).

8.7 Add a Console to Mobile Browsers

Problem

This recipe is slightly different from the others in this chapter because instead of being about automated testing, it's about manual testing—specifically manually testing code on mobile devices.

If you are testing an application on a mobile, you might stumble across a bug that doesn't appear in the desktop environment. Generally, if a bug appears, you're able to add debug messages into the JavaScript console. But mobile browsers tend not to have a visible JavaScript console. It's true that if you are using Mobile Chrome, you can try debugging it remotely with a desktop version of Chrome. But what if you discover the problem in another browser? Or if you simply don't want to go through the work of setting up a remote debug session?

Is there some way to access the JavaScript console, and other development tools, from within a mobile browser?

Solution

We are going to use a piece of software called Eruda (*https://oreil.ly/jCFSn*).

Eruda is a lightweight implementation of a development tools panel, which will allow you to view the JavaScript console, the structure of the page, and a whole heap of other plugins and extensions (*https://oreil.ly/ZUQHw*).

To enable Eruda, you will need to install a small amount of reasonably rudimentary JavaScript in the head section of your application. You can download Eruda from a content distribution network. Still, because it can be pretty large, you should enable it only if the person using the browser has indicated that they want to access it.

One way of doing this is by enabling Eruda only if *eruda=true* appears in the URL. Here's an example script that you can insert into your page container:[16]

```
<script>
    (function () {
        var src = '//cdn.jsdelivr.net/npm/eruda';
        if (!/eruda=true/.test(window.location)
            && localStorage.getItem('active-eruda') != 'true') return;
        document.write('<scr' + 'ipt src="' + src
            + '"></scr' + 'ipt>');
        document.write('<scr' + 'ipt>');
        document.write('window.addEventListener(' +
            '"load", ' +
```

---

[16] For `create-react-app` applications, this should be added to *public/index.html*.

```
'function () {' +
'  var container=document.createElement("div"); ' +
'  document.body.appendChild(container);' +
'  eruda.init({' +
'    container: container,' +
'    tool: ["console", "elements"]' +
'  });' +
'})');
      document.write('</scr' + 'ipt>');
    })();
  </script>
```

If you now open your application as *http://ipaddress/?eruda=true* or *http://ipaddress/ #eruda=true*, you will notice that an additional button has appeared in the interface, as shown in Figure 8-20.

Figure 8-20. If you add ?eruda=true *to the URL, a button will appear on the right of the page*

If you are using the example application for this chapter, then try entering a few answers into the game.[17] Then, click the Eruda button. The console will appear as shown in Figure 8-21.

---

17 The code is available in the source code repository (*https://oreil.ly/P1Tqj*) for this book.

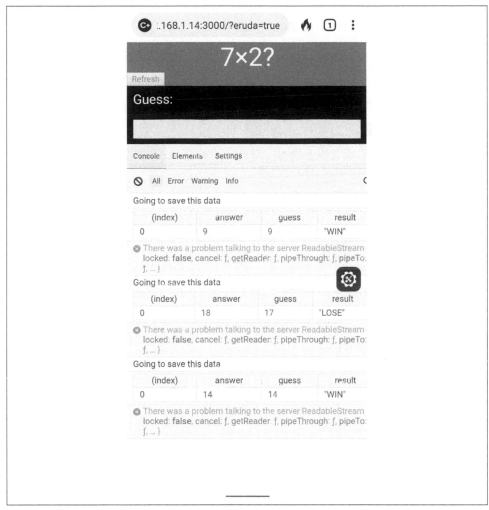

Figure 8-21. Clicking the button opens the Eruda tools

Because the endpoint the example application calls is missing, you should find some errors and other logs recorded in the console. The console even supports the much underused console.table function, which is a helpful way of displaying an array of objects in tabular format.

The Elements tab provides a fairly rudimentary view of the DOM (see Figure 8-22).

Figure 8-22. The Eruda elements view

Meanwhile, the Settings tab has an extensive set of JavaScript features that you can enable and disable while interacting with the web page (see Figure 8-23).

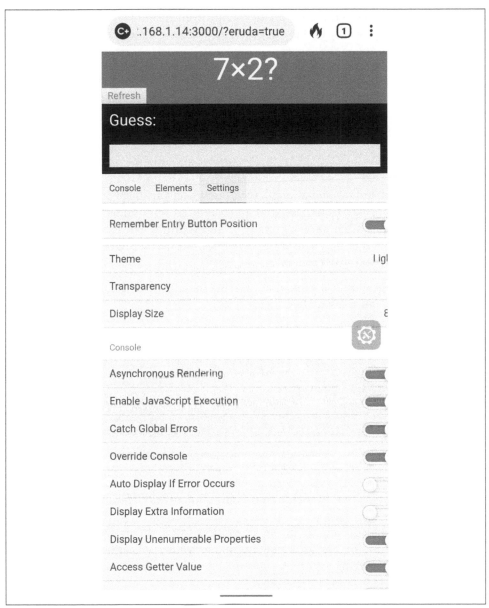

Figure 8-23. The Eruda settings view

Discussion

Eruda is a delightful tool that delivers a whole bucket of functionality, with very little work required by the developer. In addition to the basic features, it also has plugins that allow you to track performance, set the screen refresh rate, generate fake geolocations, and even write and run JavaScript from inside the browser. Once you start to use it, you probably find that it quickly becomes a standard part of your manual testing process.

You can download the source for this recipe from the GitHub site (*https://oreil.ly/ P1Tqj*).

8.8 Remove Randomness from Tests

Problem

In a perfect world, tests would always have a completely artificial environment. Tests are examples of how you would like your application to work under explicitly defined conditions. But tests often have to cope with uncertainties. For example, they might run at different times of day. The example application that we have used throughout this chapter has to deal with *randomness*.

Our example application is a game that presents the user with a randomly generated question that they must answer (see Figure 8-24).

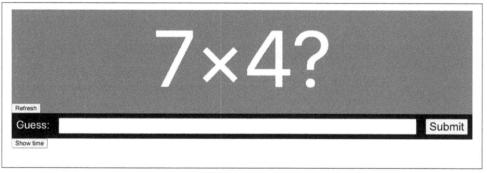

Figure 8-24. The game asks the user to calculate a random multiplication problem

Randomness might also appear in the generation of identifiers within the code or random data sets. If you ask for a new username, your application might suggest a randomly generated string.

But randomness creates a problem for tests. This is an example test that we implemented earlier in this chapter:

```
describe('Basic game functions', () => {
  it('should notify the server if I lose', () => {
    // Given I started the application
    // When I enter an incorrect answer
    // Then the server will be told that I have lost
  })
})
```

There was actually a good reason why that test looked at the case where the user entered an *incorrect* answer. The question asked is always to calculate the product of two numbers between 1 and 10. It's therefore easy to think of an incorrect answer: 101. It will *always* be wrong. But if we want to write a test to show what happens when the user enters the *correct* answer, we have a problem. The correct answer depends upon data that is randomly generated. We could write some code that finds the two numbers that appear on the screen, as in this example from the first Selenium recipe in this chapter:

```
const [number1, number2, input, submit] = await Promise.all([
  driver.findElement(By.css('.number1')).getText(),
  driver.findElement(By.css('.number2')).getText(),
  driver.findElement(By.css('input')),
  driver.findElement(By.xpath("//button[text()='Submit']")),
])
await input.sendKeys('' + number1 * number2)
await submit.click()
```

Sometimes this approach is not even possible. For example, Cypress does not allow you to capture data from the page. If we wanted to write a Cypress test to enter the correct answer to the multiplication problem, we would have great difficulty. That's because Cypress does not allow you to capture values from the page and pass them to other steps in the test.

It would be much better if we could turn off the randomness during a test.

But can we?

Solution

We will look at how we can use the Sinon library to temporarily replace the `Math.ran dom` function with a faked one of our own making.

Let's first consider how we can do this inside a unit test. We'll create a new test for the top-level `App` component, which will check that entering the correct value results in a message saying that we won.

We'll create a function that will fix the return value of `Math.random`:

```
const sinon = require('sinon')

function makeRandomAlways(result) {
  if (Math.random.restore) {
    Math.random.restore()
  }
  sinon.stub(Math, 'random').returns(result)
}
```

This function works by replacing the `random` method of the `Math` object with a stubbed method that always returns the same value. We can now use this in a test. The

Question that appears on the page always generates random numbers between 1 and 10, based upon the value of:

```
Math.random() * 10 + 1
```

If we fix `Math.random` so that it always produced the value 0.5, then the "random" number will always be 6. That means we can write a unit test like this:

```
it('should tell you that you entered the right answer', async () => {
  // Given we've rendered the app
  makeRandomAlways(0.5)
  render(<App />)

  // When we enter the correct answer
  const input = screen.getByLabelText(/guess:/i)
  const submitButton = screen.getByText('Submit')
  user.type(input, '36')
  user.click(submitButton)

  // Then we are told that we've won
  await waitFor(() => screen.findByText(/won/i), { timeout: 4000 })
})
```

And this test will always pass because the application will always ask the question, "What is 6 × 6?"

The real value of fixing `Math.random` is when we use a testing framework that explicitly *prevents* us from capturing a randomly generated value such as Cypress, as we saw earlier.

Cypress allows us to add custom commands by adding them to the *cypress/support/commands.js* script. If you edit that file and add this code:

```
Cypress.Commands.add('random', (result) => {
  cy.reload().then((win) => {
    if (win.Math.random.restore) {
      win.Math.random.restore()
    }
    sinon.stub(win.Math, 'random').returns(result)
  })
})
```

you will create a new command called `cy.random`. We can use this command to create a test for the *winning* case that we discussed in the introduction:[18]

```
describe('Basic game functions', () => {
  it('should notify the server if I win', () => {
    // Given I started the application
    cy.intercept('POST', '/api/result', {
```

_____

18 You can find out more about this test in Recipe 8.3.

```
    statusCode: 200,
    body: '',
  }).as('postResult')
  cy.visit('http://localhost:3000')
  cy.random(0.5)
  cy.contains('Refresh').click()

  // When I enter the correct answer
  cy.get('input').type('36')
  cy.contains('Submit').click()

  // Then the server will be told that I have won
  cy.wait('@postResult').then((xhr) => {
    assert.deepEqual(xhr.request.body, {
      guess: 36,
      answer: 36,
      result: 'WIN',
    })
  })
  })
 })
})
```

 After calling the cy.random command, we need to click the Refresh button in case the application generated the random numbers before the Math.random function was replaced.

Discussion

You can never remove all randomness from a test. For example, the machine's performance can significantly affect when and how often your components are re-rendered. But removing uncertainty as much as we can is generally a good thing in a test. The more we can do to remove external dependencies from our tests, the better.

We will also look at removing external dependencies in the following recipe.

You can download the source for this recipe from the GitHub site (*https://oreil.ly/ P1Tqj*).

8.9 Time Travel

Problem

Time can be the source of a tremendous number of bugs. If time were simply a scientific measurement, it would be relatively straightforward. But it isn't. The representation of time is affected by national boundaries and by local laws. Some countries have their own time zone. Others have multiple time zones. One reassuring factor is that all countries have a time zone offset in whole hours, except for places like India, where time is offset by +05:30 from UTC.

That's why it is helpful to try to fix the time within a test. But how do we do that?

Solution

We will look at how you can fix the time when testing your React application. There are some issues that you need to consider when testing time-dependent code. First, you should probably avoid changing the time on your server. In most cases, it's best to set your server to UTC and leave it that way.

That does mean that if you want to fake date and time in your browser, you will have problems as soon as the browser makes contact with the server. That means you will either have to modify the server APIs to accept an *effective date* or test time-dependent browser code in isolation from the server.[19]

We will adopt the latter approach for this recipe: using the Cypress testing system to fake any connections with the server.

We will use the same application we use for other recipes in this chapter. It's a simple game that asks the user to calculate the product of two numbers. We're going to test a feature of the game that gives the user 30 seconds to provide an answer. After 30 seconds, they will see a message telling them they've run out of time (see Figure 8-25).

Figure 8-25. The player will lose if they don't answer within 30 seconds

---

19 That is, allow the browser to say to the server *Let's pretend it's Thursday, April 14.*

We could try writing a test that somehow pauses for 30 seconds, but that has two problems. First, it will slow your test down. You don't need many 30-second pauses before your tests will become unbearable to run. Second, adding a pause is not a very precise way to test a feature. If you try to pause for 30 seconds, you might pause for 30.5 seconds before looking for the message.

To get precision, we need to take control of time within the browser. As you saw in the previous recipe, Cypress can inject code into the browser, replacing critical pieces of code with stubbed functions, which we can control. Cypress has a built-in command called cy.clock, which allows us to specify the current time.

Let's see how to use cy.clock by creating a test for the timeout feature. This will be the structure of our test:

```
describe('Basic game functions', () => {
  it('should say if I timed out', () => {
    // Given I have started a new game
    // When 29 seconds have passed
    // Then I will not see the time-out message
    // When another second has passed
    // Then I will see the time-out message
    // And the game will be over
  })
})
```

We can start by opening the application and clicking the Refresh button:

```
describe('Basic game functions', () => {
  it('should say if I timed out', () => {
    // Given I have started a new game
    cy.visit('http://localhost:3000')
    cy.contains('Refresh').click()

    // When 29 seconds have passed
    // Then I will not see the time-out message
    // When another second has passed
    // Then I will see the time-out message
    // And the game will be over
  })
})
```

Now we need to simulate 29 seconds of time passing. We can do this with the cy.clock and cy.tick commands. The cy.clock command allows you to either specify a new date and time; or, if you call cy.clock without parameters, it will set the time and date back to 1970. The cy.tick() command allows you to add a set number of milliseconds to the current date and time:

```
describe('Basic game functions', () => {
  it('should say if I timed out', () => {
    // Given I have started a new game
    cy.clock()
```

```
cy.visit('http://localhost:3000')
cy.contains('Refresh').click()

// When 29 seconds have passed
cy.tick(29000)

// Then I will not see the time-out message
// When another second has passed
// Then I will see the time-out message
// And the game will be over
  })
})
```

We can now complete the other steps in the test. For details on the other Cypress commands we're using, see the Cypress documentation (*https://oreil.ly/vahMA*):

```
describe('Basic game functions', () => {
  it('should say if I timed out', () => {
    // Given I have started a new game
    cy.clock()
    cy.visit('http://localhost:3000')
    cy.contains('Refresh').click()

    // When 29 seconds have passed
    cy.tick(29000)

    // Then I will not see the time-out message
    cy.contains(/out of time/i).should('not.exist')

    // When another second has passed
    cy.tick(1000)

    // Then I will see the time-out message
    cy.contains(/out of time/i).should('be.visible')

    // And the game will be over
    cy.get('input').should('be.disabled')
    cy.contains('Submit').should('be.disabled')
  })
})
```

If we run the test in Cypress, it passes (as you can see in Figure 8-26).

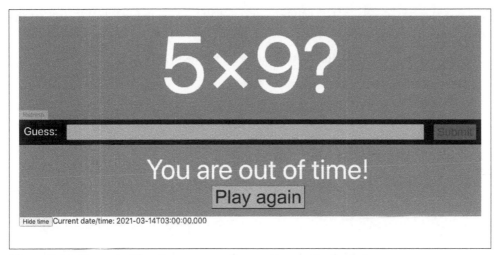

Figure 8-26. By controlling time, we can force a timeout in the test

That's a relatively simple time-based test. But what if we wanted to test something much more complex, like daylight saving time (DST)?

DST bugs are the bane of most development teams. They sit in your codebase silently for months and then suddenly appear in the spring and fall, in the early hours of the morning.

When DST occurs depends upon your time zone. And that's a particularly awful thing to deal with in client code because JavaScript dates don't work with time zones. They can certainly handle offsets; for example, you can create a `Date` object in a browser like Chrome that is set to five hours before Greenwich Mean Time:[20]

```
new Date('2021-03-14 01:59:30 GMT 0500')
```

But JavaScript dates are all implicitly in the time zone of the browser. When you create a date with a time zone name in it, the JavaScript engine will simply shift it into the browser's time zone.

The browser's time zone is fixed at the time that the browser opens. There's no way to say *Let's pretend we're in New York from now on.*

If developers create tests for DST, the tests might work only in the developer's time zone. The tests might fail if run on an integration server set to UTC.

There is, however, a way around this problem. On Linux and Mac computers (but not Windows), you can specify the time zone when you launch a browser by setting an environment variable called `TZ`. If we start the Cypress with the `TZ` variable set, any

---

20 Firefox will not generally accept this format.

browser that Cypress launches will inherit it, which means that while we can't set the time zone for a single test, we can set it for an entire test run.

First, let's launch Cypress with the time zone set to New York:

```
$ TZ='America/New_York' npx cypress open
```

The example application has a button that allows you to see the current time (see Figure 8-27).

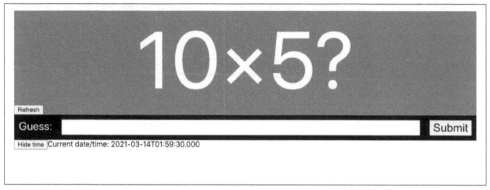

Figure 8-27. The current time is shown on the screen

We can create a test that checks that the time on the page correctly handles the change to DST. This is the test we'll create:

```
describe('Timing', () => {
  it('should tell us the current time', () => {
    cy.clock(new Date('2021-03-14 01:59:30').getTime())
    cy.visit('http://localhost:3000')
    cy.contains('Show time').click()
    cy.contains('2021-03-14T01:59:30.000').should('be.visible')
    cy.tick(30000)
    cy.contains('2021-03-14T03:00:00.000').should('be.visible')
  })
})
```

In this test, we are passing an explicit date to `cy.clock`. We need to convert this to milliseconds by calling `getTime` as `cy.clock` accepts only numeric times. We then check the initial time, and 30 seconds later, we check the time rolls over to 3 a.m., instead of 2 a.m. (as shown in Figure 8-28).

Figure 8-28. After 30 seconds, the time correctly changes from 01:59 to 03:00

Discussion

If you need to create tests that depend on the current time zone, consider placing them into a subfolder so you can run them separately. If you want to format dates into various time zones, you can use the `toLocaleString` date method:

```
new Date().toLocaleString('en-US', { timeZone: 'Asia/Tokyo' })
```

You can download the source for this recipe from the GitHub site (*https://oreil.ly/ P1Tqj*).

CHAPTER 9

Accessibility

This was a challenging chapter to write because other than wearing glasses and contact lenses, neither of us needs to use special accessibility equipment or software. We have tried to bring together a collection of tools and techniques in this chapter that will ideally help you find some of the more obvious accessibility problems in your code.

We look at how you can use landmarks and ARIA roles, which will add meaning and structure to your pages that would otherwise come only from visual grouping. We then have several recipes that show how to run manual and automated audits on your application, look for glitches in code with static analysis, and find runtime errors by automating browsers.

We then look at some of the more technical issues involved in creating custom dialogs (hint: try to use prebuilt ones from libraries), and finally, we build a simple screen reader.

For a more in-depth look at accessibility, be sure to check the Web Content Accessibility Guidelines (WCAG) (*https://oreil.ly/ie0aT*), which provide three conformance levels: A, AA, and AAA. AAA is the highest level of conformance.

If you are writing professional software, you will ideally find these recipes helpful. But nothing can replace the experience of someone who has to live with the issues caused by inaccessible software every day of their lives. Accessible software is simply good software. It maximizes your market and forces you to think more deeply about design. We would recommend, at the least, having an accessibility audit run on your code. You can contact organizations like AbilityNet (*https://oreil.ly/N7XkH*) in the UK, or just search for *accessibility software testing* wherever you are, and you will find that is the most efficient way to track down problems with your code.

9.1 Use Landmarks

Problem

Let's consider the application in Figure 9-1. It's a simple application for creating and managing tasks.

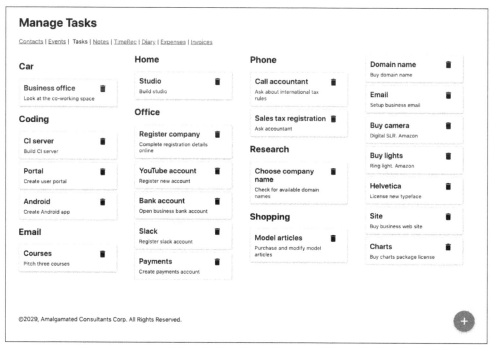

Figure 9-1. The example tasks application

If someone can see the application, they will easily distinguish between the main content (the tasks) and all of the other stuff around the edge: the links to other pages, the headings, the copyright, etc.

Let's look at the code for the main App component of this application:

```
const App = () => {
  ...
  return (
    <>
      <h1>Manage Tasks</h1>
      <a href='/contacts'>Contacts</a> | 
      <a href='/events'>Events</a> | 
      Tasks | 
      <a href='/notes'>Notes</a> | 
      <a href='/time'>TimeRec</a> | 
      <a href='/diary'>Diary</a> | 
```

```
      <a href='/expenses'>Expenses</a> | 
      <a href='/invoices'>Invoices</a>
      <button className='addButton'
          onClick={() => setFormOpen(true)}>+</button>
      <TaskContexts .../>
      &#169;2029, Amalgamated Consultants Corp. All Rights Reserved.
      <TaskForm .../>
      <ModalQuestion ...>
        Are you sure you want to delete this task?
      </ModalQuestion>
    </>
  )
}
```

The problem is that if you rely on a device to read the page to you, it can be hard to understand the page's structure. Which parts are the navigation links? Where is the main content on the page? The parsing that the human eye performs (see Figure 9-2) is difficult to replicate if you can't assess the spatial grouping of the interface.

So, how can we get around this problem? What can we use instead of visual grouping to make the structure of a page more understandable?

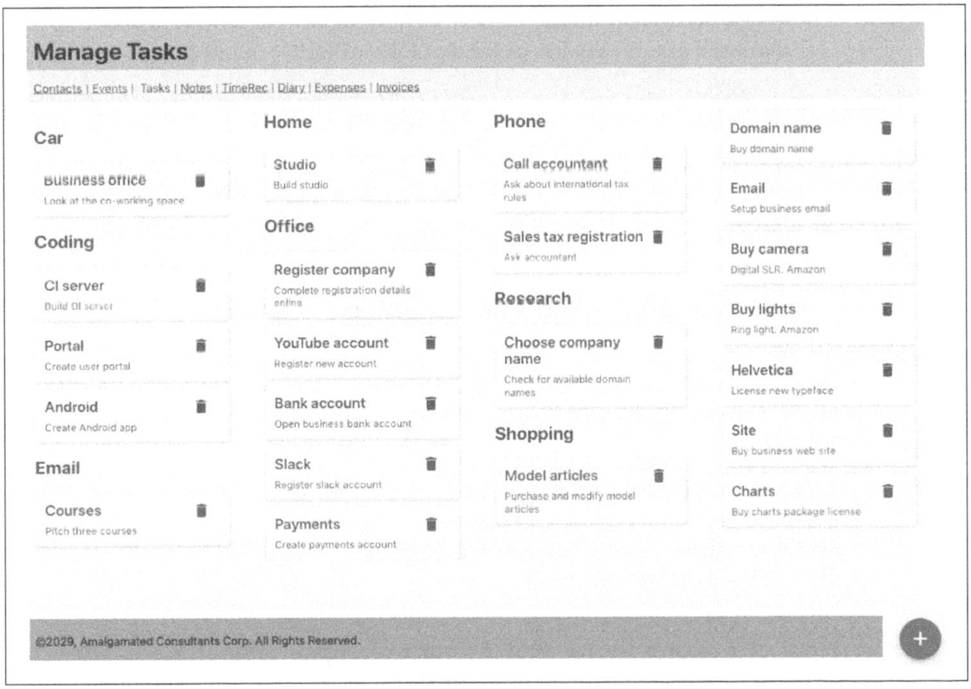

Figure 9-2. Sighted viewers can quickly identify the sections of the page spatially

Solution

We are going to introduce *landmarks* to our code. Landmarks are HTML elements that we can use to group parts of our interface structurally to mirror how they're grouped visually. Landmarks are also helpful when designing a page because they force you to think about the functions of the various types of page content.

Let's begin by highlighting the *header*. This part of the page identifies what the page is about. We would typically use an h1 heading for this, but we might also include commonly used tools, or perhaps a logo. We can identify the header using the header tag:

```
<header>
    <h1>Manage Tasks</h1>
</header>
```

We should always have an h1 heading on the page, and we should use lower-level headings to structure the content of the rest of the page without skipping any levels. For example, you should never have an h1 heading and an h3 heading without an h2 heading somewhere between the two. Headings are a handy navigation device for people using screen readers, including functions that allow the user to skip backward and forward between headings.

Next, we need to think about *navigation*. Navigation can come in many forms. It might be a list of links (as here), or it could be a series of menus or a sidebar. The navigation is a block of components that allow you to visit the major parts of a website. You will almost certainly have other links on the page that are not part of the navigation.

We can use the nav landmark to identify the navigation of our page:

```
<nav>
    <a href='/contacts'>Contacts</a> | 
    <a href='/events'>Events</a> | 
    Tasks | 
    <a href='/notes'>Notes</a> | 
    <a href='/time'>TimeRec</a> | 
    <a href='/diary'>Diary</a> | 
    <a href='/expenses'>Expenses</a> | 
    <a href='/invoices'>Invoices</a>
</nav>
```

The crucial part of a page is the content. In our tasks application, the content is the collection of tasks. The main content is what the user primarily wants to read and interact with on the page. Occasionally, the main content might also include tools—such as the floating "add" button in the tasks application—but these don't have to be in the main content, and we can move them to somewhere in the header.

We can group together the main content of the page with the `main` tag:

```
<main>
    <button className='addButton'
            onClick={() => setFormOpen(true)}>+</button>
    <TaskContexts contexts={contexts}
                tasks={tasks}
                onDelete={setTaskToRemove}
                onEdit={task => {
                    setEditTask(task)
                    setFormOpen(true)
                }}
    />
</main>
```

Finally, we have the web page's *metadata*: the data about data. In the task application, the copyright notice at the bottom of the page is an example of metadata. You will often find metadata placed in a group at the bottom of a page, and so it is grouped in a `footer` tag:

```
<footer>
    &#169;2029, Amalgamated Consultants Corp. All Rights Reserved.
</footer>
```

There are still a couple things left from our original `App` component:

```
<TaskForm .../>
<ModalQuestion ...>
    Are you sure you want to delete this task?
</ModalQuestion>
```

The `TaskForm` is a modal dialog that appears when the user wants to create or edit a task (see Figure 9-3).

Figure 9-3. The TaskForm is a modal dialog that appears above other content

The `ModalQuestion` is a confirmation box that appears if a user tries to delete a task (see Figure 9-4).

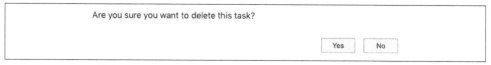
Are you sure you want to delete this task?

Yes   No

Figure 9-4. A modal question box asks the user to confirm the deletion of a task

These two components will appear only when needed. When the page is in its normal state, the modals will not appear in the page's structure, so they don't have to be included in a landmark. We will see elsewhere in this chapter that there are other ways of dealing with dynamic content, such as modals, that will make them more accessible to your audience.

This is what the final form of our `App` component looks like:

```
const App = () => {
  ....
  return (
    <>
      <header>
        <h1>Manage Tasks</h1>
      </header>
      <nav>
        <a href='/contacts'>Contacts</a> | 
        <a href='/events'>Events</a> | 
        Tasks | 
        <a href='/notes'>Notes</a> | 
        <a href='/time'>TimeRec</a> | 
        <a href='/diary'>Diary</a> | 
        <a href='/expenses'>Expenses</a> | 
        <a href='/invoices'>Invoices</a>
      </nav>
      <main>
      <button className='addButton'
          onClick={() => setFormOpen(true)}>+</button>
        <TaskContexts .../>
      </main>
      <footer>
        &#169;2029, Amalgamated Consultants Corp. All Rights Reserved.
      </footer>
      <TaskForm .../>
      <ModalQuestion ...>
        Are you sure you want to delete this task?
      </ModalQuestion>
    </>
  )
}
```

Discussion

Landmarks are part of HTML5 and so are natively supported in browsers. This means that you can start using them without needing to add special tooling or support libraries.

You will find that some automated accessibility tools might complain about landmarks rendered by React applications. The standard guidelines state that *all* content in the body of a web page should be inside a landmark. But most React applications render their content (including any landmarks) inside a single div, which instantly breaks the rules.

It is probably safe to ignore the issue. So long as the landmarks exist and they are all at the same level, it shouldn't matter that they are wrapped in an additional div.

You can download the source for this recipe from the [GitHub site].

9.2 Apply Roles, Alts, and Titles

Problem

It's common to have components in applications that behave like buttons, even if they're not buttons. Likewise, you might have components that look like pop-up dialog boxes without actually being dialog boxes. Or you might have collections of data structurally similar to lists that don't use the ol and ul tags.

Creating components that behave like standard UI elements isn't a problem if you can see the visual styling of the component. If something looks like a button to a user, they will treat it as a button, regardless of its implementation.

But there's a problem if someone can't see the visual styling of a component. Instead, you need to describe the purpose of a component for people who can't see it.

Solution

We're going to look at using *roles* within the application. The *role* describes the meaning of a component: it tells the user what purpose it serves. Roles are part of the semantics of a web page and so are similar to the semantic landmarks that we discuss in Recipe 9.1.

Here is a list of some typical roles that you can apply to rendered HTML:

Role name	Purpose
alert	Tells the user that something has happened.
article	Large block of text content, like a news story.
button	Something you can click to do something.
checkbox	A user-selectable true/false value.
comment	Like a user-submitted comment or reaction.
complementary	Additional information, perhaps in a sidebar.
contentinfo	Copyright notices, author names, publication dates.
dialog	Something floats over the other content. Often modal.
feed	Common in blogs. It's a list of articles.
figure	An illustration.
list	A sequential group of things.
listitem	Each of the things in a list.
search	A search field.
menu	A sequence of options, typically used for navigation.
menuitem	An item on a menu.

You apply roles to elements with the role attribute. Let's consider the Task component from the example application in this chapter. The Task component renders each of the tasks as a small panel, with a Delete button:

```
import DeleteIcon from './delete-24px.svg'
import './Task.css'

const Task = ({ task, onDelete, onEdit }) => {
  return (
    <div className="Task">
      <div className="Task-contents"
        ...
      >
      <div className="Task-details">
        <div className="Task-title">{task.title}</div>
        <div className="Task-description">{task.description}</div>
      </div>
      <div className="Task-controls">
        <img
          src={DeleteIcon}
          width={24}
          height={24}
          title="Delete"
          onClick={(evt) => {
            evt.stopPropagation()
            onDelete()
          }}
          alt="Delete icon"
```

```
            />
          </div>
        </div>
      </div>
    )
  }
```

We group tasks on the page under headings that describe the context in which a person would perform the task. For example, you might have a series of tasks grouped under the heading Phone (see Figure 9-5).

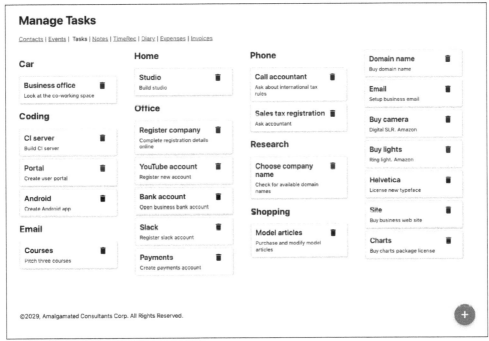

Figure 9-5. Each group contains a list of tasks

So, the tasks appear to match the `listitem` role. They are things that appear inside an ordered collection. We could therefore add that role to the first `div`:

```
return <div role='listitem' className='Task'>
    <div className='Task-details'>
        . . . .
```

If we stopped there, we would have a problem. *Roles have rules*. You cannot apply the `listitem` role to a component unless it appears inside something with a `list` role. So if we are going to mark our `Task` components as `listitems`, we will also need to give the `TaskList` parent a `list` role:

```
import Task from '../Task'
import './TaskList.css'

function TaskList({ tasks, onDelete, onEdit }) {
  return (
    <div role="list" className="TaskList">
      {tasks.map((t) => (
        <Task
          key={t.id}
          task={t}
          onDelete={() => onDelete(t)}
          onEdit={() => onEdit(t)}
        />
      ))}
    </div>
  )
}

export default TaskList
```

Using list and listitem roles is perfectly valid. But it is probably far better in practice if we have HTML that behaves like a list to change the markup and use real ul and li tags. From an accessibility point of view, it probably makes no difference. But it is always good to avoid filling your HTML with endless div tags. In general, if you can use a real HTML tag instead of a role, it's probably best to do so.

Let's remove the list role from TaskList and make a real ul:

```
import Task from '../Task'
import './TaskList.css'

function TaskList({ tasks, onDelete, onEdit }) {
  return (
    <ul className="TaskList">
      {tasks.map((t) => (
        <Task
          key={t.id}
          task={t}
          onDelete={() => onDelete(t)}
          onEdit={() => onEdit(t)}
        />
      ))}
    </ul>
  )
}

export default TaskList
```

Then we can replace the listitem role in Task with a li tag:

```
import './Task.css'

const Task = ({ task, onDelete, onEdit }) => {
  return (
    <li className="Task">
      <div
        className="Task-contents"
        ...
      >
        <div className="Task-details">...</div>
        <div className="Task-controls">...</div>
      </div>
    </li>
  )
}

export default Task
```

Using li tags will mean that we have to make a few CSS style changes to remove the list bullet points, but the code will be easier to read for any developer (and it may be you) who looks at it in the future.

Next, let's take a look at the navigation section of the example application. It has a series of links that you might almost think of as a menu of options:

```
<nav>
    <a href='/contacts'>Contacts</a>  | 
    <a href='/events'>Events</a>  | 
    Tasks  | 
    <a href='/notes'>Notes</a>  | 
    <a href='/time'>TimeRec</a>  | 
    <a href='/diary'>Diary</a>  | 
    <a href='/expenses'>Expenses</a>  | 
    <a href='/invoices'>Invoices</a>
</nav>
```

So, should you apply the menu and menuitem roles here? The answer to this is: almost certainly *no*.

Menus and menu items have expected behavior. A user who arrives at a menu will probably expect it to pop up if they select it. Once the menu is visible, they will probably use the arrow keys to navigate the options rather than move around with the Tab key.[1]

Now let's take a look at the + button in our example application that allows a user to create a new task by displaying a pop-up task form (see Figure 9-6).

---

1 For an interesting discussion on the issues surrounding menus and menu items, see this article (*https://oreil.ly/i8AMI*) by Adrian Roselli.

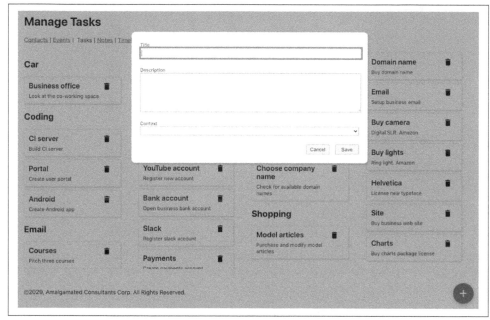

Figure 9-6. A new task form appears when the user clicks the + button

This is the code for the button:

```
<button className='addButton'
    onClick={() => setFormOpen(true)}>+</button>
```

Do we need to apply the `button` role? No. The element is already a button. But we can provide some additional information about what the user can expect to happen if they click the button. A pop-up will appear. We can make that explicit in the HTML with the `aria-haspopup` attribute:

```
<button aria-haspopup='dialog' className='addButton'
    onClick={() => setFormOpen(true)}>+</button>
```

 The value of the `aria-haspopup` attribute has to match the role of the component that will appear as a result. In this case, we're going to display a dialog. You can also set the `aria-haspopup` attribute to the value `true`. Still, a screen reader will interpret this as a `menu` because components with associated pop-ups typically are used to open menus.

Because we've set `aria-haspopup` to `dialog`, we will also need to make sure the `Task Form` that appears has the role `dialog`. This is the current code for the `TaskForm`:

```
const TaskForm = ({ task, contexts, onCreate, onClose, open }) => {
    ...
```

```
    return <Modal open={open} onCancel={close}>
      <form>
        ....
      </form>
      <ModalFooter>
        <button onClick={...}>Cancel</button>
        <button onClick={...}>Save</button>
      </ModalFooter>
    </Modal>
}
```

We will wrap the TaskForm in a Modal component, like this:

```
import './Modal.css'

function Modal({ open, onCancel, children }) {
  if (!open) {
    return null
  }

  return <div className='Modal'
        ...
    >
    <div className='Modal-dialog'
        ...
      >
        {children}
      </div>
    </div>
}

export default Modal
```

There are two parts to this Modal component:

- An external Modal wrapper, which is there to shade the other content of the page and is a semi-transparent layer
- An inner Modal-dialog div, which displays the contents in what looks like a window

Because the Modal class is reusable and might be used in things other than *dialogs* (such as *alerts*), we will give the Modal class an additional title property, which will be applied to the Modal-dialog. The title will make the purpose of the dialog clear to anyone with a screen reader.

This gives us our updated Modal component:

```
import './Modal.css'

function Modal({ open, onCancel, children, role, title }) {
```

```
    if (!open) {
      return null
    }

    return <div role='presentation' className='Modal'
          ...
    >
      <div className='Modal-dialog'
          role={role} title={title}
          ...
      >
        {children}
      </div>
    </div>
}

export default Modal
```

Here is our updated `TaskForm` component:

```
const TaskForm = ({ task, contexts, onCreate, onClose, open }) => {
  ...

  return <Modal title='Create or edit a task'
          role='dialog'
          open={open} onCancel={close}>
    <form>
      ....
    </form>
    <ModalFooter>
      <button onClick={...}>Cancel</button>
      <button onClick={...}>Save</button>
    </ModalFooter>
  </Modal>
}
```

Finally, let's consider the Delete button that appears next to each `Task` and looks like a small trash can:

```
<img src={DeleteIcon}
    width={24}
    height={24}
    alt='Delete icon'
    aria-haspopup='dialog'
    role='button'
    title='Delete'
    onClick={evt => {
      evt.stopPropagation()
      evt.preventDefault()
      onDelete()
    }}
/>
```

The trash can icon is working as a button, so we've given it that role. The trash can already has an `aria-haspopup` because a dialog will ask the user to confirm the deletion.

But just like in the case of the lists and list items, it is often better to implement buttons as buttons. We can rewrite this component as a `button` wrapping an image:

```
<button
  onClick={evt => {
    evt.stopPropagation()
    evt.preventDefault()
    onDelete()
  }}
  title='Delete'
  aria-haspopup='dialog'
>
  <img src={DeleteIcon}
    width={24}
    height={24}
    alt='Delete icon'
  />
</button>
```

Not only will this be clearer to developers, but it will also be automatically tabbable.

Discussion

Roles overlap in some ways with landmarks. There are landmark roles available, like `main` and `header`. But they serve two different purposes. Landmarks are, as the name suggests, ways of highlighting major parts of a web page. Roles, in contrast, describe the intended behavior of some part of the interface. In both cases, landmarks and roles are there to provide additional meaning to a web page.

If your interface contains components that behave like standard HTML elements, such as lists, it is often better to style the standard HTML markup than re-create the elements with custom code.

You can download the source for this recipe from the GitHub site (*https://oreil.ly/0GfgA*).

9.3 Check Accessibility with ESlint

Problem

If you don't need to use any accessibility equipment, it can be challenging to identify accessibility problems.[2] In the heat of development, it's also easy to acquire regression issues that break the accessibility of code that you've previously tested.

What you need is a way to quickly and easily find accessibility problems as you create them. You need a process that is continuously watching your code as you type and flagging them immediately while you still remember what you did.

Solution

We're going to see how you can configure the `eslint` tool to find the more obvious accessibility problems in code.

`eslint` is a tool that performs static analysis on your code. It will find unused variables, missing dependencies in `useEffect` calls, and so on. If you created your application with `create-react-app`, you probably have `eslint` running continuously on your application. The development server will rerun `eslint` each time the code needs recompiling, and any `eslint` errors will appear in the server window.

If you don't already have `eslint` installed, you can install it with this command:

```
$ npm install --save-dev eslint
```

Or you can use its `yarn` equivalent. `eslint` can be extended with *plugins*. A plugin is a collection of rules that `eslint` will apply to static code as it is saved. There is a plugin specifically created to check for accessibility problems. It's called jsx-a11y, and you can install it with the following:

```
$ npm install --save-dev eslint-plugin-jsx-a11y
```

If you want to be able to run `eslint` manually, you can add a script to your *package.json* file:[3]

```
"scripts": {
  ....
  "lint": "eslint src"
},
```

---

2 We found this ourselves while writing this chapter. As a result, we have undoubtedly missed many, many accessibility issues in the example application.

3 Particularly useful if you want to check your code in pre-commit Git hooks or on an integration server.

Before we can use the jsx-a11y plugin, we will need to configure it. We can do this by updating the eslintConfig section of *package.json*:

```
"eslintConfig": {
  "extends": [
    "react-app"
    "react-app/jest",
    "plugin:jsx-a11y/recommended"
  ],
  "plugins": [
    "jsx-a11y"
  ],
  "rules": {}
}
```

This configuration will tell eslint to use the new plugin, and it will also enable a set of recommended accessibility rules.

You can also, if you choose, configure the way each of the rules works by adding additional configuration to the rules section. And we're going to do that now, by disabling one of the rules:

```
"eslintConfig": {
  "extends": [
    "react-app"
    "react-app/jest",
    "plugin:jsx-a11y/recommended"
  ],
  "plugins": [
    "jsx-a11y"
  ],
  "rules": {
    "jsx-a11y/no-onchange": "off"
  }
}
```

Disabling rules might seem like a bad idea, but there is a reason why you might want to disable the no-onchange rule specifically.

The jsx-a11y developers created the no-onchange rule because of a problem with old browsers, which implemented onchange in disparate ways. Some would generate an onChange event every time the user typed a character into an input field. Others would generate the event only when the user left the field. The different behaviors caused a huge number of problems for people using accessibility tools.

The solution was to replace all onChange handlers with onBlur handlers, which meant that *all* browsers would fire field change events consistently: when the user left the field.

But this rule is entirely out-of-date now and is deprecated in the plugin. If you try to replace all of the onChange handlers in your React code with onBlur handlers, you will change significantly how your application works. You will also be going away from the standard way React tracks the state of form fields: to use `onChange`.

So, in this *one* case, it is a good idea to disable the rule.

We can now run `eslint`, with our accessibility rules enabled:

```
$ npm run lint
```

In an earlier version of the application, `eslint` found a number of errors:

```
$ npm run lint
> app@0.1.0 lint app
> eslint src
app/src/Task/Task.js
  6:9  error  Visible, non-interactive elements with click handlers
              must have at least one keyboard listener
              jsx-a11y/click-events-have-key-events
  6:9  error  Static HTML elements with event handlers require a role
              jsx-a11y/no-static-element-interactions
✖ 2 problems (2 errors, 0 warnings)
```

To see what the cause of these errors, let's take a look at the *Task.js* source code:

```
<li className="Task">
  <div className="Task-contents" onClick={onEdit}>
    ....
  </div>
</li>
```

The `Task` component displays the details of a task inside a small card panel (see Figure 9-7).

Figure 9-7. The app displays tasks in separate panels, each with a delete button

If the user clicks a task, they will open a form that will allow them to edit the task's details. The code that does this is the `onClick` handler on the `Task-contents` div.

To understand why `eslint` is unhappy, let's first look at this error:

```
  6:9  error  Static HTML elements with event handlers require a role
              jsx-a11y/no-static-element-interactions
```

Elements like `div`s are *static*. They have no built-in interactive behavior. By default, they are just things that layout other things. `eslint` is unhappy because the `onClick` handler suggests that this particular `div` is actually being used as an *active*

---

component. If someone is using an accessibility device, we will need to tell them the purpose of this component. `eslint` expects us to do that by giving the `div` a *role*.[4]

We will give this `div` a role of `button` to indicate that the user will use the component by clicking it. When we click a task, we will display a pop-up edit window, so we will also give the `div` an `aria-haspopup` attribute to tell the user that clicking the task will open a dialog:

```
<li className='Task'>
        <div className='Task-contents'
            role='button'
            aria-haspopup='dialog'
            onClick={onEdit}
        >
    ....
</div>
</li>
```

 It is often better to convert an element to a native `button` tag rather than use the `button` role. However, in this case, the `div` is wrapping a reasonably large block of HTML text, so it makes more sense to provide a role rather than deal with the styling consequences of making a gray button look like a card.

If we run `eslint` again, we still have two errors. But one of them is new:

```
$ npm run lint
> app@0.1.0 lint app
> eslint src
app/src/Task/Task.js
  6:9  error  Visible, non-interactive elements with click handlers
              must have at least one keyboard listener
              jsx-a11y/click-events-have-key-events
  6:9  error  Elements with the 'button' interactive role must be tabbable
              jsx-a11y/interactive-supports-focus
✖ 2 problems (2 errors, 0 warnings)
```

We've said that the task behaves like a button. But: roles have rules. If we want something to be treated like a button, it must behave like a button. One thing that buttons can do is be *tabbed* to. They need to be able to receive focus from the keyboard. We can do that by adding a `tabIndex` attribute:

```
<li className='Task'>
        <div className='Task-contents'
            role='button'
            tabIndex={0}
```

---

4 See Recipe 9.2 for details on roles and their uses.

```
          onClick={onEdit}
      >
        ....
    </div>
    </li>
```

Setting `tabIndex` to 0 means that our task will become part of the tab sequence of the page.

 `tabIndex` can have several values: –1 means that it can be focused programmatically only; 0 means that it is an ordinary tabbable component. If an element has a tabbable value greater than 0, it means the focus system should give it a higher priority. It would be best if you generally avoided values greater than 0, as they can cause accessibility problems.[5]

If we run `eslint` again, we have just one error:

```
$ npm run lint
> app@0.1.0 lint app
> eslint src
app/src/Task/Task.js
   6:9   error   Visible, non-interactive elements with click handlers
                 must have at least one keyboard listener
                 jsx-a11y/click-events-have-key-events
1 problems (1 errors, 0 warnings)
```

This error means that we have an `onClick` event to say what happens if someone clicks the task with a mouse, but we have no code to respond to the keyboard. If someone is unable to use the mouse, they will be unable to edit a task.

So we will need to add some sort of key-event handler. We'll add code to call the edit event if the user presses the Enter key or presses the spacebar:

```
<li className="Task">
  <div
    className="Task-contents"
    role="button"
    tabIndex={0}
    onClick={onEdit}
    onKeyDown={(evt) => {
      if (evt.key === 'Enter' || evt.key === ' ') {
        evt.preventDefault()
        onEdit()
      }
    }}
  >
```

---

5 See the issues involving values greater than zero in Recipe 9.8.

```
    ....
    </div>
  </li>
```

Adding the keyboard handler will fix the remaining error.

 Each of the rules in jsx-a11y has an associated page on GitHub (*https://oreil.ly/uo7Ry*), providing more details about why code might break a rule and what you can do to fix it.

Discussion

jsx-a11y is probably one of the most useful plugins available for `eslint`. Often, lint rules will check for good programming practice and can find a few coding issues. But the jsx-a11y plugin can genuinely change the design of your application.

Making sure your application allows keyboard navigation is important not only for people using accessibility tools, but it's also useful for people who might use your application frequently. If someone uses an application for a long time, they will often prefer to use a keyboard instead of a mouse because a keyboard requires less movement and is more precise.

We've also looked at how setting `tabIndex` can give elements keyboard focus. Some browsers—notably Firefox—provide subtle indicators to show which elements have keyboard focus. If you want to make it clear to users where the focus currently is, consider adding some top-level CSS to your application:

```
:focus-visible {
    outline: 2px solid blue;
}
```

This style rule will add a discernible outline to any component with keyboard focus. Some users will be more likely to choose keyboard navigation once they can see it is available.

You can download the source for this recipe from the GitHub site (*https://oreil.ly/0GfgA*).

9.4 Use Axe DevTools at Runtime

Problem

Static code analysis tools, like `eslint`, can be used to uncover many accessibility problems. But static analysis is limited. It will often miss errors that occur at runtime.

Code might dynamically behave in a way that a static analysis tool could not predict. We need to check the accessibility of an application when it is up and running in a web browser.

Solution

We're going to install the axe DevTools plugin. This is available for both Firefox (*https://oreil.ly/S1TcB*) and Chrome (*https://oreil.ly/MhiK0*).

Once it's installed, you will have an additional tab in the browser's developer console (see Figure 9-8).

Figure 9-8. The axe DevTools in the developer console

To see how it works, let's mess up some of the code in the example task application we are using throughout this chapter.

The application includes a pop-up `TaskForm` component. This component has been given a `dialog` role, but we can modify it to have some invalid value:

```
const TaskForm = ({ task, contexts, onCreate, onClose, open }) => {
  ...
  return (
    <Modal
      title="Create or edit a task"
      role="fish"
      open={open}
      onCancel={close}
    >
      <form>...</form>
      <ModalFooter>...</ModalFooter>
    </Modal>
  )
}
```

If you open *http://localhost:3000* and click the button to create a task, you will see the task form (see Figure 9-9).

Figure 9-9. The new task form appears when you press the + button

If we now open the developer tools window in the browser, switch to the axe Dev-Tools tab, and run an audit on the page, you will see two errors (see Figure 9-10).

Figure 9-10. Setting an invalid value in the modal causes two errors

There are two errors because, first, the dialog does not contain a valid *role*. Second, the modal no longer has a `dialog` role, which means it no longer acts as a landmark.

Some roles, such as `dialog`, mark an element as a vital landmark element within the page. Every part of the application must appear inside a landmark.

If you reset the code and refresh the DevTools audit, the errors will disappear.

You could imagine that some future static code analysis might include a scan of all code that checks for invalid `role` values.[6] However, DevTools can also check for other, more subtle problems.

In the example application, edit the *App.css* file, and add some code to change the color of the main heading:

```
h1 {
    color: #9e9e9e;
}
```

Figure 9-11. The result of changing the color of the first-level heading

The result doesn't appear to be too drastic (see Figure 9-11), but it does cause Dev-Tools to display this error:

```
Elements must have sufficient color contrast

Fix the following:
Element has insufficient color contrast of 2.67 (foreground color: #9e9e9e,
background color: #ffffff, font size: 24.0pt (32px), font weight: bold).
Expected contrast ratio of 3:1
```

The Chrome browser makes it relatively easy to fix contrast errors from within the developer console. If you inspect the `h1` heading, examine the `color` style of the element, and then click the small color panel, you will see the contrast problem reported in Figure 9-12.

---

6 By the time you read this book, such a rule might exist.

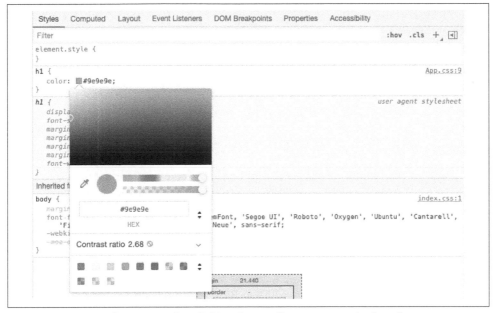

Figure 9-12. View the contrast by clicking the small gray square in the color property

If you now open the Contrast section, you can adjust the color to meet both AA and AAA accessibility standards for contrast (see Figure 9-13).

Figure 9-13. Open the contrast ratio to adjust the color to meet accessibility standards

Chrome suggests changing the color from #949494 to #767676. The difference is not hugely noticeable for most people but will be significantly easier to read for the users who are less sensitive to contrast (see Figure 9-14).

Manage Tasks

Contacts | Events | **Tasks** | Notes | TimeRec | Diary | Expenses | Invoices

Figure 9-14. The result of changing the contrast to meet the AAA standard

 Sometimes, Chrome will not display the contrast information if it cannot identify a specific background color. You can avoid this problem by temporarily assigning a `backgroundColor` to the element you are checking.

Discussion

The axe DevTools extension is straightforward to use and can find many issues that a static analysis tool will miss.

It does rely on the developer manually checking for errors, but we will see in the next chapter that there are ways of automating browser-based accessibility tests.

You can download the source for this recipe from the GitHub site (*https://oreil.ly/0GfgA*).

9.5 Automate Browser Testing with Cypress Axe

Problem

The previous recipe made clear that some accessibility problems appear only at runtime in a real web browser and so can't be found with static analysis.

If we rely on manual browser testing, we will likely acquire regression issues. It would be much better to automate the kinds of manual checks that tools like axe DevTools allow us to perform inside a browser.

Solution

We will examine how to automate browser accessibility testing with a plugin for the Cypress testing framework called `cypress-axe`. The `cypress-axe` plugin uses the same `axe-core` library as axe DevTools. Still, because we can use `cypress-axe` in browser-level tests, we can automate the auditing process so that an integration server can instantly find regression errors.

We will need to have Cypress and the `axe-core` library installed in our application:

```
$ npm install --save-dev cypress axe-core
```

We can then install the `cypress-axe` extension:

```
$ npm install --save-dev cypress-axe
```

If this is the first time you've installed Cypress, you will need to run the Cypress application, which will create the appropriate directories and initial code that you can use as the basis of your tests. You can start Cypress with this command:

```
$ npx cypress open
```

We'll need to configure the `cypress-axe` plugin. Edit the *cypress/support/index.js* file, and add this line of code:

```
import 'cypress-axe'
```

We will also need to add a couple of hooks that will allow us to record errors during a test run. We can do this by editing the *cypress/plugins/index.js* file and adding this code:

```
module.exports = (on, config) => {
  on('task', {
    log(message) {
      console.log(message)
      return null
    },
    table(message) {
      console.table(message)
      return null
    },
  })
}
```

You can then remove all of the example tests from the *cypress/integration* directory and create a new file called *cypress/integration/accessibility.js:*[7]

```
function terminalLog(violations) {
  cy.task(
    'log',
    `${violations.length} accessibility violation${
      violations.length === 1 ? '' : 's'
    } ${violations.length === 1 ? 'was' : 'were'} detected`
  )
  const violationData = violations.map(
    ({ id, impact, description, nodes }) => ({
      id,
      impact,
```

---

7 You can call this file whatever you like, so long as it has a *.js* extension and is inside the integration directory.

```
      description,
      nodes: nodes.length,
    })
  )

  cy.task('table', violationData)
  console.table(violationData)
}

describe('can be used', () => {
  it('should be accessible when starting', () => {
    cy.visit('/')
    cy.injectAxe()
    cy.checkA11y(null, null, terminalLog)
  })
})
```

This is based on the example code (*https://oreil.ly/2Exyx*) from the cypress-axe repository.

The test is inside the describe function. The terminalLog function is used to report errors.

The test has this structure:

1. Opens the page at /.
2. Injects the axe-core library into the page
3. Runs an audit of the page

The axe-core library doing most of the work is the same library used by other tools, such as the axe DevTools browser extension. The axe-core library will examine the current DOM and check it against its rule base. It will then report any failures it finds.

The cypress-axe plugin injects the axe-core library into the browser and uses the checkA11y command to run an audit. It sends the issues to the terminalLog function.

If you run this test in Cypress, by double-clicking *accessibility.js*, it will pass (see Figure 9-15).

So, let's create a problem. Let's add a second test:

```
it('should be accessible when creating a task', () => {
  cy.visit('/')
  cy.injectAxe()
  cy.contains('+').click()
  cy.checkA11y(null, null, terminalLog)
})
```

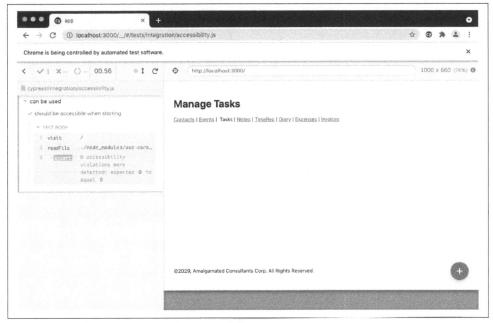

Figure 9-15. The code passing the accessibility test

The test opens the application, clicks the + button to open the form to create a task, and then performs an audit.

In its current form, the application will also pass this test. So, let's modify the `Task Form` in the example application to have an invalid `role` value:

```
const TaskForm = ({ task, contexts, onCreate, onClose, open }) => {
  ...
  return (
    <Modal
      title="Create or edit a task"
      role="hatstand"
      open={open}
      onCancel={close}
    >
      <form>...</form>
      <ModalFooter>...</ModalFooter>
    </Modal>
  )
}
```

If you rerun the test, it will now fail. You need to run the test with the JavaScript console open (see Figure 9-16) to see the failure inside a console table.

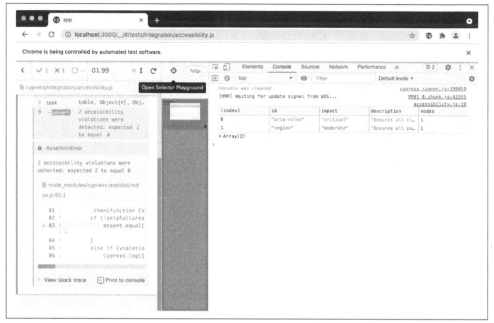

Figure 9-16. You will find the details of failures if the console is open during the test

Discussion

For a great introduction to accessibility audits and cypress-axe testing, see Marcy Sutton's talk (*https://oreil.ly/nS6R2*) at the ReactJS Girls Conference. The talk first introduced us to the plugin, and we've been using it ever since.

You can download the source for this recipe from the GitHub site (*https://oreil.ly/0GfgA*).

9.6 Add Skip Buttons

Problem

Pages often have a bunch of content right at the start. There might navigation links, quick-action menus, links to social media accounts, search fields, etc. If you can use a mouse and see the page, this won't be a problem. You will probably mentally filter them out and start using the main content of the page.

But if you are using a screen reader, you might have to listen to details of each one of those initial elements on each page you visit. Modern screen reader technology often allows users to automatically navigate through sections and headings, but it can still take some time to figure out where the important things start.

That's why many websites include hidden links and button that typically include text like "Skip to content" that allows keyboard users to get to the critical start of the page.

One example is YouTube. If you open YouTube and then hit the Tab key a few times, you see a button appear (see Figure 9-17), which will move the keyboard focus to the main content if you hit the spacebar.

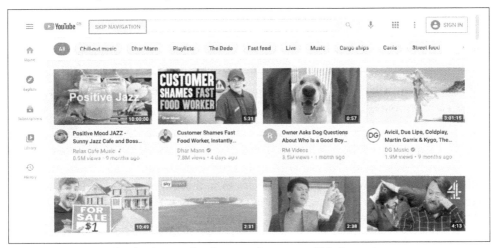

Figure 9-17. YouTube displays a skip button if you press Tab three times

How do you create a button that appears only when you Tab to it?

Solution

This recipe contains a reusable `SkipButton` component that we can include on pretty much any page without breaking the design or layout.

It needs to have several features:

- It needs to be hidden unless we tab into it. We don't just want a transparent button, just in case the user hits it if they accidentally click that part of the screen.
- It needs to float above the page content so that we don't need to leave space for it in the layout.
- It needs to work as an accessible button. That means it has to be recognized by screen readers and behave how a button behaves. If we hit the Enter key or spacebar when it's focused, we want it to work.
- It needs to disappear once we've used it.

We'll add a few other requirements along the way, but this should get us started.

Let's start by creating a new component, called `SkipButton`. We'll make it return a single `div` and allow it to include any children that are passed to it:

```
const SkipButton = (props) => {
  const { className, children, ...others } = props

  return (
    <div className={`SkipButton ${className || ''}`} {...others}>
      {children}
    </div>
  )
}
```

The component will also accept a class name and any other properties that a parent might care to pass.

We want screen readers to see it as an actual `button`. We could do this by replacing the `div` with a `button`, but we'll keep it as a `div` so that the styling is a little easier to apply. However, we will give it a `role` of `button` and—because roles have rules—we will also give it a `tabIndex` value of `0`. That's something that we'd need to do anyway, because we want the user to be able to Tab to it:

```
const SkipButton = (props) => {
  const { className, children, ...others } = props

  return (
    <div
      className={`SkipButton ${className || ''}`}
      role="button"
      tabIndex={0}
      {...others}
    >
      {children}
    </div>
  )
}
```

We need the button to do something when it's clicked. Or rather, we need it to do something when the user presses the Enter key or the spacebar. So, we'll allow it to accept a property called `onClick`, but then we'll attach it to an event handler that will trigger if the user presses the Enter key or spacebar:

```
const SkipButton = (props) => {
  const { className, children, onClick, ...others } = props

  return (
    <div
      className={`SkipButton ${className || ''}`}
      role="button"
      tabIndex={0}
      {...others}
```

```
    onKeyDown={(evt) => {
      if (evt.key === 'Enter' || evt.key === ' ') {
        evt.preventDefault()
        onClick(evt)
      }
    }}
  >
    {children}
  </div>
)
}
```

Of course, we could have named this property onKeyDown, but buttons generally have onClicks, and that will likely be easier to remember when we come to use it.

There's one final thing that we'll do to the component: we'll allow it to accept a reference, which will be useful when we reuse the component in the next recipe.

You can't pass references in the same way that you'd pass most other properties. The React renderer uses references to keep track of the generated elements in the DOM.

If we want a component to accept a reference object, we'll need to wrap everything in a call to React's forwardRef function. The forwardRef function returns a wrapped version of your component, extracting the reference from the parent component and passing it explicitly to the component it wraps. That sounds a little complicated, but it just means this:

```
import { forwardRef } from 'react'
import './SkipButton.css'

const SkipButton = forwardRef((props, ref) => {
  const { className, children, onClick, ...others } = props

  return (
    <div
      className={`SkipButton ${className || ''}`}
      role="button"
      tabIndex={0}
      ref={ref}
      {...others}
      onKeyDown={(evt) => {
        if (evt.key === 'Enter' || evt.key === ' ') {
          evt.preventDefault()
          onClick(evt)
        }
      }}
    >
      {children}
    </div>
  )
})
```

That's our completed `SkipButton`, complete with an import of some style information. It's just a button. The rest is down to styling in the *SkipButton.css* file.

We want the button to float above the other content in the page, so we'll set the `z-index` to something really high:

```
.SkipButton {
    z-index: 10000;
}
```

We want to hide the button until the user has tabbed into it. We could try to make it transparent, but that will have two problems. First, it might position itself in front of something clickable. It would block the clicks unless we also went to the trouble of setting `pointer-events` to `none`. Second, if the button is transparent but still on the screen, it might be seen as extra screen clutter for a screen reader to handle. If a screen reader is converting the screen spatially into braille, the user would hear "Skip to content" in the middle of some other piece of text.

So instead, we'll put the button way off screen until we need it:

```
.SkipButton {
    z-index: 10000;
    position: absolute;
    left: -1000px;
    top: -1000px;
}
```

So, what happens when someone tabs into the button? We can set styles that are applied only when the button has focus:

```
.SkipButton {
    z-index: 10000;
    position: absolute;
    left: -1000px;
    top: -1000px;
}

.SkipButton:focus {
    top: auto;
    left: auto;
}
```

Beyond that, we can just add some pure visual styling. It's important to remember that not everyone using this button is going to be using a screen reader. Some will want to use keyboard navigation because they are unable to use a mouse, or else they might just want to navigate with a keyboard because they find it faster:

```
.SkipButton {
    z-index: 10000;
    position: absolute;
    left: -1000px;
    top: -1000px;
```

```
        font-size: 12px;
        line-height: 16px;
        display: inline-block;
        color: black;
        font-family: sans-serif;
        background-color: #ffff88;
        padding: 8px;
        margin-left: 8px;

}

.SkipButton:focus {
    top: auto;
    left: auto;
}
```

We can now insert the SkipButton somewhere near the start of the page. It won't be visible until the user tabs into it, but positioning does matter. We want it to be within two or three Tabs from the start of the page. We'll add it to the header section:

```
<header>
    <SkipButton onClick={() => document.querySelector('.addButton').focus()}>
        Skip to content
    </SkipButton>
    <h1>Manage Tasks</h1>
</header>
```

We're just using document.querySelector here to find the element that will receive the focus. You could choose to reference the element you want to skip to or else navigate to a location. In practice, we've found that a simple document.querySelector is the most straightforward approach. It allows you to easily refer to elements that might not be in the current component. And it doesn't rely on navigating to an anchor within a page, which might break if the application changes its routing method.

If you open the example application in a browser and then press Tab, you will see the SkipButton (see Figure 9-18).

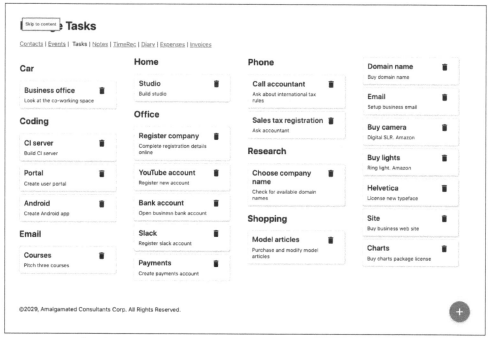

Figure 9-18. The skip button appears over the main heading if you press the Tab key

Discussion

It's a good idea to place the `SkipButton` within three Tabs of the start of the page, and it's helpful if the number of *Tabs* needed is the same on every page in your application. The user will then soon learn how to skip to the critical part of each page. We've found that `SkipButtons` are also popular with people who find using a keyboard more productive.

You could create a standard `SkipButton` for each page that also moved the focus to the first tabbable item on the `main` section of the page.[8]

You can download the source for this recipe from the GitHub site (*https://oreil.ly/0GfgA*).

---

8 See Recipe 9.1 for more information about `main` sections.

9.7 Add Skip Regions

Problem

We saw in the previous recipe that *skip buttons* are helpful if a user wants to quickly get past all of the headers and navigation at the start of a page and get into the main content.

However, even within the main content, there may be times where it would be helpful for a user to skip past a set of components. Consider the example tasks application that we are using throughout this chapter. A user can create a reasonably large number of tasks in different groups (see Figure 9-19).

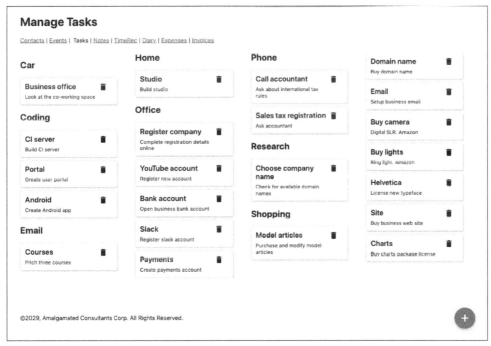

Figure 9-19. The example application displays a set of tasks, broken into groups

If they want to get to the Shopping tasks, they would potentially have to skip past 14 other tasks. And each one of those tasks would have two focus points: the task itself and the task's delete button. That means skipping past 28 focus points, even after getting into the content of the page.

What can we do to make it easier for a user to skip past a collection of components?

Solution

We're going to use the `SkipButton` component we created in the previous recipe to create skip-regions.

If we tab forward into some section of the main content of the page, such as the Office tasks, we want a button to appear that allows the user to skip past the Office tasks entirely (see Figure 9-20).

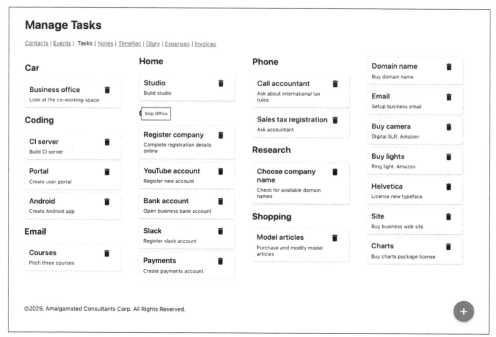

Figure 9-20. We want a skip button to appear when we tab forward into a group

Conversely, if they are tabbing backward into the Office section, we want a button to appear that allows them to skip before the Office tasks (see Figure 9-21).

We only want these buttons to appear when entering a region and not when we're leaving. That means the Skip Office button appears only when we tab forward, and the Skip before Office appears only when we tab backward.

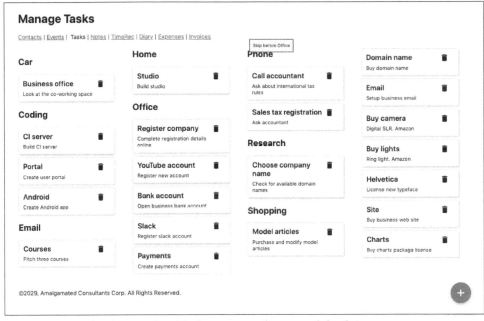

Figure 9-21. A skip button should also appear when we tab back into a group

Before looking at the implementation, let's look at how we will use a skip-region before getting into the gory details of the implementation. Our task application renders a series of groups of tasks using the TasksContexts component:

```
import TaskList from '../TaskList'
import './TaskContexts.css'

function TaskContexts({ contexts, tasks, onDelete, onEdit }) {
  return contexts.map((c) => {
    const tasksForContext = tasks.filter((t) => t.context === c.value)
    if (tasksForContext.length === 0) {
      return <div className="TaskContexts-context"> </div>
    }
    return (
      <div key={c.value} className="TaskContexts-context">
        <h2>{c.name}</h2>
        <TaskList
          tasks={tasksForContext}
          onDelete={onDelete}
          onEdit={onEdit}
        />
      </div>
    )
  })
}
```

```
    export default TaskContexts
```

Each "context" (group of tasks, for shopping, office, research, etc.) has a heading and a list of tasks. We want the user to be able to skip over each of the groups. We'll wrap each of the task-groups in a new component called Skip, like this:

```
import TaskList from '../TaskList'
import Skip from '../Skip'
import './TaskContexts.css'

function TaskContexts({ contexts, tasks, onDelete, onEdit }) {
  return contexts.map((c) => {
    const tasksForContext = tasks.filter((t) => t.context === c.value)
    if (tasksForContext.length === 0) {
      return <div className="TaskContexts-context"> </div>
    }
    return (
      <div key={c.value} className="TaskContexts-context">
        <Skip name={c.name}>
          <h2>{c.name}</h2>
          <TaskList
            tasks={tasksForContext}
            onDelete={onDelete}
            onEdit={onEdit}
          />
        </Skip>
      </div>
    )
  })
}

export default TaskContexts
```

If we wrap some tasks in our (as yet nonexistent) Skip component, the user will see the SkipButtons magically appear and disappear each time they enter the group of tasks.

All we need to pass to the Skip component is a name, which it will use in the "Skip…" and "Skip before…" text.

Now, to create the Skip component, let's begin with a simple component that renders two SkipButtons and any child components it's been given:

```
import { useRef } from 'react'
import SkipButton from '../SkipButton'
import './Skip.css'

const Skip = ({ children, name }) => {
  const startButton = useRef()
  const endButton = useRef()
```

```
      return (
        <div className="Skip">
          <SkipButton ref={startButton}>Skip {name}</SkipButton>
          {children}
          <SkipButton ref={endButton}>Skip before {name}</SkipButton>
        </div>
      )
    }
```

We have created two references that will allow us to keep track of each of the buttons. When a user clicks the startButton, the focus will skip to the endButton, and vice versa:

```
import { useRef, useState } from 'react'
import SkipButton from '../SkipButton'
import './Skip.css'

const Skip = ({ children, name }) => {
  const startButton = useRef()
  const endButton = useRef()

  const skipAfter = () => {
    if (endButton.current) {
      endButton.current.focus()
    }
  }
  const skipBefore = () => {
    if (startButton.current) {
      startButton.current.focus()
    }
  }

  return (
    <div className="Skip">
      <SkipButton ref={startButton} onClick={skipAfter}>
        Skip {name}
      </SkipButton>
      {children}
      <SkipButton ref={endButton} onClick={skipBefore}>
        Skip before {name}
      </SkipButton>
    </div>
  )
}
```

If we run this code, we will see the SkipButton when we enter a set of tasks, and we click Enter, the focus will shift to the SkipButton at the end of the list of tasks.

However, instead of jumping to the endButton, we want to focus on whatever comes *after* the endButton. It's as if we want to jump to the button at the end of the list and then immediately press Tab to get to the next thing. And we can do that if we create a function that will programmatically perform a Tab operation:[9]

```
const focusableSelector = 'a[href], ..., *[contenteditable]'

function focusNextElement() {
  var focusables = document.querySelectorAll(focusableSelector)
  var current = document.querySelectorAll(':focus')
  var nextIndex = 0
  if (current.length === 1) {
    var currentIndex = Array.prototype.indexOf.call(
      focusables,
      current[0]
    )
    if (currentIndex + 1 < focusables.length) {
      nextIndex = currentIndex + 1
    }
  }

  focusables[nextIndex].focus()
}
```

This code finds all of the elements in the DOM that we can navigate to with the Tab key. It then searches through the list until it finds the element that currently has focus, and then it sets the focus to the next element.

We can write a similar function called focusPreviousElement, which programmatically performs a back-Tab. We can then add our Skip component:

```
import { useRef, useState } from 'react'
import {
  focusNextElement,
  focusPreviousElement,
} from './focusNextElement'
import SkipButton from '../SkipButton'
import './Skip.css'

const Skip = ({ children, name }) => {
  const startButton = useRef()
  const endButton = useRef()

  const skipAfter = () => {
    if (endButton.current) {
      endButton.current.focus()
      focusNextElement()
    }
  }
  const skipBefore = () => {
```

---

[9] This is based on an answer to a question on StackOverflow (*https://oreil.ly/Li5sB*) by user Radek (*https://oreil.ly/5p8nS*).

```
      if (startButton.current) {
        startButton.current.focus()
        focusPreviousElement()
      }
    }
  }

  return (
    <div className="Skip">
      <SkipButton ref={startButton} onClick={skipAfter}>
        Skip {name}
      </SkipButton>
      {children}
      <SkipButton ref={endButton} onClick={skipBefore}>
        Skip before {name}
      </SkipButton>
    </div>
  )
}
```

When we enter a group of tasks—such as Office—we see a `SkipButton`, which will let us skip past the group entirely, onto whatever follows.

We have just one more feature to add. We only want the `SkipButtons` to appear when we are entering a skip-region, not when we're leaving one. We can do this by keeping a state variable called `inside` updated with whether the focus is currently inside or outside the current component:

```
import { useRef, useState } from 'react'
import {
  focusNextElement,
  focusPreviousElement,
} from './focusNextElement'
import SkipButton from '../SkipButton'
import './Skip.css'

const Skip = ({ children, name }) => {
  const startButton = useRef()
  const endButton = useRef()
  const [inside, setInside] = useState(false)

  const skipAfter = () => {
    if (endButton.current) {
      endButton.current.focus()
      focusNextElement()
    }
  }
  const skipBefore = () => {
    if (startButton.current) {
      startButton.current.focus()
      focusPreviousElement()
    }
  }
}
```

```
    return (
      <div
        className="Skip"
        onFocus={(evt) => {
          if (
            evt.target !== startButton.current &&
            evt.target !== endButton.current
          ) {
            setInside(true)
          }
        }}
        onBlur={(evt) => {
          if (
            evt.target !== startButton.current &&
            evt.target !== endButton.current
          ) {
            setInside(false)
          }
        }}
      >
        <SkipButton
          ref={startButton}
          tabIndex={inside ? -1 : 0}
          onClick={skipAfter}
        >
          Skip {name}
        </SkipButton>
        {children}
        <SkipButton
          ref={endButton}
          tabIndex={inside ? -1 : 0}
          onClick={skipBefore}
        >
          Skip before {name}
        </SkipButton>
      </div>
    )
  }
```

Our skip-region is now complete. If a user tabs into a group of tasks, a `SkipButton` appears. They can use the button to skip past that group and on to the next.

Discussion

It would help if you were careful about applying skip-regions too often. They are best used to skip past many components that the user would otherwise need to tab through.

There are other approaches you can take. For example, suppose your page contains a series of headings and subheadings. In that case, you might consider adding Skip Buttons that allow the user to skip to the next heading (if they are tabbing forward) or the previous heading (if they are tabbing backward).

Some users will have accessibility software that allows them to skip past groups and sections of components without any additional code required in the application. In those cases, the SkipButtons will not appear on the page, and the user will ignore them entirely.

You can download the source for this recipe from the GitHub site (*https://oreil.ly/0GfgA*).

9.8 Capture Scope in Modals

Problem

React applications frequently display pop-ups. For example, the example tasks application used in this chapter displays a pop-up dialog box when you click a task. The dialog box allows the user to edit the task's details (see Figure 9-22).

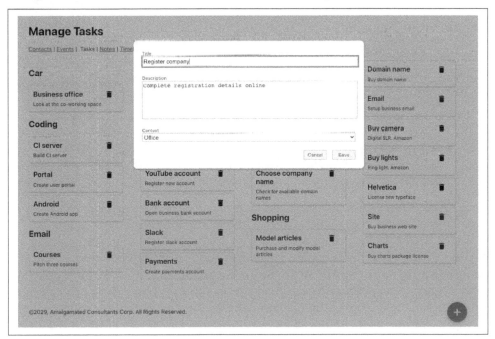

Figure 9-22. A edit dialog appears when the user clicks a task

These pop-ups are frequently *modal*, which means we will either interact with them or dismiss them before returning to the rest of the application. However, there can be a problem with custom modal dialogs: the focus can escape from them.

Let's look at the task form from the example application. An earlier version of the code suffered from this leaky-focus problem. If the user clicked a task, they would see the task form, and the first field would instantly grab the focus. But if the user then pressed back-Tab, the focus would shift into the other items in the background (see Figure 9-23).

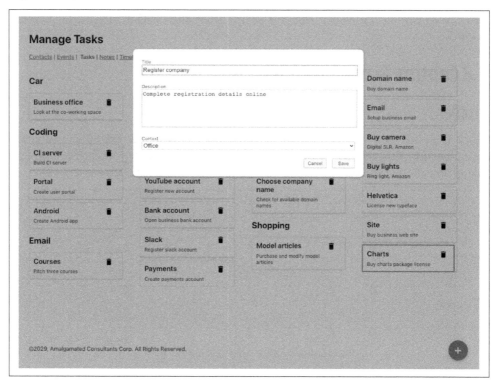

Figure 9-23. Pressing back-Tab moves the focus out of the dialog and on to the Charts task

If you can see where the focus has gone, then this is a slightly odd feature. But this would be a significant source of confusion for anyone using accessibility software, who might be completely unaware that the modal dialog is still on the screen. If someone can see the screen but cannot use a mouse, the experience might be even stranger. The user might be able to focus on a component that is hidden by the dialog.

We need a way of trapping the focus within a set of components so that the user cannot accidentally move into components that are supposed to be out of reach.

Solution

We will install the React Focus Lock library, which will trap the focus into a small subset of components. We will install it with this command:

```
$ npm install react-focus-lock
```

The React Focus Lock library works by wrapping a set of components inside a ReactFocusLock, which will watch the focus, waiting for it to move outside of itself. If that happens, it will immediately move the focus back inside.

The modal in our example application is created with the Modal component:

```
import './Modal.css'

function Modal({ open, onCancel, children, role, title }) {
  if (!open) {
    return null
  }

  return (
    <div role="presentation" className="Modal" ...>
      <div className="Modal-dialog" role={role} title={title} ...>
        {children}
      </div>
    </div>
  )
}
```

We pass the entire contents of the modal as child components. We can use the React Focus Lock library to trap the focus within those child components by wrapping them in a ReactFocusLock:

```
import ReactFocusLock from 'react-focus-lock'
import './Modal.css'

function Modal({ open, onCancel, children, role, title }) {
  if (!open) {
    return null
  }

  return (
    <div role="presentation" className="Modal" ...>
      <div className="Modal-dialog" role={role} title={title} ...>
        <ReactFocusLock>{children}</ReactFocusLock>
      </div>
    </div>
  )
}
```

Now, if a user opens the `TaskForm` and starts hitting the Tab key, they will cycle through the buttons and fields within the dialog box. If they Tab past the last button, they will move to the first field, and vice versa.

 The library works by creating a hidden button with `tabIndex` set to 1, breaking the tabindex rule in axe-core, stating that no tabindex should be greater than 0. If this causes a problem, then you can disable the tabindex rule. For example, in cypress-axe, you can run `cy.configureAxe({rules: [{ id: 'tabindex', enabled: false }]})` before performing an audit on the page.

Discussion

Our example application uses a custom-mode dialog box and, in so doing, demonstrates why that is often a bad idea. If you use dialog boxes and other components from libraries like Material UI, you will often get many accessibility features for free. Also, libraries will often create floating elements outside of the "root" `div` of the React application. They will then set the `aria-hidden` attribute of the entire "root" `div` to `true`, which effectively hides the whole rest of the application from screen readers and other accessibility software.

For an excellent example of an accessible modal, take a look at React Modal (*https://oreil.ly/2nI5x*) from the ReactJS team.

You can download the source for this recipe from the GitHub site (*https://oreil.ly/0GfgA*).

9.9 Create a Page Reader with the Speech API

Problem

You can use many tools to check for accessibility, but it is hard to get a feel for what it is like for a person with particular needs to use your application. That is why the best way to create an accessible application is to involve people who have to use accessibility devices to build and test your code.

For the rest of us, getting a "feel" for the experience of using the application with accessibility software is still helpful. But there are problems. Braille readers rely on the ability of the user to read Braille. Software that reads out your application is a good option, but most screen readers are pretty expensive. The Mac comes with a built-in screen reader called VoiceOver, which has a whole host of features that allow you to skip around a screen. But not everyone uses a Mac.

Chrome has an extension called ChromeVox, which works well, but it's available only for Chrome and no longer appears to be actively developed.

In addition to all of those issues, screen readers will want to tell you about *everything*. You might want to use the screen reader to see what some part of your application is like to use, but it will continue to read to you when you switch back to your IDE or some reference material in another browser tab.

Even with all of those issues, it is still worth trying to experience an audio version of your application. If nothing else, it will give you some sense of what a poor job most of us do at writing software that people can use.

What can we do to try our application with a screen reader?

Solution

We're going to create a simple screen reader—a very, *very* simple screen reader. It won't be professional quality, but it will provide some sense of using our application with only a keyboard and audio feedback. It will also work on our local React application and won't affect our machine's other pages or desktop applications. It's called TalkToMe.[10]

We will add a small amount of code to the example tasks application we are using throughout this chapter. We don't want the screen reader code to be included in the production version of our code, so we'll begin by adding a file called *talkToMe.js* to the main source folder:

```
function talkToMe() {
  if (
    process.env.NODE_ENV !== 'production' &&
    sessionStorage.getItem('talkToMe') === 'true'
  ) {
    ...
  }
}
```

By checking the NODE_ENV value, we can limit the code to our development environment. We're also checking for the session-storage variable called talkToMe. We will run the screen reader only if this exists and has the value "true".

We need the code to read out the details of the current element that has the focus. Focus events don't bubble, which means we cannot simply attach an onFocus event handler to a high-level element and start tracking focus.

---

10 Thanks to Terry Tibbs for his help in writing this tool.

However, we *can* listen to focusin events. We can attach a focusin listener to the document object, and it will be called every time the user moves to a new component:

```
function talkToMe() {
  if (
    process.env.NODE_ENV !== 'production' &&
    sessionStorage.getItem('talkToMe') === 'true'
  ) {
    document.addEventListener('focusin', (evt) => {
      if (sessionStorage.getItem('talkToMe') === 'true') {
        ....
      }
    })
  }
}
```

Notice that we do an additional check for the talkToMe item, just in case the user has switched it off while using the application.

We need some way of describing the currently focused element. This function will provide a rough description of the current element, based upon its name, its role, and so on:

```
function getDescription(element) {
  const nodeName = element.nodeName.toUpperCase()
  const role = element.role
    ? element.role
    : nodeName === 'BUTTON'
    ? 'button'
    : nodeName === 'INPUT' || nodeName === 'TEXTAREA'
    ? 'text field ' + element.value
    : nodeName === 'SELECT'
    ? 'select field ' + element.value
    : element.getAttribute('role') || 'group'
  const title = element.title || element.textContent
  const extraInstructions =
    nodeName === 'INPUT' || nodeName === 'TEXTAREA'
      ? 'You are currently in a text field. To enter text, type.'
      : ''
  return role + '. ' + title + '. ' + extraInstructions
}
```

We can get now get a description of the currently focused element:

```
function talkToMe() {
  if (
    process.env.NODE_ENV !== 'production' &&
    sessionStorage.getItem('talkToMe') === 'true'
  ) {
    document.addEventListener('focusin', (evt) => {
      if (sessionStorage.getItem('talkToMe') === 'true') {
        const description = getDescription(evt.target)
        ....
```

```
    }
  })
  }
}
```

Now we need to convert the text of the description into speech. For this, we can use the Web Speech API, which most browsers now include. The speech synthesizer accepts an object called an *utterance*:

```
window.speechSynthesis.speak(
  new SpeechSynthesisUtterance(description)
)
```

Before we start to read out a piece of text, we first need to check if we are already in the process of reading something else. If we are, we will cancel the old utterance and begin the new one, which will allow the user to quickly skip from component to component as soon as they have heard enough information:

```
if (window.speechSynthesis.speaking) {
  window.speechSynthesis.cancel()
}
window.speechSynthesis.speak(
  new SpeechSynthesisUtterance(description)
)
```

This gives us the final version of `talkToMe`:

```
function talkToMe() {
  if (
    process.env.NODE_ENV !== 'production' &&
    sessionStorage.getItem('talkToMe') === 'true'
  ) {
    document.addEventListener('focusin', (evt) => {
      if (sessionStorage.getItem('talkToMe') === 'true') {
        const description = getDescription(evt.target)
        if (window.speechSynthesis.speaking) {
          window.speechSynthesis.cancel()
        }
        window.speechSynthesis.speak(
          new SpeechSynthesisUtterance(description)
        )
      }
    })
  }
}
```

We can now add `talkToMe` to our application, by calling it from the *index.js* file at the top of our application:

```
import React from 'react'
import ReactDOM from 'react-dom'
import './index.css'
import App from './App'
```

```
import reportWebVitals from './reportWebVitals'
import talkToMe from './talkToMe'

talkToMe()

ReactDOM.render(
  <React.StrictMode>
    <App />
  </React.StrictMode>,
  document.getElementById('root')
)

// If you want to start measuring performance in your app, pass a function
// to log results (for example: reportWebVitals(console.log))
// or send to an analytics endpoint. Learn more: https://bit.ly/CRA-vitals
reportWebVitals()
```

If you now open your application in a browser, open the developer console, and create a new session-storage variable called talkToMe set to the string "true," you should now hear elements described as you Tab between them.

Discussion

The *talkToMe* screen reader is little more than a toy, but it will help you create concise titles and other metadata in your code, stressing how important it is to "front-load" information in descriptions. The sooner the user can decide that an element is not what they're looking for, the sooner they can move on. It will also make it abundantly clear which parts of your application are challenging to navigate and allow you to try your application without looking at the screen.

You can download the source for this recipe from the GitHub site (*https://oreil.ly/ 0GfgA*).

CHAPTER 10

Performance

One of us had a computer science lecturer who began one class by saying, "You should never, ever, ever try to optimize your code. But when you do optimize your code, here's how you should do it."

Premature optimization, as Donald Knuth once said, is the root of all evil. It would be best if you first made your code work. Then make your code maintainable. And only then—if you have a problem—should you worry about making your code fast. Slow code that works will always beat fast code that doesn't.

That said, there are times when performance can be a significant issue. If your application takes more than a few seconds to load, you may lose users who will never return. Slow can become unusable on low-powered devices. This chapter will take what we like to call an *essentialist* approach to performance. You should rarely tune your code, but when you do, you should tune the right code. We look at various tools and techniques that will allow you to track down and measure performance bottlenecks so that if you do need to apply performance fixes, they will be in the right place, and you will have some way of measuring the difference they make.

All performance fixes come at a cost. If you make your client code faster, it might cost more memory or more server time. You will almost always have to add more code and more complexity.

The recipes in this chapter follow the order in which we would suggest you approach performance problems. We begin with high-level measurements in the browser and look at ways that you can objectively identify performance bottlenecks. If you find a bottleneck, we will show you how you can use React's built-in `Profiler` component to track down the individual components that are the source of the problem. We then look at lower-level and more precise ways of measuring performance down to the sub-millisecond level.

Only once you can precisely measure performance can you even think about improving the speed of your code.

We then show you just a few ways that you can improve the performance of your application. Some are simple, such as splitting your code into smaller bundles or combining asynchronous network calls. Others are more complex, such as prerendering your pages on a server.

In summary: this chapter is far more about performance measurement than performance tuning. Because you should never, ever, ever optimize your code, but when you do, you should begin with measurement.

10.1 Use Browser Performance Tools

Problem

It is worth delaying performance tuning until you know you have a problem. In a sense, the only time you have a problem is if a user notices that your application isn't performing. But if you wait until a user notices, that might be too late. For that reason, it would be helpful to have some objective measure for when an application needs tuning, something that realistically measures performance and isn't just looking for code that could run faster. You can almost always make code faster, and many developers have wasted many hours tuning code that results in no noticeable effect on the user experience.

It would be helpful to have a tool that will focus on where you might need to optimize your code.

Solution

The best way to check for performance is by using a browser. In the end, the user's experience is the only thing that matters. So, we will look at the various in-browser tools that will provide objective measures and find potential bottlenecks in your code.

The first thing we will look at is a tool built into Chrome called Lighthouse.

 Google produces an add-in for Firefox called Google Lighthouse. Although this works well, it is simply a frontend for the Google Page Speed service, so you can use it only on public-facing web pages. However, you can use the Lighthouse extension in Chrome on any page that Chrome can read.

The Lighthouse extension is a great way to check the basic road-worthiness of your application. As well as checking performance, Lighthouse will look at the accessibility of your web page and whether you are following best practices for the web. It will check whether your pages are optimized for search engine robots and will look to see if your web application meets the standards required to consider it a progressive web application (see Figure 10-1).

Figure 10-1. The metrics checked by Lighthouse

You can run a Lighthouse audit in two ways: either on the command line or in a browser.

If you want to run audits on the command line, you will first need to install the Lighthouse command:

```
$ npm install -g lighthouse
```

You can then run an audit with the `lighthouse` command:

```
$ lighthouse http://localhost:3000
```

The command-line version of Lighthouse is simply an automated script for the Google Chrome browser. It has the advantage that it generates an HTML report of the audit, which makes it suitable for use on a continuous integration server.

You can also use Lighthouse interactively, within Google Chrome. It's best to do this in an incognito window, as this will reduce the likelihood of other extensions and storage interfering with the Lighthouse audit. Once you have started Chrome and opened your application, go to developer tools and then switch to the Lighthouse tab (see Figure 10-2).

Figure 10-2. The Lighthouse tab with Chrome DevTools

Then click the Generate audit button. Lighthouse will refresh your page several times and perform a series of audits. The performance audit will concentrate on six different metrics (see Figure 10-3).

Figure 10-3. The six web vitals measured by the Lighthouse performance audit

These metrics are known as *web vitals*. The web vitals are metrics that you can use to track performance when applications are running in production.

The *First Contentful Paint* (FCP) is the time taken for the browser to start to render content. The FCP will significantly affect the user's perception of performance. Before the FCP, the user will see only a blank screen, and if this lasts for too long, the user might close down the browser and go elsewhere.

Lighthouse measures the time taken for the FCP and then compares that against the performance statistics Google records globally. If your application is in the top 25% of FCPs globally, it will mark you as green. Currently, a green rating means that the first content renders within two seconds. If you are within the top 75%, it will give you an orange grade, which means your page started to render within four seconds. Lighthouse will give anything else a red grade.

The *Speed Index* (SI) measures how long it takes until your page stabilizes visually. It performs this check visually by recording a video and checking for differences between frames.

Lighthouse will compare the SI metric to website performance globally. If the SI takes less than 4.3 seconds, you are in the top 25% of web pages globally, and Lighthouse will give a green rating. If you take less than 5.8 seconds, you will be in the top 75%, and Lighthouse will give you an orange rating. It will give everything else a red grade.

The *Largest Contentful Paint* (LCP) occurs when the browser's viewport is completely loaded. Other content might still be loading out of view, but the LCP is when the user will feel that the page is visible. To be rated green, the LCP needs to be within 2.5 seconds. It needs to be less than 4 seconds for an orange rating. Everything else is rated red. Server-side rendering can significantly improve the LCP rating.

Time to interactive (TTI) is how long it takes before you can interact with the page using the mouse and keyboard. In React, this happens after the first complete render, when React has attached the event handlers. You want this to be less than 3.8 seconds to get a green rating. If you can get a TTI of 7.3 or less, you will be rated orange. Everything else is rated red. You can improve the TTI by deferring the loading of third-party JavaScript or by code splitting.[1]

Total blocking time (TBT) is the sum of all blocking tasks that occur between the FCP and TTI. A blocking task is anything that takes longer than 50 ms. That's about how long it takes to display a frame in a movie, and anything longer than 50 ms starts to become noticeable. If you have too many blocking tasks, the browser will start to feel like it's freezing up. For this reason, the grades for TBT cover short periods. If TBT is less than 300 ms, Lighthouse will grade your page as green. Anything up to 600 ms is orange, and everything else is graded red. A high TBT score will feel to the user like the browser is being overloaded. TBT is generally improved by running less JavaScript code or reducing the number of scans of the DOM. The most effective technique is probably code splitting.

Cumulative Layout Shift (CLS) is a measure of the *jumpiness* or visual stability of your web page. If your application inserts additional content that moves other content around during a page load, this will start to affect the CLS metric. The CLS is the proportion of the page that moves during loading.

---

1 See Recipe 10.5.

Not included in the Lighthouse report is the *First Input Delay* (FID) metric, which is how long it takes between a user sending an event to the page—such as by clicking a button—and the JavaScript handler receiving the event. You want an FID of no more than 300 ms. The FID is closely related to the TBT because blocking events are typically created by event handlers.

As well as providing an audit of the primary metrics of your page, the Lighthouse report will also include advice for how to fix any problems it finds.

Lighthouse is an excellent starting point when checking for performance issues. It's not an exhaustive check, but it will highlight problems that you might not otherwise notice.

 Many factors (bandwidth, memory, CPU, and so on) can affect a Lighthouse audit, so expect your results to vary from run to run. Online services such as WebPageTest (*https://www.webpagetest.org*) and GTmetrix (*https://gtmetrix.com*) can run audits on your application from various locations around the world, which will give you a more realistic view of your application's speed than a Lighthouse audit running against *http://localhost:3000*.

While Lighthouse is good at highlighting the existence of performance problems, it's less helpful at finding the cause of those problems. It might be that code for a web page is too large or too slow. It might be that the server is responding sluggishly. It might even be a resource problem, such as low memory or large cache size.

To find out *why* a bottleneck exists, we can next visit the performance tools of the browser itself.

If you are using Firefox or Chrome, you can get to the performance console by opening your page in an incognito window and then going to the Performance tab in the development tools (see Figure 10-4).

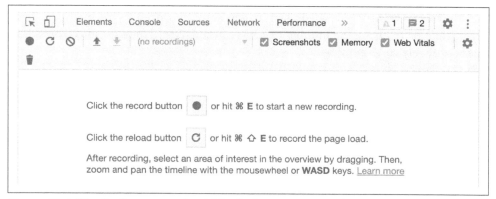

Figure 10-4. The Performance tab within the browser DevTools

The Performance tab is like the engine management system of the browser. There, you can track the memory usage, any CPU blockers, the number of elements within the DOM, and so on. To gather statistics, you will need to click the Record button on the toolbar and then interact with your page for a few seconds before stopping the recording. The performance system will trace everything you selected. In the example in Figure 10-5, you can see that a blocking operation (see TBT earlier) occurred when the user clicked a button, and the browser blocked for 60.92 ms until the event handler returned.

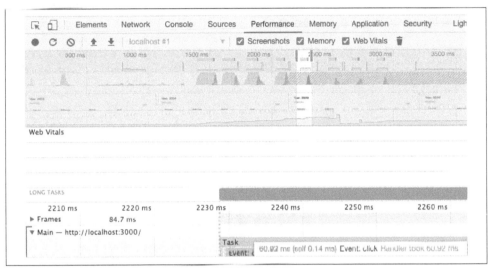

Figure 10-5. Zooming in to investigate a long-running task

The Performance tab gives you all the statistics you are ever likely to want when performance tuning. It probably has far more detail than you are ever likely to need. For that reason, you might want to install the React Developer Tools, which are available for Chrome (*https://oreil.ly/vvCLp*) and Firefox (*https://oreil.ly/mw1yn*).

When you install the React Developer Tools, you may find that they cannot run in incognito mode by default. It's worth enabling them to have access (see Figure 10-6 for Chrome and Figure 10-7 for Firefox).

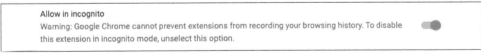

Figure 10-6. Enabling React Dev Tools in incognito mode in Chrome

Run in Private Windows   ○ Allow   ○ Don't Allow

When allowed, the extension will have access to your online activities while private browsing. Learn more

Figure 10-7. Enabling React Dev Tools in private mode in Firefox

In a similar way to the browser's performance tools, the React Developer Tools need you to record a performance session by clicking the Record button in the top left of the developer panel (see Figure 10-8).

Figure 10-8. The React Profiler tab in Chrome DevTools

Once you have recorded a session, the performance statistics will be displayed and related to the React components that rendered the web page. If a component took a long time to display, you can hover over it in the performance results and see it highlighted on the page (see Figure 10-9).

The React Developer Tools are often the best interactive tool to identify the underlying cause of a performance issue. But, as ever, you should consider tuning performance only if a user or some higher-level tool such as Lighthouse discovers that a performance bottleneck exists.

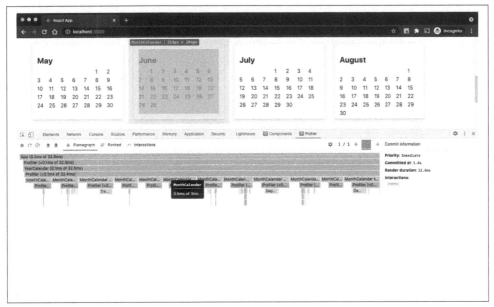

Figure 10-9. If you hover over a component in the flamegraph, it will be highlighted on the page

Discussion

If you are taking an *essentialist* approach to performance, you should always begin in the browser, either by using the application or by using one of the built-in tools or extensions we discuss here.

10.2 Track Rendering with Profiler

Problem

Browser tools provide a wealth of performance detail, and they should always be the first place you look to discover the cause of underlying performance problems.

Once you have identified a problem, it can be helpful to get more detailed performance statistics for a small part of the application. The only way to boost performance is by gathering actual performance figures before and after a change. That can be difficult to do with browser extensions because they will flood you with information about everything.

How do we get performance statistics for the part of the application we are tuning?

Solution

We are going to use the React `Profiler` component. You can wrap the `Profiler` component around any part of your application that you will tune. It will record performance statistics whenever React renders it and will tell you several vital pieces of information:

Statistic	Purpose
Phase	Whether a mount or an update caused the render
Actual duration	How long the render would take to complete if no internal caching was applied
Base duration	How long the render took with caching
Start time	The number of milliseconds since the page loaded
Commit time	When the results of the render find their way into the browser's DOM
Interactions	Any event handlers that we are currently tracing

To see how the `Profiler` component works, let's start to examine the example application you can see in Figure 10-10.

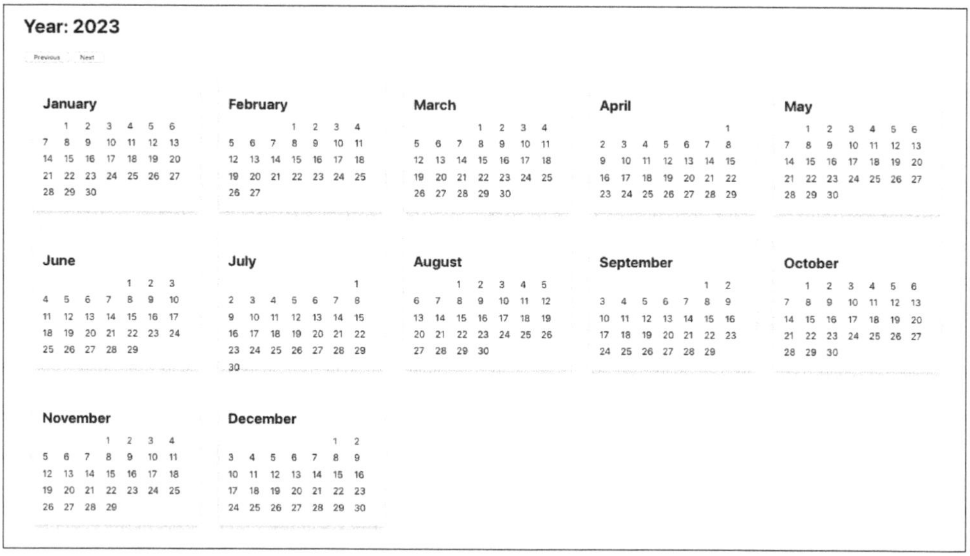

Figure 10-10. The example Calendar application

This is the code for the App component:

```
import { useState } from 'react'
import { unstable_trace as trace } from 'scheduler/tracing'
import './App.css'

function App({ onRender }) {
  const [year, setYear] = useState(2023)
```

```
    return (
      <div className="App">
        <h1>Year: {year}</h1>
        <button onClick={() => setYear((y) => y - 1)}>Previous</button>
        <button onClick={() => setYear((y) => y + 1)}>Next</button>
        <br />
        <YearCalendar year={year} onRender={onRender} />
      </div>
    )
}

export default App
```

The application displays two buttons: one for moving forward a year and one for moving back.

We can begin by wrapping the buttons and the calendar component in a `Profiler` component:

```
import { useState, Profiler } from 'react'
import { unstable_trace as trace } from 'scheduler/tracing'
import './App.css'

function App({ onRender }) {
  const [year, setYear] = useState(2023)

  return (
    <div className="App">
      <h1>Year: {year}</h1>
      <Profiler id="app" onRender={() => {}}>
        <button onClick={() => setYear((y) => y - 1)}>
          Previous
        </button>
        <button onClick={() => setYear((y) => y + 1)}>Next</button>
        <br />
        <YearCalendar year={year} onRender={onRender} />
      </Profiler>
    </div>
  )
}

export default App
```

The `Profiler` takes an id and a callback function onRender. Each time the `Profiler` is rendered, it sends back statistics to the onRender function. So, let's fill out the details of the onRender function a little more:

```
import { useState, Profiler } from 'react'
import { unstable_trace as trace } from 'scheduler/tracing'
import './App.css'

let renders = []
```

```
let tracker = (
  id,
  phase,
  actualDuration,
  baseDuration,
  startTime,
  commitTime,
  interactions
) => {
  renders.push({
    id,
    phase,
    actualDuration,
    baseDuration,
    startTime,
    commitTime,
    interactions: JSON.stringify(Array.from(interactions)),
  })
}

function App({ onRender }) {
  const [year, setYear] = useState(2023)

  return (
    <div>
      ....
      <Profiler id="app" onRender={tracker}>
        ....
      </Profiler>
      <button onClick={() => console.table(renders)}>Stats</button>
    </div>
  )
}
```

The tracker function will record each of the results from the Profiler in an array called renders. We've also added a button to the interface, which will display the renders in the console in tabular format whenever we click it.

If we reload the page and click the Previous and Next buttons a few times, followed by the Stats button, we will see the profile statistics on the console (see Figure 10-11).

The data is in tabular format, which makes it a little easier to read. It also means that we can sort by any of the columns. We can also copy the entire table and paste it into a spreadsheet for more analysis.

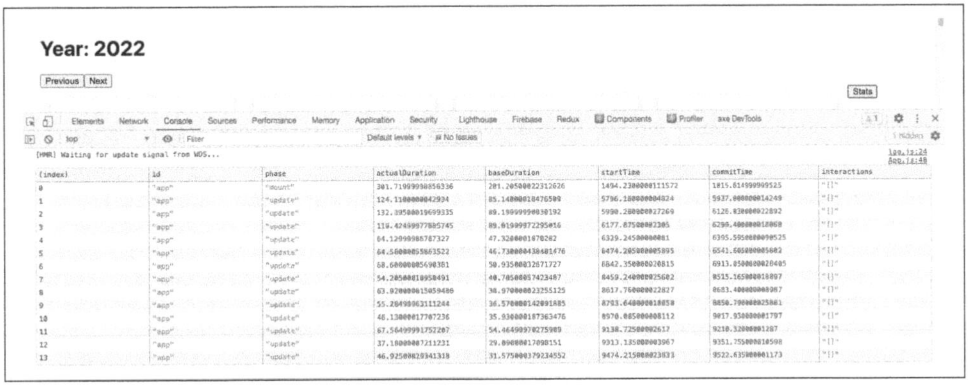

Figure 10-11. The render statistics displayed in the JavaScript console

You will notice that the *interactions* column is always an empty array. That's because we are not currently tracking any event handlers or other pieces of code. If we want to see which event handlers are currently running during a render, we can import a tracing function and wrap it around any piece of code that we want to track. For example, this is how we can start to track the user clicking the Previous button:

```
import { unstable_trace as trace } from 'scheduler/tracing'
...
<button
  onClick={() => {
    trace('previous button click', performance.now(), () => {
      setYear((y) => y - 1)
    })
  }}
/>
```

The `trace` function takes a label, a timestamp, and a callback containing the code it is tracing. The timestamp could be a date, but it is often better to use the milliseconds returned from `performance.now()`.

If we reload the web page, click Next a few times, and then click Previous a few times, we will start to see the interactions appearing in the table of results (see Figure 10-12).

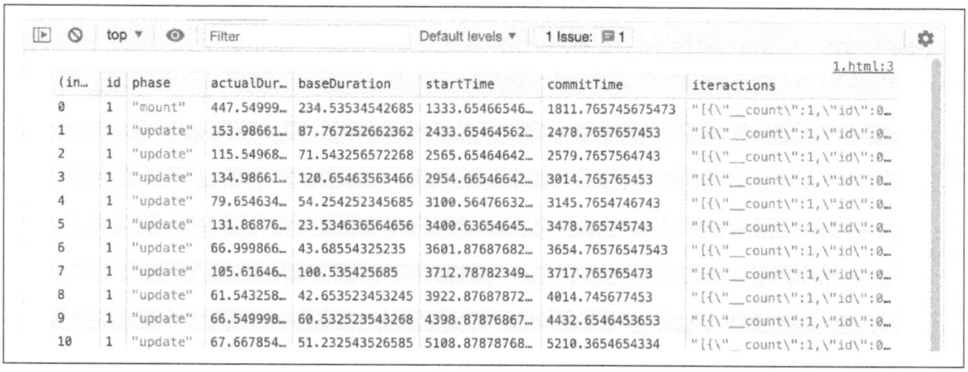

(in…	id	phase	actualDur…	baseDuration	startTime	commitTime	iteractions
0	1	"mount"	447.54999…	234.53534542685	1333.65466546…	1811.765745675473	"[{\"__count\":1,\"id\":0…
1	1	"update"	153.98661…	87.767252662362	2433.65464562…	2478.7657657453	"[{\"__count\":1,\"id\":0…
2	1	"update"	115.54968…	71.543256572268	2565.65464642…	2579.7657564743	"[{\"__count\":1,\"id\":0…
3	1	"update"	134.98661…	120.65463563466	2954.66546642…	3014.765765453	"[{\"__count\":1,\"id\":0…
4	1	"update"	79.654634…	54.254252345685	3100.56476632…	3145.7654746743	"[{\"__count\":1,\"id\":0…
5	1	"update"	131.86876…	23.534636564656	3400.63654645…	3478.765745743	"[{\"__count\":1,\"id\":0…
6	1	"update"	66.999866…	43.68554325235	3601.87687682…	3654.76576547543	"[{\"__count\":1,\"id\":0…
7	1	"update"	105.61646…	100.535425685	3712.78782349…	3717.765765473	"[{\"__count\":1,\"id\":0…
8	1	"update"	61.543258…	42.653523453245	3922.87687872…	4014.745677453	"[{\"__count\":1,\"id\":0…
9	1	"update"	66.549998…	60.532523543268	4398.87876867…	4432.6546453653	"[{\"__count\":1,\"id\":0…
10	1	"update"	67.667854…	51.232543526585	5108.87878768…	5210.3654654334	"[{\"__count\":1,\"id\":0…

Figure 10-12. Traced interactions are shown as JSON strings within the results table

We stringify the output because `trace` stores interactions as JavaScript sets, which often don't display correctly in the console. Even though the interaction data looks truncated in the table, you can still copy the results. Here is the example of the data returned by a single trace interaction:

```
[
    {
        "__count":1,
        "id":1,
        "name":"previous button click",
        "timestamp":4447.909999988042
    }
]
```

Discussion

The `Profiler` component has been in React since version 16.4.3. The `trace` function is still experimental, but it is tremendously powerful. Although we are using it for only a simple event handler in our example, it can also provide real-world timing for larger pieces of code, such as network requests. React container components will often have many network requests "in-flight" during a render, and the `trace` function gives you the ability to see what was going on at the time of a particularly slow render. It will also give you some idea of how many renders resulted from a whole chain of different network processes.

You can download the source for this recipe from the GitHub site (*https://oreil.ly/XhJLR*).

10.3 Create Profiler Unit Tests

Problem

The React `Profiler` is a powerful tool. It gives you access to the same profiling information that is available within the React Developer Tools. It has the advantage that you can focus on the code that you are trying to optimize.

However, it still relies on the interactions that you make with the web page. You will want to test performance before and after you make a code change. But how can you be sure that the timings you take before and after are measuring the same things? If you perform a manual test, how can you guarantee that you will perform the same set of actions each time?

Solution

This recipe will look at how to create unit tests that call the `Profiler` code. Automated tests will allow us to create repeatable performance tests that we can run to check that any optimizations we make are having a real impact on performance.

In a unit test, we can render a React component outside of a web browser because the Testing Library provides a headless implementation of the DOM.

To see how to use the `Profiler`, we will take another look at the example calendar application (see Figure 10-13).

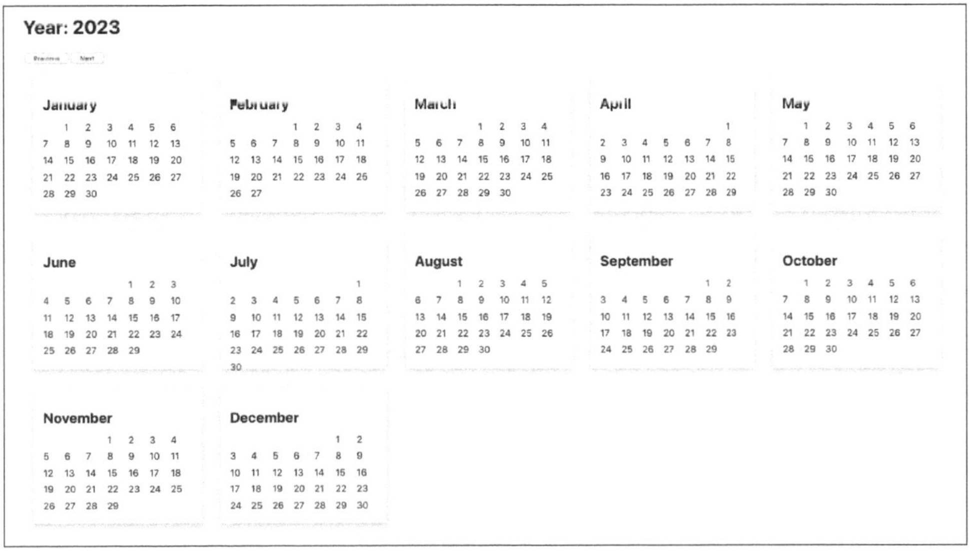

Figure 10-13. The example Calendar application

We can add a `Profiler` component to the main code for the `App` component and then allow any other code to pass in an `onRender` method that can be used to track render performance:

```
import { useState, Profiler } from 'react'
import YearCalendar from './YearCalendar'
import { unstable_trace as trace } from 'scheduler/tracing'
import './App.css'

function App({ onRender }) {
  const [year, setYear] = useState(2023)

  return (
    <div className="App">
      <h1>Year: {year}</h1>
      <Profiler id="app" onRender={onRender || (() => {})}>
        <button
          onClick={() => {
            trace('previous button click', performance.now(), () => {
              setYear((y) => y - 1)
            })
          }}
        >
          Previous
        </button>
        <button onClick={() => setYear((y) => y + 1)}>Next</button>
        <br />
        <YearCalendar year={year} onRender={onRender} />
      </Profiler>
    </div>
  )
}

export default App
```

We can also pass the `onRender` function down to child components to track their render performance. In the preceding code, we're passing `onRender` to `YearCalendar`, which can then use it in its own `Profiler` component or pass it further down the component tree.

 You can avoid the need to pass the `onRender` to child components by creating a provider component that will inject the `onRender` into the current context. We are not doing that here to keep the code simple. But there are various other examples using providers elsewhere in the book. For example, see the `SecurityProvider` in Recipe 7.1.

The `Profiler` component must be given an `id` property and an `onRender` property. When the application is run normally, no `onRender` property will be passed to the `App` component, so we need to provide a default function:

```
<Profiler id='app' onRender={onRender || (() => {})}>
```

 The `Profiler` component is relatively lightweight and does not generally slow down the application's performance. If you forget to remove the `Profiler` from your code, it won't matter. The `Profiler` runs only in development mode. It will be removed from the code when you create a production build.

We can now start to build a unit test:

```
import { render, screen } from '@testing-library/react'
import user from '@testing-library/user-event'
import App from './App'

let renders = []
let tracker = (
  id,
  phase,
  actualDuration,
  baseDuration,
  startTime,
  commitTime,
  interactions
) => {
  renders.push({
    id,
    phase,
    actualDuration,
    baseDuration,
    startTime,
    commitTime,
    interactions: JSON.stringify(Array.from(interactions)),
  })
}

let startTime = 0

describe('App', () => {
  beforeEach(() => {
    renders = []
    startTime = performance.now()
  })
  afterEach(() => {
    console.log('Time taken: ', performance.now() - startTime)
    console.table(renders)
  })
```

```
it('should move between years', async () => {
  render(<App onRender={tracker} />)
  user.click(screen.getByRole('button', { name: /previous/i }))
  user.click(screen.getByRole('button', { name: /previous/i }))
  user.click(screen.getByRole('button', { name: /previous/i }))
  user.click(screen.getByRole('button', { name: /next/i }))
  user.click(screen.getByRole('button', { name: /next/i }))
  user.click(screen.getByRole('button', { name: /next/i }))
}, 30000)
})
```

Tests that last longer than five seconds are likely to breach the Jest timeout limit. The easiest way to avoid this limit is by adding a timeout parameter to the it function call, as we do here, to set the timeout to 30,000 ms. You will need to adjust this value according to the complexity of your test.

When you run this test, an enormous amount of data is captured in the console (see Figure 10-14).

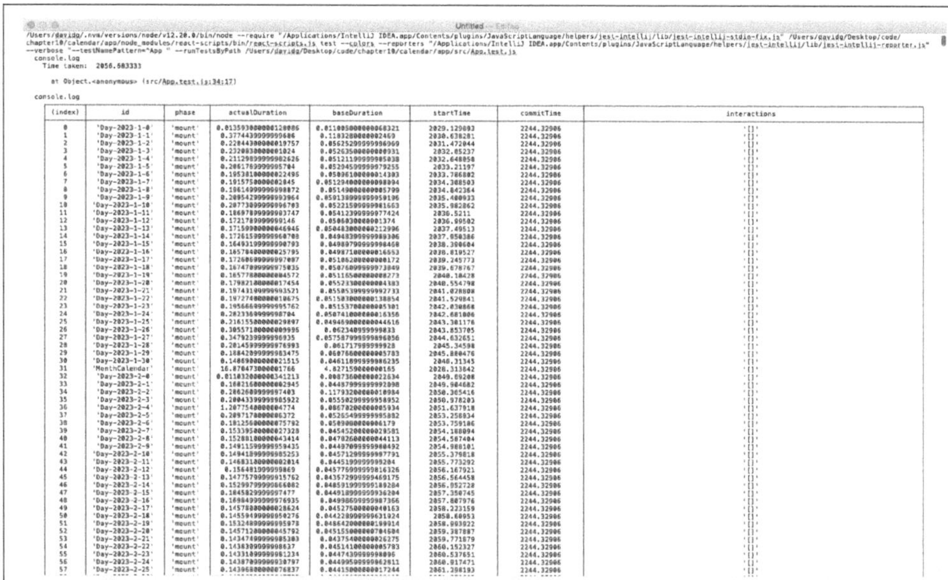

Figure 10-14. The unit test will capture an enormous amount of rendering information

Notably, the test is *repeatable*. It will perform the same actions each time. We've found that unit tests tend to be far more consistent than code run in the browser. Repeated runs of the previous test gave overall times of 2,100 ms +/– 20 ms. That's a variation of less than 1%. They also produced exactly 2,653 profile scores each time.

It's unlikely that we'd get repeatable results in a browser with a manual test.

In the example here, we are simply displaying the capture results. In an actual performance situation, you might want to process the results in some way to find the average render time of a particular component, for example. Then, when you start to tune the component, you can be more confident that any performance gains result from actual performance changes rather than variations in the browser's behavior.

Discussion

Even though we are writing this performance testing code in a Jest unit test, it is not a *test* in the same way that a regular functional test is; we are not performing any assertions. Assertions can still be helpful,[2] but it is not good to write performance tests that assert that some operation is faster than a given time. Performance tests are highly dependent upon the environment. If you write a test on a development that asserts that something will take less than three seconds, you should not be surprised if it fails on an integration server, where it took nine seconds.

If you do want to track performance automatically, you might consider adding regression checks. A regression check will record a set of performance statistics in some central repository and record the ID of the environment that produced them. You can check that future runs in the same environment are not significantly slower than historic runs in the same environment.

In general, though, it is better to report performance results rather than assert what you want the performance to be.

You can download the source for this recipe from the GitHub site (*https://oreil.ly/XhJLR*).

10.4 Measure Time Precisely

Problem

Once you get to the point where you need to optimize quite low-level JavaScript code, what should you use to measure performance? You could, for example, use the Date() function to create a timestamp at the start and end of some JavaScript code:

```
const beforeDate = new Date()
for (let i = 0; i < 1000; i++) {}
const afterDate = new Date()
console.log(
  '1,000 loops took',
```

---

2 For example, by checking that the component is in a particular state before performing some action.

```
    afterDate.getTime() - beforeDate.getTime()
)
```

We can convert each date into milliseconds, so we can see how long it takes if we subtract one date from another.

This was such a common technique that the console object was given to new methods called time and timeEnd, to make the code shorter:

```
console.time('1,000 loops')
for (let i = 0; i < 1000; i++) {}
console.timeEnd('1,000 loops')
```

The time function accepts a label parameter, and if we call timeEnd with the same label, it displays the results on the console. Let's run the code:

```
1,000 loops: 0ms
```

That's a problem. React applications rarely contain long-running functions, so you typically need to optimize small pieces of JavaScript code only if the browser calls them many times. For example, you might want to optimize game code that is rendering animation on a screen. It can be hard to measure short pieces of code because they might run in less than a millisecond. We can't measure the performance with Date objects because they resolve down to the millisecond only, even though the machine's internal clock is far more precise than that.

We need something that we can use for measuring times of less than a millisecond.

Solution

We are going to use performance.now(). This function call returns a high-resolution timestamp measured in fractions of milliseconds. For example, if you open the Chrome console and type performance.now(), you will see something like this:

```
> performance.now()
< 10131.62500000908
```

The time is measured differently from the time in JavaScript dates. JavaScript dates measure time from January 1, 1970. Instead, performance.now() measures time from when the current web page loaded.[3]

An interesting thing happens if you try to run performance.now() inside Firefox:

```
> performance.now()
< 4194
```

---

3 If you run it in Node, performance.now() measures the time from the start of the current process.

By default, Firefox will return only whole numbers of milliseconds for `performance.now()`, effectively removing most of the advantages of using it. Firefox rounds to the whole milliseconds because of security. Technically, if JavaScript can time tiny amounts of code precisely, this can provide a signature for the browser.

You can enable high-resolution time within Firefox by opening `about:config`, searching for the property called `privacy.reduceTimerPrecision`, and setting it to `false`. If you do this, you will start to get high-resolution times:

```
performance.now()
151405.8
```

Be sure you disable this property if you want to avoid third parties using it to track you.

To go back to our example code, we can measure the time taken to perform loops like this:

```
const before0 = performance.now()
for (let i = 0; i < 1000; i++) {}
const after0 = performance.now()
console.log('1,000 loops took', after0 - before0)
const before1 = performance.now()
for (let i = 0; i < 100000; i++) {}
const after1 = performance.now()
console.log('100,000 loops took', after1 - before1)
```

When we run this code, we see the following:

```
1,000 loops took 0.03576700000007804
100,000 loops took 1.6972319999999854
```

These answers are far more precise and provide more information about the underlying performance of JavaScript. In this case, we can see that adding more iterations to a loop does not scale linearly, which suggests that the JavaScript engine starts to optimize the code on the fly once it realizes that each of the loop iterations is the same.

Discussion

`performance.now()` has several advantages over JavaScript dates. Aside from the additional precision, it is unaffected by clock changes, which is good if you decide to add some performance monitoring to long-running code. It also starts at zero when the page starts to load, which is useful for optimizing page load times.

One word of caution when using `performance.now()`: be wary of using it to build some higher-level timing function. For example, we once created a simple JavaScript generator function to make it a little easier to use `performance.now()`:

```
function* timekeeper() {
  let now = 0
```

```
    while (true) yield -now + (now = performance.now())
  }
```

This function was created to avoid the need to calculate the difference between start and end times. Instead of writing this:

```
const before0 = performance.now()
for (let i = 0; i < 1000; i++) {}
const after0 = performance.now()
console.log('1,000 loops took', after0 - before0)
const before1 = performance.now()
for (let i = 0; i < 100000; i++) {}
const after1 = performance.now()
console.log('100,000 loops took', after1 - before1)
```

we could instead write this:

```
const t = timekeeper()
t.next()
for (let i = 0; i < 1000; i++) {}
console.log('1,000 loops took', t.next().value)
for (let i = 0; i < 100000; i++) {}
console.log('100,000 loops took', t.next().value)
```

No need for all of those ugly `before` and `after` variables. The time would reset to zero after each call to `t.next().value`, doing away with the need for the calculation.

The problem? The act of wrapping the `performance.now()` call inside another function adds a significant amount of time to the measure, destroying the precision of `performance.now()`:

```
1,000 loops took 0.05978800000002593
100,000 loops took 19.585223999999926
```

In this case, even though it takes only 1.69 ms to run 100,000 loops, the function reports the time as over 19 ms.

> Never hide a call to `performance.now()` inside another function if you want it to be accurate.

You can download the source for this recipe from the GitHub site (*https://oreil.ly/baiOr*).

10.5 Shrink Your App with Code Splitting

Problem

One of the biggest drains on performance for an SPA is the amount of JavaScript code that needs to be downloaded and run. Not only does the JavaScript take time to render, but the amount of network bandwidth required can slow your app down significantly on devices connected to a mobile network.

Let's consider the *synchronized routes* application we used in Chapter 2 (see Figure 10-15).

Figure 10-15. The synchronized routes application

The example application is tiny, but it contains some quite large JavaScript bundles:

```
$ ls -l build/static/js
total 1336
-rw-r--r--  1 davidg  admin  161800 12:07 2.4db4d779.chunk.js
-rw-r--r--  1 davidg  admin    1290 12:07 2.4db4d779.chunk.js.LICENSE.txt
-rw-r--r--  1 davidg  admin  461100 12:07 2.4db4d779.chunk.js.map
-rw-r--r--  1 davidg  admin    4206 12:07 3.307a63d5.chunk.js
-rw-r--r--  1 davidg  admin    9268 12:07 3.307a63d5.chunk.js.map
-rw-r--r--  1 davidg  admin    3082 12:07 main.e8a3e1cb.chunk.js
-rw-r--r--  1 davidg  admin    6001 12:07 main.e8a3e1cb.chunk.js.map
-rw-r--r--  1 davidg  admin    2348 12:07 runtime-main.67df5f2e.js
-rw-r--r--  1 davidg  admin   12467 12:07 runtime-main.67df5f2e.js.map
$
```

The largest (*2.4db4d779.chunk.js*) contains the main React framework code, and the app-specific code is limited to the small *main.e8a3e1cb.chunk.js* file. That means this application is about as small as a React application can be. Most React applications will be significantly larger: often totaling 1 Mb in size, which will be a significant problem for users on slow connections.

So, what can we do to reduce the size of JavaScript bundles in React?

Solution

We will use *code splitting*, which involves breaking the main code for our application into several smaller bundles. The browser will then load these bundles *lazily*. A particular bundle will load only when one of the components it contains is needed.

The example application we are using for this recipe is most certainly *not* one that requires code splitting. As with all performance changes, you should only really try to split your code if doing so makes a significant change to web performance. We will split the code in this application because it will be easier to see how it works.

We split code in React with a function called `lazy`:

```
import { lazy } from 'react'
```

The `lazy` function accepts a factory function, which, when called, will import a component. The `lazy` function returns a placeholder component, which will do nothing until the browser renders it. The placeholder component will run the factory function and dynamically load whichever bundle contains the actual component.

To see how this works, consider this component from our example application:

```
import { NavLink, Redirect, Route, Switch } from 'react-router-dom'
import People from './People'
import Offices from './Offices'
import './About.css'

const About = () => (
  <div className="About">
    <div className="About-tabs">
      <NavLink
        to="/about/people"
        className="About-tab"
        activeClassName="active"
      >
        People
      </NavLink>
      <NavLink
        to="/about/offices"
        className="About-tab"
        activeClassName="active"
      >
        Offices
      </NavLink>
    </div>
    <Switch>
      <Route path="/about/people">
        <People />
      </Route>
      <Route path="/about/offices">
        <Offices />
      </Route>
```

```
        <Redirect to="/about/people" />
      </Switch>
    </div>
  )

export default About
```

The browser will render the `People` and `Offices` components only when the user visits a given route. If the application is currently on the path */about/people*, the `Offices` component will not render, which means that we could potentially delay loading the `Offices` component until later. We can do this with the `lazy` function.

We'll replace the import of the `Offices` component with a call to `lazy`:

```
//import Offices from "./Offices"
const Offices = lazy(() => import('./Offices'))
```

The object now stored in the `Offices` variable will appear to the rest of the application as just another component. It's a lazy placeholder. Internally it contains a reference to the factory function, which it will call when the browser renders it.

If we try to refresh the web page, we will see an error (see Figure 10-16).

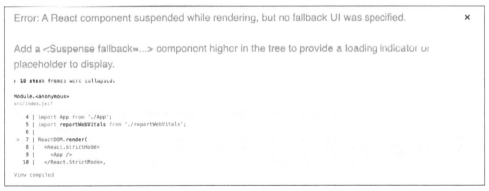

Figure 10-16. You will get a lazy loading error if you forget to add a Suspense component

The placeholder will not wait for the actual component to load before returning. Instead, it will substitute some other HTML while it is waiting for the actual component to load.

We can set this "loading" interface with the `Suspense` container:

```
import { lazy, Suspense } from 'react'
import { NavLink, Redirect, Route, Switch } from 'react-router-dom'
import People from './People'
// import Offices from './Offices'
import './About.css'

const Offices = lazy(() => import('./Offices'))
```

```
const About = () => (
  <div className="About">
    <div className="About-tabs">
      <NavLink
        to="/about/people"
        className="About-tab"
        activeClassName="active"
      >
        People
      </NavLink>
      <NavLink
        to="/about/offices"
        className="About-tab"
        activeClassName="active"
      >
        Offices
      </NavLink>
    </div>
    <Suspense fallback={<div>Loading...</div>}>
      <Switch>
        <Route path="/about/people">
          <People />
        </Route>
        <Route path="/about/offices">
          <Offices />
        </Route>
        <Redirect to="/about/people" />
      </Switch>
    </Suspense>
  </div>
)

export default About
```

The lazy placeholder will check its context to find the fallback component provided by Suspense, and it will display this on the page while waiting for the additional JavaScript bundle to load.

We are using a simple "Loading…" message here, but there's no reason why you can't instead show some fake replacement interface to give the impression that the new component has loaded before it has. YouTube uses the same technique on its front page. When YouTube is loading content, it displays a set of blocks and rectangles in place of the videos it's about to load (see Figure 10-17). Videos will often take two to three seconds to load, but this technique gives the user the impression that they load instantly.

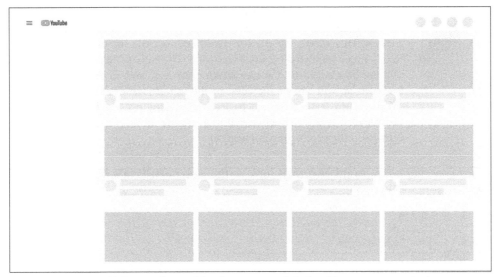

Figure 10-17. YouTube renders a fake front page while loading recommendations

In our application, if you refresh the page now, you should see the application go back to normal, as shown in Figure 10-18.

Figure 10-18. Adding a Suspense component removes the error

Behind the scenes, the Webpack development server will split off the Offices code into a separate JavaScript bundle.

Webpack will also split out the bundles when you generate a build. It will use tree shaking to identify which components can safely appear in which JavaScript bundles.

Tree shaking is a process that recursively analyzes which code files are imported by other files, starting from some initial file, such as *index.js*. This allows Webpack to avoid adding code into a bundle that is never imported by any other code. The calls to `React.lazy` will not be tracked by the tree shaking process, and so the lazily loaded code will not be included in the initial JavaScript bundle. Webpack will instead run a separate tree shaking process for each lazily loaded file, which will result in a large number of small code bundles in the production application.

If we generate a new build and then look at the generated JavaScript code, we will now see some extra files:

```
$ yarn build
...Builds code
$ ls -l build/static/js
total 1352
-rw-r--r--  1 davidg  admin     628 12:09 0.a30b3768.chunk.js
-rw-r--r--  1 davidg  admin     599 12:09 0.a30b3768.chunk.js.map
-rw-r--r--  1 davidg  admin  161801 12:09 3.f7664178.chunk.js
-rw-r--r--  1 davidg  admin    1290 12:09 3.f7664178.chunk.js.LICENSE.txt
-rw-r--r--  1 davidg  admin  461100 12:09 3.f7664178.chunk.js.map
-rw-r--r--  1 davidg  admin    4206 12:09 4.a74be2bf.chunk.js
-rw-r--r--  1 davidg  admin    9268 12:09 4.a74be2bf.chunk.js.map
-rw-r--r--  1 davidg  admin    3095 12:09 main.e4de2e45.chunk.js
-rw-r--r--  1 davidg  admin    6089 12:09 main.e4de2e45.chunk.js.map
-rw-r--r--  1 davidg  admin    2361 12:09 runtime-main.9df06006.js
-rw-r--r--  1 davidg  admin   12496 12:09 runtime-main.9df06006.js.map
```

Because this is such a small application, this is unlikely to affect the performance, but let's check anyway.

Loading performance is easiest to check using Chrome's Lighthouse tool. You can see the performance of the original version of this application in Figure 10-19.

Figure 10-19. The application's performance without code splitting

If we add some lazy loading, we do get a slight performance increase, primarily because of the time taken to complete the FCP (see Figure 10-20).

Figure 10-20. The application's performance with code splitting

It's not a massive increase in performance, but it does indicate that you can get some benefit from lazy loading even in tiny applications.

Discussion

All optimizations have a price, but code splitting takes minimal effort to implement, and it's the one that we find we use most often. It will often improve web-vitals metrics for FCP and TTI. You should avoid using it too aggressively because the framework needs to do more work to download and evaluate each of the scripts. But for most reasonably large applications, you will get some immediate benefit from splitting the code.

 It is often best to split code at the route level. Routes control which components are visible and so are a good place to divide the code you need to load now from the code you need to load later. It will also mean that if anyone bookmarks a location in your application, they will only download the code required for that location when they return to it.

You can download the source for this recipe from the GitHub site (*https://oreil.ly/Pj2Bu*).

10.6 Combine Network Promises

Problem

Many React applications make asynchronous network calls, and a lot of application lethargy results from waiting for responses to those asynchronous requests. The application is probably doing very little during those calls, so the application is not busy; it's just waiting.

Over time, client applications have become more complex, and server APIs have become simpler. In the case of *serverless* applications, the server APIs are so generic that no custom code is required, which leads to an increase in the number of API calls that the client code makes.[4]

Let's look at an example. We have an application that reads the details of several people from a backend API. The server has an end point that, if a browser sends a GET request to */people/1234*, will return the details of a person with the id of 1234. The developer has written a hook to make these requests:

```
import { useEffect, useState } from 'react'
import { get } from './fakeios'

const usePeopleSlow = (...ids) => {
  const [people, setPeople] = useState([])

  useEffect(() => {
    let didCancel = false
```

---

4 An exception to this is in the case of GraphQL services. In GraphQL, the client can make a complex query to the backend, and a standardized query resolver will "stitch together" the results of low-level queries on the server. GraphQL can produce faster network responses without needing to tune the client.

```
;(async () => {
  const result = []
  for (let i = 0; i < ids.length; i++) {
    const id = ids[i]
    result.push(await get('/people/' + id))
  }
  if (!didCancel) {
    setPeople(result)
  }
})()
return () => {
  didCancel = true
}
// eslint-disable-next-line react-hooks/exhaustive-deps
}, [...ids])

  return people
}
```

```
export default usePeopleSlow
```

The hook is called like this:

```
const peopleSlow = usePeopleSlow(1, 2, 3, 4)
```

The code calls the server for each ID. It waits for each response to complete before storing the results in an array. If the API endpoint takes 5 seconds to respond, the usePeopleSlow hook will take 20 seconds to return all of the data.

Is there anything we can do to speed things up?

Solution

We will combine asynchronous promises so that multiple API requests can be in flight at the same time.

Most asynchronous request libraries work by returning promises. If you wait for a promise, it will return the payload of the response. But in the example usePeople Slow code earlier, these promises are waited for in sequence:

```
const result = []
for (let i = 0; i < ids.length; i++) {
  const id = ids[i]
  result.push(await get('/people/' + id))
}
```

The request for the second person is not even sent until the response for the first person is received, which is why a 5-second delay results in a 20-second response time when we are reading the details of four people.

There is another way we can do this. We could send the requests without waiting and have all of them in-flight simultaneously. We then need to wait for all the responses, and when we receive the last one, we can return the data from the hook.

You can make parallel requests with a JavaScript function called `Promise.all`.

The `Promise.all` function accepts a list of promises and combines them into a single promise. That means we could combine several `get()` calls like this:

```
const [res1, res2, res3] = await Promise.all(
  get('/people/1'),
  get('/people/2'),
  get('/people/3')
)
```

`Promise.all` combines not just promises, but also results. If you wait for an array of promises with `Promise.all`, you will receive an array containing each of the promises.

We can now write a new version of the `usePeopleSlow` hook, using `Promise.all`:

```
import { useEffect, useState } from 'react'
import { get } from './fakeios'

const usePeopleFast = (...ids) => {
  const [people, setPeople] = useState([])

  useEffect(() => {
    let didCancel = false
    ;(async () => {
      const result = await Promise.all(
        ids.map((id) => get('/people/' + id))
      )
      if (!didCancel) {
        setPeople(result)
      }
    })()
    return () => {
      didCancel = true
    }
    // eslint-disable-next-line react-hooks/exhaustive-deps
  }, [...ids])

  return people
}

export default usePeopleFast
```

The key to this code is these three lines:

```
const result = await Promise.all(
  ids.map((id) => get('/people/' + id))
)
```

By *mapping* the ids into an array of the promises returned by network requests, we can wait for the `Promise.all` result and receive an array of all the responses.

If you time the two hooks, then `usePeopleFast` will read the details of four people in just over five seconds. Effectively, we have made five requests in the time taken to make one. In the example application, these were the comparative timings of the two versions of the code:

Version	Time Taken (ms)
usePeopleSlow	5000.99999998929
usePeopleFast	20011.224999994738

Discussion

This approach will significantly improve performance if you have multiple independent asynchronous requests. If you make many parallel requests, then the browser, the network card, or the server might start to queue responses. However, it will still generate a response more rapidly than a series of independent responses.

If you send parallel requests, it will intensify the load on the server, but this is unlikely to be a huge issue. First, as we just noted, servers often queue requests when they are busy. Second, the server will still be performing the same total amount of work. All you are doing is concentrating that work into a shorter period.

You can download the source for this recipe from the GitHub site (*https://oreil.ly/LhVY8*).

10.7 Use Server-Side Rendering

Problem

SPAs do a great job of making websites as feature-rich as desktop applications. If you use an application like Google Docs, the experience is almost indistinguishable from using a desktop word processor.

But all things come at a price. One of the major performance issues for SPAs is that the browser has to download a large bundle of JavaScript code before it can build an interface. If you create a React application with a tool like `create-react-app`, the only thing you will have in the body of the HTML is an empty `DIV` called `root`:

```
<div id="root"></div>
```

That empty `DIV` is all the browser will see until the JavaScript engine downloads the code, runs it, and updates the DOM.

Even if we reduce the bundle size with code splitting and the browser has cached the JavaScript, it can still take a couple of seconds to read the code and set up the interface.

Building the entire interface from JavaScript means that SPAs typically suffer from two main issues. First, and most important, the user experience can degrade, particularly for large React applications. Second, your application will have poor search engine optimization (SEO). Search engine robots will often not wait for the JavaScript to render an interface when scanning your site. They will download the basic HTML of the page and index its contents. For many business applications, this might not matter. But if you are building, say, a shopping site, you will probably want as many of the pages indexed as possible to capture passing traffic.

Therefore, it would be helpful if, instead of displaying an empty DIV when the HTML is loaded, we could begin by including the initial HTML of our page *before* the browser downloads and runs the application's JavaScript.

Solution

We will look at using server-side rendering to replace the empty DIV of a React page with a prerendered HTML version. We'll be able to do this because of the way that React interacts with the DOM of a web page.

When you render a component in React, you are not directly updating the DOM. Instead, when you run a piece of code like this:

```
ReactDOM.render(
  <React.StrictMode>
    <App />
  </React.StrictMode>,
  document.getElementById('root')
)
```

the render method updates a virtual DOM, which, at intervals, we will synchronize with the actual HTML elements on the page. React does this efficiently, so it will only update elements in the real DOM that don't match the elements in the virtual DOM.

Server-side rendering works by rendering not to the React virtual DOM, but to a string. When the browser sends a request for the HTML page to the server, we will render a version of the React contents to a string and then insert that string into the HTML, before returning it to the browser. This means that the browser will immediately render HTML of the page before it even starts to download the JavaScript of the application. Our server-side code will look something like this:

```
let indexHTML = <contents of index.html>
const app = <render App to string>
indexHTML = indexHTML.replace(
  '<div id="root"></div>',
```

```
  `<div id="app">${app}</div>`
)
res.contentType('text/html')
res.status(200)
return res.send(indexHTML)
```

Let's begin by creating an application with `create-react-app` to see how this works in more detail.

There are many React tools and frameworks that support server-side rendering. `create-react-app` is *not* one of those tools. So looking at how to convert a `create-react-app` application will allow us to understand all the steps required to enable SSR in React:

```
$ npx create-react-app ssrapp
```

We'll be building a server to host the SSR code. Let's start by creating a folder for the server code:

```
$ mkdir server
```

We'll build the server using Express. Our server code will be rendering the components of our application.

We'll need some additional libraries that will be useful when loading the React components. In the main application directory (not the *server* subdirectory), install the following:

```
$ npm install --save-dev ignore-styles url-loader @babel/register
```

The `create-react-app` tool generates code that uses a lot of modern JavaScript features that are not available out of the box, so the first thing we'll need to do in our server code is enable those JavaScript features for the server to run our React components. Within the new *server* folder, create a file called *index.js* and put this into it:

```
require('ignore-styles')
require('url-loader')
require('file-loader')
require('regenerator-runtime/runtime')
require('@babel/register')({
  ignore: [/(node_modules)/],
  presets: [
    '@babel/preset-env',
    [
      '@babel/preset-react',
      {
        runtime: 'automatic',
      },
    ],
  ],
  plugins: [],
```

```
})
require('./ssr')
```

This file will configure language features that we are going to use in the server code. We're loading the `preset-react` Babel plugin that is installed automatically in every `create-react-app` application. At the end of the script, we load a file called *ssr.js*, where we'll put our main server code.

Create the *server/ssr.js* file and add the following code to it:

```
import express from 'express'
import fs from 'fs'
import path from 'path'

const server = express()

server.get(
  /.(js|css|map|ico|svg|png)$/,
  express.static(path.resolve(__dirname, '../build'))
)

server.use('*', async (req, res) => {
  let indexHTML = fs.readFileSync(
    path.resolve(__dirname, '../build/index.html'),
    {
      encoding: 'utf8',
    }
  )

  res.contentType('text/html')
  res.status(200)

  return res.send(indexHTML)
})

server.listen(8000, () => {
  console.log(`Launched at http://localhost:8000!`)
})
```

Our custom server will work similarly to the development server that comes with `create-react-app`. It creates a web server with this line:

```
const server = express()
```

If the server receives a request for a JavaScript, stylesheet, or image file, it will look for the file in the *build* directory. The *build* directory is where `create-react-app` generates the deployable version of our application:

```
server.get(
  /.(js|css|map|ico|svg|png)$/,
  express.static(path.resolve(__dirname, '../build'))
)
```

If we receive a request for anything else, we will return the contents of the *build/index.html* file:

```
server.use('*', async (req, res) => {
  ...
})
```

Finally, we start the server running on port 8000:

```
server.listen(8000, () => {
  console.log(`Launched at http://localhost:8000!`)
})
```

Before we can run this server, we need to build the application. We can do this with the following command:

```
$ yarn run build
```

Building the application generates all of the static files in the *build* directory that our server will need. We can now run the server itself:

```
$ node server
Launched at http://localhost:8000!
```

If we open a browser at *http://localhost:8000*, we will see our React application (see Figure 10-21).

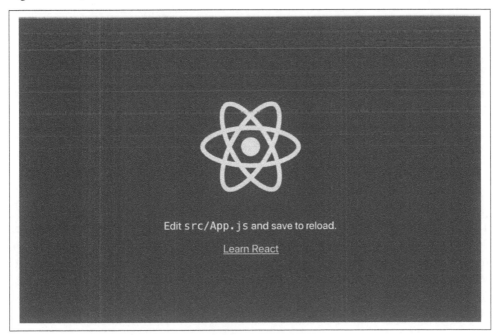

Figure 10-21. The application running on our new server

So far, so good. But we aren't actually doing any server-side rendering. For that, we will need to load some React code to load and render the App component:

```
import express from 'express'
import fs from 'fs'
import path from 'path'
import { renderToString } from 'react-dom/server'
import App from '../src/App'

const server = express()

server.get(
  /.(js|css|map|ico|svg|png)$/,
  express.static(path.resolve(__dirname, '../build'))
)

server.use('*', async (req, res) => {
  let indexHTML = fs.readFileSync(
    path.resolve(__dirname, '../build/index.html'),
    {
      encoding: 'utf8',
    }
  )

  const app = renderToString(<App />)

  indexHTML = indexHTML.replace(
    '<div id="root"></div>',
    `<div id="app">${app}</div>`
  )

  res.contentType('text/html')
  res.status(200)

  return res.send(indexHTML)
})

server.listen(8000, () => {
  console.log(`Launched at http://localhost:8000!`)
})
```

This new code uses the `renderToString` function from React's SSR library `react-dom/server`. The `renderToString` function does what you would expect. Instead of rendering the App component into a virtual DOM, it simply renders it into a string. We can replace the empty DIV in the *index.html* content with the HTML generated from the App component. If you restart the server and then reload the web browser, you will find that the application still works. Mostly (see Figure 10-22).

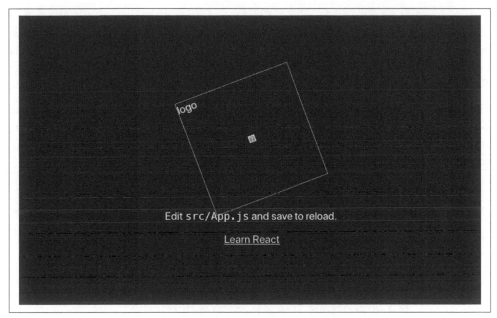

Figure 10-22. The React application showing a broken SVG image

Instead of seeing the rotating React logo, we instead see a broken image symbol. We can see what happens if we look at the generated HTML returned by the server:

```
<div id="app">
  <div class="App" data-reactroot="">
    <header class="App-header">
      <img src="[object Object]" class="App-logo" alt="logo"/>
      <p>Edit <code>src/App.js</code> and save to reload.</p>
      <a class="App-link" href="https://reactjs.org"
         target="_blank" rel="noopener noreferrer">
        Learn React
      </a>
    </header>
  </div>
</div>
```

Something odd has happened to the `img` element. Instead of rendering an SVG image, it tries to load the URL "[object Object]." What's happening here?

In the React code, we are loading the logo like this:

```
import logo from './logo.svg'
...
<img src={logo} className="App-logo" alt="logo" />
```

This code relies on some Webpack configuration from `create-react-app`. When you access the application through the development server, Webpack will use a library called *svgr* to replace any imports of SVG files with generated React components that contain the raw SVG contents. *svgr* allows SVG images to be loaded just like any other React components. That's what allows us to import them as we might import a *.js* file.

However, in our hand-built server, we have no such Webpack configuration. Instead of going to the trouble of configuring Webpack, we can avoid the problem by copying the *logo.svg* file to the *public* folder and then changing the code in the App component to the following:

```
// import logo from './logo.svg'
import './App.css'

function App() {
  return (
    <div className="App">
      <header className="App-header">
        <img src="/logo.svg" className="App-logo" alt="logo" />
        <p>
          Edit <code>src/App.js</code> and save to reload.
        </p>
        <a
          className="App-link"
          href="https://reactjs.org"
          target="_blank"
          rel="noopener noreferrer"
        >
          Learn React
        </a>
      </header>
    </div>
  )
}

export default App
```

If we now rebuild the application and restart the server:

```
$ yarn build
$ node server
```

the SSR application will display the application correctly (see Figure 10-23).

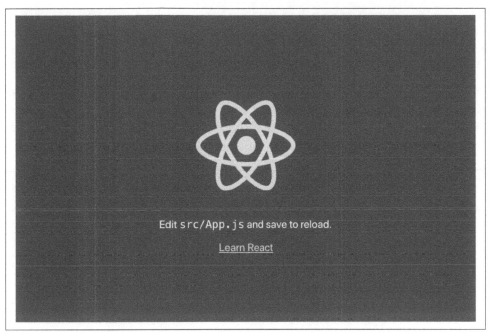

Figure 10-23. The application now displays the SVG image correctly

There is actually just one step left, which we should implement. In the *src/index.js* file, we render the single-page version of the application like this:

```
ReactDOM.render(
  <React.StrictMode>
    <App />
  </React.StrictMode>,
  document.getElementById('root')
)
```

Remember, this code will still run, even when we access our application through the SSR server. The browser will download the prerendered version of the web page, and it will then download the JavaScript for the SPA. When the SPA code runs, it will execute the preceding code from *index.js*. The browser still needs to load and run the JavaScript to make the interface interactive. The `ReactDOM.render` method may replace all of our prerendered HTML when it doesn't need to. So if we replace the call to `ReactDOM.render` with `ReactDOM.hydrate`, we will only replace the HTML in the DOM if it is different from the HTML in the virtual DOM. For our server-side rendered page, the content of the static web page and the content of the virtual DOM should be the same. The result is that `hydrate` will not update the elements on the page; it will just attach a set of event listeners to make the page interactive.

So, we now have a server-side rendered application. But has it made the page load any faster?

The simplest way to test page load time is to run a Lighthouse performance audit within Chrome. Lighthouse, remember, performs a basic audit of a web page, checking performance, accessibility, and a bunch of other features. It will give us a metric that we can use to compare the two versions of the application.

When we tried this on a development laptop when accessing the ordinary React development server that comes bundled with `create-react-app`, we got a performance grade of 91 out of 100 and a *first contentful paint* (FCP) time of 1.2 seconds (see Figure 10-24).

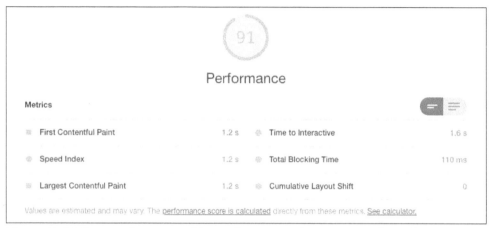

Figure 10-24. Base performance of the application, without server-side rendering

That's not a bad performance score. But we are running a small React application.

What happens when we test the SSR version of the application? After all, the server will still have to spend some time rendering the React code. Will it run any faster? You can see the results of our test in Figure 10-25.

The overall score has increased to 99 out of 100. The time to FCP has dropped to 0.6 seconds: half that of our original version. Also, if you load the original SPA version of the application in a browser and keep hitting Refresh, you will see the page will often flash white for a moment before rendering the web page. The flash occurs because the downloaded HTML is just an empty `DIV`, which the browser displays as a white page before the JavaScript can render the application.

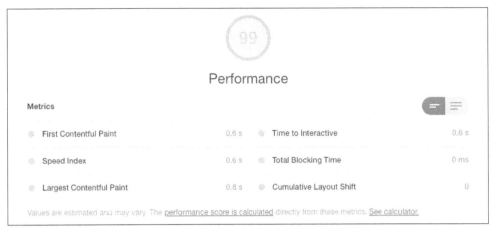

Figure 10-25. Performance of the application with server-side rendering

Compare that to the SSR version of the application. If you keep hitting Refresh on the SSR version, the only thing you should notice is that the rotation of the logo keeps resetting. You will see almost no flashing.

Even though there is still a render process occurring on the server, the time needed to render a string version of the HTML is less than the time needed to render the same set of DOM elements.

Discussion

In this recipe, we have taken you through the basics of how you might set up basic server-side rendering for your application. The details for *your* application are likely to vary quite a lot, dependent upon which additional libraries your application uses.

Most React applications use some form of routing, for example. If you are using `react-router`, then you will need to add some additional code on the server side to handle the fact that different components will need to be rendered, based upon the path that the browser has requested. For example, we can use the `StaticRouter` from `react-router` like this:

```
import { StaticRouter } from 'react-router-dom'
...
const app = renderToString(
  <StaticRouter location={req.originalUrl} context={{}}>
    <App />
  </StaticRouter>
)
```

The `StaticRouter` renders its child components for a single, specific route. In this case, we use the `originalURL` route from the browser request. If the browser asks for */person/1234*, the `StaticRouter` will render the App component for this route.

Notice that we can also use the `StaticRouter` to pass any additional context for the rest of the application. We could use the context to pass content to the rest of the application.

If you are using code splitting in your application with `React.lazy`, you need to be aware that this will not work on the server side. Fortunately, there is a workaround. The Loadable Components (*https://oreil.ly/v8zan*) library does the same job as `React.lazy`, but it can also run on the server side. Therefore, Loadable Components gives you all of the advantages of server-side rendering with all the benefits of code splitting.

As with all optimizations, there is a price to pay with server-side rendering. It will require additional complexity in your code, and it will also require additional load on your server. You can deploy an SPA as static code on any web server. That's not true for server-side rendered code. It will need a JavaScript server and may well increase your cloud hosting costs.

Also, if you know from the outset that you want to use server-side rendering for your application, you should probably consider a tool like Razzle or Next.js for your application and build server-side rendering from day one.

Finally, there are alternative approaches to SSR that can boost the performance of your web page without the need for server-side rendering. Consider using Gatsby. Gatsby can prerender your pages at *build time*, giving you many of the advantages of SSR without needing server-side code.

You can download the source for this recipe from the GitHub site (*https://oreil.ly/Mfzex*).

10.8 Use Web Vitals

Problem

It is more important to have code that works and is readable than it is to have highly tuned code. Tuning, as we've seen, always comes with an associated cost.

But if there *are* noticeable performance issues, it is essential to become aware of them and fix them as quickly as possible. Much of the Internet relies upon *passing trade*. If people go to your website and it doesn't immediately respond, they may leave and never return.

Developers often track server performance using trackers—known as *beacons*—embedded within the code. If there's a performance issue, the beacons can generate an alert, and the developer can fix the problem before it affects a lot of users.

But how do we embed a tracking beacon into our client code?

Solution

We're going to look at how to track *web vitals*. We mentioned web vitals in Recipe 10.1. They are a small set of metrics that measure your application's most important performance features, such as the *Cumulative Layout Shift* (CLS), which measures how much your application jumps around when it first loads.

Several tools, such as the Lighthouse Chrome extension, track web vitals. The name *web vitals* is intended to remind you of vital signs, like heart rate and blood pressure, because they tell you about an underlying issue that you need to address.

If you created your application with `create-react-app`, you probably already have code embedded that can automatically track the web vitals of your application. If you look in the *src/index.js* file, you will see a call to report the web vitals at the end:

```
import React from 'react'
import ReactDOM from 'react-dom'
import './index.css'
import App from './App'
import reportWebVitals from './reportWebVitals'

ReactDOM.render(
  <React.StrictMode>
    <App />
  </React.StrictMode>,
  document.getElementById('root')
)

reportWebVitals()
```

The `reportWebVitals` function can be given a callback function that can be used to track the various metrics while the application is running. For example, if you pass it `console.log`:

```
reportWebVitals(console.log)
```

you will then see metrics appearing in your JavaScript console as a series of JSON objects (see Figure 10-26).

```
[HMR] Waiting for update signal from WDS...
▶ {name: "TTFB", value: 8895.58000001125, delta: 8895.58000001125, entries: Array(1), id: "v1-1619375289115-2756702094238"}
▶ {name: "FCP", value: 12343.090000009397, delta: 12343.090000009397, entries: Array(1), id: "v1-1619375289114-8463971860890"}
▶ {name: "FID", value: 12.084999994840473, delta: 12.084999994840473, entries: Array(1), id: "v1-1619375289114-6129894643559"}
▶ {name: "LCP", value: 12343.09, delta: 12343.09, entries: Array(1), id: "v1-1619375289114-8994253857417"}
  >
```

Figure 10-26. The web vitals in the JavaScript console

This is not really how you are intended to track web vitals. A better option is to send the data back to some backend store. For example, you might choose to POST them to send API endpoint:

```
reportWebVitals((vital) => {
  fetch('/trackVitals', {
    body: JSON.stringify(vital),
    method: 'POST',
    keepalive: true,
  })
})
```

Many browsers have a built-in function that is intended for use when recording vital measurements. The browser will cancel normal network requests, such as those made by calling `fetch`, if the user leaves the page. Given that the most important web vitals happen when the page loads, it would be a pity to lose these metrics. For that reason, you should consider using the `navigator.sendBeacon` function when it's available:

```
reportWebVitals((vital) => {
  if (navigator.sendBeacon) {
    navigator.sendBeacon('/trackVitals', JSON.stringify(vital))
  } else {
    fetch('/trackVitals', {
      body: JSON.stringify(vital),
      method: 'POST',
      keepalive: true,
    })
  }
})
```

If the user briefly opens the page and then goes elsewhere, the `navigator.sendBea con` will be allowed to complete its `POST` request before dying.

Discussion

There are commercial tracking services available that you can use to record web vitals, such as sentry.io (*https://sentry.io*). If you have a performance monitoring system installed, you might also be able to wire it up using web vitals to provide additional performance monitoring for your system.

Finally, consider tracking web vitals with Google Analytics as described on the `create-react-app` site (*https://oreil.ly/wImZt*).

CHAPTER 11

Progressive Web Applications

Progressive web applications (PWAs) are web applications that try to behave like locally installed applications. They can work offline, integrate with the native notification system, and have the ability to run long background processes, which can continue even after you leave the website. They're called *progressive* because they smoothly downgrade their functionality if some feature is not available in the current browser.

This chapter focuses almost exclusively on one feature of PWAs: service workers. You will occasionally encounter the term *progressive web application* used to describe any JavaScript-rich browser application. The truth is that unless that application uses service workers, it isn't a PWA.

Service workers are, in effect, a locally installed server for the application. The backend server is a software distribution mechanism and a provider of live data services, but the service worker is really in charge because it provides access to the network. It can choose to satisfy network requests from its own local cache. If the network is not available, it can choose to replace network resources with local placeholders. It can even queue data updates offline and synchronize with the backend server when the network connection reappears.

This is a good topic for the final chapter because it has been the most enjoyable chapter to write. Service workers are one of the most fascinating features found in modern browsers. We hope you have fun.

11.1 Create Service Workers with Workbox

Problem

PWAs can work even when you're offline. They can cache any content or code they require, and the cache will survive the user refreshing the page. They can run background operations independently of the code that runs in the browser.

PWAs can do this because of *service workers*. Service workers are a kind of web worker. A *web worker* is a piece of JavaScript that runs in a separate thread from the JavaScript running in a web page. Service workers are specialized web workers that can intercept network traffic between a web page and the server, giving them a tremendous amount of control over the page that registers them. You can think of a service worker as a kind of local proxy service that's available even when you've disconnected from the network.

Service workers are most often used to cache content locally. Browsers will cache most content they see, but a service worker can do so much more aggressively. For example, hitting force-refresh in a browser will often force it to reload assets from the network. But the force-refresh function will not affect service workers, no matter how many times a user uses it.

You can see a service worker in operation in Figure 11-1.

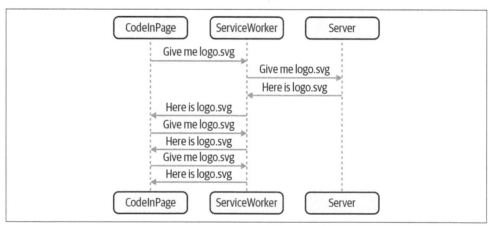

Figure 11-1. A service worker will intercept all network requests

In this case, the service worker will cache files the first time they are downloaded. If the page asks for the *logo.svg* file more than once, the service worker will return it from its private cache rather than from the network.

How a service worker caches data and how it decides if it needs to return data from its cache or the network is called a *strategy*. We will look at various standard strategies in this chapter.

Service workers are stored on the server as separate JavaScript files, and the browser will download and install them from a URL. There is nothing to prevent you from handcrafting a service worker and storing it in the public folder of your application, but there are several problems with writing service workers from scratch.

First, service workers are notoriously difficult to create. Not only can they include complex code, but they also have complex life cycles. It's far too easy to write a service worker that fails to load or caches the wrong files. Even worse, it's possible to write a service worker that will isolate your application from the network.

Second, you can use service workers to precache application code. For a React application, this is a fantastic feature. Instead of downloading several hundred kilobytes of JavaScript, a service worker can return it all in a split second from a local cache, which means that your application can start almost immediately, even on a low-powered device with a bad network connection.

But code caching has its own set of problems. Let's say we have a React application that includes the following generated JavaScript files:

```
$ ls build/static/js/
2.d106afb5.chunk.js              2.d106afb5.chunk.js.map
3.9e79b289.chunk.js.map          main.095e14c4.chunk.js.map
runtime-main.b175c5d9.js.map     2.d106afb5.chunk.js.LICENSE.txt
3.9e79b289.chunk.js              main.095e14c4.chunk.js
runtime-main.b175c5d9.js
$
```

If we want to precache these files, the service worker will need to know the names. That's because it will download the files in the background, even before the browser has asked for them. So if you create a service worker by hand, you will need to include the names of each of the files that it will precache.

But then what happens if you make a small change to your source code and then rebuild the application?

```
$ yarn run build
$ ls build/static/js/
2.d106afb5.chunk.js              2.d106afb5.chunk.js.map
3.9e79b289.chunk.js.map          main.f5b66cc7.chunk.js.map
runtime-main.b175c5d9.js.map     2.d106afb5.chunk.js.LICENSE.txt
3.9e79b289.chunk.js              main.f5b66cc7.chunk.js
runtime-main.b175c5d9.js
$
```

The filenames *change*, which means you will now have to update the service worker script with the latest generated filenames.

How can you create stable service workers that are always in sync with the latest application code?

Solution

We're going to use a set of tools from Google called Workbox (*https://oreil.ly/9dPXh*). The Workbox tools allow you to generate service workers that are up-to-date with your latest application files.

Workbox includes a set of standard strategies to handle the details of common service worker use cases. If you want to precache your application, you can do so with a single line of code into Workbox.

To see how to use Workbox, consider the application you can see in Figure 11-2.

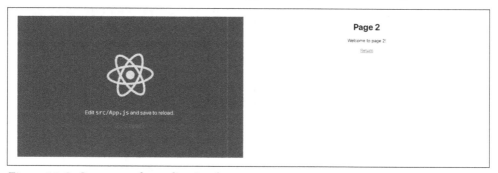

Figure 11-2. Our example application has two pages

It's a simple two-page application based on the default application generated by `create-react-app`. We're going to build a service worker that will precache all of the application's code and files.

We'll begin by installing a few of the libraries from Workbox:

```
$ yarn add workbox-core
$ yarn add workbox-precaching
$ yarn add workbox-routing
```

You will see what each of these libraries is for as we build the service worker.

In our application, we will create a new file for the service worker called *service-worker.js*. We can place this file in the same directory as the rest of the application code:

```
import { clientsClaim } from 'workbox-core'
import { precacheAndRoute } from 'workbox-precaching'
```

```
clientsClaim()

precacheAndRoute(self.__WB_MANIFEST)
```

 If we were creating a service worker by hand, we would have to create it in the same directory we use to store other static content. For example, in a `create-react-app` application, we would have to create it in the *public* directory.

Our service worker will precache all of the application code. That means it will automatically cache any CSS, JavaScript, HTML, and images that are part of the application.

The service worker calls the `clientsClaim` function from *workbox-core*, which will make the service worker the controller for all clients within its scope. A *client* is a web page, and the *scope* is any web page with a URL within the same path as the service worker. Workbox will generate our service worker at *https://host/service-worker.js*, which means the service worker will be the controller for all pages that begin with *https://host/*.

The `precacheAndRoute` function will handle all of the gory details of the precaching process. It will create and manage the local cache, and it will intercept network requests for application files and load them from the local cache rather than the network.

 Service workers will function only if loaded with HTTPS. Most browsers make an exception for sites loaded from *localhost*. For security reasons, browsers will not run service workers in private tabs.

As we've created our service worker, we need to register it from the main application code. Registration is a complex process, but the good news is that it's almost always the same. Once you've written the registration code for one application, you can copy it, unchanged, to another. Also, if you are building your application using the *cra-template-pwa* template, it will generate the registration code for you.[1]

It is still worth understanding the details of the registration process; it will give you insight into the life cycle of a service worker. That will make it a lot easier to understand any seemingly odd behavior that occurs after you deploy your application.

---

1 See Recipe 11.2.

Create a new file called *registerWorker.js* in the main source directory of the application:

```
const register = (pathToWorker, onInstall, onUpdate, onError) => {
  // We will write this code shortly
}

const registerWorker = () => {
  register(
    '/service-worker.js',
    (reg) => console.info('Service worker installed', reg),
    (reg) => console.info('Service worker updated', reg),
    (err) => console.error('Service worker failed', err)
  )
}

export default registerWorker
```

Leave the `register` function empty for now.

We will call the `registerWorker` function from the *index.js* file in our application:

```
import React from 'react'
import ReactDOM from 'react-dom'
import './index.css'
import App from './App'
import registerWorker from './registerWorker'

ReactDOM.render(
  <React.StrictMode>
    <App />
  </React.StrictMode>,
  document.getElementById('root')
)

registerWorker()
```

The `registerWorker` function will call `register` with the path of our generated service worker: *service-worker.js*.

We can now start to write the `register` function:

```
const register = (pathToWorker, onInstall, onUpdate, onError) => {
  if (
    process.env.NODE_ENV === 'production' &&
    'serviceWorker' in navigator
  ) {
    const publicUrl = new URL(
      process.env.PUBLIC_URL,
      window.location.href
    )
    if (publicUrl.origin !== window.location.origin) {
      return
```

```
    }
    // Do the loading and registering here
  }
}
```

We'll check that we're in *production* mode and that the browser can run service work-ers. The *progressive* in *progressive web application* means that we should always check that a feature is available before using it. Almost all browsers (with the notable excep-tion of Internet Explorer) support service workers, but we can skip the service worker entirely if a browser doesn't. It will mean that the application will lose its ability to work offline, but other than that, the application should still work.

We also add an extra check to ensure we are running on the specified PUBLIC URL of the application, which will avoid cross-domain issues that arise when loading code from content distribution networks.[2]

Now we can download and register the service worker:

```
const register = (pathToWorker, onInstall, onUpdate, onError) => {
  if (
    process.env.NODE_ENV === 'production' &&
    'serviceWorker' in navigator
  ) {
    const publicUrl = new URL(
      process.env.PUBLIC_URL,
      window.location.href
    )
    if (publicUrl.origin !== window.location.origin) {
      return
    }

    window.addEventListener('load', async () => {
      try {
        const registration = await navigator.serviceWorker.register(
          process.env.PUBLIC_URL + pathToWorker
        )

        // Code to check progress goes here
      } catch (err) {
        if (onError) {
          onError(err)
        }
      }
    })
  }
}
```

---

2 The code we will build here is a simplified version of the code in the cra-template-pwa library. For further information, see this issue on GitHub (*https://oreil.ly/dKJE0*).

Once we know the web page is loaded, we can register the service worker with the navigator.serviceWorker.register function, passing it the full URL of the service worker: *https://host/service-worker.js*.

It returns a *registration* object, which can be used to track and manage the service worker. For example, you can use the registration object to find out when the service worker is updated or installed:

```
const register = (pathToWorker, onInstall, onUpdate, onError) => {
  if (
    process.env.NODE_ENV === 'production' &&
    'serviceWorker' in navigator
  ) {
    const publicUrl = new URL(
      process.env.PUBLIC_URL,
      window.location.href
    )
    if (publicUrl.origin !== window.location.origin) {
      return
    }

    window.addEventListener('load', async () => {
      try {
        const registration = await navigator.serviceWorker.register(
          process.env.PUBLIC_URL + pathToWorker
        )

        registration.onupdatefound = () => {
          const worker = registration.installing
          if (worker) {
            worker.onstatechange = () => {
              if (worker.state === 'installed') {
                if (navigator.serviceWorker.controller) {
                  if (onUpdate) {
                    onUpdate(registration)
                  }
                } else {
                  if (onInstall) {
                    onInstall(registration)
                  }
                }
              }
            }
          }
        }
      } catch (err) {
        if (onError) {
          onError(err)
        }
      }
    })
```

```
        }
    }
```

The `onupdatefound` handler runs when the browser starts to install the service worker. Once the browser has installed the service worker, we can check `navigator.serviceWorker.controller` to see if a previous service worker is still running. If not, we know that this is a fresh installation and not an update.

 One of the most confusing things about service workers is the way that they are updated. If an old service worker is already in control of a page, the browser will put the new service worker into a *waiting* state, which means it will do *absolutely nothing* until the old service worker stops. A service worker stops when the user closes all the pages that it controls. Consequently, if you update your service worker, you will not run the new code until you open, close, and then open the page again.

This process can be confusing for anyone manually testing a new service worker feature.

Before we build the application, we will need to configure the build tools to convert our *service-worker.js* source file into a densely written service worker script.

If you're building your application with Webpack, you should install the Workbox Webpack Plugin:

```
$ yarn install -D workbox-webpack-plugin
```

 You will not need to install the Workbox Webpack Plugin or configure its use if you created your application with `create-react-app`, which includes and configures the plugin for you.

You can then add the following to your *webpack.config.js* configuration:

```
const { InjectManifest } = require('workbox-webpack-plugin')

module.exports = {
  ....
  plugins: [
    ....
    new InjectManifest({
      swSrc: './src/service-worker.js',
    }),
  ],
}
```

This configuration will tell Webpack to generate a service worker from the *src/service-worker.js* file. It will also generate a file called *asset-manifest.json* in your built application, which will list all of the application files. The service worker will use the information in *asset-manifest.json* when it's precaching the application.

Now you build the application:

```
$ yarn run build
```

In your *build* directory, you will see a generated *service-worker.js* file and the *asset-manifest.json* file:

```
asset-manifest.json  logo192.png          service-worker.js.map
favicon.ico          manifest.json        static
index.html           robots.txt
logo512.png          service-worker.js
```

The *asset-manifest.json* file will contain something like this:

```
{
  "files": {
    "main.css": "/static/css/main.8c8b27cf.chunk.css",
    "main.js": "/static/js/main.f5b66cc7.chunk.js",
    "main.js.map": "/static/js/main.f5b66cc7.chunk.js.map",
    "runtime-main.js": "/static/js/runtime-main.b175c5d9.js",
    "runtime-main.js.map": "/static/js/runtime-main.b175c5d9.js.map",
    "static/js/2.d106afb5.chunk.js": "/static/js/2.d106afb5.chunk.js",
    "static/js/2.d106afb5.chunk.js.map": "/static/js/2.d106afb5.chunk.js.map",
    "static/js/3.9e79b289.chunk.js": "/static/js/3.9e79b289.chunk.js",
    "static/js/3.9e79b289.chunk.js.map": "/static/js/3.9e79b289.chunk.js.map",
    "index.html": "/index.html",
    "service-worker.js": "/service-worker.js",
    "service-worker.js.map": "/service-worker.js.map",
    "static/css/main.8c8b27cf.chunk.css.map":
        "/static/css/main.8c8b27cf.chunk.css.map",
    "static/js/2.d106afb5.chunk.js.LICENSE.txt":
        "/static/js/2.d106afb5.chunk.js.LICENSE.txt",
    "static/media/logo.6ce24c58.svg": "/static/media/logo.6ce24c58.svg"
  },
  "entrypoints": [
    "static/js/runtime-main.b175c5d9.js",
    "static/js/2.d106afb5.chunk.js",
    "static/css/main.8c8b27cf.chunk.css",
    "static/js/main.f5b66cc7.chunk.js"
  ]
}
```

You can now run the application. You can't just start the development server with this:

```
$ yarn run start
```

That will only run the application in development mode, and the service worker will not start. You will need to run a server on the contents of the *build* directory. The simplest way to do this is by installing the *serve* package globally and then running it against the *build* directory:

```
$ npm install -s serve
$ serve -s build/
```

```
|                                                           |
|    Serving!                                               |
|                                                           |
|    - Local:            http://localhost:5000              |
|    - On Your Network:  http://192.168.1.14:5000           |
|                                                           |
|    Copied local address to clipboard!                     |
|                                                           |
```

The -s option is for running SPAs. If the server can't find a matching file, it will return the *build/index.html* file.

You can now open a browser at *http://localhost:5000*. The application will appear, and if you open the developer tools and switch to the Application tab, under Service Workers, you should see the *service-worker.js* script running (see Figure 11-3).

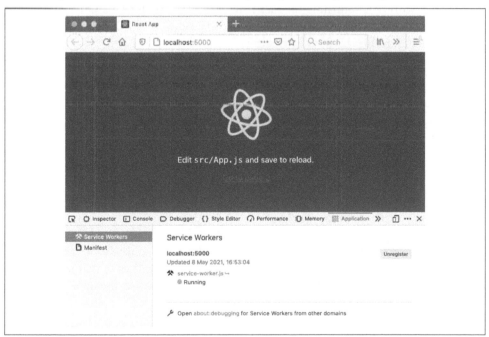

Figure 11-3. The service worker installed and running in the application

The service worker will download all of the application files into a local cache so that the next time the page is loaded, the files will come from the local cache rather than the server. You can see this happen if you switch to the *Network* tab in developer tools and then reload the page (see Figure 11-4). The service worker will supply each of the network responses, except those that fall outside its scope. Any file that belongs at the site level rather than page level, such as *favicon* icons, will still be downloaded in the usual way.

Figure 11-4. After refresh, the files are downloaded using the service worker

The service worker is returning the files from a local cache. If you are using Chrome, you can see the cache on the Application tab. For Firefox, you will find it on the Storage tab (see Figure 11-5).

Figure 11-5. A cache stores the files locally

The cache doesn't contain a copy of *all* the application files, only those that the application has requested. In this way, it will avoid downloading files that are not needed and will download files into the cache only after the browser or the application code has requested them.

So the first time you load the application, the cache might be empty. It depends on when the service worker becomes active. If the page loads *before* the service worker is active, the service worker won't intercept the network requests and cache the responses. As a result, you might have to refresh a page before you see the caches appear.

To prove that the files are genuinely coming from the service worker, you can stop the server and refresh the web page. Even though the server is no longer there, the page should load as usual (see Figure 11-6).

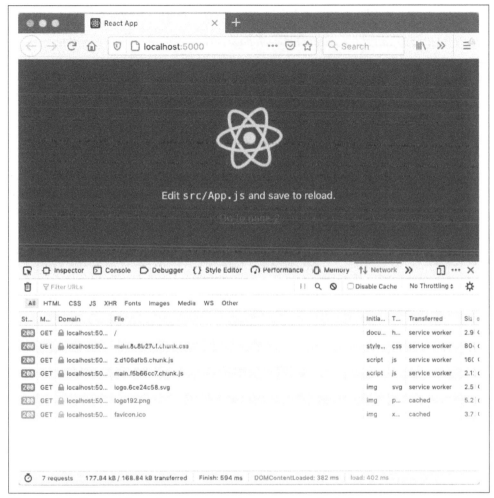

Figure 11-6. Even without the server running, you can refresh the page

You should now think of the React application as a local application rather than a network application. It's served from the service worker rather than the backend server. It will even let you get to navigate to page 2 (see Figure 11-7).

Figure 11-7. You can still navigate between pages even when the server is offline

 Using code splitting can interfere with some offline functionality. If the code to display page 2 in the example application was stored in a separate JavaScript file that was not initially loaded, the browser will not return it from the local cache. It will be available once the browser has visited that page when the server is online.

While we are looking at page 2, we can examine a current problem with the service worker. Make sure the server is *not* running, and navigate to page 2. It should load normally. Then reload the page. Instead of seeing page 2, you will get an error page from the browser (see Figure 11-8).

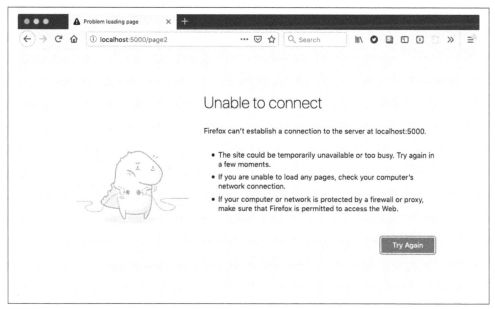

Figure 11-8. Page 2 will not reload when the server is offline

We can reload the front page of the application while offline, so why isn't this true for page 2? It's because this is an SPA. When we navigate to page 2, the browser isn't loading a new web page from the server; instead, it uses the history API to update the URL in the address bar and then modify the DOM to show page 2.

However, when you reload the page, the browser will make a new request to the server for *http://localhost:5000/page2*. When the server is running, it will return the contents of *index.html* for all page requests, and the React router will render the components to look like page 2.

This process falls apart when the server is no longer online. The service worker will not be able to respond to a request for *http://localhost:5000/page2* using cached data. There is nothing in the cache for *page2*. So, it will forward the request to the server, which is no longer running. That's why you get the error page.

We can fix this by adding a little more code to *service-worker.js*:[3]

```
import { clientsClaim } from 'workbox-core'
import {
  createHandlerBoundToURL,
  precacheAndRoute,
} from 'workbox-precaching'
import { registerRoute } from 'workbox-routing'

clientsClaim()

precacheAndRoute(self.__WB_MANIFEST)

const fileExtensionRegexp = new RegExp('/[^/?]+\\.[^/]+$')
registerRoute(({ request, url }) => {
  if (request.mode !== 'navigate') {
    return false
  }
  if (url.pathname.startsWith('/_')) {
    return false
  }
  if (url.pathname.match(fileExtensionRegexp)) {
    return false
  }
  return true
}, createHandlerBoundToURL(process.env.PUBLIC_URL + '/index.html'))
```

We are now registering an explicit *route* using `workbox-routing`. A route decides how the service worker will deal with requests for a set of paths. We're registering a new route using a filter function and a handler in the previous example code. The filter function is the first value passed to the `registerRoute` call. It will return true if

---

3 This code is based on the example service worker is `cra-template-pwa`, which we will look at in the following recipe.

this route deals with a given request. The filter function in the preceding code will deal with any navigation requests to new web pages. So if you open the browser at *http://localhost:5000/* or *http://localhost:5000/page2*, this route will return the same cached copy of *index.html*.

The function `createHandlerBoundToURL` will create a handler to treat any of these requests as if they were requests for *http://localhost:5000/index.html*, which means that if we reload the application while we're on page 2, the service worker should load the HTML the same way it does when we are on the front page.

Let's try this. After saving the change to *service-worker.js*, rebuild the application:

```
$ yarn run build
```

Now make sure that your local server is running:

```
$ serve -s build/
```

Open the browser at *http://localhost:5000*, and you should see the application. If you check the developer tools, you will find that it has loaded the new version of the service worker, but the old version of the service worker is still running (see Figure 11-9).

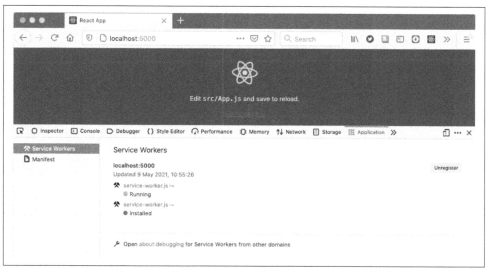

Figure 11-9. The old and new service workers are both visible in the tools

The previous version of the service worker is still in control of the application. The browser has installed the new service worker, but it's in a *waiting* state. It won't take over until the old service work disappears, and that will happen if you close down the tab and then reopen it (see Figure 11-10).

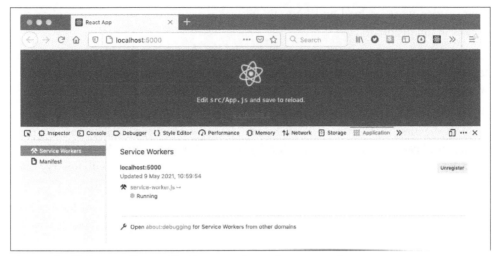

Figure 11-10. Reopen the application to activate the new worker

If you now stop your local server and navigate to page 2, you should be able to reload it with no problems (see Figure 11-11).

Figure 11-11. Once you've registered a route handler, you can reload page 2

Discussion

We've gone into quite a lot of depth in this recipe, looking at how to create, register, and use service workers. In the following recipe, you will see that you can automatically generate a lot of this code when you first build the application. But it's still worth digging into the messy details of how service workers operate. It helps to understand the life cycle of a worker: how a browser installs a service worker and how it becomes active.

We have found that service workers can confuse anyone who is manually testing the code. If the browser is still running an old version of a service worker, it may still be running an old version of your application. This confusion can lead to failed test reports because an old bug might still appear to be there. Once you understand how new service workers load and how old service workers disappear, you can quickly diagnose the problem.

Out-of-date service workers are not an issue with automated browser tests, which will tend to run in a *clean* state at the start of a test, with no caches or running service workers.

Progressive web applications with service workers are a kind of hybrid between a local application and a remote application. The server becomes a distribution server for an application that is installed locally. When the application is updated, it will install a new version in the browser, but that new application will not typically become available until the browser reopens it.

Now that we've gone through service workers in a detailed way, we can look at how you can quickly add them to a new application.

You can download the source for this recipe from the GitHub site (*https://oreil.ly/ su224*).

11.2 Build a PWA with Create React App

Problem

You need two things before you can run service workers in your application. First, you need a service worker, and Recipe 11.1 looked at how the Workbox library would help simplify the creation and management of service workers. Second, you need code that will register the service worker in your application. Although complex to create, you can copy registration code to new applications with few changes.

However, as patterns evolve in the use of service workers, it would be helpful to avoid the need to create our own registration code. How can we do that?

Solution

We will look at how to use templates in `create-react-app` to build an application that includes service workers.

Even if you don't intend to use `create-react-app`, it can be worth generating an application with it and then reusing the service worker code in your project.

We briefly saw how to use application templates in Chapter 1 when we generated TypeScript projects with `create-react-app`. Templates are the boilerplate code that `create-react-app` uses when it generates a new application.

If we want to create a progressive web application, we can do it by typing the following:

```
$ npx create-react-app appname --template cra-template-pwa
```

 If you want to create a TypeScript application, replace cra-
template-pwa with cra-template-pwa-typescript.

If we do that, it will generate a React application in a new folder called *appname*. The
application will look virtually the same as any other CRA application, but it will
install several Workbox libraries. It will add two additional source files. In the *src*
directory, you will find an example *service-worker.js* script:

```javascript
import { clientsClaim } from 'workbox-core'
import { ExpirationPlugin } from 'workbox-expiration'
import {
  precacheAndRoute,
  createHandlerBoundToURL,
} from 'workbox-precaching'
import { registerRoute } from 'workbox-routing'
import { StaleWhileRevalidate } from 'workbox-strategies'

clientsClaim()

precacheAndRoute(self.__WB_MANIFEST)

const fileExtensionRegexp = new RegExp('/[^/?]+\.[^/]+$')
registerRoute(({ request, url }) => {
  if (request.mode !== 'navigate') {
    return false
  }

  if (url.pathname.startsWith('/_')) {
    return false
  }

  if (url.pathname.match(fileExtensionRegexp)) {
    return false
  }

  return true
}, createHandlerBoundToURL(process.env.PUBLIC_URL + '/index.html'))

registerRoute(
  ({ url }) =>
    url.origin === self.location.origin &&
    url.pathname.endsWith('.png'),
  new StaleWhileRevalidate({
    cacheName: 'images',
    plugins: [new ExpirationPlugin({ maxEntries: 50 })],
  })
```

```
  )

  self.addEventListener('message', (event) => {
    if (event.data && event.data.type === 'SKIP_WAITING') {
      self.skipWaiting()
    }
  })
})
```

The service worker is similar to the one we created in Recipe 11.1.

You will also find a new file in the *src* directory called *serviceWorkerRegistration.js*. This file is very long, so we won't include the contents here. But it serves the same purpose as the *registerWorker.js* script we wrote in Recipe 11.1. It registers the service worker as the controller of the application. The *serviceWorkerRegistration.js* file is valuable, even if you don't intend to use `create-react-app` for your application. It has several additional features that the registration code in the previous recipe did not. For example, suppose you are running on *localhost*. In that case, it will unregister any service workers that look like they belong to a different application, which is helpful if you're working on several React applications.

Even though the service worker and the registration code are created for you in your new application, they won't actually be configured. In the *index.js* file, you will find that the application will actually unregister any service workers:

```
import React from 'react'
import ReactDOM from 'react-dom'
import './index.css'
import App from './App'
import * as serviceWorkerRegistration from './serviceWorkerRegistration'
import reportWebVitals from './reportWebVitals'

ReactDOM.render(
  <React.StrictMode>
    <App />
  </React.StrictMode>,
  document.getElementById('root')
)

serviceWorkerRegistration.unregister()

reportWebVitals()
```

If you want to enable the *service-worker.js* script, you will need to change `serviceWorkerRegistration.unregister` to `serviceWorkerRegistration.register`.

The `register` function allows you to pass callbacks into the registration process so that you can track the current status of the service worker installation. To do this, pass an object with `onInstall` and `onUpdate` functions:

```
serviceWorkerRegistration.register({
  onInstall: (registration) => {
```

```
    console.log('Service worker installed')
  },
  onUpdate: (registration) => {
    console.log('Service worker updated')
  },
})
```

The callbacks are helpful if you want to defer some processing until after the browser has installed the service worker or if you would like to run code when the new service worker is an update to a previous one. If onUpdate is called, you will know that your new service worker is waiting for an old service worker to disappear.

Discussion

Recipe 11.1 helps you understand how service workers operate. When you are finally building a real application, templated code will be far more polished and feature-rich.

You can download the source for this recipe from the GitHub site (*https://oreil.ly/ hHAC9*).

11.3 Cache Third-Party Resources

Problem

Many of the resources used in a modern application come from third-party servers: payment libraries, fonts, images, etc. Third-party resources can consume a lot of bandwidth and might grow in size over time. If they come from slow servers, then they might slow down your application in a way that's out of your control.[4]

Is it possible to use a service worker to cache third-party resources?

Solution

Service workers have limited scope because they are allowed to control pages only within the same URL path. That's why service workers are generally at the root of an application; it allows them to control every page.

But there is no such limitation on the URLs that they are allowed to contact. They can talk to any endpoint that your page or code can. That means you can start to cache resources that come from third-party servers.

---

4 A recent project we worked on relied on a third-party payment library. When we were testing the application's performance, the payment library was by far the slowest component, not simply because it was large but because its server often took several 100 ms to start downloading the code.

The application you can see in Figure 11-12 is using a font downloaded from Google Fonts.

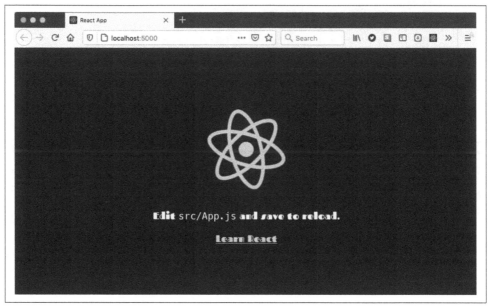

Figure 11-12. An application with a Google font—beautiful!

The font was added using these two lines in the header of the page:

```
<link rel="preconnect" href="https://fonts.gstatic.com">
<link href="https://fonts.googleapis.com/css2?family=Fascinate&display=swap"
    rel="stylesheet">
```

The first link imports the web font, and the second imports the associated stylesheet.

To cache this in the application, we will first need to register a service worker. The example application was created with the *cra-template-pwa* template, so we will need to call the register function in the *index.js* file:

```
import React from 'react'
import ReactDOM from 'react-dom'
import './index.css'
import App from './App'
import * as serviceWorkerRegistration from './serviceWorkerRegistration'
import reportWebVitals from './reportWebVitals'

ReactDOM.render(
  <React.StrictMode>
    <App />
  </React.StrictMode>,
  document.getElementById('root')
)
```

```
serviceWorkerRegistration.register()
```

```
reportWebVitals()
```

We will now add some routes into the *service-worker.js* script, which contains the service worker for the application. The service worker uses the Workbox library.

We need to cache the stylesheet and the downloadable font.

We saw in Recipe 11.1 that we could precache the application code, which is such a common requirement that Workbox lets you do it with a single line of code:

```
precacheAndRoute(self.__WB_MANIFEST)
```

This command will create a route that will cache any application code locally. We need to do a little more work if we want to cache third-party resources. Let's create a route to cache the stylesheet:

```
registerRoute(
  ({ url }) => url.origin === 'https://fonts.googleapis.com'
  // TODO Add handler
)
```

When we call `registerRoute`, we have to pass it a filter function and a handler. The filter function is given a request object and returns true if the handler should process it. The handler is a function that decides how to satisfy the request. It might look in a local cache, pass the request onto the network, or do some combination of the two.

Handlers are quite complex functions to build, but they typically follow some standard *strategy*, such as checking the cache before downloading a file from the network. Workbox has functions that will provide implementations of several strategies.

When we're downloading stylesheets, we'll use a `stale-while-revalidate` strategy (*https://oreil.ly/Ct1K3*), which means that when the browser wants to download the Google stylesheet, we will send a request for the stylesheet and also check the local cache to see if we already have a copy of the stylesheet file. If not, we'll wait for the stylesheet network request to return. This strategy is helpful if you make frequent requests for a resource but don't care if you have the latest version. We'll prefer to use the cached version of the stylesheet because that will be faster. But we will also always request a new version of the stylesheet from the network. We'll cache whatever comes back from Google, so even if we don't get the latest version of the stylesheet this time, we will the next time we load it.

This is how we create a handler for the `stale-while-revalidate` strategy:

```
registerRoute(
  ({ url }) => url.origin === 'https://fonts.googleapis.com',
  new StaleWhileRevalidate({
    cacheName: 'stylesheets',
```

```
  })
)
```

The `StaleWhileRevalidate` function will return a handler function that will cache the stylesheet in a cache called `stylesheets`.

 When loading third-party requests, you might find that your request might fail with a cross-origin resource sharing (CORS) error. This error can occur even if the third-party resource is returned with a valid CORS header because the `GET` request comes from JavaScript code rather than the HTML of the page. You can fix it by setting the `crossorigin` to `anonymous` on the HTML element using the resource, for example, the `link` reference that is downloading a stylesheet.

We could apply the same strategy when downloading the Google font. But font files can be large, and the `stale-while-revalidate` strategy will always download the latest version of the resource, even if it does so only to update the local cache.

Instead, we'll use a *cache-first* strategy (*https://oreil.ly/c8aa5*). In a cache-first strategy, we first check the cache for the resource, and if it's there, we use it. If we don't find the resource locally, we will send a network request. This is a helpful strategy for large resources. It does have a downside: you will download a new version of the resource only if the cache doesn't contain it. That means you might never be able to download any updated versions.

For that reason, we usually configure the cache-first strategy to cache resources for only a given period. If the handler finds the resource in the local cache but it's too old, it will request the resource from the network and then cache the updated version.

Whatever we cache, we'll be using until the cache times out. So if there's some temporary problem on the third-party server and we receive a 500 status,[5] we don't want to cache the response. So, we will also need to check the status before we decide to cache a response.

The following code shows how we will register a route to cache the Google font:

```
registerRoute(
  ({ url }) => url.origin === 'https://fonts.gstatic.com',
  new CacheFirst({
    cacheName: 'fonts',
    plugins: [
      new CacheableResponsePlugin({
        statuses: [0, 200],
```

---

5 "Internal Server Error."

```
    }),
    new ExpirationPlugin({
      maxAgeSeconds: 60 * 60 * 24 * 7,
      maxEntries: 5,
    }),
  ],
})
)
```

This code will cache up to five font files in a local cache called fonts. The cached copies will time out after a week, and we will cache the response only if the status is either 200 or 0. A 0 status indicates a cross-origin issue with the request, and in this case, we cache the response. A CORS error will not go away without a code change, and if we cache the error, we will avoid sending future requests that are doomed to fail.

Discussion

Third-party resource caching can significantly improve the performance of your application, but much more importantly, it will make resources available when your application is offline. It doesn't matter too much if the application cannot read something cosmetic like a font file. Still, if you're using third-party code to generate a payment form, it would be helpful to keep doing so, even if the user's device is temporarily off the network.

You can download the source for this recipe from the GitHub site (*https://oreil.ly/QaFYG*).

11.4 Automatically Reload Workers

Problem

The way that service workers are updated can be confusing for anyone using or testing an application. If we make a change to a service worker, the application will download the new version and set its status to Installed (see Figure 11-13).

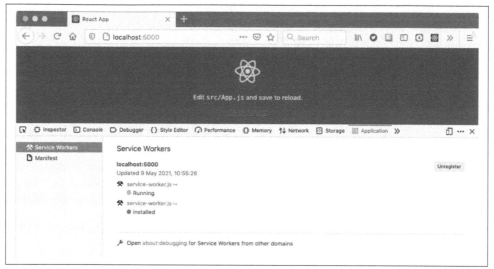

Figure 11-13. The updated worker is installed, but the old version is still running

The old service worker will go away only if the user closes the tab and then reopens it. The old worker disappears, and the new worker can stop waiting and start running (see Figure 11-14).

Figure 11-14. The new worker will start only if you close and re-open the application

The service worker may be caching the application's code, so if the service worker does not start running, it will not download the latest code from the server. You might find that you are using an old version of the entire client application. To run the new application, you need to reload the page (to install the new worker) and then close and reopen the tab (removing the old worker and starting the new one).

Testers will soon get used to this slightly odd sequence, but the same is not true for real users. In reality, the fact that new code will only update the next-but-one time that it's available is usually not a big problem. It *can* be a problem if you have made a significant change to the code, such as an update to an API.[6]

In some cases, you want to use the new code immediately. Is there a way to clear out the old service workers and upgrade to the new version of the application?

Solution

There are two things that we need to do to switch to a new service worker:

If you've created your application with `create-react-app` or you are using the code from the *cra-template-pwa* template,[7] then you will be registering your service worker, using the `serviceWorkerRegistration.register` function. For example, you might have code in the *index.js* file of your application that looks like this:

```
import React from 'react'
import ReactDOM from 'react-dom'
import './index.css'
import App from './App'
import * as serviceWorkerRegistration from './serviceWorkerRegistration'
import reportWebVitals from './reportWebVitals'

ReactDOM.render(
  <React.StrictMode>
    <App />
  </React.StrictMode>,
  document.getElementById('root')
)

serviceWorkerRegistration.register()

reportWebVitals()
```

Even if you've written your own registration code, you will likely have something similar.

The `serviceWorkerRegistration.register` function allows you to pass a couple of callbacks, which will tell you when a service worker has been installed or updated:

```
serviceWorkerRegistration.register({
  onInstall: (registration) => {},
  onUpdate: (registration) => {},
})
```

---

6 This is not the case if you use semantic versioning of API endpoints.

7 See Recipe 11.2.

The callbacks receive a *registration* object: a wrapper for the service worker that the browser has just installed or updated.

A service worker is installed when it is downloaded. But if an existing service worker is running, the new service worker will wait for the old service worker to disappear. If a service worker is waiting, the onUpdate function will be called.

We want to automatically remove the old service worker whenever the onUpdate function is called. That will allow the new service worker to start operating.

Service workers are a specialized form of *web worker*. A web worker is a piece of JavaScript that runs in a separate thread from the JavaScript running in the web page. You communicate with all web workers by posting asynchronous messages to them. Service workers can intercept network requests because the browser will convert network requests into messages.

So, we can ask a service worker to run an arbitrary piece of code by sending it a message. We can make our service worker respond to messages by giving it a message event listener:

```
self.addEventListener('message', (event) => {
  // handle messages here
})
```

The self variable contains the global scope for the service worker. It's like window is for page code.

The page code can send a message to the new service worker, telling it that we want it to stop waiting and replace the old service worker:

```
serviceWorkerRegistration.register({
  onUpdate: (registration) => {
    registration.waiting.postMessage({ type: 'SKIP_WAITING' })
  },
})
```

registration.waiting is a reference to the service worker, and registration. waiting.postMessage will send it a message.

When the browser installs a new version of a service worker but the old service worker is still running, the application code will send a SKIP_WAITING message to the new service worker.

Service workers have a built-in function called skipWaiting, which will kill the old service worker and allow the new one to take over. So, we can call skipWaiting in the service worker, when it receives a SKIP_WAITING message:

```
self.addEventListener('message', (event) => {
  if (event.data && event.data.type === 'SKIP_WAITING') {
    self.skipWaiting()
  }
})
```

If the application is now updated, the new service worker will immediately replace the old service worker.

There's just one step remaining: we need to reload the page so that we can download the new application code through the new service worker. This means that the updated version of the *index.js* file in the application looks like this:

```
import React from 'react'
import ReactDOM from 'react-dom'
import './index.css'
import App from './App'
import * as serviceWorkerRegistration from './serviceWorkerRegistration'
import reportWebVitals from './reportWebVitals'

ReactDOM.render(
  <React.StrictMode>
    <App />
  </React.StrictMode>,
  document.getElementById('root')
)

serviceWorkerRegistration.register({
  onUpdate: (registration) => {
    registration.waiting.postMessage({ type: 'SKIP_WAITING' })
    window.location.reload()
  },
})

reportWebVitals()
```

Once you've installed this new version of the code, the application will automatically update itself each time the application changes. Instead of seeing the old service worker alongside a patiently waiting version of the new service worker, you will instead just see the newly loaded version (see Figure 11-15).

Figure 11-15. The new service worker will now immediately replace the old version

Discussion

By adding a page reload, you will find that the page "blinks" when the new code is downloading. If you have a large application, this might be jarring for the user, so you might choose to ask the user if they want to upgrade to the new version of the application before reloading. Gmail does this whenever a significant update is available.

You can download the source for this recipe from the GitHub site (*https://oreil.ly/Lbal7*).

11.5 Add Notifications

Problem

One of the advantages of service workers, and web workers in general, is that they don't stop running just because the user leaves the page. If a service worker performs a slow operation, it will continue to run in the background, so long as the browser itself is still running. That means you can leave the page or close the tab and be sure that your worker will have time to finish.

However, what if the user wants to know when the background task has finally finished? Service workers don't have any visual interface. They might control web pages, but they can't update them. The only way that a web page and a service worker can communicate is by sending messages.

Given that service workers have no visual interface, how can they let us know when something important has happened?

Solution

We're going to create notifications from a service worker. Our example application (see Figure 11-16) will start a long-running process, taking around 20 seconds, when you click the button.

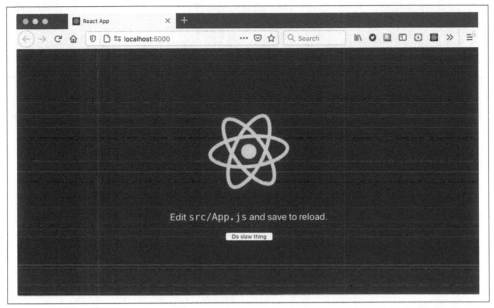

Figure 11-16. The example application starts a slow process when you click the button

The user will have to grant permission to be sent a completion notification (see Figure 11-17). If they deny permission, the background task will still run, but they won't see anything when it's complete.

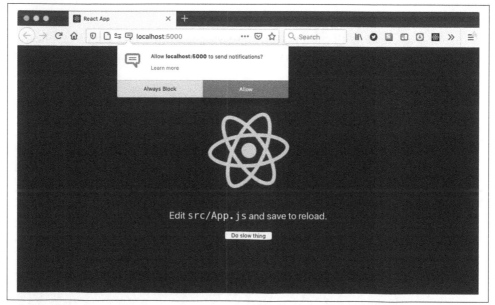

Figure 11-17. You will have to grant permission to receive notifications

 Notifications have a poor reputation. You usually see them when a site wants to spam you with information. In general, if you're using notifications, it's best to defer asking for permission until it's apparent to the user why you want it. Avoid asking for permission to send notifications when the page first loads because the user will have no idea why you want to send them.

The service worker will then run some code that will pause for 20 seconds, and then it will display a notification (see Figure 11-18).

Figure 11-18. The notification that appears when the task is finished

Let's start to look at the code. In the App component, we'll add a button to run the background but make sure we make it visible only if the browser supports service workers:

```
function App() {
  const startTask = () => {
    // Start task here
  }
  return (
```

```
    <div className="App">
      <header className="App-header">
        <img src={logo} className="App-logo" alt="logo" />
        <p>
          Edit <code>src/App.js</code> and save to reload.
        </p>
        {'serviceWorker' in navigator && (
          <button onClick={startTask}>Do slow thing</button>
        )}
      </header>
    </div>
  )
}
```

When the user clicks the button, they will call the startTask function. We can ask for permission to show notifications in there:

```
const startTask = () => {
  Notification.requestPermission((permission) => {
    navigator.serviceWorker.ready.then(() => {
      const notifyMe = permission === 'granted'
      // Then run task
    })
  })
}
```

If the user grants permission, the permission string will have the value granted, which will set the notifyMe variable to true. We can run the task in the service worker and tell it whether it's allowed to send a notification when it's complete.

We cannot talk to service workers directly. Instead, we have to post messages because service workers run in a separate thread from web page code.

We can get the current service worker controlling the page from navigator.service Worker.controller. So, we can send a message to the service worker like this:

```
const startTask = () => {
  Notification.requestPermission((permission) => {
    navigator.serviceWorker.ready.then(() => {
      const notifyMe = permission === 'granted'
      navigator.serviceWorker.controller.postMessage({
        type: 'DO_SLOW_THING',
        notifyMe,
      })
    })
  })
}
```

In the example application, our service is in *service-worker.js*. It can receive messages by adding a message event handler:

```
self.addEventListener('message', (event) => {
  ...
```

```
    if (event.data && event.data.type === 'DO_SLOW_THING') {
      // Code for slow task here
    }
  })
```

In a service worker, `self` refers to the global scope object. It's the equivalent of `window` in web page code. Let's simulate a slow task, with a call to `setTimeout`, which will wait for 20 seconds before sending a message to the console:[8]

```
self.addEventListener('message', (event) => {
  ...
  if (event.data && event.data.type === 'DO_SLOW_THING') {
    setTimeout(() => {
      console.log('Slow thing finished!')
      // TODO: Send notification here
    }, 20000)
  }
})
```

All that's left to do now is show the notification. We can do this with the service worker's *registration* object, which has a `showNotification` method:

```
self.addEventListener('message', (event) => {
  ...
  if (event.data && event.data.type === 'DO_SLOW_THING') {
    setTimeout(() => {
      console.log('Slow thing finished!')
      if (event.data.notifyMe) {
        self.registration.showNotification('Slow thing finished!', {
          body: 'Now get on with your life',
          icon: '/logo512.png',
          vibrate: [100, 100, 100, 200, 200, 200, 100, 100, 100],
          // tag: 'some-id-if-you-do-not-want-duplicates'
        })
      }
    }, 20000)
  }
})
```

Notice that we check `event.data.notifyMe` before attempting to show a notification; this is the variable we added to the message in the web page code.

The notification takes a `title` and an `options` object. The options allow you to modify the behavior of the notification. In this case, we're giving it some body text and an icon and setting a vibration sequence. If the user's device supports them, they should feel a set of *dot-dot-dot-dash-dash-dash-dot-dot-dot* vibrations when the notification appears.

---

8 You will see the message in Chrome. You will not see it if you use Firefox because Firefox does not give service workers access to the JavaScript console.

There's also a `tag` option, which we've commented out in the example code. We can use the `tag` to uniquely identify a notification and prevent the user from receiving the same notification multiple times. If you omit it, each call to `showNotification` will make a new notification appear.

To try the code, you will first need to build the application because service workers will run only in production mode:

```
$ yarn run build
```

You will then need to run a server on the contents of the generated *build* directory. You can do this by installing the *serve* module and then running this command:

```
$ serve -s build
```

If you open the application at *http://localhost:5000* and click the button, the slow process will start. You can then go to a different page or close the tab, and the slow task will continue running. It will stop only if you close the browser.

After 20 seconds, you should see a notification appear that looks similar to Figure 11-19.

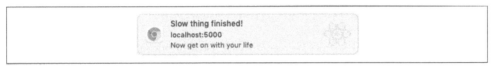

Slow thing finished!
localhost:5000
Now get on with your life

Figure 11-19. A notification as it appears on a Mac

It's tempting to access your server from a mobile device to check that the vibrations work in the notification. Be aware that service workers are enabled only if you access *localhost* or are using HTTPS. If you want to test your application over HTTPS, see Recipe 7.3 to enable it on a server.

Given that notifications can appear after you've closed the page, it's helpful if you give the user a simple way of navigating back to your application. You can do this by adding a notification-click handler to your service worker. If a service worker creates a notification and the user clicks it, the browser will send a `notificationclick` event to the service worker. You can create a handler for it like this:

```
self.addEventListener('notificationclick', (event) => {
  event.notification.close()
  // TODO Go back to the application
})
```

You can close the notification by calling `event.notification.close`. But how do you send the user back to the React application?

The service worker is the controller of zero or more browser tabs, which are called its *clients*. These are tabs whose network requests are intercepted by the service worker. You can get access to the list of clients using `self.clients`. This object has a utility function called `openWindow` that can be used to open a new tab in the browser:

```
self.addEventListener('notificationclick', (event) => {
  event.notification.close()
  if (self.clients.openWindow) {
    self.clients.openWindow('/')
  }
})
```

If the user now clicks the notification, the browser will return them to the front page of the React application.

But we can do a little better than that. If the user has switched to a different tab but the React application is still open, we can switch the focus back to the correct tab.

To do this, we will need to get hold of an array of each of the open tabs that our service worker controls. Then we can look to see if any match the correct path. If we find one, we can switch focus to that tab:

```
self.addEventListener('notificationclick', (event) => {
  event.notification.close()

  event.waitUntil(
    self.clients
      .matchAll({
        type: 'window',
      })
      .then((clientList) => {
        const returnPath = '/'

        const tab = clientList.find((t) => {
          return t.url === self.location.origin + returnPath
        })
        if (tab && 'focus' in tab) {
          tab.focus()
        } else if (self.clients.openWindow) {
          self.clients.openWindow(returnPath)
        }
      })
  )
})
```

If we click the notification, we will switch back to an open tab rather than always create a new one (see Figure 11-20).

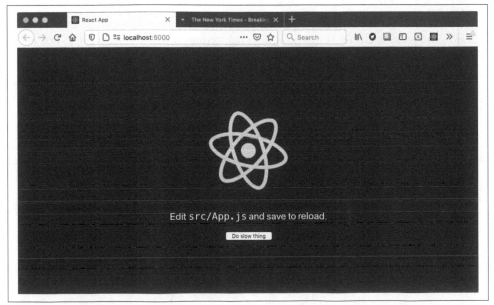

Figure 11-20. The notification can switch back to our application if it's still open

Discussion

Notifications are a great way of keeping the user informed about important events. The critical thing is to clarify *why* they should agree to receive notifications and then send them only if something significant has happened.

You can download the source for this recipe from the GitHub site (*https://oreil.ly/ZkcrR*).

11.6 Make Offline Changes with Background Sync

Problem

Imagine someone is using an application in a place where a network connection is not available, for example, on a subway train.[9] Precaching of application code means that there should be no problem opening an application without a network connection. The user can also move from page to page, and everything should appear normal.

But what if they do something that will send data to a server? What if they try to post a message?

---

9 Admittedly, more and more subways now have mobile repeater stations.

Solution

Background sync is a way of queuing network requests when the server is not available and then resending them automatically at a later time.

Our example application will send some data to a backend server when the user clicks a button (see Figure 11-21).

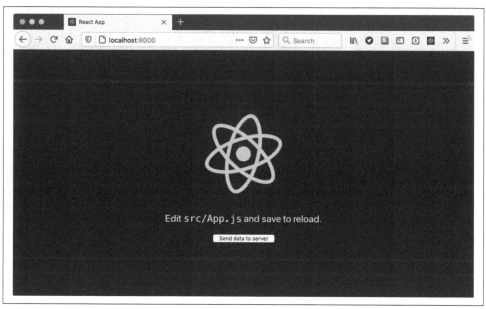

Figure 11-21. The example application sends data to the server when the user clicks a button

To start the application, you will first need to build it with this command:

```
$ yarn run build
```

The example project includes this server in *server/index.js*:

```
const express = require('express')
const app = express()

app.use(express.json())
app.use(express.static('build'))

app.post('/endpoint', (request, response) => {
  console.log('Server received data', request.body)
  response.send('OK')
})

app.listen(8000, () => console.log('Launched on port 8000!'))
```

The server will deliver content from the *build* directory, where the generated code is published. It also displays the data from any POST requests sent to *http://localhost:8000/endpoint*.

You can start the server with this command:

```
$ node server
```

If you now open the application in a browser at *http://localhost:8000* and click the button on the front page a few times, you will see data appearing in the server window:

```
$ node server
Launched on port 8000!
Server received data { timeIs: '2021-05-09T18:59:37.280Z' }
Server received data { timeIs: '2021-05-09T18:59:37.720Z' }
Server received data { timeIs: '2021-05-09T18:59:38.064Z' }
Server received data { timeIs: '2021-05-09T18:59:38.352Z' }
```

This is the application code that sends data to the server. It uses the `fetch` function to POST the current time when the button is pressed:

```
import React from 'react'
import logo from './logo.svg'
import './App.css'

function App() {
  const sendData = () => {
    const options = {
      method: 'POST',
      body: JSON.stringify({ timeIs: new Date() }),
      headers: {
        'Content-Type': 'application/json',
      },
    }
    fetch('/endpoint', options)
  }
  return (
    <div className="App">
      <header className="App-header">
        <img src={logo} className="App-logo" alt="logo" />
        <p>
          Edit <code>src/App.js</code> and save to reload.
        </p>
        <button onClick={sendData}>Send data to server</button>
      </header>
    </div>
  )
}

export default App
```

If you now stop the server, clicking the button on the web page will generate a series of failed network requests, as shown in Figure 11-22.

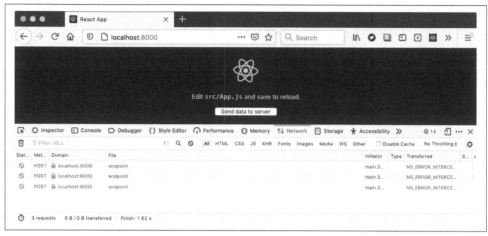

Figure 11-22. If the server cannot be contacted, the network requests fail

Stopping the server simulates what would happen if the user was temporarily out of network contact and then tried to send data from the application.

We can fix this problem using service workers. A service worker can intercept the network requests made by a web page in a progressive web application. In the other recipes in this chapter, we have used service workers to handle network failures by returning locally cached versions of files. We now need to handle data going in the opposite direction: from the browser to the server.

We need to cache the POST requests that we try to send to the server and then resend them when we are back in contact with the server.

To do this, we will use the workbox-background-sync library. *Background sync* is an API for diverting network requests onto a queue in those cases where we cannot contact the server. It's a complex API, and not all browsers support it.

The workbox-background-sync library makes the API far easier to use, and it will also work on browsers like Firefox that don't support Background Sync natively.

The service worker for the example application is in the *service-worker.js* file. We can add background syncing by adding this code:

```
import { NetworkOnly } from 'workbox-strategies'
import { BackgroundSyncPlugin } from 'workbox-background-sync'

// Other service worker code here....

registerRoute(
  //endpoint/,
```

```
  new NetworkOnly({
    plugins: [
      new BackgroundSyncPlugin('endPointQueue1', {
        maxRetentionTime: 24 * 60,
      }),
    ],
  }),
  'POST'
)
```

This code will register a new *route* in the service worker, saying how to deal with network requests to particular URLs. In this case, we are creating a route to handle all requests to *http://localhost:8000/endpoint*. We're using a regular expression to match the path. We're then using a Network Only (*https://oreil.ly/rLqLq*) strategy, which means that the browser will send all requests to the service worker, and all responses will come from the network. But we're configuring that strategy to use the background sync plugin. The third parameter in the route says that it is interested only in POST requests to the endpoint.

When the application sends a POST request to *http://localhost:8000/endpoint*, the service worker intercepts it. The service worker will forward the request to the server, and if successful, it will return the response to the web page. If the server is unavailable, the service worker will return a network error to the web page and then add the network request to a retry queue called endPointQueue1.

Workbox stores queues in indexed databases within the browser. Setting the max RetentionTime to *24 * 60* stores the requests in the database for a maximum of one day.

The workbox-background-sync library will resend the requests in the queue whenever it thinks the server might have become available, for example, if the network connection comes online. Retries will also happen every few minutes.

If you restart the server and then wait about five minutes, you should see the failed network requests appearing in the server:

```
$ node server
Launched on port 8000!
Server received data { timeIs: '2021-05-09T21:26:11.068Z' }
Server received data { timeIs: '2021-05-09T21:02:44.647Z' }
Server received data { timeIs: '2021-05-09T21:02:45.647Z' }
```

You can force Chrome to resend the requests immediately if you open the Application tab in the developer tools, select the service worker, and then send a sync message to workbox-background-sync:endPointQueue1 (as shown in Figure 11-23).

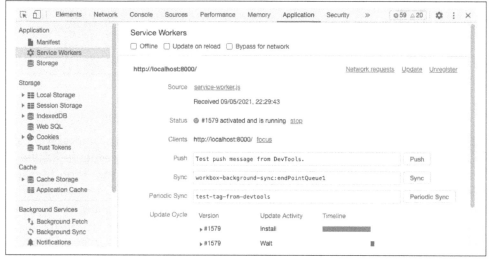

Figure 11-23. Forcing a sync to occur in Chrome

Discussion

Background sync is a tremendously powerful feature, but you need to think carefully before enabling it. The order in which the client code sends requests will not necessarily be the order they are processed at the server.

The exact order will probably not matter if you are creating a simple set of resources with `POST` requests. For example, if you buy books from an online bookstore, it doesn't matter what sequence you buy them in.

But if you create dependent resources or apply multiple updates to the same resource,[10] then you need to careful. If you amend your credit card number to *1111 1111 1111 1111* and then to *2222 2222 2222 2222*, the order of updates will completely change the final result.

You can download the source for this recipe from the GitHub site (*https://oreil.ly/ NFVAY*).

11.7 Add a Custom Installation UI

Problem

PWAs behave, in many ways, like locally installed applications. You *can* install them alongside other applications on a desktop machine or a mobile device. Many

---

10 In a RESTful API, you would probably perform updates with a PUT or PATCH request.

browsers allow you to create a shortcut on the current device to launch your application in a separate window. If you're using a desktop machine, you can add the shortcut to the dock or launch menus. If you're on a mobile device, you can add the application to the home screen.

But many users miss the fact that that they can install PWAs, a situation that is not helped by the low-key interface used in browsers to indicate that installation is possible (see Figure 11-24).

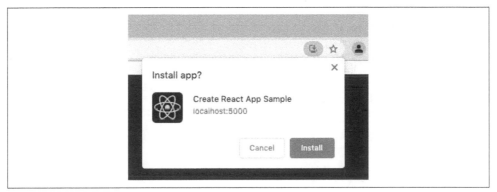

Figure 11-24. PWAs are installed with a small button in the address bar

Browsers do this to maximize the amount of screen estate available for your website. However, if you think that a local installation would be helpful to your users, you might choose to add a custom installation UI. But how can you do that?

Solution

Some browsers[11] will generate a JavaScript beforeinstallprompt event if they detect that your application is a fully fledged PWA.[12]

You can capture this event and use it to display your custom installation UI.

Create a component called *MyInstaller.js* and add this code:

```
import React, { useEffect, useState } from 'react'

const MyInstaller = ({ children }) => {
  const [installEvent, setInstallEvent] = useState()

  useEffect(() => {
```

---

11 At the time of writing, Chrome, Edge, and Samsung Internet support this event.

12 You can check if your application meets the requirements of a PWA by running the Lighthouse tool in Chrome Developer Tools. Not only will it tell you if your application qualifies, it will also give you reasons why, if it doesn't.

```
      window.addEventListener('beforeinstallprompt', (event) => {
        event.preventDefault()
        setInstallEvent(event)
      })
  }, [])

  return (
    <>
      {installEvent && (
        <button
          onClick={async () => {
            installEvent.prompt()
            await installEvent.userChoice
            setInstallEvent(null)
          }}
        >
          Install this app!
        </button>
      )}
      {children}
    </>
  )
}

export default MyInstaller
```

This component will capture the onbeforeinstallprompt event and store it in the installEvent variable. It then uses the existence of the event to display a custom user interface. In the code here, it displays a simple button on the screen. You can then insert this component into your application, for example:

```
function App() {
  return (
    <div className="App">
      <MyInstaller>
        <header className="App-header">
          <img src={logo} className="App-logo" alt="logo" />
          <p>
            Edit <code>src/App.js</code> and save to reload.
          </p>
          <a
            className="App-link"
            href="https://reactjs.org"
            target="_blank"
            rel="noopener noreferrer"
          >
            Learn React
          </a>
        </header>
      </MyInstaller>
    </div>
```

```
    )
  }
```

If you now build and run the application:

```
$ yarn run build
$ serve -s build
```

you will see the install button at the top of the front page (see Figure 11-25). You won't see the install button if you run the application with the development server, like this:

```
$ yarn run start
```

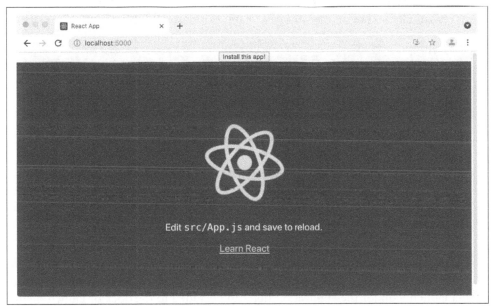

Figure 11-25. The custom install button appears at the top of the page

That's because the application will qualify as a PWA only if it has a service worker running. The service worker will run only in production code.

If you click the Install button, the MyInstaller component will run the install Event.prompt method. This will display the usual installation dialog (see Figure 11-26).

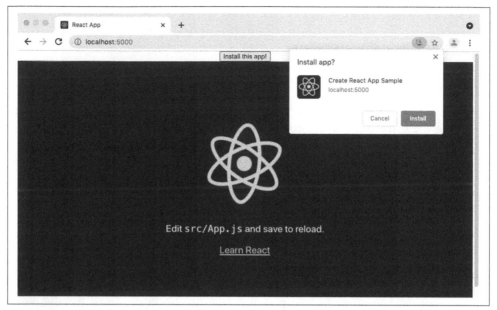

Figure 11-26. The install prompt will appear when you click the custom install button

If your device has already installed the application, the browser will not fire the `onbeforeinstallprompt` event.

If the user chooses to install the application, it will launch a separate application window.[13] If they are using a desktop machine, a finder or explorer window might appear, with a launch icon for the application that can be added to the dock or launch menus on your machine (see Figure 11-27). On a mobile device, the icon will appear on the home screen.

---

13 While it will create a separate application window, it will disappear if you close the web browser. If you launch the application directly, it will also launch the web browser if it's not already running.

Figure 11-27. The browser will create a launch icon for the application

Discussion

Local installation is an excellent feature for users who want to run your application often. In our experience, many users don't realize that the installation option is available for some sites, so adding a custom interface is a good idea. However, you should be wary of creating an intrusive interface if you think your users are likely to be one-time visitors. It's probably also best to avoid triggering the appearance of the instance automatically when the page loads. Doing so is likely to irritate your users and deter them from returning to your site.

You can download the source for this recipe from the GitHub site (*https://oreil.ly/Dbmpc*).

11.8 Provide Offline Responses

Problem

You won't want to cache all third-party resources in your application; it would take too much space. That means there will be times when your code will be unable to load all the resources it needs. For example, you can see in Figure 11-28 an application we created in an earlier chapter that displayed a series of images from a third-party image site.

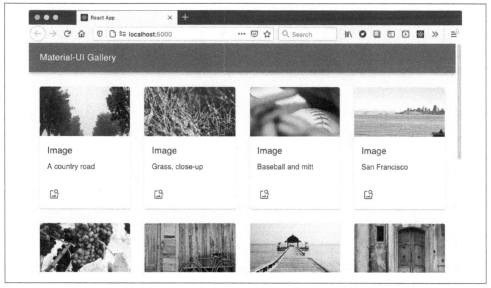

Figure 11-28. The application displays images from http://picsum.photos

You can use a service worker to cache all of this application's code to work offline. You probably wouldn't want to cache the third-party images because there will be too many. That means that if you disconnect from the network, the application will still open but without images (see Figure 11-29).

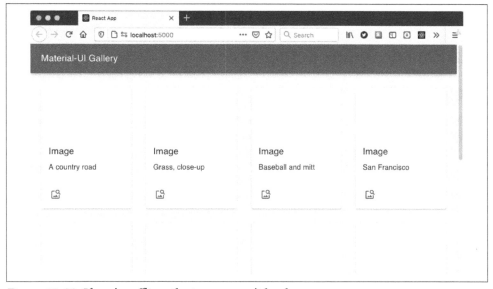

Figure 11-29. If you're offline, the images won't load

It would be helpful to replace the missing image with a locally served replacement. That way, when the user is offline, they will still see a placeholder image.

This is a particular case of a general problem: you may want to have placeholder files when a sizable external file is unavailable. You might want to replace video files, audio files, or even complete web pages with some temporary replacement.

Solution

To solve this problem, we'll use a couple of service worker techniques that together will return a local replacement with a cached file.

Let's say we want to replace all failed image loads with the replacement image shown in Figure 11-30.

Figure 11-30. Replacement for images that fail to load

The first thing we need to do is make sure that the image file is available in the local cache. We'll add the image to static files used by the application, but we can't rely on the replacement image being cached automatically. Precaching will store any files we download from the server. We will not need the placeholder image until the network is offline, so we will have to use *cache warming* to load the image into a local cache explicitly.

In the service worker, we're going to run some code as soon as the service worker is installed. We can do this by adding an `install` event handler:

```
self.addEventListener('install', (event) => {
  // Cache image here
})
```

We can explicitly open a local cache—which we'll call `fallback`—and then add the file to it from the network:

```
self.addEventListener('install', (event) => {
  event.waitUntil(
    caches.open('fallback').then((cache) => {
      cache.add('/comingSoon.png')
    })
  )
})
```

You can use this technique if you ever want to cache files when your application is installed, which is helpful for files that will be needed when you're offline but that are not immediately loaded by the application.

Now that we have the replacement image stored, we need to return it when the real images are not available. We'll need to add code that will run when network requests fail. We can do this with a *catch handler*. A catch handler is executed when a Workbox strategy fails:[14]

```
setCatchHandler(({ event }) => {
  if (event.request.destination === 'image') {
    return caches.match('/comingSoon.png')
  }
  return Response.error()
})
```

The catch handler receives the failed request object. We could check the URL of the request, but it is better to check the request's `destination`. The destination is the thing that will consume the file, and the destination is helpful when selecting a placeholder for the file. If the destination is `image`, the request happened because the browser was trying to load an `img` element. Here are some other examples of request destinations:

Destination	Generated by
""	JavaScript network requests
"audio"	Loading an <audio>
"document"	Navigation to a web page
"embed"	Loading an <embed>
"font"	Loading a font in CSS
"frame"	Loading a <frame>
"iframe"	Loading an<iframe>
"image"	Loading an <img>, /favicon.ico, SVG <image>, or a CSS image
"object"	Loading an <object>
"script"	Loading a <script>
"serviceworker"	Loading a service worker

---

14 For more details about the Workbox library, see the other recipes in this chapter.

Destination	Generated by
"sharedworker"	Loading a shared worker
"style"	Loading CSS
"video"	Loading a <video>
"worker"	Loading a worker

If our catch handler is called, we will return the *comingSoon.png* image from the cache. We're using `caches.match` to find the file in any of the available caches.

But now that we have a catch handler, we need to make sure that we define a Workbox strategy for every request. If not, a failed request might not trigger the catch handler. If we set a default handler, it will apply a strategy to every request not handled in some other way:

```
setDefaultHandler(new NetworkOnly())
```

This command will ensure that the service worker forwards all requests to the network unless some more specific handler is defined.

Each of the `img` tags on the page will generate a request with a destination of `image`. The default handler will forward them to a third-party server, which will cause an error because the application can't contact the network. The catch handler will then return the replacement image file to each `img` element. You can see the result of this process in Figure 11-31.

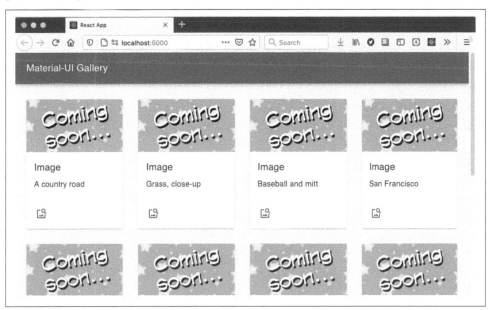

Figure 11-31. When offline, all images are replaced by a placeholder

Discussion

This technique is beneficial for large media files that are difficult or impossible to cache locally. If, for example, you have built an application to play podcasts, you could replace a missing episode with a short audio clip, explaining that the episode will be available only when you are next online.

Warming the cache with files can increase the time needed for the service worker to install. For this reason, if you're warming a cache with reasonably large files, you should also add this line to your service worker:

```
import * as navigationPreload from 'workbox-navigation-preload'
...
navigationPreload.enable()
```

Navigation preload is a browser optimization that will run network requests in the background if they begin when a service worker is installing. Not all browsers support navigation preload, but the workbox-navigation-preload library will use it if it's available.

You can download the source for this recipe from the GitHub site (*https://oreil.ly/ 5nN80*).

Index

reducing number of scans to improve TBT, 387

render method updating virtual DOM, 416

standalone implementation for unit tests in React Testing library, 275

updating real DOM elements not matching virtual DOM, 416

viewing in Eruda Elements tab, 317

virtual DOM in Preact, 15

DST (daylight saving time), testing, 327

duration parameter, 151

E

effective date, 324

ejecting applications, 5

element (block element modifier naming), 141

email input type attribute, 269

empty object ({}), 127

error handlers

building centralized error handler, 113-118

ErrorContainer, 115

ErrorHandlerContext, 114

ErrorHandlerProvider component, 114

information to pass on to end user, 114

useErrorHandler hook, 116

wrapping bulk of application in Error-Container, 116

errors, 156

accessibility, found by eslint, 348

cross-origin resource sharing (CORS), 452

error object from SEARCH_RESULTS action, 177

error state, 157

failures to cope with missisng properties or data, 286

network call failures, testing in Cypress, 295

network request converted to hook, 160

not tracking in create function of useForum, 167

unauthorized access, 222

Eruda, 315-320

eslint

checking accessibility with, 346-351

configuring jsx-ally plugin, 347

errors found, 348

extending eslint with plugins, 346

jsx-a11y plugin, 346

running with rules enabled, 348

checking security with, 266-269

enabling eslint, 267

installing plugin with security rules, 267

no-dangerously-set-innerhtml rule, 267

running checks with Git pre-commit hooks, 268

event.data.notifyMe, 462

exceptions

handling consistently in React applications, 114

network request throwing exception, 117

F

fade out animations, 144

FCP (First Contentful Paint), 386, 424

Feed component, 218

fetch command, 157

fetch function, 171

fetch request, dropping into useMessages hook, 158

filter methods, screen object, 277

fingerprints, authenticating with, 244-251

First Contentful Paint (FCP), 386, 424

First Input Delay (FID), 388

FixedSizeList, 204

flows in web authentication, 231

focus

buttons receiving from keyboard, 349

describing currently focused elemet in screen reader, 380

escaping from custom modal dialogs, 376

finding element receiving with document.querySelector, 365

function performing Tab operation, 372

listener for focusin events, 380

making clear to users where it is, 351

SkipButtons in Skip component, 371

style for skip button having focus, 364

trapping within small subset of components, 376-378

footer tag, page metadata grouped in, 335

forms

adding form to post messages to forum, 162

building in Semantic UI, 217

creating and laying out with Bootstrap, 200-202

creating and validating, 83-91

InputField component with validation, 89

About the Authors

David Griffiths is an author and trainer who has written code professionally in React for five years. *React Cookbook* is his sixth book. He has created applications for startups, retail stores, vehicle manufacturers, and national sports bodies. He lives and works in the United Kingdom.

Dawn Griffiths is an author and trainer with more than 20 years of software development experience creating desktop and web applications. She has written about Android development, Kotlin, and statistics.

Together, David and Dawn have written several books in the Head First series, including *Head First Android Development* and *Head First Kotlin*, and are contributors to the book *97 Things Every Java Programmer Should Know*. They developed the Agile Sketchpad video course as a way of teaching fundamental concepts and techniques in a way that keeps your brain active and engaged, and they deliver live, online training for O'Reilly.

Colophon

The animal on the cover of *React Cookbook* is a great blue heron (*Ardea herodias*). These birds, sometimes called "cranes," are found across much of North America: breeding in Canada, wintering in Mexico, and spending most of the year in the United States. Great blue herons frequent both fresh- and saltwater shorelines, river banks, and the edges of marshes, estuaries, and ponds. They can also be found foraging in meadows, agricultural fields, and other open grasslands.

Great blue herons are the largest of the herons in North America. They are characterized by their long legs and neck, and a thick bill often described as "daggerlike." They appear blue-gray from a distance and their plumage can make them appear shaggy. An all-white form known as the great white heron can be found in Southern Florida and the Caribbean—though there is some debate as to whether these birds constitute a separate species. Populations in the Eastern US will migrate to the Caribbean, Central America, or northern South America—by day or night, alone or in flocks. Those living along the Pacific Coast are less likely to migrate and may reside permanently in one location, even as far north as southeastern Alaska. Great blue herons are opportunistic when it comes to their diet and will eat almost anything they can catch or impale with their bills, including fish, amphibians, reptiles, small mammals, insects, and even other birds!

When breeding, great blue herons will nest within a few miles of their feeding areas. Colonies of several hundred pairs may build stick nests in trees, on bushes, or on the ground near isolated swamps, islands, ponds, and lakes. These herons perform elaborate courtship and pair-bonding displays that can include a ritualized greeting, stick transfers, and nest relief ceremonies. Pairs can be monogamous for a season but will choose new partners each year. Both parents feed their young by regurgitation. Young herons are capable of flight at about 60 days and will leave the nest within a month of fledging.

Populations of great blue herons have been increasing in the US since 1966, with the exception of the "great white heron" group in southern Florida where elevated mercury levels in local waterways may be contributing to a notable population decline. Like most birds in the US, herons are legally protected by the Migratory Bird Treaty Act. Many of the animals on O'Reilly covers are endangered; all of them are important to the world.

The cover illustration is by Karen Montgomery, based on a black and white engraving from *Audubon*. The cover fonts are Gilroy Semibold and Guardian Sans. The text font is Adobe Minion Pro; the heading font is Adobe Myriad Condensed; and the code font is Dalton Maag's Ubuntu Mono.

O'REILLY®

There's much more where this came from.

Experience books, videos, live online training courses, and more from O'Reilly and our 200+ partners—all in one place.

Learn more at oreilly.com/online-learning